palgrave macmillan law masters

company law

D0491969

Series editor: **Marise Cremona**

Company Law (6th edn)   Janet Dine and Marios Koutsias
Constitutional and Administrative Law (6th edn)   John Alder
Contract Law (7th edn)   Ewan McKendrick
Conveyancing (3rd edn)   Priscilla Sarton
Criminal Law (5th edn)   Jonathan Herring
Employment Law (5th edn)   Deborah J. Lockton
Evidence (3rd edn)   Raymond Emson
Family Law (5th edn)   Kate Standley
Housing Law and Policy   David Cowan
Intellectual Property Law (4th edn)   Tina Hart, Linda Fazzani and
    Simon Clark
Land Law (5th edn)   Kate Green and Joe Cursley
Landlord and Tenant Law (5th edn)   Margaret Wilkie, Peter Luxton,
    Jill Morgan and Godfrey Cole
Law of the European Union (3rd edn)   Jo Shaw
Law of Succession   Catherine Rendell
Legal Method (6th edn)   Ian McLeod
Legal Theory (4th edn)   Ian McLeod
Social Security Law   Robert East
Torts (3rd edn)   Alastair Mullis and Ken Oliphant

palgrave macmillan law masters

company law

janet dine

Professor of International Economic Law
Centre for Commercial Law Studies
Queen Mary, University of London

and

marios koutsias

PhD University of Essex
Research Assistant, Centre for Commercial Law
Studies, Queen Mary, University of London

Sixth edition

Series editor: Marise Cremona
Professor of European Law
European University Institute
Florence
Italy

palgrave
macmillan

First edition 1991
Second edition 1994
Third edition 1998
Fourth edition 2001
Fifth edition 2005

This edition published 2007 by
PALGRAVE MACMILLAN
Houndmills, Basingstoke, Hampshire RG21 6XS and
175 Fifth Avenue, New York, N.Y. 10010
Companies and representatives throughout the world

PALGRAVE MACMILLAN is the global academic imprint of the Palgrave Macmillan division of St. Martin's Press, LLC and of Palgrave Macmillan Ltd. Macmillan® is a registered trademark in the United States, United Kingdom and other countries. Palgrave is a registered trademark in the European Union and other countries.

ISBN-13: 978–0–230–01877–8
ISBN-10: 0–230–01877–7

This book is printed on paper suitable for recycling and made from fully managed and sustained forest sources. Logging, pulping and manufacturing processes are expected to conform to the environmental regulations of the country of origin.

A catalogue record for this book is available from the British Library.

11   10   9   8   7   6   5
16   15   14   13   12   11   10   09   08

Printed and bound in Great Britain by
Creative Print & Design (Wales), Ebbw Vale

Contents

Preface		xiii
Table of cases		xiv
Table of Statutes and Directives		xxvi

1	**The reasons for forming companies**	**1**
1.1	The elements of a company	3
1.2	Outsiders	5
1.3	'Parent' and 'subsidiary' company	6
1.4	Single member companies	6
	Hot Topic: Corporate governance	7
	Summary	7
	Case note	8
	Exercises	10

2	**Starting a company**	**11**
2.1	Limited and unlimited companies	11
2.2	Public and private companies	12
2.3	Minimum capital requirements for a public company	14
2.4	Change of status from public to private company and vice versa	14
2.5	Groups	15
2.6	The memorandum of association and registration	16
2.7	Incorporation	18
2.8	Duty of Registrar	18
2.9	Off-the-shelf companies	19
	Hot Topic: Community interest companies	19
	Summary	19
	Exercises	20

3	**Corporate personality**	**21**
3.1	The legal basis for the separate personality doctrine	22
3.2	Problems caused by the personality doctrine and exceptions	26
3.3	Statutory intervention	27
3.4	Lifting the veil	27
3.5	Fraud	30
3.6	Groups	31
3.7	The criminal and civil liabilities of companies	39
3.8	What crimes?	39

3.9 Why convict companies? 40
3.10 Identification of the company's *alter ego* 41
3.11 Civil liability 41
Hot Topic: Performance of Companies and Government
Departments (Reporting) Bill (2004) (1) 42
Summary 43
Case notes 43
Exercises 44

4 The memorandum of association 46
4.1 *Ultra vires* – the old law 47
4.2 Constructive notice 47
4.3 Justification of the doctrine 48
4.4 How to determine whether an act is *ultra vires* 48
4.5 The new law 49
4.6 Ratification 50
4.7 The old case law 50
4.8 Objects and powers 52
4.9 *Ultra vires* and objects 53
4.10 Knowledge by an outsider that a transaction is outside
objects or powers 54
4.11 Can borrowing ever be an object? 54
4.12 1980s cases 55
Summary 58
Exercises 58

5 The articles of association 59
5.1 The articles as a contract 60
5.2 What rights are governed by the contract in the articles? 61
5.3 Outsiders 62
5.4 Entrenched provisions 65
5.5 The articles as evidence of a contract 65
5.6 Alteration of the articles of association 67
5.7 *Bona fide* for the benefit of the company 68
5.8 Remedies 71
Summary 73
Case notes 73
Exercises 74

6 Power to represent the company 75
6.1 Power of directors to bind the company 75
6.2 Protection 78
6.3 Transaction and dealing 78
6.4 Decided on by the directors 78
6.5 Good faith 78
6.6 Unauthorised agents 80

6.7	Usual authority	83
6.8	Promoters	83
6.9	Who are promoters?	83
6.10	Duties of promoters	84
6.11	Disclosure	85
6.12	The loss of the right to recission	86
6.13	Actions for damages	87
6.14	Remuneration of promoters	87
6.15	Pre-incorporation contracts	87
6.16	Liability of the company	89
	Summary	89
	Exercises	90

7 Public issue of securities **91**

7.1	Shares	92
7.2	Direct offers, offers for sale, issuing houses	92
7.3	The two regimes	92
7.4	Rights offers and public offers	92
7.5	Placing	93
7.6	Pre-emption rights	93
7.7	Authority to issue shares	94
7.8	Directors' duties	94
7.9	The structure of the rules	94
7.10	Admission to Stock Exchange Listing	95
7.11	Contents of listing particulars	95
7.12	Continuing obligations	96
7.13	Remedies for defective listing particulars	96
7.14	Prospectus issues	99
7.15	Remedies for defective prospectuses	99
7.16	Liabilities for misstatements in prospectuses and listing particulars	99
7.17	The EC Prospectus Directive	101
	Summary	102
	Case notes	103
	Exercises	105

8 The regulation of investment business **106**

8.1	Financial Services and Markets Act 2000 – 'regulated business'	108
8.2	How the range of regulatory tools is used in practice	112
8.3	Financial Services Authority: authorisation provisions	113
8.4	Complaints	114
8.5	The Investment Services Directive	116
	Summary	116
	Case notes	117
	Exercises	118

9	**Maintenance of capital**	**119**
9.1	Fundamental rule	119
9.2	Payment of money to members	120
9.3	Distributions	121
9.4	Rules governing distributions	121
9.5	Dividends	122
9.6	Public companies	123
9.7	Members' liability	123
9.8	Other permitted payments to members	123
9.9	Reductions of capital	124
9.10	Interests of creditors	126
9.11	Procedure	126
9.12	Bonus shares	127
9.13	Redeemable shares	127
9.14	Purchase of own shares	129
9.15	Illegal transactions	130
9.16	Serious loss of capital by a public company	134
9.17	Accounts	134
9.18	Company accounts	135
9.19	FRSs and FREDs	135
9.20	The obligation to prepare accounts	136
9.21	Keeping the records	136
9.22	Duty to prepare individual company accounts and 'true and fair view'	136
9.23	Group accounts	137
9.24	Conclusion	139
	Summary	140
	Exercises	140
10	**The balance of power inside the company: corporate governance**	**141**
10.1	Proxy voting	142
10.2	Solicitation of proxies	142
10.3	Formality of procedure	143
10.4	Meetings	143
10.5	Management of the company	149
10.6	Appointment of directors	151
10.7	Removal of a director	155
10.8	Validity of directors' acts	157
10.9	Disqualification	157
10.10	Directors' meetings	157
10.11	Managing director	158
10.12	Relationship between the board of directors and the general meeting	159

10.13	Where the board of directors ceases to function	161
10.14	The Secretary	162
10.15	Employees	162
	Hot Topic: International debate on corporate social responsibility	164
	Summary	165
	Case notes	166
	Exercises	184
11	**Directors' duties: the general duties**	**185**
11.1	The Cadbury, Hampel and Combined Code initiatives	187
11.2	Duty owed to the company	189
11.3	What is the company?	190
11.4	Duties of care and skill	192
	Hot Topic: Performance of Companies and Government Departments (Reporting) Bill 2004 (2)	196
11.5	Fiduciary duties	197
11.6	Are the prohibitions absolute?	199
11.7	The categories of duties	200
11.8	Consequences of a breach	211
	Hot Topic: Performance of Companies and Government Departments (Reporting) Bill 2004 (3)	211
	Summary	212
	Case notes	213
	Exercises	218
12	**Specific duties of directors**	**219**
12.1	Disqualification of directors	220
12.2	Insider dealing	233
	Summary	242
	Case notes	243
	Exercises	249
13	**Suing the company, suing for the company, enforcing directors' duties**	**250**
13.1	Suing the company	250
13.2	Suing for the company (the exceptions to the rule in *Foss* v. *Harbottle* and derivative actions)	251
13.3	Ratification	252
13.4	The statutory remedy in section 994	262
13.5	Unfair prejudice	262
13.6	The relief that can be granted	267
13.7	Winding-up orders	268
13.8	When a winding-up order is likely to be made	269
13.9	Department of Trade investigations	269
13.10	When inspectors have been appointed	271

13.11 Following investigations   271
       Summary   272
       Case notes   272
       Exercises   276

14 Shares   278
    14.1   Ordinary shares   278
    14.2   Preference shares   279
    14.3   Voting rights   281
    14.4   The exercise of voting powers   282
    14.5   Variation of class rights   283
    14.6   Alteration of articles to insert a variation clause   287
    14.7   Statutory right to object   287
           Summary   288
           Exercises   288

15 Lending money and securing loans   289
    15.1   Debenture-holders' receiver   290
    15.2   Fixed and floating charges   290
    15.3   The characteristics of fixed and floating charges   293
    15.4   Crystallisation of the floating charge   293
    15.5   Legal and equitable charges   294
    15.6   Floating charges and other claims against the company   295
    15.7   Retention of title clauses   296
    15.8   Registration of company charges   297
    15.9   Which charges are registrable?   297
    15.10 Salient points   298
    15.11 Delivery of particulars and priorities   298
    15.12 Priorities under the registration scheme   299
    15.13 Effect of registration   299
    15.14 Duty to register and effect of non-registration   299
    15.15 Payment of money secured by unregistered charge   300
           Summary   300
           Case note   301
           Exercises   301

16 Takeovers, reconstructions and amalgamations   302
    16.1   Public offers   302
    16.2   Monopolies   302
    16.3   The Takeover Panel   303
    16.4   General principles and rules   303
    16.5   Partial offers   304
    16.6   Compulsory purchase provisions   305
    16.7   Sell-out right   305
    16.8   Reconstructions   306
    16.9   Meetings   306

16.10	Approval of the court	306
16.11	Reconstruction in a liquidation	307
	Hot Topic: International takeovers	308
	Summary	311
	Case note	311
	Exercises	312

17 Insolvency   313

17.1	Voluntary arrangements	313
17.2	Proposal	313
17.3	The involvement of the court	314
17.4	Contents of the proposal	314
17.5	Meetings	314
17.6	Challenges	314
17.7	Administrative receivership	314
17.8	Liquidations	315
17.9	Voluntary winding-up	316
17.10	The liquidator	316
17.11	Order of payment of debts	317
17.12	Avoiding antecedent transactions	317
17.13	Fraudulent trading	321
17.14	Summary remedy against delinquent directors – Section 212 Insolvency Act 1986	321
17.15	Wrongful trading	321
17.16	The destination of the money	323
17.17	Dissolution	323
	Summary	324
	Case notes	324
	Exercises	330

18 The effect of the EU on English company law   331

18.1	The making of a Directive	331
18.2	The extent of the influence of EU rules	332
18.3	Sources of EU law	333
18.4	The institutions of the EU	335
18.5	The EU Company Law Harmonisation Programme	337
	Hot Topic: The European Company	338
18.6	Company Law Directives	339
18.7	Securities regulation	344
18.8	Insolvency	345
18.9	Conclusion	348
	Hot Topic: Takeover Directive	350
	Summary	351
	Exercises	352

19 Transglobal corporations and world development   353
    19.1   Development issues   354
    19.2   The displacement of domestic production   355
    19.3   The effects of the international money and banking systems   356
    19.4   The undermining of political systems and the absence of
           control of transnationals   358
    19.5   Environmental issues   359
    19.6   Labour law issues   361
           Hot Topic: Saro-Wiwa family v. Royal Dutch/Shell 361

    Bibliography and further reading   364

    Index   368

Preface

In accordance with the aims of the Palgrave Macmillan Law Masters series, this book is intended as an introduction to the basic principles of company law. We have endeavoured to state the law in clear and simple terms throughout.

In common with the other books in the series, the book contains features designed to help those studying this subject for the first time. These include Key words highlighted at the start of each chapter, Hot Topics where an issue is currently under review or very recent, and Case notes at the end of most chapters which give a short account of the facts and decisions in key cases. A number of points for further consideration are included in the Exercises at the end of each chapter.

I am very happy to have as joint author Dr Marios Koutsias who has taught company law with me at Essex University for a number of years and is currently a research assistant at Queen Mary College London. The sixth edition of the book proved to be particularly challenging as the Companies Act 2006 received royal assent in December 2006. It will be implemented over the next two years and the government is forecasting that it will be fully in force in 2008. During this period of uncertainty we have chosen to alter the text to take account of the new law in most cases. The exceptions are areas where we are awaiting implementing legislation (such as model articles) and areas such as registration of charges where there is a long history of legislation which was passed but never came into force. Readers are cautioned to check whether the relevant sections have been implemented before relying on the text as representing the law in force. This can be done by referring to the website of the Department of Trade and Industry: **www.dti.gov.uk/**

January 2007   JANET DINE and MARIOS KOUTSIAS

Table of cases

A Company, Re [1983] Ch 178 — 267
A Company, Re [1983] 1 WLR 927 — 268
A Company, Re (1986) 2 BCC 98 & 952 — 267
A Company, Re [1986] BCLC 376 — 263
A Company, Re (1988) 4 BCC 506 — 267
A Company No. 00996 of 1979, Re [1980] Ch 138 — 222
A Company (No. 001761 of 1986), Re [1987] BCLC 141 — 263
AB Trucking and BAW Commercials Ch D, 3 June 1987,
 unreported — 225, 228
Abbey Malvern Wells v. Minister of Local Government [1951]
 Ch 728 — 37
Aberdeen Railway Co. v. Blaikie Bros (1854) 1 Macq 461 — 205
Acatos and Hutcheson plc v. Watson [1995] 1 BCLC 218; [1995]
 BCC 441 — 133
Adams v. Cape Industries PLC [1990] BCLC 479 — 36, 37
AIB Finance Ltd v. Bank of Scotland [1995] 1 BCLC 185 — 295
Alexander v. Automatic Telephone Co. [1990] 2 Ch 56 — 94, 260
Alexander Ward & Co. Ltd v. Samyang Navigation Co. Ltd [1975]
 2 All ER 424 — 161
Allen v. Gold Reefs of West Africa Ltd [1900] 1 Ch 656 — 67, 68, 73
Al-Nakib Investments (Jersey) Ltd v. Longcroft [1990] 1 WLR 1390 — 100
Alpine Investments BV v. Minister van Financien [1995] 2 BCLC 214 — 337
Aluminium Industrie Vaassen BV v. Romalpa Aluminium Ltd
 [1976] 1 WLR 676 — 296
Amaron Ltd, Re [1998] BCC 264 — 224
Anglo Continental Supply Co., Re [1922] 2 Ch 723 — 307
Arbuthnot Leasing International Ltd v. Havelet Leasing Ltd (No. 2)
 [1990] BCC 636 — 319
Arctic Engineering Ltd, Re [1986] 1 WLR 686 — 221
Armagh Shoes Ltd, Re [1982] NI 59 — 291
Ashbury Railway Carriage and Iron Co. (1875) LR 7 HL 653 — 50, 51
Asprey & Garrard Ltd v. WRA (Guns) Ltd & Another [2001]
 EWCA Civ 1499 (11 October 2001) — 17
Attorney-General's Reference (No. 1 of 1975) [1975] 2 All ER 684 — 237

Attorney-General's Reference (No. 2 of 1982), Re [1984] 2 WLR 447   198
Attorney-General's Reference (No. 1 of 1988) [1989] BCLC 193   237
Attorney-General's Reference (No. 2 of 1999) [2000] 3 WLR 195   40
Atwool v. Merryweather (1867) 5 Eq 464   260
Augustus Barnett & Son Ltd, Re [1986] BCLC 170   32
Automatic Bottle Makers Ltd, Re [1926] Ch 412   295
Automatic Self Cleansing Filter Syndicate Company Ltd v.
    Cunningham [1906] 2 Ch 34   159

M. C. Bacon Ltd, Re [1990] BCLC 324   318
Baillie v. Oriental Telephone and Electric Company Ltd [1915] 1
    Ch 503   145
Bamford v. Bamford [1970] Ch 212   251, 161
Barings plc, Re [1999] 1 BCLC 433   230
Barings plc and Another v. Coopers and Lybrand and Others [1997]
    1 BCLC 427   258
Barnett, Hoares & Co. v. South London Tramways Co. (1887) 18
    QBD 815   83
Barrett v. Duckett and Others [1995] 1 BCLC 243   251
Bath Glass, Re [1988] BCLC 329   225, 228
Beattie v. Beattie [1938] Ch 708   64, 73
Bell Houses Ltd v. City Wall Properties Ltd [1966] 2 QB 656   52
Belmont Finance Corporation v. Williams Furniture Ltd (No. 2)
    [1980] 1 All ER 393   131, 132
Benjamin Cope & Sons, Re [1914] 1 Ch 800   295, 296
Bhullar v. Bhullar [2003] EWCA Civ 424   207
Birch v. Sullivan [1958] 1 All ER 56   253
Bisgood v. Henderson's Transvaal Estates [1908] 1 Ch 743   307
Bishopgate Investment Management (in liquidation) v. Maxwell
    [1993] BCC 120   202
H. L. Bolton (Engineering) Co. Ltd v. T. J. Graham & Sons Ltd
    [1957] 1 QB 159   41
Bond Worth, Re [1980] Ch 228   297
Borden (UK) Ltd v. Scottish Timber Products [1979] 3 WLR 672   297
Bovey Hotel Ventures, Re (31 July 1981) unreported   262
Brady v. Brady [1989] 1 AC 755   132, 133, 191
Braymist Ltd & Others v. Wise Finance Company Ltd [2002] EWCA
    Civ 127   88
Breckland Group Holdings Ltd v. London and Suffolk Properties Ltd
    [1989] BCLC 100   160
Brenfield Squash Racquets Club Ltd, Re [1996] 2 BCLC 184   268
Brightlife Ltd, Re [1987] Ch 200   292, 294, 298

British America Nickel Corporation Ltd *v.* M. J. O'Brien Ltd [1937]
AC 707   283

British and American Trustee & Finance Corporation Ltd *v.* Couper
[1894] AC 229   125, 126

British Midland Tool Ltd *v.* Midland International Tooling Ltd [2003]
2 BCLC 523   209

British Murac Syndicate *v.* Alperton Rubber Co. [1915] 2 Ch 186   71, 72

Broderip *v.* Salomon [1895] 2 Ch 323   22, 26, 30, 37

Brown *v.* British Abrasive Wheel [1919] 1 Ch 290   68, 69

Browne *v.* La Trinidad (1888) 37 Ch D 1   63

BSB Holdings, Re [1996] 1 BCLC 155   265

Bugle Press Ltd, Re [1961] Ch 270   305, 311

Bushell *v.* Faith [1970] AC 1099   4, 156, 157, 161

Cairney *v.* Black, Re [1906] 2 KB 746   296

Campbell *v.* Paddington Corporation [1911] 1 KB 869   42

Cane *v.* Jones [1981] 1 WLR 1451   143, 146

Cape Breton, Re (1885) 29 Ch D 795   87

Capital Finance Co. Ltd *v.* Stokes [1968] 1 All ER 573   323

Carrington Viyella PLC, Re (1983) 1 BCC 98   264, 267

Carruth *v.* Imperial Chemical Industries Ltd [1937] AC 707   124, 145,
                                                                          287, 307

Centrafarm BV et Adriaan de Peijper *v.* Winthrop BV [1974] EVECJ
R-16/74 (31 October 1974)   33

Centros Ltd *v.* Erhuerus- og Selskabsstyrelsen [2000] 2 BCLC 68   337

Chartmore, 12 October 1989, Re [1990] BCLC 673   232

Chequepoint SARL *v.* McClelland and Another [1997] 1
BCLC 117   337

Chohan *v.* Saggar and Another [1994] 1 BCLC 706   319

Christensen *v.* Scott [1996] 1 NZLR 273   258

City Equitable Fire Insurance, Re [1925] Ch 407   193, 195, 225, 228

Civicia Investments Ltd, Re [1983] BCLC 456   226

Clark *v.* Mid Glamorgan County Council [1996] 1 BCLC 407   293

Clemens *v.* Clemens Bros Ltd [1976] 2 All ER 268   147

Climex Tissues, Re [1995] 1 BCLC 409   293

Clough Mill Ltd *v.* Geoffrey Martin [1985] 1 WLR 111   297

CMS Dolphin Ltd *v.* Simonet [2002] BCC 600   206

Commission *v.* Italy (1992) ECR I-06337   347

Continental Assurance Co. of London plc, Re [2001] BPIR 733   229

Cook *v.* Deeks [1916] 1 AC 554   204, 260

Cory Bros & Co. [1927] 1 KB 810   40

Cosslett (Contractors) Ltd, Re [1998] 2 WLR 131 (CA)   293

Cotman *v*. Brougham [1918] AC 514   51, 52, 54
Cotronic (UK) Ltd *v*. Dezonie [1991] BCLC 721   88
Crestjoy Products Ltd, Re [1990] BCC 23; [1990] BCLC 677   227
Crichton's Oil, Re [1902] 2 Ch 86   280
Criterion Properties Plc *v*. Stratford UK Properties LLC [2004]
    UKHL 28   201
Crown Bank, Re (1890) 44 Ch D 634   51, 52
Cumbrian Newspapers Group Ltd *v*. Cumberland & Westmorland
    Herald Newspaper & Printing Co. Ltd [1987] Ch 1   284
Curtain Dream plc, Re [1990] BCLC 925   297

Dafen Tinplate Co. Ltd *v*. Llanelly Steel Co. (1907) Ltd [1920]
    2 Ch 124   69
Daimler *v*. Continental Tyre Co. [1916] AC 307   38
Daniels *v*. Daniels [1978] Ch 406   261, 274
Darby, Re [1911] 1 KB 95   31
David Payne & Co. Ltd, Re [1904] 2 Ch 608   54, 57
Dawson Print Group, Re [1987] BCLC 601   224, 225, 248
Day *v*. Cook [2001] EWCA Civ 592   259
Destone Fabrics, Re [1941] Ch 319   320
DHN Food Distributors *v*. Tower Hamlets Borough Council [1976]
    1 WLR 852   36
Dimbula Valley (Ceylon) Tea Co. *v*. Laurie [1961] Ch 353   286
D'Jan of London Ltd, Re [1993] BCC 646   194, 321
Dorchester Finance Co. Ltd *v*. Stebbing [1989] BCLC 498   193
Dovey *v*. Cory [1901] AC 477   192
DPP *v*. Kent and Sussex Contractors Ltd [1944] KB 146   41

Ebrahami *v*. Westbourne Galleries Ltd, Re [1973] AC 360   269, 275–6
EIC Services Ltd & Another *v*. Phipps & Others [2004] EWCA
    Civ 1069   79
El Ajou *v*. Dollar Land Holdings Plc [1994] 1 BCLC 464   41
El Sombrero Ltd, Re [1958] Ch 900   144
Elder *v*. Elder and Watson (1952) SC 49   264
Eley *v*. Positive Government Security Life Association (1876)
    1 Ex D 88   62, 63
ELS Ltd, Re; Ramsbottom *v*. Luton Borough Council [1994] BCC 449   294
Engel *v*. Netherlands (1976) 1 ECHR 647   116
English, Scottish and Australian Chartered Bank, Re [1893] 3 Ch 385   307
Erlanger *v*. New Sombrero Phosphate Co. (1878) 3 App Cas 1218   85
Estmanco (Kilner House) Ltd *v*. GLC [1982] 1 WLR 2   261, 273
Evans *v*. Brunner Mond [1921] 1 Ch 359   53
Expanded Plugs Ltd, Re [1960] 1 WLR 514   269

Exxon Corporation *v.* Exxon Insurance Consultants International Ltd
[1982] Ch 119   17

Fargo Ltd *v.* Godfroy [1986] 3 All ER 279   255
F. G. Films, Re [1953] 1 WLR 483   38
Firestone Tyre Co. *v.* Llewellin [1957] 1 WLR 464   36
Foss *v.* Harbottle (1843) 2 Hare 461   251, 254, 256, 261, 262, 264, 272
Framlington Group Plc and Another *v.* Anderson and Others [1995]
1 BCLC 475   208
Francovich and Boniface *v.* Italian Republic [1992] ECR 133   334, 346
Freeman & Lockyer *v.* Buckhurst Park Properties Ltd [1964]
2 QB 480   76, 81
Fulham Football Club and Others *v.* Cabra Estates Plc [1994]
1 BCLC 363   202

Gencor ACP Ltd *v.* Dalby [2000] 2 BCLC 734   206
George Fischer (Great Britain) *v.* Multi Construction Ltd,
Dexion Ltd [1995] 1 BCLC 260   258
George Newman and Co., Re [1895] 1 Ch 674   153
Georgiou, Re (1988) 4 BCC 322   220
Gerber Garment Technology Inc *v.* Lectra Systems Ltd and Another
[1997] RPC 443   258
German Date Coffee Co., Re (1882) 20 Ch D 169   268, 269
Giles *v.* Rhind [2002] EWCA Civ 1428   259
Gilford Motor Co. *v.* Horne [1933] Ch 935   31
Gluckstein *v.* Barnes [1900] AC 240   85
Gover's Case [1875] 1 Ch D 182   87
Gramophone and Typewriter Ltd *v.* Stanley [1908] 2 KB 89   161
Graphical Paper and Media Union *v.* Derry Print and Another [2002]
IRLR 380, 7 January 2002   37
Great Northern Salt and Chemical Works Co., Re (1890) 44 Ch D 472   151
Greenhalgh *v.* Arderne Cinemas Ltd [1946] 1 All ER 512; [1951]
Ch 286   70, 73–4, 285, 286
Grierson, Oldham and Adams Ltd, Re [1968] Ch 17   305

H, Re [1966] 2 BCLC 500   31
H and Others (restraint order: realisable property), Re [1966]
2 BCLC 500   31
Halifax Building Society *v.* Meridian Housing Association [1994]
2 BCLC 540   57
Halifax Sugar Refining Co. *v.* Franklyn (1890) 59 LJ Ch 591   158
Halt Garage (1964) Ltd, Re [1982] 3 All ER 1016   55, 120

Harman and Another *v.* BML Group Ltd [1994]
    2 BCLC 674   144, 146, 149
Harold Houldsworth & Co. (Wakefield) Ltd *v.* Caddies [1955]
    1 WLR 352   158
Harrods *v.* Lemon [1931] 2 KB 157   28
Hellenic and General Trust Ltd, Re [1976] 1 WLR 123   306
Heron International *v.* Lord Grade [1983] BCLC 244   258
Hickman *v.* Kent and Romney Marsh Sheepbreeders [1915]
    1 Ch 881   63, 64
Hinchcliffe *v.* Secretary of State for Trade and Industry [1999]
    BCC 226   228
Hogg *v.* Cramphorn Ltd [1967] Ch 254   261
Holder's Investment Trust Ltd, Re [1971] 1 WLR 583   283
Horsley & Weight Ltd, Re [1982] Ch 442   55
Houldsworth *v.* City of Glasgow Bank (1880) 5 App Cas 317   72, 99
Howard *v.* Patent Ivory Co. (1888) 38 Ch D 156   89
R. P. Howard Ltd & Richard Alan Witchell *v.* Woodman Matthews
    and Co. [1983] BCLC 117   258
Howard Smith Ltd *v.* Ampol Petroleum Ltd [1974] AC 821   94, 200
Huggins (1730) 2 Stra 883   39
Hutton *v.* West Cork Railway Company (1883) 23 Ch D 654   8, 53, 54
Hydrodan (Corby) Ltd, Re [1994] BCC 161   152

In Plus Group Ltd *v.* Pyke [2002] EWCA Civ 370   209
Industrial Developments *v.* Cooley [1972] 1 WLR 443   206
International Sales and Agencies *v.* Marcus [1982] 3 All ER 551   78, 79
Introductions Ltd *v.* National Provincial Bank Ltd [1970] Ch 199   54
Island Export Finance Ltd *v.* Umunna and Another [1986] BCLC
    460   208
Item Software (UK) *v.* Fassihi [2004] EWCA Civ 1244   207

John Morley Building Co. *v.* Barras [1891] 2 Ch 386   151
Johnson *v.* Gore Wood & Co. [2000] UKHL 65   257, 258, 259, 260
Jon Beauforte (London) Ltd, Re [1953] Ch 131   54
Jones *v.* H. F. Ahmanson & Co. (1993) 1 Cal 3d   35
Jones *v.* Lipman [1962] 1 All ER 442   30
Jupiter House Investments (Cambridge) Ltd, Re [1985] BCLC 222   125

Karella *v.* Minister of Industry, Energy and Technology (1991)
    ECR I-02691 (judgment of 30 May 1991), OJ C166/12;
    [1994] 1 BCLC 774   334, 340
Keenan Brothers Ltd, Re [1986] BCLC 242   291

Lady Gwendolen, The [1965] P 294   42
Lagunas Nitrate v. Lagunas Syndicate [1899] 2 Ch 392   86
Larvin v. Phoenix Office Supplies Ltd [2002] EWCA Civ 1740   265
Lee v. Lee's Air Farming [1916] AC 12   29, 37
Lee v. Sheard [1956] 1 QB 192   258
Lee, Behrens & Co. Ltd, Re [1932] 2 Ch 46   9
Leeds United Holdings plc, Re [1996] 2 BCLC 545   263, 264
Legal Costs Negotiators Ltd, Re [1999] BCC 547   266
Lennard's Carrying Company Ltd v. Asiatic Petroleum Co. Ltd
  [1915] AC 705   42
H. Leverton Ltd v. Crawford Offshore (Exploration) Services Ltd
  (in liquidation) (1996) The Times, November 22nd   31, 43
Levy v. Abercorris Slate and Slab Co. (1883) 37 Ch D 260   289
Lifecare International PLC, Re [1990] BCLC 222   305
Littlewoods Stores v. IRC [1969] 1 WLR 1241   38
Living Images Ltd, Re [1996] 1 BCLC 348   227
Lo-Line Electric Motors Ltd, Re (1988) 4 BCC 415; Re [1988]
  BCLC 698   227, 229, 232
London Sack and Bag v. Dixon [1943] 2 All ER 763   61
London School of Electronics Ltd, Re [1986] Ch 211   263
Lonrho v. Shell Petroleum [1980] 1 WLR 627   36, 43–4, 190
Looe Fish Ltd, Re [1993] BCC 368   202

Macaura v. Northern Assurance Co. [1925] AC 619   28
Mackenzie & Co. Ltd, Re [1916] 2 Ch 450   285
Maclaine Watson & Co. v. DTI (International Tin Council) [1990]
  BCLC 102   36
Macro (Ipswich) Ltd, Re [1994] 2 BCLC 354   263
Majestic Recording Studios Ltd, Re [1989] BCLC 1   226, 231
Malyon v. Plummer [1963] 2 All ER 344   28, 29, 37
Marleasing SA v. La Comercial International de Alimentation SA
  (1990) ECR I-4135   341
Marquis of Bute's Case, The [1892] 2 Ch 100   192
Marshall's Valve Gear Co. v. Manning Wardle & Co. [1909] 1 Ch 267   162
Matthew Ellis, Re [1933] Ch 458   320
McNulty's Interchange Ltd & Another, Re (1988) 4 BCC 533   229
Melhado v. Porto Alegre Ry Co. (1874) LR 9 CP 503   63
Melton Medes v. SIB (1994) The Times, July 27th   107
Menier v. Hooper's Telegraph Works [1874] LR 9 Ch D 350   204, 260
Meridian Global Funds Management Asia Ltd v. Securities
  Commission (PC) [1995] 2 BCLC 116   42, 44
Meux's Brewery Co. Ltd, Re [1919] 1 Ch 28   126

Mitchell & Hobbs (UK) *v.* Mill [1996] 2 BCLC 102 — 159
Moffatt *v.* Farquhar (1878) 7 Ch D 591 — 72
Moore *v.* Bresler Ltd [1944] 2 All ER 559 — 41
Mosly *v.* Koffyfontein [1904] 2 Ch 108 — 289
Movitex Ltd *v.* Bulfield and Others [1988] BCLC 104 — 199, 205

National Dock Labour Board *v.* Pinn & Wheeler Ltd & Others
  [1989] BCLC 647 — 36
National Motor Mail Coach Co., Re [1908] 2 Ch 515 — 87
Nelson *v.* James Nelson & Sons Ltd [1914] 2 KB 770 — 66, 155, 158
New British Iron Company *Ex Parte* Beckwith, Re [1898]
  1 Ch 324 — 65, 154
New Bullas Trading Ltd [1993] BCC 251 — 292
New Generation Engineers Ltd, Re [1993] BCLC 435 — 225
Newhart Developments Ltd *v.* Co-operative Commercial Bank Ltd
  [1978] QB 814 — 315
Neptune (Vehicle Washing Equipment) Ltd *v.* Fitzgerald [1995]
  1 BCLC 352 — 27
Neptune (Vehicle Washing Equipment) Ltd *v.* Fitzgerald (No. 2),
  Re [1995] BCC 1000 — 7
R. A. Noble & Son (Clothing) Ltd, Re [1983] BCLC 273 — 262, 268
North West Transportation *v.* Beatty (1887) 12 App Cas 589 — 147
Northumberland Avenue Hotel Co., Re (1866) 33 Ch D 16 — 89
Nurcombe *v.* Nurcombe [1985] 1 All ER 65 — 255, 272

Oakdale (Richmond) Ltd *v.* National Westminister Bank plc [1997]
  1 BCLC 63 — 337
Official Receiver *v.* Brady and Others [1999] BCLC 258 — 220
Old Silkstone Collieries, Re [1954] Ch 169 — 285
Omnium Electric Palace *v.* Baines [1914] 1 Ch 332 — 85
O'Neill and Another *v.* Phillips [1999] 2 BCLC 1 — 265, 266
Oshkosh B'Gosh Inc *v.* Dan Marbel Inc Ltd [1989] BCLC 507 — 88

P&O European Ferries Ltd (1990) 93 Cr App R 72 — 40
Pamstock Ltd, Re [1994] 1 BCLC 736 — 225
Panagis Pafitis and Others *v.* Bank of Central Greece and Others
  (12 March 1996) Lexis 6244 — 340
Panorama Developments Ltd *v.* Fidelis Furnishing Fabrics [1971]
  3 WLR 440 — 77, 83, 162
Parke *v.* Daily News [1962] Ch 927 — 5, 6, 8–9
Paul & Frank Ltd *v.* Discount Bank (Overseas) Ltd [1967] Ch 348 — 298
Pavlides *v.* Jensen [1956] Ch 565 — 253, 261

Peel *v.* London and North Western Rly Co. [1907] 1 Ch 5   143
Pender *v.* Lushington (1877) 6 Ch D 70   147
Percival *v.* Wright [1902] 2 Ch 421   94, 189
Pergamon Press, Re [1970] 3 WLR 792   271
Peter's American Delicacy Company Ltd (High Court of Australia),
    Re (1939) 61 CLR 457   60, 70
Phonogram *v.* Lane [1981] 3 WLR 736   88
Piercy *v.* S. Mills & Co. Ltd [1920] 1 Ch 77   200, 215
Polly Peck International Plc (in administration), Re [1996]
    2 All ER 433   37
Portuguese Copper Mines, Re (1889) 42 Ch D 160   158
Possfund Custodian Trustee *v.* Diamond [1996] 2 BCLC 665   100
Prichard's Case (1873) LR 8 Ch 956   63
Produce Marketing Consortium Ltd [1989] 1 WLR 745   322
Prudential Assurance Co. Ltd *v.* Newman Industries Ltd (No. 2)
    [1982] Ch 204; [1982] 1 All ER 354   253, 256, 258
Pudas *v.* Sweden (1988) 10 ECHR 380   115
Puddephatt *v.* Leith [1916] 1 Ch 200   148
Punt *v.* Symonds & Co. [1903] 2 Ch 506   200, 214–15

R *v.* Farmizer (Products) Ltd [1995] 2 BCLC 462   322
R *v.* Gomez [1992] 3 WLR 1067   120, 198
R *v.* Goodman [1994] BCLC 349   220
R *v.* Panel on Takeovers *Ex Parte* Datafin [1987] 2 WLR 699   303
R *v.* Panel on Takeovers and Mergers *Ex Parte* Guinness PLC [1989]
    BCLC 255   303
R *v.* Phillipou [1989] Crim LR 559 and 585   198
R *v.* Secretary of State for Trade, *Ex Parte* Perestrello [1981] QB 19   271
R *v.* SIB [1995] 2 BCLC 76; [1996] 2 BCLC 342   107
R *v.* Smith [1996] 2 BCLC 109   321
R & H Electric and Another *v.* Haden Bill Electrical Ltd [1995]
    2 BCLC 280   266
Rayfield *v.* Hands [1960] Ch 1   62
J. H. Rayner (Mincing Lane) Ltd *v.* Department of Trade and Industry
    [1987] BCLC 667; [1988] 3 WLR 1033 (CA)   36, 44
Read *v.* Astoria Garage (Streatham) Ltd [1952] 2 All ER 292   65, 66, 156
Reckitt & Colman Ltd *v.* Borden Inc [1990] 1 All ER 873   17
Red Label Fashions Ltd, Re [1999] BCC 308   263
Regal (Hastings) Ltd *v.* Gulliver [1942] 1 All ER 378   205, 206, 207, 260
Richmond Gate Property Co. Ltd, Re [1965] 1 WLR 335   66, 154
Rights and Issue Investment Trust Ltd *v.* Stylo Shoes Ltd [1965]
    Ch 250   71

Robbie *v.* Whitney Warehouses [1963] 3 All ER 613   296
Rolled Steel Products *v.* British Steel Corporation [1985] Ch 246   56
Rolus Properties Ltd & Another, Re (1988) 4 BCC 446   229, 232
Royal British Bank *v.* Turquand (1856) 6 E&B 327   75, 76
Royal Trust Bank *v.* National Westminster Bank plc and Another
    [1996] 2 BCLC 682   293
Russell *v.* Northern Bank Development Corporation Ltd [1992]
    BCLC 1016   149

Salisbury Gold Mining Co. *v.* Hathorn [1897] AC 268   148
Salmon *v.* Quinn & Axtens [1909] AC 442   63, 64, 73
Salomon *v.* Salomon [1897] AC 22   22, 26, 29, 30, 36, 37, 39, 85
Saltdean Estate Co. Ltd, Re [1968] 1 WLR 1844   126
Sam Weller & Sons Ltd, Re (Re A Company (No. 823 of 1987))
    [1990] BCLC 80   264
Saul D Harrison & Sons plc, Re [1995] 1 BCLC 14   264, 265
Saunders *v.* UK (Case 43/1994/490/572) [1977] BCC 872   271
Schweppes Ltd, Re [1914] 1 Ch 322   286
Scott *v.* Frank F. Scott (London) Ltd [1940] Ch 794   72
Scottish Co-operative Wholesale Society Ltd *v.* Meyer
    [1959] AC 324   32, 189, 204, 213
Secretary of State for Trade and Industry *v.* Bottrill [1999] BCC 177   29
Secretary of State for Trade and Industry *v.* Ettinger; Re Swift
    736 Ltd [1993] BCLC 896   230
Secretary of State for Trade and Industry *v.* Gray and Another [1995]
    1 BCLC 276   225, 227, 229, 230, 232
Secretary of State for Trade and Industry *v.* Hickling and Others
    [1996] BCC 678   229
Secretary of State for Trade and Industry *v.* McTighe and Another
    (No. 2) [1996] 2 BCLC 477   226
Secretary of State for Trade and Industry *v.* Rosenfield [1999] BCC
    413   231
Selangor United Rubber Estates *v.* Craddock [1968] 1 WLR 1555   130
Sevenoaks Stationers, Re [1991] BCLC 325   224, 226, 230, 231, 232
M. J. Shanley Contracting Ltd, Re (1979) 124 SJ 239   146
Shindler *v.* Northern Raincoat Co. Ltd [1960] 1 WLR 1038   72, 155
Shuttleworth *v.* Cox Bros & Co. (Maidenhead) Ltd [1927] 2 KB 9   69
Sidebottom *v.* Kershaw, Leese & Co. Ltd [1919] 1 Ch 290   68, 69
Smith *v.* Croft (No. 2) [1988] Ch 114   254, 256, 272–3
Smith *v.* England and Scottish Mercantile Investment Trust [1896]
    WN 86   296
Smith *v.* Henniker-Major & Co. [2002] EWCA Civ 762   79, 80

Smith *v.* Van Gorkom [1985] 488 A.2d 858   195, 213–14

Smith New Court Securities Ltd *v.* Citibank NA and Others [1996]
    4 All ER 769   87

Smith New Court Securities *v.* Scrimgeour Vickers (Asset
    Management) Ltd and Another (1996) *The Times*, November
    22nd   100, 102

Smith, Stone & Knight *v.* Birmingham Corporation [1939] 4 All
    ER 116   36, 43

Southard & Co. Ltd, Re [1979] 3 All ER 556   32

Southern Foundries Ltd *v.* Shirlaw [1940] AC 701   71, 155

Southern Pacific Co. *v.* Bogert (1919) 250 US 483   34

Specialist Plant Services Ltd *v.* Braithwaite Ltd [1987] BCLC 1   297

Standard Chartered Bank *v.* Walker [1992] 1 WLR 561   191

Stanford Services, Re [1987] BCLC 607   224, 225, 248

Stein *v.* Blake [1998] 1 BCLC 573   258

Stirling *v.* Maitland (1864) 5 B&S 840   155

Syndesmos EEC, Vasco *et al. v.* Greece *et al.* (1992) ECR I-2111
    (judgment of 24 March 1992)   340

Tesco Supermarkets *v.* Nattrass [1972] AC 153   41

Thomas Marshall (Exports) Ltd *v.* Guinle [1979] Ch 227   210

L. Todd (Swanscombe) Ltd, Re [1990] BCC 125   321

Tomberger *v.* Gebruder von der Wettern GmbH [1996] 2 BCLC 457   341

Tottenham Hotspur plc, Re [1994] 1 BCLC 655   264

Trevor *v.* Whitworth (1887) 12 App Cas 409   119

Trustor AB *v.* Smallbone [2001] 1 WLR 1177   31

Trustor AB *v.* Smallbone and Others (No. 2) [2001] 3 All ER 987   37

G. E. Tunbridge Ltd, Re [1995] 1 BCLC 409   293

Tunstall *v.* Steigman [1962] QB 593   29

Twycross *v.* Grant (1877) 2 CPD 469   83

Unisoft Group Ltd (No. 2), Re [1994] BCC 766   152

Unit Construction Co. *v.* Bullock [1960] AC 351   36

Viho Europe BV *v.* Commission of the European Communities
    (supported by Parker Pen Ltd, Intervener) (1996) *The Times*,
    December 9th   33

Walker *v.* Stones [2001] BCC 757   258

Welch (1946) 62 LQR 385   41

Welton *v.* Saffery [1987] AC 299   63

West Mercia Safetywear Ltd, The Liquidator of the Property
   of *v*. Dodd and Another [1988] BCLC 250 — 190
Westburn Sugar Refiners Ltd, *Ex Parte* [1951] AC 625 — 125
Wheatley *v*. Silkstone and Haigh Moor Coal Company (1885)
   29 Ch D 715 — 295
White *v*. Bristol Aeroplane Company [1953] Ch 65 — 286
Will *v*. Murray (1850) 4 Ex 843 — 148
William Gaskell Group *v*. Highley [1994] 1 BCLC 197 — 292
Williams *v*. Natural Life Health Foods Ltd [1998] 2 All ER 577 — 30
Wilson *v*. Kelland [1910] 2 Ch 306 — 299
Windward Islands (Enterprises) UK Ltd, Re [1983] BCLC 293 — 143
Winkworth *v*. Edward Baron [1987] BCLC 193 — 191
Wood *v*. Odessa Waterworks (1889) 42 Ch D 636 — 61, 63
Wood Skinner & Co., Re [1944] Ch 323 — 280
Woodroffes (Musical Instruments) Ltd, Re [1986] Ch 366 — 294

Yenidje Tobacco Co. Ltd, Re [1916] 2 Ch 426 — 269
Yorkshire Woolcombers Association Ltd, Re [1903]
   2 Ch 284 — 290, 292, 301

Table of Statutes and Directives

Amendment to the Fourth and Seventh Directives (SI 1992/2452)   341

Bank of England Act 1998   106
Bankruptcy (Scotland) Act 1985   329
Betting and Gaming Duties Act 1981   327
   Schedule 2   327
   s. 12.1   327
   s. 14   327

Canada Business Corporations Act of 1975   3
Community Interest (Audit, Investigations and Community
   Enterprise) Act 2004   11, 19
   s. 35   19
Companies Act 1948
   s. 54   131
   s. 210   213
   Table A, Art. 80   159, 160
Companies Act 1967   270
Companies Act 1980   119, 122, 339, 340, 341
Companies Act 1981   119, 131, 340, 341
Companies Act 1985   3, 50, 101, 224
   Part VII   341
   Part X   219
   Schedule 4   134
     para. 51(3)   135
   s. 2(1)(c)   47
   s. 9   61, 67
   s. 14   60, 61, 62, 64, 65, 72
   s. 23   282
   s. 35   252, 339
   s. 35A   79, 80
   s. 35A(2)(b)   79

s. 35A(2)(c)	79
s. 36C	88
s. 36C(1)	90
s. 97	87
s. 111A	72, 100
s. 125	284
s. 125(7)	287
s. 151	131, 132, 133
s. 153	132
s. 175	294
s. 196	328
ss. 228–230	343
s. 300	224, 231, 248
s. 303	155, 156, 157
s. 309	5, 162, 164, 199
s. 322A	80
s. 371	143, 144
s. 395(1)	297, 298, 300
s. 395(2)	300
s. 396(1)	297
s. 398	299
s. 398(4)	299
s. 410	294
s. 416	299
s. 416(1)	299
s. 416(2)	299
s. 425	307
s. 431(2)(c)	270
s. 432(1)	270
s. 432(1)(b)	270
ss. 433–435	271
s. 436	271
s. 437	274
s. 438	271
s. 440	271
s. 441(1)	271
s. 447	274
ss. 447–452	270
s. 448	274
s. 459	44, 71, 193, 264, 265, 266, 267, 268, 269, 311
ss. 459–461	99, 213, 262
ss. 459(2)	267

s. 460	267
s. 711A(1)	299
s. 711A(4)	299
s. 719	6
s. 736	15
s. 755	13
s. 756	13
Table A	59, 64, 151, 166–84
Arts. 1–118	166–84
Art. 45	148, 172
Art. 51	148, 173
Art. 64	152, 175
Arts. 64–98	151, 175–81
Art. 70	151, 159, 160, 176
Art. 72	158, 159, 176
Art. 73	151, 176
Art. 81	157, 177–8
Art. 82	154, 178
Art. 84	151, 154, 158, 178
Arts. 88–98	157, 179–81
Art. 110	127, 182
Companies Act 1989	15, 47, 72, 82, 294, 297, 341, 343
Schedule 19	
Art. 11	267
s. 108	339
s. 131	100
s. 145	267
Companies Act 2006	3, 42, 47, 58, 64, 75, 79, 119, 126, 142, 150, 161, 197, 250, 272, 311
Chapter 3	16
Part 7	14
Part 10	6
Part 15	246
Part 30	274–5
s. 3(2)	12
s. 3(3)	12
s. 5	11
s. 7	3, 6, 12, 16, 23
s. 8	12, 16
s. 9	12, 18
s. 9(4)	12
s. 10	12

s. 14	18
s. 15	18
s. 15(4)	18
s. 16	18
s. 18	59
s. 20	59
s. 20(1)(b)	59
s. 21	67, 146
s. 22	62, 65
s. 25	67
s. 31	46
ss. 31–41	76
s. 33	61, 65, 73, 154, 157
s. 39	46
s. 39(2)	46
ss. 39–41	76
s. 40	46, 49, 76, 77, 78, 89
s. 40(1)	78
s. 40(2)(a)	78
s. 40(2)(b)(ii)	78
s. 40(2)(b)(iii)	79
s. 40(4)	46
s. 41	49, 77, 80
s. 41(3)	50
s. 41(5)	50
s. 51	88
s. 53	16
s. 54	16
s. 55	16
s. 58	13
s. 60	13
s. 61	13
s. 62	13
s. 66	16
ss. 77–81	17
s. 90	15
s. 98	15
s. 98(4)	15
s. 98(5)	15
s. 152	151
s. 154	151
s. 154(2)	151

s. 155	152
s. 157	153
s. 161	76, 77, 157
s. 168	143, 155, 157, 158, 166
s. 168(5)	155
s. 169	157
s. 170	203
s. 170(3)	24, 191
s. 170(4)	24, 191
s. 171	200
s. 172	23, 24, 26, 139, 163, 190, 196, 198, 215, 254, 255
ss. 172–177	215
s. 173	202, 211, 216
s. 174	194, 216
s. 175	203, 216–17
s. 175(2)	208
s. 176	204, 205, 211, 217
s. 177	217–18, 243
s. 178	211
s. 182	158, 243
s. 183	158, 211, 243–4
s. 184	217, 243
s. 185	217, 243
s. 188	156, 219, 244–5
s. 189	219
s. 190	245–6
ss. 190–196	219
s. 191	245, 246
s. 197	246–7
ss. 197–214	219
s. 199	247
s. 215	246, 247–8
ss. 215–222	219
ss. 217–221	248
s. 239	50, 199, 252, 283
s. 239(3)	256
s. 239(4)	256
s. 239(7)	199, 255
s. 247	6, 9
s. 248	158
s. 249	158
s. 250	151, 152

s. 251	151, 152
s. 252	153
s. 253	153
s. 260	262
s. 260(3)	261
s. 261	254
s. 262	254
s. 262(3)	256
s. 262(4)	257
s. 263	254, 255
s. 263(4)	254
s. 270	162
s. 271	162
s. 273	162
s. 281(2)	146
s. 282	146
s. 283	146
s. 288	143
s. 296(4)	143
s. 302	143
s. 303	143
s. 305	143
s. 306	143
s. 318	145
s. 321	147
s. 324	142
s. 336	143, 144
s. 336(3)	144
s. 336(4)	144
ss. 381–385	136
s. 382(3)	136
s. 383(4)	137
s. 386	136
s. 387	136
s. 388	136
s. 393	136
ss. 394–396	136
s. 398	137
s. 399	137
s. 411	138
s. 412	138
s. 413	138

s. 415	138
s. 416	138
s. 417	138
s. 417(2)	138
s. 424	246
s. 465	137
s. 465(3)	137
ss. 475–484	138
s. 477	137
s. 510	143
s. 541	278
s. 542	278
s. 551	93, 94
ss. 560–577	93
s. 561	94
s. 562	93
s. 562(5)	93
s. 567	93
s. 570	93
s. 582	127
s. 586	14
s. 629	284
s. 630	284, 286, 288
ss. 630–634	286
ss. 630 *et seq.*	67
s. 630(5)	287
s. 630(6)	284
s. 633	287
s. 633(4)	287
s. 634	287
s. 641	124
s. 641(4)	124
ss. 641–657	124
s. 645	126
s. 645(4)	126
s. 646	126
s. 646(5)	126
s. 647	126
s. 648(2)	126
s. 649	127
s. 656	134
s. 658	129

s. 659	129
s. 677	130
s. 678	130, 132, 133
s. 679	130
s. 681	133
s. 682	134
s. 684	127
s. 685	127
s. 686(1)	128
s. 710	128
s. 712	128
s. 714	128
s. 715	129
s. 716	128
s. 717	128
s. 738	289
s. 754	290
s. 755	91
s. 756	91
s. 761	14
s. 763	14
s. 793	304
s. 829	121, 123
s. 829(2)	121
s. 830(2)	122
s. 831	123
s. 847	123
s. 860	297
ss. 860–877	297
ss. 902–941	306
s. 917	306
s. 931	306
s. 932	306
s. 934	306
s. 939	306
ss. 942–946	303
s. 943(1)	303
s. 943(2)	303, 304
s. 943(3)	304
s. 952	304
s. 955	304
s. 979	305

s. 981   305
s. 983   305
s. 986   305
s. 993   321
s. 994   262, 268, 274
ss. 994–996   252, 262, 272, 274–5
ss. 994 *et seq.*   287
s. 995   274–5
s. 996   267, 275
ss. 1035–1039   271
s. 1159   16, 137
s. 1161   138
s. 1162(2)   138
Companies (Mergers and Divisions) Regulations 1987 (SI 1987
    No. 1991)   341
Companies (Single Member Private Limited Companies) Regulations
    1992 (SI 1992/1699)   315, 343, 344
Companies (Tables A to F) Regulations 1985, SI 1985 No. 805
    (as amended by SI 1985 No. 1052)   160
Company Directors Disqualification Act 1986   121, 157
    Schedule 1   225
        Part I   223
        Part II   223
    s. 1   224
    s. 2   220
    ss. 2–5   220
    s. 3   221
    s. 3(2)   221
    s. 3(3)   221
    s. 4   221
    s. 4(1)(a)   221
    s. 4(1)(b)   222
    s. 5   221
    s. 6   44, 220, 222, 223, 224, 231, 232, 233, 248
    s. 6(2)   223
    s. 6(4)   220
    s. 8   202, 233
    s. 9   223
Company Law Reform Bill 2005   59
Company Securities (Insider Dealing) Act 1985   235
    s. 2   236
    s. 3   239

s. 9	236
Consequential Provisions Act 1985	315
Criminal Justice Act 1993	234, 348
Part V	234
Schedule 1	238
Schedule 2	234
s. 52	237
s. 52(2)	239
s. 52(2)(a)	238
s. 52(2)(b)	238
s. 52(3)	238
s. 53	238
s. 53(3)	239
s. 53(6)	239
s. 54	234, 235
s. 54(2)	234
s. 55	237
s. 56	235
s. 57	235, 236, 237
s. 57(1)(b)	235
s. 58	235
s. 59	238
s. 62	240
s. 63	239
Decision 3/52 of the High Authority of the Coal and Steel Community	329
Art. 6	329
Delaware Corporation Law	199
s. 102(b)(7)	199
s. 174	199
Disclosure of Interests in Shares (Amendment) Regulations 1993, SI 1993/1819	344
Disclosure of Interests in Shares (Amendment) (No. 2) Regulations 1993, SI 1993/2689	344
ECSC (European Coal and Steel Community) Treaty	
Art. 49	329
Art. 50	329
Art. 50(3)	329

Employment Protection Act 1975
  s. 101   328
Employment Protection (Consolidation) Act 1978
  s. 12(1)   328
  s. 19   328
  s. 27(3)   328
  s. 31(3)   328
  s. 31A(4)   328
Employment Rights Act 1996   29
Enterprise Act 2002   303
European Communities Act 1972
  s. 2   334
  s. 9   339
European Community amending Directive (SI 1992/2452)   344
European Community Amendment to the Fourth and Seventh
  Directives (Directive 90/605/EEC, OJ 1990 L317/60)   341
European Community Amsterdam Treaty 1999   333, 335
European Community Companies (Accounts of Small and
  Medium-Sized Enterprises and Publication of Accounts in ecu)
  Regulations 1992 (90/604 EEC, OJ 1990 L317/57)   341, 342
European Community Council Directive 80/987/EEC of 20 October
  1980 on the approximation of the laws of the Member States
  relating to the protection of employees in the event of the
  insolvency of their employer (Francovich Directive) (OJ 1980
  L283/23)   346–7
  Art. 11   347
European Community Council Directive of 23 July 1990 on the
  Common System of Taxation Guidelines in the Case of a Parent
  Company and Subsidiaries of Different Member States   349
European Community Council Directive 91/308 EEC on Money
  Laundering (OJ 1991 L166/77)   347, 349
European Community Directive 68/151/EEC
  Art. 9   48
European Community Directive 77/197   340
European Community Directive 94/8   342
European Community Directive 2001/34/EC   116, 345
European Community Directive for informing and consulting
  employees of groups (Directive 94/95; OJ 1994 L254/64)   348
European Community Directive on Insider Dealing
  (89/592/EEC)   234, 345
  Art. 2   236
  Art. 2(2)   237

Art. 2(3) 238
Art. 2(4) 239
Art. 5 240
Art. 13 240
European Community Directive on the information to be published when a major holding in a listed company is acquired or disposed of 344
European Community Draft Proposal for a Ninth Directive 344
European Community Draft Proposal for a Thirteenth Directive on takeovers 310
Art. 9(2) 310
European Community Eighth Directive (OJ 1984 L126/30) 342
European Community Eleventh Directive on the disclosure requirements of branches of certain types of company (OJ 1989 L395/36) 343
European Community Fifth Directive 26, 150
European Community First Directive (68/151/EEC) 79, 339, 342
Art. 11 339
European Community Fourth Directive (OJ 1978 L222/11) 122, 341, 343
Art. 11 342
Art. 15(3)(a) 342
Art. 15(4) 342
Art. 53(2) 342
European Community Investment Services Directive 116
Art. 1 116
Art. 4 116
European Community Maastricht Treaty 1993 332, 333, 335
European Community Market Abuse Directive 234
European Community Market Abuse Directive (2003/6/EC) 234, 345
European Community proposed Ninth Directive on Company Law 33, 34, 36
European Community Prospectus Directive (OJ 32 L124, 5 May 1989) 99, 101, 102, 116
Art. 11(2) 99
European Community Prospectus Directive (2003/71/EC; OJ L345, 31 December 2003) 344
European Community Regulation on Insolvency Proceedings (1346/2000 OJ L160/1) 345
European Community Second Directive (OJ 1977 L26/1) 14, 134, 139, 334, 339
Art. 25 340

Arts. 25–29   340
Art. 29   340
European Community Seventh Directive (OJ 1983 L193/1)   341, 343
European Community Sixth Directive (OJ 1982 L378/47)   341
European Community Tenth Directive (OJ 1985 C23 28/11)   344
European Community Third Directive (OJ 1978 L295/36)   340
European Community Twelfth Directive (OJ 1989 L395/40)   6, 343
Art. 7   343
European Company Statute (Regulation (EC) 2157/2001, OJ 2001
   L294/1; Directive 2001/86/EC, OJ 2001 L294/22)   26, 150,
                                                              167, 338–9, 349
Annex   338
Art. 7   338
European Convention on Human Rights   115
Art. 6(1)   115
European Economic Community Treaty (Treaty of Rome)   333, 335, 336
Art. 59   337
Art. 61   345
Art. 67   345
Art. 82   303
Art. 85 (now Art. 81)   32, 33, 333, 337
Art. 86 (now Art. 82)   333, 337
Art. 100   348
Art. 169   347
Art. 177   336, 347
Art. 249   334
European Economic Interest Grouping (EEIG) Regulation
   (OJ 28 L199/1)   337
European Parliament and Council Directive 2004/25/EC of
   21 April 2004 on Takeover Bids   303, 305, 350–1

Financial Services Act 1986   101, 106, 107, 108, 239
Financial Services Act 1986 (EEA Regulated Market) (Exemption)
   Order 1995   116
Financial Services Act 1986 (Investment Services) (Extension of
   Scope) Order 1995   116
Financial Services and Markets Act 2000 (FSMA 2000)   92, 94, 99,
                                                   101, 102, 106, 108, 116, 234
Part V   101
Part VI   92
Part 11   274
Schedule 1   108

Schedule 2	107, 108, 234
para. 11	108
Part 1	108
Schedule 6	113
Schedule 10	97, 98, 99, 103–5
para. 2	98
Schedule 11	102
ss. 2–6	106
s. 5	109
s. 6	110
s. 19	107, 108
s. 20	113
s. 23	113
s. 24	113
s. 31	113
s. 33	113
s. 41	113
s. 66	113
s. 79	96
s. 80	96, 97, 103
s. 80(1)	94
s. 80(2)	94
s. 80(3)(b)	97
s. 80(4)	97
s. 80(4)(c)	97
s. 81	94, 97, 103
s. 82	94, 97
s. 84	102
s. 90	94, 96, 97
s. 90(1)	103, 104
s. 90(4)	104
s. 91	96, 99
s. 119	115
s. 132	114
s. 137	114
s. 144(2)	101
s. 228	115
s. 426	113
s. 427	113
Human Rights Act 1998	113, 115, 228, 271

Income and Corporation Taxes Act 1988
    s. 203   326
    s. 559   326
Insider Dealing Act 1986
    s. 7   239
Insolvency Act 1986   120, 275, 313
    Part I   134
    Part XVIII   329–30
    Schedule 1   315, 325–6
    Schedule 1A   313
    Schedule 6   290, 317, 326–9
    s. 1   313
    s. 1A   313
    ss. 1–7   222
    s. 2(2)   314
    s. 6(1)   314
    s. 8   222
    s. 14   324–5
    s. 14.42   325
    s. 40   328
    s. 42(1)   315
    s. 53(6)   328
    s. 54(5)   328
    s. 84   316
    s. 89   316
    s. 94   323
    s. 95   317
    s. 96   317
    s. 107   316
    s. 110   134, 308
    ss. 110–111   307, 311
    s. 122(1)(g)   268
    s. 124A   316
    s. 125(2)   268
    s. 129   316
    s. 143   316–17
    s. 175   317
    s. 201   323
    s. 205   323
    s. 212   321, 323
    s. 213   321
    s. 214   44, 194, 319, 322

s. 214(2)	321
s. 214(5)	322
s. 238	120, 317, 319
s. 239	318, 319
s. 239(4)(b)	318
s. 241	318
s. 244	319
s. 245	320
s. 249	320
s. 251	320
s. 386	317
s. 390(1)	316
s. 423	319
s. 435	320, 329–30
s. 651	323
s. 652	323
Insolvency (No. 2) Act 1994	318
Insolvency (Northern Ireland) Order 1989 (SI 1989/2405 (NI 19))	275
Insolvency Rules	
r. 1.20(1)	314
Investment Services Regulations 1995	116
Landlord and Tenant Act 1954	
s. 30	30
Law of Property Act 1925	
s. 85(1)	295
s. 86(1)	295
Law of Property Act 1969	
s. 6	30
Limitation Act 1980	
s. 991	322
Mental Health Act 1983	177
Mental Health (Scotland) Act 1960	177
Money Laundering Regulations 1993, SI 1993 No. 1933	348
Oversea Companies and Credit Financial Institutions (Branch Disclosure) Regulations 1992	343
Performance of Companies and Government Departments (Reporting) Bill 2004	42, 196–7, 211–12

Public Offers of Securities Regulations (POSR) 1995 (SI 1995
    No. 1537)   92, 94, 99, 101, 102
    Reg. 8(1)   99
    Reg. 9   94, 99
    Reg. 10   94
    Reg. 14   99
    Reg. 14(1)   94
    Reg. 15   99
    Reg. 93   99
    Schedule 1   99
Public Offers of Securities Amendment Regulations 1999   99, 101

Reserve Forces (Safeguard of Employment) Act 1985   327

Single European Act (SEA) 1986   333
Social Security Act 1975   327
Social Security (Northern Ireland) Act 1975   327
Social Security Pensions Act 1975
    Schedule 3   327
Statutory Water Companies Act 1991   274

Theft Act 1968
    s. 15   99
    s. 19   99
Theft Act 1978
    s. 1   99
    s. 2   99
Trade Descriptions Act 1968   41

Value Added Tax Act 1983   326
'Vredling' Directive (OJ Vol 26C 217/3)   348

Chapter 1

The reasons for forming companies

Key words

▶ **Corporate personality** – the company is regarded in law as separate from the humans who invest in it and make it work.

▶ **Directors** – persons (in big companies usually men!) who are elected to look after the day-to-day running of the company.

▶ **Limited liability** – shareholders are not obliged to pay more than is due to purchase their shares even if the company cannot pay its debts.

▶ **Shareholders or members** – pay money to the company in return for a 'share' which gives them specified rights (often voting rights) and the possibility of receiving a share of the profits.

'The limited liability corporation is the greatest single discovery of modern times. Even steam and electricity are less important than the limited liability company,' said Professor N. M. Butler, President of Columbia University (quoted by A. L. Diamond in Orhnial (ed.), *Limited Liability and the Corporation* (Law Society of Canada, 1982) p. 42; see also Sealy, *Company Law and Commercial Reality* (Sweet & Maxwell, 1984) p. 1).

Why so important? Well, a huge proportion of the world's wealth is generated by companies, and companies are most often used by people as a tool for running a commercial enterprise. Many of these businesses start in a small way, often by co-operation between a small number of people.

If such a commercial undertaking prospers, the persons involved will wish to expand the undertaking, which will generally require an injection of money. This can be achieved by inviting more people to contribute to the capital sum which the business uses to fund its activities. The alternative is to raise a loan. The latter course has the disadvantage of being expensive because the lender will charge interest. On the other hand, the option of inviting a large number of persons to be involved in a business may have considerable disadvantages. One is that they may disagree with each other as to how the business should best be run. They may even disagree with each other as to who should make the decisions about how the business is to be run. This is partially solved in a company by the necessity of having a formal constitution (the memorandum and articles of association) which sets out the voting and other rights of all the members (shareholders) of a company.

Another disadvantage of expansion of a business is that as the amounts dealt with increase, so also do the risks. One great advantage of the most widely used type of company is that it has 'limited liability'. This means that if the company becomes unable to pay its debts, the members of that company will not have to contribute towards paying the company's debts out of their own private funds: they are liable to pay only the amount they have paid, or have promised to pay, for their shares. This means that contributors to the funds of businesses which are run on this limited liability basis may be easier to find. Limited liability is also said to encourage greater boldness and risk-taking among the business community, so that new avenues to increasing commerce are explored. The advantage of limited liability may lead quite small businesses to use a company, although this may not be advantageous from a tax point of view and does lead to a number of obligations to file accounts and so on, which create a considerable burden for a small concern. Further, if a very small business wishes to raise a loan from a bank, the bank will normally require a personal guarantee from the people running the business. This means that the advantage of limited liability will, practically speaking, be lost.

A further disadvantage of attempting to run a business with a large number of people involved is that considerable difficulties may be experienced when some of those people die, wish to retire or simply leave the business. There may be great difficulties for a person dealing with the business in deciding precisely who is liable to pay him. In a shifting body of debtors, an outsider may experience extreme difficulty in determining which people were actually involved in the business at the time that is relevant to his claim against it. This difficulty is solved by the invention of the legal fiction of corporate personality. The idea is that the company is an entity separate from the people actually involved in it. This fictional 'legal person' owns the property of the business, owes the money that is due to business creditors and is unchanging even though the people involved in the business come and go. The importance of the invention was emphasised when in 1971 a team of Canadian lawyers (principally Robert Dickerson, John Howard, Leon Getz and Robert Bertrand) undertook a comprehensive review of Canadian corporation law. Their aim was not piecemeal reform but a fundamental review of company law in order to determine what the purpose behind the existence of the current rules was, whether that purpose was being achieved, and where necessary to suggest improvements to the system. Because the review started from fundamentals it contains many lessons for those who seek to formulate law to govern the behaviour of corporations and their relationship with the public and the state.

The first point made in the introduction to the Canadian review (*Proposals for a New Business Corporations Law of Canada* (Canadian Government

Publications, 1971), authors as above) is the importance of the corporation in the economic system: it can 'scarcely be exaggerated'.

Those reformers came to the conclusion that Canadian companies were subject to too much regulation and proposed a drastic reduction of the number and complexity of rules applying to companies. Their recommendations were largely accepted and became the Canada Business Corporations Act of 1975. The United Kingdom company law rules were the subject of a Department of Trade and Industry review during 2001–2. Although it was publicised as a 'fundamental review' of company law, the changes that resulted are quite modest in substance. However, the Companies Act 2006 almost completely replaces the previous Companies Act 1985 so that many sections have been slightly changed in substance and bear a different number in the new Act.

As we examine the company law of the UK, it is useful to consider the purpose behind the various rules and whether they are sufficiently effective in achieving their purpose; also whether they justify the expense which is incurred by companies to ensure that their operations stay within the complicated framework that has grown up. Section 7 of the Companies Act 2006 describes 'the method of forming a company':

'(a) A company is formed under this Act by one or more persons subscribing their names to a memorandum of association . . ., and

(b) complying with the requirements of this Act as to registration.'

If only it were as simple as that! That, of course, describes only the requirements for forming a company. Many and greater complications will arise when we look at how the company makes decisions and does business in the course of its active life.

1.1 The elements of a company

The people who provide the money to run the business of the company are called members or shareholders. They put money into the business by buying shares from the company. Their rights and liabilities are governed by the constitution of the company contained in the memorandum and articles of association (see Chapters 2, 4 and 5 for the contents and further discussion of these documents). It is usual (though not universal) for a share to carry voting rights. Many of the decisions necessary for the running of a company can be arrived at by a majority vote of the shareholders taken at a meeting. However, it would be cumbersome for the everyday running of the business to be conducted in this way, so the company votes that certain people should be 'directors' of the company and should take care of the everyday running of the company. The meeting of shareholders has the right to appoint and remove directors by majority vote. This procedure is not as democratic as it first appears, however, as the person who is suggested as a director may himself hold a majority of the shares and be able to vote himself into office. Alternatively, a director may be able to prevent his removal from office by special multiple voting rights which operate when there is an attempt to remove him (*Bushell* v. *Faith* [1970] AC 1099) or by making it very expensive for the company to get rid of him.

If there is a disagreement between the shareholders of the company and the management in the form of the directors, complicated issues arise. This is particularly the case when the directors have a majority of the shares. If they were permitted to use that majority in any way they wished they would be able to authorise themselves to use the company assets for any purpose, perhaps even to deprive other shareholders of any valuable stake they had in the company. This would amount to an unjust expropriation of the property of a minority and the court will intervene to prevent such a thing happening (see Chapter 13). However, the court will be cautious not to intervene too readily in the running of the company, partly because many of the judgments that must be made by directors are of a commercial nature and the courts have little expertise in making such assessments. Another reason is that the directors would be hampered if they constantly had to look over their shoulders when commercial judgments had to be made, in case an action could be brought against them. Another balancing act has to occur because the directors are similar to trustees in that they are engaged in handling money in which other people have a considerable stake – both the shareholders and the creditors of the company. They should therefore behave honestly and fairly. However, if the rules making them responsible for mistakes or breaches of duty are too strict, directors may become too cautious in performing an entrepreneurial role and the business may fail from that cause.

The law has sought to balance these interests by use of the idea that the company is a thing separate from any of the humans involved in the business (see Chapter 2). If a company is seen as a person, albeit a legal person, the directors owe it a duty to act in the correct fashion. If they do not do so, it is the company's right to sue them. This theory means that the directors will only be sued if a majority vote is in favour of such action. To prevent this from allowing directors too much power, particularly where they have control of the majority of votes, the court will overturn the result of such a majority vote where it feels that in the particular circumstances the result is very unfair to other shareholders (see Chapters 11, 12 and 13). It is very difficult to get the balance between these groups right, but it is important to view the law as holding the line between the various interest groups, as the jargon involved with the law sometimes obscures the reality.

Another tension is created between shareholders and creditors where the subject of disposal of the assets of the company is concerned. The law in the UK follows the European Union rules and takes the line that attempts must be made to keep a sum of money in the company which will be available to pay debts if the company fails. To this end an elaborate system regulating the raising and maintenance of capital has grown up (see Chapter 9). Furthermore there are elaborate accounting rules which are expensive for the company to maintain. These may be of use to a potential investor or someone who is contemplating doing business with the company, but are against the interests of current shareholders who would usually prefer either to have the money paid to them or to use it in the business.

There are many other tensions which will appear in a study of this subject. The technicalities of the subject become more comprehensible if the law is seen as struggling to hold a fair line between competing interest groups. The debate as to the proper degree and method of regulating this balance of interests is often referred to as the 'corporate governance debate'. It has been carried on vigorously in recent years (see Chapter 10).

1.2   Outsiders

It is important to draw a distinction between the relationships which occur between the inside factions within a company and the relationships between a company and those who are 'outsiders'. Identification of 'outsiders' may be complicated, as a single person may be both a member and an outsider at the same time. Consider someone who is owed money by the company on a commercial transaction; in his capacity as a commercial creditor he is an outsider. If he also owns shares he will have rights as a member, but the two bundles of rights are quite separate and the one will not usually affect the other.

It may be surprising to some that employees are also (in that capacity) outsiders. Until recently directors were not entitled to give any priority to the welfare of the employees unless this could be shown to be in the ongoing interests of the company (*Parke* v. *Daily News* [1962] Ch 927) (see Case note, p. 8). Section 309 of the Companies Act 1985 introduced the idea of a duty to employees although it was generally agreed to be ineffective. This section provided:

'(1) The matters to which the directors of a company are to have regard in the performance of their functions include the interests of the company's employees in general, as well as the interests of its members.

(2) Accordingly, the duty imposed by this section on the directors is owed by them to the company (and the company alone) and is enforceable in the same way as any other fiduciary duty owed to a company by its directors.

(3) This section applies to shadow directors as it does to directors.'

Although it appears at first sight that this could have made a significant change in the interests of employees, the duty was enforceable only if a majority of shareholders voted to sue the directors for non-compliance, an unlikely event. In fact the letter of the law was often observed by the interests of employees being on the agenda at directors' meetings, the chairman remarking, 'We are now considering the interests of employees', before passing to the next business. This section has now been replaced by the more comprehensive statutory statement of directors' duties in Part 10 of the Companies Act 2006. Whether or not the employees' position has been improved is doubtful and is discussed in Chapter 11.

A more substantial change in the law was effected by s. 719 Companies Act 1985, now s. 247 Companies Act 2006, which gives the company power to make provision for its present or past employees, or those of its subsidiaries, on cessation of the business of the company. This provision will prevent payments to employees made in those circumstances being challenged on the grounds that it is a misuse of money which should have been paid to the shareholders and therefore not in the interests of the company. It was the latter argument which succeeded in *Parke* v. *Daily News* (see Case note, p. 8). This case will not now be followed, because s. 247 permits a company to make these payments. However the case is still useful as an illustration of the competing interest groups within a company.

1.3 'Parent' and 'subsidiary' company

It may be convenient for different parts of a business to be managed by separate but connected companies. In this case one company may cause another to be formed. If the first company wishes to retain a measure of control over the new company, it will take shares in it. If the shareholding gives the first company control over the new company, the first company will be a 'parent' company and the new company a 'subsidiary'. In certain circumstances the financial affairs of subsidiary companies must be disclosed by the parent company in its accounts. Chapter 2 discusses the definition of parent and subsidiary. However, group activities still cause problems and the courts have sometimes ignored the separate personality of companies within a group (see Chapter 3).

1.4 Single member companies

The EC Twelfth Directive (see Chapter 18) provides that all Member States must allow the formation of single member companies. This Directive has now been implemented in the Companies Act 2006 which provides for formation of a company by a single person (s. 7).

However, it is still important to recognise the separation between the director and member and the company itself. In *Re Neptune (Vehicle Washing Equipment) Ltd* v. *Fitzgerald (No. 2)* [1995] BCC 1000 it was held that a sole director and shareholder of a single member company was under an obligation to disclose an interest in a contract which he was contemplating terminating with the company (in this case, his own service contract). The importance lies in the fact that directors must understand that, when they are dealing with corporate property, they are dealing with the property of the company rather than their own personal property and several other interest groups (creditors, employees) may have an interest in the outcome of the decision. Single member companies must not be regarded as 'my company' by that sole member.

Hot Topic . . .
CORPORATE GOVERNANCE

The collapse of the giant American corporation ENRON has brought into sharp focus some of the ways in which companies can be misused. In that case the finances of the company were manipulated in order to persuade the public that the company was extraordinarily successful and that the share price would continue to rise. Many people, including employees, were persuaded to buy shares which became almost worthless overnight. Many employees also lost their pensions. The fraud was not spotted by the company's accountants who were making huge sums of money doing 'consultancy' work for ENRON. This points to the importance of having both internal control within a company and external scrutiny of what is going on.

Further Reading: B. McClean and P. Elkind, *The Smartest Guys in the Room: The Amazing Rise and Scandalous Fall of ENRON* (Harmondsworth, Penguin, 2003).

Summary

Companies are a useful tool for conducting business, particularly when that business has grown bigger than can usefully be managed by a few people and also requires an increase in funding. The laws governing companies seek to achieve a balance between the various interested groups within companies and also between the protection of people dealing with companies and the freedom to act of those managing companies. If too many regulations are imposed on companies, these may be counterproductive in that they may make the organisation inefficient and thus liable to fail.

Case note

Parke v. Daily News Ch 927

The *Daily News* sold a significant part of its business and proposed to distribute the money received to employees who would be made redundant by the sale. Although most shareholders supported this distribution, the plaintiff (who was also a shareholder) objected. The question was whether the majority vote in favour of the distribution entitled the directors to give away the money of the company (and thus money which would eventually be returned to shareholders, including Mr Parke). The court held that such an action could only be justified if the company would benefit from the distribution. As the company had sold the main part of its business, the kindness to employees could not be justified as having any future effect in securing loyalty or attracting good staff. The distribution was held to be invalid despite the majority vote in favour. Plowman J referred to a previous case which had arisen on similar facts, *Hutton* v. *West Cork Railway Company* (1883) 23 Ch D 654. He said:

'That was a case where a company had transferred its undertaking to another company and was going to be wound up. After completion of the transfer, a general meeting of the transferor company was held at which a resolution was passed to apply (among other sums) a sum of 1000 guineas in compensating certain paid officials of the company for their loss of employment, although they had no legal claim for compensation
. . . In an oft-cited judgement, Bowen

LJ said: "Now the directors in this case have done, it seems to me, nothing at all wrong . . . Not only have they done nothing wrong but I confess I think the company have done what nine companies out of ten would do, and do without the least objection being made. They have paid, perhaps liberally, perhaps not at all too liberally, persons who have served them faithfully." But that, of course, does not get rid of the difficulty. As soon as a question is raised by a dissentient shareholder . . . sympathy must be cut adrift, and we have simply to consider what the law is. In this particular instance the plaintiff is a person who stands *prima facie* in the condition of those who are bound by the vote of a general meeting acting within the powers of a general meeting, but he complains that the majority propose to expend certain purchase money which the company are receiving . . . in two ways which he thinks are beyond their powers . . . Now can a majority compel a dissentient unit in the company to give way and to submit to these payments? We must go back to the root of things. The money which is going to be spent is not the money of the majority. That is clear. It is the money of the company, and the majority want to spend it. What would be the natural limit of their power to do so? They can

only spend money which is not theirs but the company's if they are spending it for the purposes which are reasonably incidental to the carrying on of the business of the company. That is the general test. *Bona fides* cannot be the sole test, otherwise you might have a lunatic conducting the affairs of the company, and paying away its money with both hands in a manner perfectly *bona fide* yet perfectly irrational . . . one must "ask oneself what is the general law about gratuitous payments which are made by the directors or by a company so as to bind a dissentient. It seems to me you cannot say the company has only got power to spend the money which it is bound to pay according to law, otherwise the wheels of business would stop, nor can you say that directors . . . are always to be limited to the strictest possible view of what the obligations of the company are. They are not to keep their pockets buttoned up and defy the world unless they are liable in a way which would be enforced at law or in equity. Most businesses require liberal dealings. The test there again is not whether it is *bona fide*, but whether, as well as being done *bona fide*, it is done within the ordinary scope of the company's business, and whether
it is reasonably incidental to the carrying on of the company's business for the company's benefit. Take this sort of instance. A railway company, or the directors of the company, might send down all the porters at a railway station to have tea in the country at the expense of the company. Why should they not? It is for the directors to judge, provided it is a matter which is reasonably incidental to the carrying on of the business of the company, and a company which always treated its employees with Draconian severity, and never allowed them a single inch more than the strict letter of the bond, would soon find themselves deserted – at all events, unless labour was very much more easy to obtain in the market than it often is. The law does not say that there are to be no cakes and ale, but that there are to be no cakes and ale except such as are required for the benefit of the company . . . [*Re Lee, Behrens & Co. Ltd.* [1932] 2 Ch 46 was also cited] . . . The conclusions which, I think, follow from these cases are: first that a company's funds cannot be applied in making *ex gratia* payments as such; secondly, that the court will inquire into the motives actuating any gratuitous payment; and the objectives which it is intended to achieve" . . .'

In the event, the distribution in *Parke* was held to be invalid. The case would not be decided in the same way today, as s. 247 Companies Act 2006 gives express power to provide for employees where the business is to cease or be substantially lessened as a result of transfer to another party.

Exercises

1. Why are companies a useful form of business association?

2. Identify the different interest groups involved in *Parke* v. *Daily News* (see Case note). What is the best method of resolving the potential conflicts between these groups?

3. After reading Chapters 3 and 11, consider the implications of the separate corporate personality of companies within a group on the duties of directors.

Chapter 2

Starting a company

Key words

> **Community interest company (CIC)** – this type of company was created by the Community Interest (Audit, Investigations and Community Enterprise) Act 2004. It is a new form of company designed for community enterprises which are not charities.
>
> **Private company (Ltd)** – this type of company may not advertise in order to sell shares.
>
> **Public company (PLC)** – this type of company may offer shares to the public by advertisement.
>
> **Quoted company** – a company whose shares are quoted on a recognised stock exchange.

The first decision that must be made by those considering incorporation of a business is the type of company that will be suitable.

2.1 Limited and unlimited companies

An unlimited company has the advantage of being a legal entity separate from its members, but lacks the advantage that most people seek from incorporation, that is the limited liability of the members. Thus, the members of an unlimited liability company will be held responsible for all of the debts of the company without limit. Unlimited companies therefore form only a small proportion of the number of registered companies.

Limited liability companies have the advantage that the members' liability to contribute to the debts of the company has a fixed limit which is always clear. There are two ways of setting the limit, by issuing shares or by taking guarantees from the members that they will contribute up to a fixed amount to the debts of the company when it is wound up or when it needs money in particular circumstances. The first type of company is a company limited by shares, the second is a company limited by guarantee (s. 5 Companies Act 2006). No new companies limited by guarantee and having a share capital to provide working money can be formed (s. 5 Companies Act 2006). This means that a guarantee company formed in the future cannot have any contributed capital. This form is therefore unsuitable for commercial enterprises although the form has been extensively used to carry out semi-official functions, particularly in the sphere of regulation of the financial services market.

In a company limited by shares, the members know that they will never have to pay more into the company than the full purchase price of their shares. This need not necessarily be paid when they are first purchased. When some money is outstanding on shares, the company may issue a 'call' for the remainder to be paid, but it can never demand more than the full price due to the company for that share. Such a company will be registered as a 'company limited by shares'. By s. 3(2) Companies Act 2006 if the liability of shareholders 'is limited to the amount, if any, unpaid on the shares held by them', the company is 'limited by shares'. By s. 3(3) if the liability is limited to such amount 'as the members undertake to contribute to the assets of the company in the event of it being wound up', it is a company 'limited by guarantee'. By s. 7 a company is formed by 'one or more persons subscribing their name to a memorandum of association and complying with the requirements' of the Act as to registration. Section 8 requires the memorandum of association to state that those submitting it wish to form a company and agree to become members. If the company is to have a share capital they must take at least one share each. The memorandum must be delivered to the registrar of companies together with an application for registration (s. 9 Companies Act 2006). Section 9 sets out the basic requirements which must be included in the application for registration. These include:

- the name of the company;
- whether the registered office is to be in England and Wales, in Wales, in Scotland or Northern Ireland;
- whether it is to be limited and if so by shares or guarantee;
- whether it is to be a private or public limited company.

By s. 9(4) Companies Act 2006 in the case of a company limited by share capital, the application must state the amount of share capital with which the company proposes to be registered (further details in s. 10). This is known as its 'authorised share capital', 'registered share capital' or 'nominal share capital'. It does not represent the amount actually contributed at the time when the company is formed, which may only be part of the share price.

2.2   Public and private companies

As we have seen, where a company is to be registered as a public company, this must be stated in the application for registration and the words 'public limited company' (or the abbreviation PLC or plc) must come at the end of its name, unless it is Welsh or a community interest company (s. 58 Companies Act 2006). A private limited company must normally have a name ending in ltd unless it is a community interest company, a charity or otherwise exempted by ss. 60, 61 or 62 Companies Act 2006. The application must also contain a statement of the proposed officers.

The fundamental difference between public and private companies is that only public companies may invite the public to subscribe for shares. Section 755 Companies Act 1985 prohibits a private company from offering, allotting or agreeing to allot securities to the public or with a view to them being offered to the public. Section 756 defines 'offer to the public' as including an offer to any section of the public, however selected. However, it is not an offer to the public if it can properly be regarded, in all the circumstances, as –

(a) being calculated to result, directly or indirectly, in securities of the company becoming available to persons other than those receiving the offer, or

(b) otherwise being a private concern of the person receiving it and the person making it.

In other words, the offeror and offeree must either be known to each other or be part of a close network of friends, family or acquaintances.

Public companies are therefore more suitable for inviting investment by large numbers of people. A private company is particularly suitable for running a business in which a small number of people are involved. Professor Len Sealy describes the situation as follows:

> 'During the nineteenth century (and indeed for a considerable period before that) the formation of almost all companies was followed immediately by an appeal to the public to participate in the new venture by joining as members and subscribing for "shares" in the "joint stock" . . . The main reason for "going public" in this way was to raise funds in the large amounts necessary for the enterprises of the period – often massive operations which built a large proportion of the world's railways, laid submarine cables, opened up trade to distant parts and provided the banking, insurance and other services to support such activities. The promoters would publish a "prospectus", giving information about the undertaking and inviting subscriptions. This process is often referred to as a "flotation" of the company or, more accurately, of its securities.' (Sealy, *Cases and Materials in Company Law*, 6th edn, Butterworths, 1996)

It would now be most unusual for a new enterprise to 'float' immediately. The Stock Exchange controls the rules for flotation and requires an established business record before it will permit it to occur. Another market, whose requirements are similar but not quite so strict, is the Alternative Investment Market (AIM). (For further discussion see Chapter 7.)

As one would expect, the regulations governing public companies are more extensive than those governing private companies. In many areas, however, no distinction is made between the two types of company.

2.3 Minimum capital requirements for a public company

We have seen that a private company need have only a very small amount of capital. However, the European Community Second Directive set a minimum capital for a public company. Section 763 Companies Act 2006 sets the minimum for UK companies at £50,000 or the euro equivalent and gives the power to the Secretary of State to specify a different sum by statutory instrument. The company is not obliged to have received the full £50,000. However, by s. 586 Companies Act 2006, public companies must receive at least one-quarter of the nominal value of the shares. The amount of capital actually contributed could be as little as £12,500, although the company would have a right to make a 'call' on the shareholders demanding payment of the unpaid capital (that is, the outstanding £37,500).

By s. 761 it is a criminal offence committed by the public company and any officer of it in default, to do business or to borrow money before the Registrar of Companies has issued a trading certificate to the effect that he is satisfied that the nominal value of the company's allotted share capital is not less than the prescribed minimum and that he has received a statutory declaration which must be signed by a director or secretary of the company and must:

(a) state that the nominal value of the company's allotted share capital is not less than the authorised minimum;
(b) specify the amount, or estimated amount, of the company's preliminary expenses;
(c) specify any amount or benefit paid or given, or intended to be paid or given, to any promoter of the company, and the consideration for the payment or benefit (see Chapter 6).

2.4 Change of status from public to private company and vice versa

A change of status from private to public company is much more common than registration as a public company on initial incorporation. Part 7 of the Companies Act 2006 provides for this change of status from private to public and from public to private status. In both cases the members of the company must pass a special resolution (a resolution passed by at least 75 per cent of the votes cast) to effect the change. In the case of a change from private to public, the Registrar of Companies must be provided with a statutory declaration that the minimum capital requirements for public companies have been satisfied and that the requisite special resolution has been passed (s. 90).

If the reverse change of status from public to private is undertaken, the members may find that it is more difficult to sell their shares. There are safeguards in the Act aimed at protecting a minority who object to such a change of status. Under s. 98 Companies Act 2006, the holders of 5 per cent or more of the nominal value of a public company's shares, any class of the company's issued share capital or 50 members may apply to the court for the cancellation of a special resolution to request re-registration as a private company. The court has an unfettered discretion to cancel or approve the resolution on such terms as it thinks fit (ss. 98(4) and 98(5) Companies Act 2006).

2.5 Groups

The old definition of this relationship was to be found in s. 736 Companies Act 1985. That read:

'(1) For the purposes of this Act, a company is deemed to be a subsidiary of another if (but only if) –
   (a) that other either –
      (i) is a member of it and controls the composition of its board of directors, or
      (ii) holds more than half in nominal value of its equity share capital, or
   (b) the first-mentioned company is a subsidiary of any company which is that other's subsidiary.'

This definition of the parent–subsidiary relationship caused two main difficulties. The first was that it concentrated on the number of shares held by (1)(a)(ii). This ignores the fact that control is exercised through voting rights, which need have no relationship to the number of shares held.

The second difficulty lay with the reference to the control of the board of directors. Under the original sections in the 1985 Act, a company was deemed to control the composition of the board of directors if it could appoint or remove the holders of all or a majority of the directorships. If one company could appoint less than a majority of the directors, but those it was able to appoint had extra voting rights so that they could outvote the other directors, then control of the board's activities was effectively achieved, while the arrangement was still outside the scope of the section.

By these and other methods it was possible to avoid the intended effect of the section, which was to treat a group of companies as a single business for various purposes, including accounting purposes.

Because of this the Companies Act 1989 introduced new definitions of this relationship. These sections have now been adopted by the Companies Act 2006 in s. 1159:

'(1) A company is a "subsidiary" of another company, its "holding company", if that other company –

(a) holds a majority of the voting rights in it, or

(b) is a member of it and has the right to appoint or remove a majority of its board of directors, or

(c) is a member of it and controls alone, pursuant to an agreement with other shareholders or members, a majority of the voting rights in it.

(2) A company is a "wholly owned subsidiary" of another company if it has no members except that other and that other's wholly owned subsidiaries or persons acting on behalf of that other or its wholly owned subsidiaries.'

The emphasis has shifted from ownership of shares to control of voting rights which are further defined by the Act. This gives a more realistic picture of a group of companies.

2.6 The memorandum of association and registration

It is essential that a company have a memorandum of association (ss. 7 and 8 Companies Act 2006) but the constitution of the company comprises the company's articles and any resolutions made under Chapter 3 of the Act which essentially are 'important' resolutions passed by special majorities or by unanimous agreement. It is very important to note that a company must have articles of association but if none are drafted or not all of the provisions of the 'model articles' are excluded then those model articles apply by default.

Name

The choice of a name for a company is of considerable importance and subject to a number of restrictions. As we have seen, with exceptions for companies of charitable or 'social' nature, if it is to have limited liability the name must end with 'Limited' (permitted abbreviation 'Ltd') for a private company, and 'Public Limited Company' (permitted abbreviation 'PLC' or 'plc') for a public company (or Welsh equivalents).

By s. 53 Companies Act 2006 a company may not be registered with a name which, in the opinion of the Secretary of State, would constitute a criminal offence or be offensive and the Secretary of State's approval is required for the use of a name which would be likely to give the impression that the company is connected with the government or any local authority, or which includes any word or expression specified in regulations made by the Secretary of State (ss. 54 and 55 Companies Act 2006). The name must not be the same as any other kept in the index of company names held by the Registrar (s. 66 Companies Act 2006).

By ss. 77–81 Companies Act 2006 a company can change its name by special resolution, by any other means provided for by its articles and by a resolution of its directors.

Passing off

One further restriction on the selection of names is imposed by the rules against using a name so similar to the name used by an existing business as to be likely to mislead the public into confusing the two concerns. Thus in *Exxon Corporation* v. *Exxon Insurance Consultants International Ltd* [1982] Ch 119 the court granted an injunction restraining the defendants from using the word Exxon in their company's name.

In *Reckitt & Colman Ltd* v. *Borden Inc* [1990] 1 All ER 873, Lord Oliver reaffirmed the test for passing off. The plaintiff in a passing-off action has to:

> 'establish a goodwill or reputation attached to the goods or services which he supplies in the mind of the purchasing public by association with the identifying "get-up" (whether it consists simply of a brand name or a trade description, or the individual features of labelling or packaging) under which his particular goods or services are offered to the public, such that the get-up is recognised by the public as distinctive specifically of the plaintiff's goods or services. Second, he must demonstrate a misrepresentation by the defendant to the public (whether or not intentional) leading or likely to lead the public to believe that goods or services offered by him are the goods or services of the plaintiff. ... Third, he must demonstrate that he suffers or ... that he is likely to suffer damage by reason of the erroneous belief engendered by the defendant's misrepresentation that the source of the defendant's goods or services is the same as the source of those offered by the plaintiff.'

So, the three basic elements of passing off are reputation, misrepresentation and damage to goodwill.

In *Asprey & Garrard Ltd* v. *WRA (Guns) Ltd & Another* [2001] EWCA Civ 1499 (11 October 2001), the issue was the defence arising from the use of one's own name in business. Although Mr Asprey was using his own name, the latter could be associated with a different retail shop, so causing confusion. The court stated that in this case the use of the name not only caused confusion but deception as well, as the name had been used as a trade mark. Thus, it is evident that an individual cannot carry on business in his own name if he is not honest and he causes deception. The principle is that anyone using his own name in business cannot prevent a passing-off claim by a company already operating under the same or very similar name.

2.7 Incorporation

Section 9 Companies Act 2006 requires delivery of the memorandum of association, the application for registration of the company and a statement of compliance to the Registrar of Companies for England and Wales, if the registered office is to be situated in either England or Wales, and for Scotland if the registered office is to be situated in Scotland.

The statement must be signed by or on behalf of the subscribers to the memorandum and the intended address of the company's registered office must be stated.

2.8 Duty of Registrar

Section 14 Companies Act 2006 provides that if the Registrar is satisfied that the requirements of the Act have been complied with he must register the documents delivered to him; and (s. 15) certify that the company is incorporated. The effect of this process of registration is set out in the remainder of s. 16 Companies Act 2006:

'From the date of incorporation mentioned in the certificate,
(2) The subscribers of the memorandum, together with such other persons as may from time to time become members of the company, are a body corporate by the name contained in the memorandum.
(3) That body corporate is capable of exercising all the functions of an incorporated company.
(4) The status and registered office of the company are as stated in, or in connection with, the application for registration.
(5) In the case of a company having a share capital, the subscribers to the memorandum become holders of the shares specified in the statement of capital and initial shareholdings.
(6) The persons named in the statement of proposed officer
 (a) as director, or
 (b) as secretary or joint secretary of the company,
 are deemed to have been appointed to that office.'

Section 15(4) provides that the certificate of incorporation is conclusive evidence that the requirements of the Act have been met and the company is duly registered. Thus, the company's existence as such is unchallengeable from the date of the issue of the certificate of incorporation.

2.9   Off-the-shelf companies

Ready-made companies can be acquired from enterprises which register a number of companies and hold them dormant until they are purchased by a customer. This may save time when a company is needed quickly for a particular enterprise. There used to be a potential problem in that the objects clause of such a company might not precisely cover the enterprise in question, with the result that such a company would be precluded from carrying on the desired business. Contracts made in pursuance of such an enterprise would be of no effect (see Chapter 4). However, many such companies will be formed in the future with the objects of a general commercial company and with unlimited powers. This will prevent any problems arising under the old law of *ultra vires* (see Chapter 4).

Hot Topic . . .

COMMUNITY INTEREST COMPANIES

The Community Interest (Audit, Investigations and Community Enterprise) Act 2004 provides for a new type of company to be known as a community interest company (CIC). This is for social enterprises who want to use their profits and assets for the benefit of the public. It is more flexible than a charity which is not able to generate profits. The most difficult problem is to provide for a test of community interest. Section 35 of the Act specifies that 'a company satisfies the community interest test if a reasonable person might consider that its activities are being carried on for the benefit of the community'. The Act also provides for a new regulator to which a CIC will report.

Summary

1. There are several types of company. The most common company is a limited company, the liability of the members being limited to the amount they have previously agreed. There are some unlimited companies where members are liable to pay the whole of the debts of the company.

2. Companies may have a share capital or be limited by guarantee. In the former case members buy shares. In the latter case members agree to contribute to the debts of the company up to a certain amount.

3. Companies may be public companies (PLCs) or private companies (normally having Ltd after their names). Only public companies can sell shares to the public. Public companies are subject to more regulations than private companies. Quoted companies are those whose shares are quoted on a recognised stock exchange.

Summary cont'd

4. There is a minimum capital requirement for public companies of £50,000.

5. Companies can change from public to private status and vice versa.

6. A company must have a memorandum of association.

7. The choice of the name of a company is important and subject to a number of restrictions.

8. Incorporation is achieved after the memorandum and articles are delivered to the Registrar of Companies.

9. Ready-made companies can be bought.

Exercises

1. What is the difference between the various types of companies?

2. What matters should be considered when choosing a name for a company?

3. What information is needed by the Registrar on the incorporation of a company?

4. When does a company come into existence?

Chapter 3

Corporate personality

Key words

> ▶ **Alter ego** – a device which attributes the acts of important managers to the company so that the company can be sued for compensation or convicted of crimes.
> ▶ **Lifting the veil** – looking at the fact situation and disregarding the effect of the legal fiction that all companies are completely separate from their shareholders.

The essence of a company is that it has a legal personality distinct from the people who compose it. This means that even if the people running the company are continuously changing, the company itself retains its identity and the business need not be stopped and restarted with every change in the managers or members (shareholders) of the business. If the company is a limited liability company, not only is the money owned by the company regarded as wholly distinct from the money owned by those running the company, but also the members of the company are not liable for the debts of the company (except where the law has made exceptions to this rule in order to prevent fraudulent or unfair practices by those in charge). Members can only be called upon to pay the full price of their shares. After that a creditor must depend on the company's money to satisfy his claim. This limitation of the liability of the members has led to careful rules being drawn up to attempt to prevent a company from wasting its money (Chapter 9). It is one of the disadvantages of incorporation that a number of formal rules, designed to protect people doing business with companies, have to be complied with. A partnership which consists of people carrying on a business with a view to making profits has many fewer formalities to be complied with. On the other hand, the members of an ordinary partnership are liable for all the debts incurred by the business they run. (It is possible now to form a limited liability partnership.) If large losses are made partners in an ordinary partnership must contribute their own money to clear the debts of the business. In practice this may be a distinction without a difference since, where small businesses are concerned, banks will not lend money to a company without first securing guarantees from those running the business so that if the company cannot pay its debts, such debts will be met from the personal assets of those in charge.

The separate personality of a company creates a range of problems because although the company is regarded as a person in law it can, of course, only function through the humans who are running the business in which the company is involved. The law must regulate the relationships between a company and its creators and members or shareholders as well as the relationship between a company and 'outsiders' who do business with the company.

3.1   The legal basis for the separate personality doctrine

The case of *Salomon* v. *Salomon* [1897] AC 22 is by no means the first case to depend on the separate legal personality of a company, but it is the most widely discussed in this context. Mr Salomon was a boot and shoe manufacturer who had been trading for over 30 years. He had a thriving business. He also had a large family to provide for. To enable the business to expand, he turned it into a limited liability company. As part of the purchase price he took shares in the company and lent the company money in return for 'debentures', which are paid off preferentially in the event of a liquidation. The company did not last very long. Almost immediately there was a depression in the boot and shoe trade and a number of strikes. Mr Salomon tried to keep the company afloat by lending it money and by transferring his debentures to a Mr Broderip for £5,000, which he handed over to the company on loan. However, liquidation was not long in coming. The sale of the company's assets did not realise enough to pay the creditors. The liquidator claimed that the debentures had been fraudulently issued and were therefore invalid. He also denied that the business had been validly transferred from Mr Salomon to the company. The grounds for both these claims were that the business had been overvalued at £39,000 instead of its true worth of around £10,000 and that the whole transfer to a limited company amounted to a scheme to defeat creditors. The judge who heard the case first admitted that the transfer had been legally carried out and could not be upset. However, he suggested (*Broderip* v. *Salomon* [1895] 2 Ch 323) that Mr Salomon had employed the company as an agent and that he was therefore bound to indemnify the agent. He said that the creditors of the company could have sued Mr Salomon despite the existence of the company to whom the business had been legally transferred. In the Court of Appeal, Mr Salomon's appeal was dismissed. However, the House of Lords took a different view. Lord MacNaughten said:

compensate

> 'The company is at law a different person altogether from [those forming the company] and, though it may be that after incorporation the business is precisely the same as it was before, and the same persons are managers, and the same hands receive the profits, the company is not in law the agent of the subscribers or trustee for them. Nor are the subscribers as members liable, in any shape or form, except to the extent and in the manner provided by the Act . . . If the view

of the learned judge were sound, it would follow that no common law partnership could register as a company limited by shares without remaining subject to unlimited liability.'

Thus was established the complete separation between a company and those involved in its operation. As with many principles of English law, having established first the principle we must then look at the problems caused by and the exceptions to that principle.

The fundamental importance of separate personality

The invention of the company as separate is vital as it means that it is free to develop as an instrument of business shaped by both the people involved in its running and those regulating its existence. That different models of companies have come to exist is a direct result of the fact that the company's separate personality sets it apart from the individuals that are running it. The models that have developed say a great deal about the society in which they operate.

What models exist?

The contractual theory

This is usually accepted as the philosophy underlying UK company law, which generally adheres rather strictly to a contractual theory of companies, regarding a company as primarily, if not solely, the property of and co-extensive with the members. This theory is exemplified by the idea in the Companies Act 2006 that a company is formed by 'one or more persons'. Section 7 Companies Act 2006 reads:

'(1) A company is formed under this Act by one or more persons –
    (a) subscribing their names to a memorandum of association . . ., and
    (b) complying with the requirements of this Act.'

Thus, at formation the owners alone are involved. The UK courts have tended to carry this theory into the period when the company is in full operation. This has the major consequence that the wishes of the shareholders are seen as the overriding consideration for management, who are obliged to act 'in the best interests of the company'. The apparent change to this structure contained in s. 172 Companies Act 2006 is unclear in scope. That section requires a director to act 'in a way he considers, in good faith, would be most likely to promote the success of the company for the benefit of its members as a whole', and in doing so have regard (among other matters) 'to a range of concerns including the interests of employees, long-term consequences of the decisions, impact on the environment etc.' (see Chapter 11 for a detailed discussion). However, this section is said to be based on the pre-existing common law and should be interpreted in accordance with those principles (ss. 170(3) and 170(4)) which seems to indicate that the law has not changed. However, numerous cases equate the interests of the shareholders alone with the interests of the company. The most logical explanation of the new rules is that the sensible director could not benefit shareholders without some concern for the other interests set out in s. 172. However, those interests are only to be considered through the lens of shareholder benefit. This has the effect of excluding other interests from consideration in the way the company is run, in particular leaving creditors, employees and the environment as 'outsiders', their interests only to be considered to the extent that failing to take account of them will destroy share value. This model is reflected in the structure of UK companies where employee directors are rare and shareholders elect the whole of the management team. Although this model would seem at first sight to be a simple one, it has inbuilt complications. For example, shareholders are not an amorphous body. Different shareholders will have different interests at any one time. The interest of an aged shareholder intent on enjoying the good life before departure may differ radically from the young shareholder just starting out in business life. Thus attempts by the UK courts to pin down the true meaning of the 'interests of the company', even applying this simple theory, have been fraught with difficulty and division. Much debate centres round whether a dissentient minority of shareholders should be considered when the 'interests of the company' are at stake. The interests of the company have been equated with 'the single individual hypothetical shareholder', but commentators have pointed out that this formulation does not solve the problem, because the hypothetical shareholder could be in the majority or in the minority. A hypothetical future shareholder has been suggested as the benchmark, but even this formulation does not solve the potential conflict between short-term and long-term policies. Thus even the simple model meets difficulties in its application.

Separation of ownership and control

The famous research of Berle and Means (in A. Berle and G. Means, *The Modern Corporation and Private Property*, New York, 1932) showed that the ownership and control of companies were increasingly in different hands. The identification of the shareholders with the company no longer represented reality. This could have led to a re-identification of the company as the creature of its professional managers, but instead the tendency has been to regard the company more and more as a creature in its own right and to struggle to identify the interests of the company as an entity clearly distinct from its shareholders. Critical theorists have argued from a Marxist perspective that the separation of ownership and control necessarily leads to a depersonalisation of the relationship between capital and labour, but this need not be the case provided that an inclusive model of this separate legal entity is chosen, rather than a divisive one. What are the alternatives?

The constituency or stakeholder model

In order to read other interested parties into the decision-making of directors, some have suggested a move to a constituency or stakeholder model of company law. There are two variants of this model. The adoption of one or the other variant will have little practical effect on the actual decisions made, but the different theoretical underpinning has important implications for determining which parties should have a corporate governance role. The first variant of the model sees the company as run in the interests of shareholders, it being in the interests of shareholders to take account of other interest groups, because to ignore them would damage shareholder interests. This approach is exemplified by legislation which details the interests which must be considered by directors in determining their actions while enforcement is left in the hands of shareholders. The importance of the routing of the constituency interests through the interests of the shareholders is that the logical group to enforce those interests is the shareholders themselves. In the second variant of the model it is accepted that interests of other groups must be taken into account, because such an approach directly benefits the company. In this variant the company is seen as encompassing interests other than those of shareholders. Then 'interests of the company' are seen as including at least the interests of employees and creditors as well as shareholders. The distinction between the two variants is that in the second it is more clearly the company which has the corporate governance role and it is less clear that shareholders should have an exclusive role in acting on behalf of the company to ensure that it is run in its best interests. It could be argued that the company should be able to depend on other interested groups to ensure its proper management. Both variants of this model are able to absorb the tendency of the courts to give different weight to the degree of interest of the constituencies, which will vary at different times in the history of the company, reflecting not least the financial health of the company; thus it is likely that creditors will be considered more important than shareholders when the company is insolvent. This model is hard to control because groups of interested parties are considered relevant since they comprise a described group and not because of any analysis of how closely they are in fact involved with the interests of the company.

The enterprise model

An enterprise model differs from a constituency model in that the directors not only have to take into account the interests of others as well as the shareholders; those interests are also regarded as part of the company, having a corporate governance role of their own inside the decision-making process. The contrast can be drawn between the obligation of directors to take account of the interests of employees under s. 172 Companies Act 2006 (which has no enforcement mechanism open to employees, only to shareholders) and the election of employees to the boards of companies. A further example would be the ability of a person named in the articles of association to nominate members of the supervisory board, a provision which would probably be used by banks to involve themselves in corporate decision-making. This model is the classic one developed in Germany and the Netherlands and originally reflected by the draft EC Fifth Directive and European Company Statute.

3.2 Problems caused by the personality doctrine and exceptions

The first 'personality' problem that can arise is that experienced by those seeking to form a company in order to carry on a business. While they are completing the formalities which will lead to registration of the company and the consequent gain of legal personality for the company, its creators may wish to sign contracts for the benefit of the company when it is formed. The difficulty is that the company does not exist as a legal person until registration and therefore cannot be party to any contract, nor can it employ agents to act on its behalf. The law on such 'pre-incorporation contracts' is explained in Chapter 6.

The second problem was the one under discussion in *Salomon*'s cases. A limited liability company can be a very powerful weapon in the hands of one determined on fraud and on defeating a creditor's rightful claims. Will the courts make no exceptions to the rule that a company is wholly separate from those who manage and control it?

A survey of the case law shows that the courts do contravene the strict principle of the separateness of the company from time to time. There is general agreement among those who have sought to analyse the relevant cases that the only principle that can be gleaned from them is that the courts will look at the human reality behind the company if the interests of justice provide a compelling reason for doing so. This may sound an excellent principle, but when the huge variety of fact situations that are likely to arise is considered, such a vague notion makes it extremely difficult to predict what a court will do in any given case. When the existence of the company is disregarded, commentators have called it the 'lifting' or 'piercing' of the veil of incorporation. There are a number of cases, discussed below, which are clearly relevant to the sanctity of the 'veil' of incorporation, but the whole of company law is riddled with examples of the validity of acts depending on the effect they will have on the members of a company.

An example would be where the part of the constitution of a company known as the articles of association is changed, that change can be challenged unless it can be justified as in good faith and for the benefit of the company as a whole. In order to determine the latter, the effect of the decision on the members of the company must be examined.

It is also said that the proper person to sue to redress a wrong done to the company is the company itself. However, there is an exception to this rule to prevent those in charge of the company causing damage to shareholders in a powerless minority, for example by taking the company's property. The examples in Chapter 13 clearly show the difficult task which those seeking to regulate a company have because of the doctrine of legal personality. The company must be given as much independence from its operators as possible, otherwise it would always be subject to interference from a large number of (probably disagreeing) voices and therefore be no less cumbersome than a partnership trying to operate by consensus. On the other hand, the law must always recognise the reality of the fact that the company can do nothing without human operators and that those human operators may wish to hijack the company for their own ends, to the detriment of others who have money at stake.

3.3 Statutory intervention

The personality of the company is recognised and ignored at will by the legislature. Those drafting legislation do not seem to respect the principle as being sacrosanct in itself and look merely to the end sought to be achieved by particular provisions. This is a highly practical approach. The courts might do well to admit that the only principle running through their decisions is 'justice in the individual case' and thus adopt a similarly pragmatic approach. Examples of statutory interference with the principle of legal personality are listed below (see Case notes, pp. 43–4). It should be noted that these are only examples. Many more can be found.

3.4 Lifting the veil

The separate personality of the company can have some unexpected and sometimes unwelcome effects. In *Neptune (Vehicle Washing Equipment) Ltd* v. *Fitzgerald* [1995] 1 BCLC 352 the defendant was a sole director of a company. Despite this he was obliged to make disclosure of a personal interest in a resolution which he passed purporting to terminate his contract of employment, although the court held that 'it may be that the declaration does not have to be out loud'. Although this sounds strange it emphasises that the contract was one between the director and the company so that in his capacity as an official acting in the interests of the company, the director must remind himself of his personal interest before determining a course of action. In *Macaura* v. *Northern Assurance Co.* [1925] AC 619 the court refused to ignore the separateness of the company and 'lift the veil' despite the fact that the consequence of so doing was to deny a remedy to someone whose personal fortune had gone up in smoke. Macaura had sold the whole of the timber on his estate to a company. He owned almost all of the shares in the company and the company owed him a great deal of money. Macaura took out an insurance policy on the timber in his own name. When almost all the timber was later destroyed by fire he claimed under the insurance policy. The House of Lords held that he could not do so. He no longer had any legal interest in the timber and so fell foul of the rule that an insurance policy cannot normally be taken out by someone who has no interest in what is insured.

Sometimes other rules of law can be used to mitigate the effects of the strict application of the doctrine. This was done in *Harrods* v. *Lemon* [1931] 2 KB 157. The estate agents' division of Harrods was acting as agent in the sale of the defendant's house. A purchaser was introduced and subsequently instructed surveyors to examine the house. The surveyors that were instructed were Harrods' surveyors' department. The survey disclosed defects as a result of which a reduced price was negotiated. The defendant had been informed prior to this of the fact that Harrods were acting on both sides of the sale. This would normally be a breach of the agency contract between the estate agents' department and the defendant. The defendant, however, agreed to Harrods continuing to act for her. The two departments of Harrods were in fact completely separate. The judge (Avory J) agreed that there had been a technical breach of the agency contract between Harrods and the defendant. Although the two departments were completely separate, the company in fact was one single person in the eyes of the law. However, he also insisted that the defendant should pay Harrods, despite the breach, as she had agreed to them continuing to act despite having full knowledge of the breach.

The following cases provide a prime example of the way the courts will disregard the separate personality of the company if that will achieve a just result, but will equally keep the veil of personality firmly in place where that will benefit someone for whom the court feels sympathy. In *Malyon* v. *Plummer* [1963] 2 All ER 344 a husband and wife had full control of a company. The husband was killed by the defendant in a car accident and the widow was unable to continue the business of the company. An insurance policy had been taken out on the man's life and £2,000 was paid to the company on his death. The shares of the company were therefore more valuable than they had been prior to his death. The plaintiff (widow) had received an inflated salary from the company prior to her husband's death. The court had to assess the future financial situation of the widow in order to set the amount of damages payable to her. It was decided that the excess of the plaintiff's salary over the market value of her services was a benefit derived from the plaintiff's relationship as husband and wife. It was therefore a benefit lost by his death and only the market value of her services should be taken into account in assessing her future position. This ignores the fact that she was employed by a company which should, in accordance with *Salomon's* case, have been regarded as a completely separate entity from both husband and wife. It did mean, however, that the widow got more. Similarly, the court held that the insurance money was money which should be regarded as having been paid to the wife as a result of the death of the husband. The shares owned by the wife should therefore be valued at the lower value before the £2,000 was paid.

It is very difficult to see a distinction in principle between *Malyon* v. *Plummer* where the veil was not just pierced but torn to shreds and *Lee* v. *Lee's Air Farming* [1916] AC 12 where the emphasis was laid heavily on the separate legal personality of the company. In this case the widow would have lost everything if the *Malyon* v. *Plummer* approach had been adopted. In *Lee* the appellant's husband was the sole governing director and controlling shareholder of a company. He held all but one of the shares in the company. He flew an aircraft for the company which had taken out an insurance policy which would entitle his widow to damages if when he died he was a 'worker' for the company. He was killed in a flying accident. It was held that the widow was entitled to compensation. Lee's position as sole governing director did not make it impossible for him to be a servant of the company in the capacity of chief pilot because he and the company were separate and distinct legal entities which could enter and had entered into a valid contractual relationship. The reasoning in *Lee* was followed in *Secretary of State for Trade and Industry* v. *Bottrill* [1999] BCC 177 where the Court of Appeal affirmed that a controlling shareholder could also be an employee of the company for the purposes of claiming under the Employment Rights Act 1996. The approach in *Lee* was followed in *Tunstall* v. *Steigman* [1962] QB 593. There a landlord was unable to terminate a tenancy on the ground that he was going to carry on a business on the premises because the business was to be carried on by a limited company. This was despite the fact that the landlord held all the shares in the company except for two which were held by her nominees and of which she had sole control.

The result in this case would be different if it fell to be decided now, because s. 6 Law of Property Act 1969 provides that where a landlord has a controlling interest in a company, any business to be carried on by the company shall be treated for the purposes of s. 30 Landlord and Tenant Act 1954 as a business carried on by him. The case remains useful as an illustration of the way in which the courts have approached the question of corporate personality. The corporate veil remained firmly in place in *Williams* v. *Natural Life Health Foods Ltd* [1998] 2 All ER 577 where the House of Lords held that a managing director was not liable for negligent advice given by the company. Liability would only arise where personal responsibility for the advice, based on objective factors, had been assumed and there had been reliance on the assumption of responsibility. This had not been established, despite the fact that the director had played a significant part behind the scenes in negotiations leading up to the grant of a franchise which the plaintiff purchased on the faith of financial projections furnished by someone introduced by the director and misrepresented as having relevant expertise. A brochure issued by the director's company had placed particular emphasis on the personal expertise and experience of the director. There were, however, no personal dealings between the managing director and the plaintiff.

3.5 Fraud

The ability to hide behind the corporate veil could be a powerful weapon in the hands of those with fraudulent tendencies. The courts have therefore always reserved the right to ignore a company which is formed or used merely to perpetrate a dishonest scheme. In *Salomon*'s cases both the Court of Appeal and the judge in the first instance thought that they had before them just such a case of fraud. Since there was no evidence of dishonest intent in that case it seems that these courts were using 'fraud' in a very wide sense. Indeed, they seem to have regarded the formation of the company so that the business could henceforth be carried on with limited liability as sufficient evidence of 'fraud'. To take such a wide view would defeat the whole notion of the separate existence of the company and make it impossible for small private companies to function in any way differently from partnerships. The importance of the decision in *Salomon* in the House of Lords is clear. A mere wish to avail oneself of the benefits of limited liability is not of itself to be regarded as fraudulent. A different view was taken of the conduct in *Jones* v. *Lipman* [1962] 1 All ER 442. In that case the first defendant agreed to sell land to the plaintiffs. When he later wished to avoid the sale he formed a company and transferred the land to it. The court held that the company was a 'cloak' for the first defendant, that he had the power to make the company do as he wished and therefore the court would order the transfer of land to the plaintiff. In *Trustor AB* v. *Smallbone* [2001] 1 WLR 1177 the defendant, the managing director of Trustor AB, transferred funds from the account of Trustor AB to another company, Introcom Ltd incorporated in Gibraltar, which was owned and controlled by him via a Liechtenstein trust. The board of directors did not authorise such a transaction. A part of these funds had found their way, via Introcom, to the defendant personally. The Court stated that: 'Introcom is liable, as constructive trustee, to account for and repay to Trustor the Trustor moneys that were paid to it . . . Introcom was the creature of the defendant. He owned and controlled Introcom. The payments out by Introcom of Trustor money were payments made with the knowing assistance of him . . . the defendant would be liable jointly and severally with Introcom for the repayment of that money with interest thereon. The defendant's joint and several liability would not be confined to the part that he personally received . . . the defendant is, in my view, clearly liable, jointly and severally with Introcom, for the whole of the sums for which Introcom is accountable.' The defendant was therefore found personally liable to return the funds in question on the basis that Introcom functioned as a façade used by him principally to misappropriate Trustor's funds. He tried to hide behind the corporate veil to escape his obligation to return the misappropriated funds but the court held him personally liable. Similarly, in *Gilford Motor Co.* v. *Horne* [1933] Ch 935 the court refused to allow the defendant to avoid an agreement that he would not compete with former employers. He had attempted to do so by competing with them in the guise of a limited company. Even clearer cases were *Re Darby* [1911] 1 KB 95 and *Re H* [1996] 2 BCLC 500. In *Re Darby* the corporation was simply a device whereby a fraudulent prospectus was issued and the directors of the company pocketed the public's money. The directors were prosecuted for fraud and convicted. The court held that the directors were liable to repay all the money that had been received by them via the company. In *Re H and Others (restraint order: realisable property)* [1996] 2 BCLC 500 two family companies had been used to defraud the revenue. The assets of the company could be treated as the assets of their fraudulent owners and seized. See also *H. Leverton Ltd* v. *Crawford Offshore (Exploration) Services Ltd (in liquidation)* (1996) *The Times*, November 22nd and Case note 1, p. 43.

3.6 Groups

The courts have sometimes to make difficult decisions about the circumstances in which a group of companies is to be regarded as one entity. Different jurisdictions have reached different answers. In UK case law there is no formal or informal recognition of group interests.

Do companies with a significant cross-shareholding have a special relationship? In the UK, while for many tax and accounting purposes groups of companies are treated as one unit, the courts are reluctant to admit the reality of interrelated companies acting in any way other than as a number of separate entities tied together by their relationship as significant shareholders in each other. Thus in *Scottish Co-operative Wholesale Society Ltd* v. *Meyer* [1959] AC 324 three directors of a subsidiary company were also directors of the parent company. Lord Denning said:

'So long as the interests of all concerned were in harmony, there was no difficulty. The nominee directors could do their duty by both companies without embarrassment. But, so soon as the interests of the two companies were in conflict, the nominee directors were placed in an impossible position. It is plain that, in the circumstances, these three gentlemen could not do their duty by both companies, and they did not do so. They put their duty to the co-operative society above their duty to the textile company . . .'

The approach of the UK courts is epitomised by Templeman LJ in *Re Southard & Co. Ltd* [1979] 3 All ER 556:

'English company law possesses some curious features, which may generate curious results. A parent company may spawn a number of subsidiary companies, all controlled directly or indirectly by the shareholders of the parent company. If one of the subsidiary companies, to change the metaphor, turns out to be the runt of the litter and declines into insolvency to the dismay of its creditors, the parent company and the other subsidiary companies may prosper to the joy of the shareholders without any liability for the debts of the insolvent subsidiary.'

The approach is confirmed by the cavalier treatment by the courts of 'letters of comfort'. Thus in *Re Augustus Barnett & Son Ltd* [1986] BCLC 170 the company was a wholly owned subsidiary of a Spanish company. The subsidiary traded at a loss for some time but the parent company repeatedly issued statements that it would continue to support the subsidiary. Some of the statements were made in letters written to the subsidiary's auditors and published in the subsidiary's annual accounts for three successive years. Later the parent company allowed the subsidiary to go into liquidation and failed to provide any financial support to pay off the debts of the subsidiary. In deciding that this did not constitute fraudulent trading on the part of the parent company Hoffman J accepted that the assurances of the parent were without legal effect.

Community law and concepts of 'undertaking' or 'enterprise'

The 'economic unit' approach is exemplified by a number of cases concerning Article 85 of the EEC Treaty of Rome which seeks to control unfair competition by *inter alia* outlawing 'agreements between undertakings, decisions by associations of undertakings' the object or effect of which is distortion of competition. It has become necessary on occasion to determine the nature of an 'undertaking' and it is clear that the EC (European Court of Justice or ECJ) will not adopt the somewhat simplistic approach of the UK courts and will investigate the reality of the economic unit rather than rely on the technical boundaries drawn by incorporation. Thus the definition includes non-profit-making associations and the reality of the parent–subsidiary relationship will always be investigated by the court. In *Centrafarm BV et Adriaan de Peijper* v. *Winthrop BV* [1974] EVECJ R-16/74 (31 October 1974) the court said:

> 'Article 85, however, is not concerned with agreements or concerted practices between undertakings belonging to the same concern and having the status of parent and subsidiary, if the undertakings form an economic unit within which the subsidiary has no real freedom to determine its course of action on the market, and if the agreements or practices are concerned merely with the internal allocation of tasks as between undertakings.'

Similarly, in *Viho Europe BV* v. *Commission of the European Communities (supported by Parker Pen Ltd, Intervener)* (1996) *The Times,* December 9th, the European Court of Justice held that where a company and its subsidiaries formed a single economic unit, Art. 85 (new Art. 81) did not apply. The subsidiaries enjoyed no autonomy and were obliged to follow the instructions of the parent company.

German law and the EC proposed Ninth Directive

In Germany there is a law of groups which has been placed on a statutory footing. It is this *Konzernrecht* which formed the model for the draft EC Ninth Directive on Company Law. The *Konzernrecht* is applicable only to stock corporations although a vigorous body of developing law applies it to other companies.

Under this law a distinction is made between contractual and *de facto* groups of companies. In contractual groups the creditors of the subsidiary are protected by a legal obligation of the parent towards the subsidiary to make good any losses at the end of the year. Shareholders other than the parent company have a right to periodic compensation payments and must be offered the opportunity of selling their shares to the parent at a reasonable price. They have a right to an annual dividend which is calculated according to (a) the value of their shares at the time of the formation of the contractual group and (b) the likelihood of such dividends without the formation of the group. The board of the subsidiary has to give a report on all transactions, measures and omissions during the past year which result from its membership of the group. The conclusion of the contract between members of the group is encouraged by the ability of the parent company to induce the subsidiary to act against its own interests, thus legitimising the concept of the interests of the group as a whole. However, the concept has been little used. Hopt (Schmittoff and Wooldridge (eds.), *Groups of Companies* (Sweet & Maxwell, 1991)) observed that most groups have chosen 'cohabitation without marriage certificates'.

Despite problems experienced in the operation of the German law, the draft proposal for an EC Ninth Company Law Directive took a similar route. The proposal would have affected groups of companies and public limited companies controlled by any other undertaking (whether or not that undertaking was itself a company). The proposal was that there should be a harmonised structure for the 'unified management' of groups of such companies and undertakings. Under the proposal, rules would be laid down for the conduct of groups which were not managed on a 'unified' basis. Unless an undertaking which exercised a dominant interest over a public limited company formalised its relationship and provided for some prescribed form of 'unified' management', it would be liable for any losses suffered by a dependent company provided the losses could be traced to the exercise of the influence or to action which was contrary to the dependent company's interest. Although loosely based on the German Konzernrecht, the proposal would have been less effective. Not only did it rely on a satisfactory definition of dominance or control being found (see below) but it failed to give adequate incentives to persuade companies to adopt a formal 'unified management' approach. The German law on which it was based permits a parent company to induce a subsidiary to act against its own interests if the contractual 'unified management' approach is adopted.

Approaches in the United States of America

In the USA it is recognised that dominant shareholders have fiduciary duties towards both the company and other shareholders. Thus, dominant shareholders are distinguished from other shareholders. The latter, as in the UK, are permitted to vote their shares according to their own selfish interests. In *Southern Pacific Co.* v. *Bogert* (1919) 250 US 483 the Supreme Court stated:

> 'The rule of corporation law and of equity invoked is well settled and has been often applied. The majority has the right to control; but when it does so, it occupies a fiduciary relation toward the minority, as much so as the corporation itself or its officers or directors.'

The principle is widely, if not unanimously, accepted by States. However the implications of the doctrine vary widely. Two States have adopted by legislation a general principle which authorises contracts between parent and subsidiary companies subject to certain conditions of fairness and procedural requirements for adoption or ratification. In other States a voluminous body of case law is evidence of the different and uncertain effects of the doctrine. Part V of the *American Law Institute's Principles of Corporate Governance: Analysis and Recommendations* deals with the duties of dominating shareholders. Ability to control over 25 per cent of the voting equity would give rise to a presumption of control. It is a strange feature of the definition of control that it focuses solely on control of shareholder votes. In Tentative Draft No. 5, control is defined as:

> 'the power directly or indirectly, either alone or pursuant to an arrangement or understanding with one or more other persons, to exercise a controlling influence over the management or policies of a business organization through the ownership of equity interests, through one or more intermediary persons, by contract or otherwise.'

Transactions between a dominating shareholder and the corporation are valid if:

(a) the transaction is fair to the corporation when entered into; or
(b) the transaction is authorised or ratified by disinterested shareholders, following disclosure concerning the conflict of interest and the transaction, and does not constitute a waste of corporate assets at the time of the shareholder transaction.

If the transaction is ratified according to (b) the burden of proving unfairness is on the challenging party. Otherwise it is for the dominant shareholder to prove the fairness of the transaction. A transaction is 'fair' if it falls 'within a range of reasonableness'.

Conflicting duties of loyalty owed by directors who sit on boards of parents and subsidiaries are also judged on a 'fairness' scale: 'In the absence of total abstention of an independent negotiating structure, common directors must determine what is best for both parent and subsidiary.'

This rule is intended to reflect the decision in *Jones* v. *H. F. Ahmanson & Co.* (1993) 1 Cal 3d in which a majority of shareholders had enhanced their investments in a scheme which was not open to the minority investors. Delivering the judgment of the Supreme Court of California, Chief Justice Roger Traynor determined that the conduct of the majority had been unfair. Although he emphasised the duty of the majority towards the corporation as well as to minority shareholders, in fact the relevant opportunity would not have been available to the corporation so that, on the facts, only the majority's duty to the minority was an issue. What is interesting and may provide further insight into a way forward is that the minority did not suffer a loss but were denied an opportunity which was available exclusively to the majority.

United Kingdom

In many circumstances, statutes dictate where groups should act as if they were one enterprise (see Chapter 8). The matter may be formalised if the EC Ninth Directive on the conduct of groups becomes law (see Chapter 18). Where there are no statutory rules, the principles that will guide the court are to be found in *Smith, Stone & Knight* v. *Birmingham Corporation* [1939] 4 All ER 116 (Case note **2**, p. 43). Atkinson J reviewed previous cases on the point and said:

> 'I find six points which were deemed relevant for the determination of the question: Who was really carrying on the business? In all the cases, the question was whether the company, an English company here, could be taxed in respect of all the profits made by some other company, being carried on elsewhere. The first point was: Were the profits treated as the profits of the company? – when I say "the company" I mean the parent company – secondly, were the persons conducting the business appointed by the parent company? Thirdly, was the company the head and brain of the trading venture? Fourthly, did the company govern the adventure, decide what should be done and what capital should be embarked on the venture? Fifthly, did the company make the profits by its skill and direction? Sixthly, was the company in effectual and constant control?'

Where these questions can be answered in the affirmative it is likely that the group will be treated as a single entity. However, the answers to these questions can only provide guidelines and the court will determine each case according to its own facts and the context in which the case arises. The background to such cases can be varied. One involved the determination of the residence of a company registered in Kenya but managed by a parent in the UK. The company was held to be resident in the UK (*Unit Construction Co.* v. *Bullock* [1960] AC 351). In *Firestone Tyre Co.* v. *Llewellin* [1957] 1 WLR 464 an English subsidiary was held to be the means whereby the American parent company traded in the UK. A similar decision was arrived at in *DHN Food Distributors* v. *Tower Hamlets Borough Council* [1976] 1 WLR 852. In *Lonrho* v. *Shell Petroleum* [1980] 1 WLR 627 it was decided that documents could not be regarded as in the 'power' of a parent company when they were in fact held by a subsidiary (see Case note **3**, pp. 43–4). In *National Dock Labour Board* v. *Pinn & Wheeler Ltd & Others* [1989] BCLC 647 the court emphasised that it is only in 'special circumstances which indicate that there is a mere façade concealing the true facts that it is appropriate to pierce the corporate veil'. Similarly, the rule in *Salomon* was approved and relied on in *J. H. Rayner (Mincing Lane) Ltd* v. *Department of Trade and Industry* (Court of Appeal Judgment) [1988] 3 WLR 1033 (see also Case note **4**, p. 44). This approach was upheld by the House of Lords in *Maclaine Watson & Co.* v. *DTI (International Tin Council)* [1990] BCLC 102 and applied in *Adams* v. *Cape Industries PLC* [1990] BCLC 479. *Adams* v. *Cape Industries* provides a particularly stark example of the application of the *Salomon* principle. Several hundred employees of the group headed by Cape Industries had been awarded damages for injuries received as a result of exposure to asbestos dust. The injuries had been received in the course of their employment. The damages had been awarded in a Texan court. The English Court of Appeal held that the awards could not be enforced against Cape even though one of the defendants was a subsidiary of Cape and there was evidence that the group had been restructured so as to avoid liability. Slade J said:

> 'Our law, for better or worse, recognises the creation of subsidiary companies, which, though in one sense the creation of their parent companies, will nevertheless under the general law fail to be treated as separate legal entities with all the rights and liabilities which would normally attach to separate legal entities . . . We do not accept as a matter of law that the court is entitled to lift the corporate veil as against a defendant company which is the member of a corporate group merely because the corporate structure has been used so as to ensure that the legal liability (if any) in respect of particular future activities of the group . . . will fall on another member of the group rather than the defendant company. Whether or not this is desirable, the right to use a corporate structure in this way is inherent in our law.'

A similar approach was taken in *Re Polly Peck International Plc (in administration)* [1996] 2 All ER 433 where the court held that where companies were insolvent the separate legal existence of each within the group became more, not less, important. The courts consistently repeat the finding in *Cape* that the veil cannot be lifted 'simply because the consequences of not doing so are unfair or even absurd' (*Graphical Paper and Media Union* v. *Derry Print and Another* [2002] IRLR 380, 7 January 2002; see also *Trustor AB* v. *Smallbone and Others (No. 2)* [2001] 3 All ER 987).

Agency and trust

Other cases that are often cited on this issue are sometimes put into categories such as 'agency' or 'trust' cases. This can give the impression that the reason for interfering with the corporate veil in those cases was because the court made a finding that an agency or trust relationship had developed between the company in question and some other body. In fact it may well be that, as in the *Malyon* and *Lee* cases, the interests of justice required the court to ignore the corporate veil. The finding of agency or trust may be a convenient excuse for a refusal to follow the rule in *Salomon*'s cases. Thus, in *Abbey Malvern Wells* v. *Minister of Local Government* [1951] Ch 728 the company owned a school which was managed by a board of trustees who were bound by the terms of the trust to use the assets of the company for educational purposes. The company applied to the Minister for Town and

Country Planning for a ruling that the land they held was exempt from development charges because it was held for charitable (educational in this case) purposes. The Minister ruled against them but on appeal from that decision, the court held: (1) that the land was occupied by the company for the educational purposes of the school; (2) that the trusts in the trust deed were charitable; (3) that the company was controlled by trustees who were bound by the trust deed; so that (4) the property and assets of the company could only be applied to the charitable purposes of the trust deed. Accordingly the company's interest in and use of the land were charitable and fell within the exemption provisions of the tax statute. In this case it was because the very strict control over the use of the land that was imposed by the trust deed bound the controllers of the company both as trustees and directors. In consequence the legally separate nature of the trust and the company could safely be ignored. Similarly, in *Littlewoods Stores* v. *IRC* [1969] 1 WLR 1241 it was held that a subsidiary company held an asset on trust for the holding company, Littlewoods, because Littlewoods had provided the purchase price. Littlewoods could therefore not take advantage of the separate legal identity of its subsidiary to avoid the tax consequences of ownership of the asset.

The decision in *Re F. G. Films* [1953] 1 WLR 483 is sometimes regarded as an instance of lifting the veil where the company concerned is acting as an agent for another. Although the judgment mentions agency, the true basis for the decision is that the interests of justice required the court to have regard to the realities behind the situation. The case concerned an application to have a film registered as a British film. To succeed, the applicant company had to show that they were the 'makers' of the film. Vaisey J said:

> 'The applicants have a capital of £100 divided into 100 shares of £1 each, 90 of which are held by the American director and the remaining 10 by a British one . . . I now understand that they have no place of business apart from their registered office and they do not employ any staff . . . it seems to me to be contrary, not only to all sense and reason, but to the proved and admitted facts of the case, to say or to believe that this insignificant company undertook in any real sense of that word the arrangements for the making of this film. I think that their participation in any such undertaking was so small as to be practically negligible, and that they acted, in so far as they acted at all in the matter, merely as the nominee of and agent for an American company called Film Group Incorporated . . . The applicant's intervention in the matter was purely colourable.'

A similar motive lies behind the decision in *Daimler* v. *Continental Tyre Co.* [1916] AC 307, where an English company was held to be an enemy alien because of the nationality of its shareholders.

It is impossible to find a legally consistent basis for the cases in which the courts have decided to ignore the separate legal personality of the company.

All that can be said with certainty is that unless there are compelling considerations of justice and fairness, the courts will follow *Salomon* and respect the doctrine which declares a company to be a body quite distinct from its members.

3.7 The criminal and civil liabilities of companies

If a company is to be regarded as a person under the law, it follows that it can incur liabilities as can any other person. The courts have held that a company can be convicted of crimes. There are two ways in which this may happen. A company may be *vicariously liable* for a crime which is committed by an employee. This will occur when the law says that if a crime is committed by an employee, the employer will bear criminal liability for that act even though the employer may have known nothing about the action in question. The general rule about vicarious liability in criminal law was laid down in the case of *Huggins* (1730) 2 Stra 883. It was made clear that as a general rule the civil doctrine of vicarious liability was not going to be adopted into criminal law. There are two exceptions to this rule which judges have made. In public nuisance and criminal libel an employer can be liable for his employees' crimes on the basis of the relationship alone. Many statutes also impose criminal liability. However, the courts were not content with this relatively narrow basis for the criminal liability of companies and have found that if the criminal acts were committed by persons of sufficient importance in the company, those acts will be seen as the acts of the company itself. This is the wrongly named *alter ego* (other self) doctrine. Those committing the crime, if of sufficient standing, are said to be the 'other self' of the company. In fact they are the only 'self' as the company has no other physical existence. There are two difficulties: (1) are there crimes which a company cannot commit? and (2) who are the individuals of sufficient status to be the *alter ego* of the company?

3.8 What crimes?

It seems most likely that a company can only be convicted of criminal offences that can be punished by a fine. This would not exclude many offences. Murder, however, is punishable only by life imprisonment and would therefore be excluded. In their textbook on criminal law (*Criminal Law*, 8th edn, Butterworths, 1996), Professors John Smith and Brian Hogan state:

> 'There are other offences which it is quite inconceivable that an official of a corporation should commit within the scope of his employment; for example, bigamy, rape, incest, and possibly perjury.'

It is arguable that even these crimes might be committed by an important official in a company who aided or abetted another in the commission of such a crime.

The above seem to be the only limitations on the potential criminal liability of companies. It was at one time thought that a company could not be convicted of a crime involving personal violence (*Cory Bros & Co.* [1927] 1 KB 810) but in *P&O European Ferries Ltd* (1990) 93 Cr App R 72, Turner J held that an indictment for manslaughter could lie against a company in respect of the Zeebrugge disaster. The company was acquitted on the merits.

Similarly in *Attorney-General's Reference (No. 2 of 1999)* [2000] 3 WLR 195, the Court of Appeal held that on a charge of manslaughter by gross negligence, a corporation could only be convicted where there was evidence to establish the guilt of an identified human individual. In the light of this narrow view the government is considering legislation to broaden the offence of corporate manslaughter, based on the Law Commission Report, *Criminal Law: Involuntary Manslaugher: an overview* (Law Commission, 1994, No. 135).

3.9 Why convict companies?

There are three possible justifications for this rather curious procedure. The most convincing one is that the public is thereby informed of wrongdoing by companies. They might read in the press that Mr Smith had been guilty of selling contaminated milk or pies and this would mean little. If it is a well-known supermarket which is convicted, the attendant publicity might well affect sales. This possibility might have a significant deterrent effect on the company's controllers. This argument may be significant in the decision to prosecute companies implicated in disasters.

The second justification is that a company can be made to pay a larger fine than an individual so that serious breaches, for example of pollution regulations, can be met with large fines to denote public condemnation. The problem with this approach is that the shareholders are those who ultimately shoulder the burden of the fine, since money leaving the company will cause the devaluation of their shares. As we will see elsewhere (Chapter 13), the idea that the controllers of the company can be effectively disciplined by shareholders is far-fetched, particularly in a large company.

The third justification is that there may be crimes which have obviously been authorised by the controllers of a company but it may be very difficult to prove individual liability. Convictions are difficult in such cases because of the need to establish the mental state necessary for conviction of a crime. Smith and Hogan find none of these arguments convincing. The present authors feel that the first and third justifications have considerable force.

However, while the 'identification' policy is adhered to, conviction in cases where the policy of the company leads to disaster but the finger does not point to identifiable individuals will be impossible.

3.10　Identification of the company's *alter ego*

In *H. L. Bolton (Engineering) Co. Ltd* v. *T. J. Graham & Sons Ltd* [1957] 1 QB 159 Denning LJ said:

> 'A company may in many ways be likened to a human body. It has a brain and nerve centre which control what it does. It also has hands which hold the tools and act in accordance with directions from the centre. Some of the people in the company are mere servants and agents who are nothing more than hands to do the work and cannot be said to represent the mind or will. Others are directors and managers who represent the directing mind and will of the company, and control what it does. The state of mind of these managers is the state of mind of the company and is treated by the law as such.'

Examples

In *Tesco Supermarkets* v. *Nattrass* [1972] AC 153, Tesco had been convicted of an offence under the Trade Descriptions Act 1968 for selling a product at a price higher than the advertised price. Tesco was entitled to a defence if it could be shown (among other things) that the offence was committed by 'another person'. Tesco alleged that the 'other person' in this case was the manager of the branch involved who had been in sole command of that store. It was held that the manager was not the 'brains' of the company so that he was indeed 'another person' for the purposes of the offence. In *DPP* v. *Kent and Sussex Contractors Ltd* [1944] KB 146, the Divisional Court held that a company could properly be convicted of an offence which required proof of an intent to deceive. The intention was that of the transport manager of the company.

Each case will turn on its own facts and depend upon the precise nature of the distribution of power within the particular company. The case of *Moore* v. *Bresler Ltd* [1944] 2 All ER 559 has been criticised on the grounds that the court went 'too far down the scale' in convicting a company of tax fraud where that fraud was carried out by the company secretary and the manager of one branch (see *Welch* (1946) 62 LQR 385). In view of the enhanced status of the company secretary (see Chapter 10) that criticism may be of less force today.

3.11　Civil liability

A precisely similar test is used to determine the civil liability of a company (see *El Ajou* v. *Dollar Land Holdings Plc* [1994] 1 BCLC 464). It must be remembered, however, that the principle of vicarious liability in civil law is much more widely used and so there may be that route to liability as well as the use of the *alter ego* doctrine. In *Lennard's Carrying Company Ltd* v. *Asiatic Petroleum Co. Ltd* [1915] AC 705, the *alter ego* doctrine was the basis of the company's liability. The question was whether damage had occurred without 'the actual fault or privity' of the owner of the ship. The owners were a company. The fault was that of the registered managing owner who managed the ship on behalf of the owners. It was held that Mr Lennard was the directing mind of the company so that his fault was the fault of the company. (See also *Campbell* v. *Paddington Corporation* [1911] 1 KB 869 and *The Lady Gwendolen* [1965] P 294; but for a different test see *Meridian Global Funds Management Asia Ltd* v. *Securities Commission (PC)* [1995] 2 BCLC 116 (Case note 5, p. 44).)

Hot Topic . . .

PERFORMANCE OF COMPANIES AND GOVERNMENT DEPARTMENTS (REPORTING) BILL (2004) (1)

As a result of a lengthy review of company law the government introduced the concept of an 'Operating and Financial Review' (OFR) for 'major' companies. This was introduced by Regulation but the Regulation was repealed a matter of months after it came into force. The companies concerned were companies where, in one financial year, two or more of the criteria listed were fulfilled: turnover of at least £50 million; balance sheet total at least £25 million at the end of the year; at least 500 employees on average.

The OFR included the employment impact, environmental impact, and social and community impact of the company's operations, policies, products and procurement practices; the company's performance in carrying out employment, environmental, and social and community policies.

The Companies Act (2006) also requires a director of any company to act in good faith in a way most likely to promote the company's success for the benefit of shareholders as a whole. Clause 9 Companies Bill required directors

to 'take all reasonable steps to minimize the impact of the company on the communities it affects and on the environment'.

These changes might have altered the 'contractual' model of UK companies by including the concerns of other stakeholders but cynics felt that it would only give the public relations departments of companies another chance to show how well their corporate social responsibility policies are working without giving stakeholders other than shareholders any effective voice in company decisions. In any event, these minor concessions to the 'stakeholder' approach to company law have now gone, replaced only by the requirement to include employee and environmental matters in a directors' report (see Chapter 9).

Summary

1. A company has the advantage that it continues to exist despite a change in the persons carrying on the business. A limited company has the advantage that the liability of the members is limited to an amount agreed by them. Companies have the disadvantage that they have to comply with more regulations than do partnerships.

2. A company is a separate legal person, with an existence independent of its members.

3. Because a company does not exist until registered, it cannot be a party to contracts entered into before that registration.

4. The courts will 'lift the veil' in cases where a company's separate legal personality is being used unjustly or as a fraudulent device.

5. A company may incur criminal or civil liability as a result of the action of someone important enough in the company to be regarded as the directing 'mind and will' of the company.

Case notes

1. *H. Leverton Ltd* v. *Crawford Offshore (Exploration) Services Ltd (in liquidation)* (1996) *The Times*, November 22nd

Garland J held that the director who managed a company should be personally liable for the costs of the action. The director was the sole decision-maker, had kept its only records, had been present throughout the action and had improperly caused the company to defend the action and prosecute a falsely concocted counterclaim.

2. *Smith, Stone & Knight* v. *Birmingham Corporation* [1939] 4 All ER 116

The claim was for compensation for a factory which was to be the subject of a compulsory purchase by the defendants. The plaintiffs had let the premises to a subsidiary company and the question arose as to whether the parent company could claim compensation for what would, in fact, be damage done not to its business but to the business of a subsidiary. The court held that in this case it could.

3. *Lonrho* v. *Shell Petroleum* [1980] 1 WLR 627

The case involved UK companies. However, the plaintiffs sought to obtain documents that were in the possession of wholly owned foreign subsidiaries of the defendant. The Court of Appeal refused to order this. Lord Denning said:

'These South African and Rhodesian companies were very much self-controlled. The directors were local directors – running their own show, operating it, with comparatively little interference from London.'

That, together with the fact that the foreign companies had in fact refused to give up the documents, led to the conclusion that these companies were separate entities.

4. *J. H. Rayner (Mincing Lane) Ltd* v. *Department of Trade and Industry* [1987] BCLC 667; [1988] 3 WLR 1033 (CA)

This case involved the International Tin Council (ITC) whose members were the UK, 22 other sovereign states and the EC. The ITC had corporate status under UK law. Because of this the Court of Appeal refused to hold that the members had personal liability for the debts of the ITC. This was later affirmed by the House of Lords.

5. *Meridian Global Funds Management Asia Ltd* v. *Securities Commission (PC)* [1995] 2 BCLC 116

Meridian's funds were used by two senior investment managers to provide finance for an attempted takeover of a New Zealand company. The funds were used to purchase shares. The New Zealand legislation required immediate notification of acquisition of more than 5 per cent of the shares of a public company. Meridian was held liable for non-disclosure despite the fact that the investment managers had been acting without the authority of the directors. The court held that the knowledge of the investment managers was to be attributed to the company. The test of 'directing mind and will' was not appropriate in all cases and here would defeat the purpose of the Act, which was to encourage immediate notification of acquisition of substantial shareholdings (Meridian's board met only once a year), and restricting the company's knowledge to the knowledge of those directing the company could encourage the board to pay as little attention as possible to what its investment managers were doing.

As possible examples of statutory 'lifting the veil', consider s. 214 Insolvency Act 1986, s. 459 Companies Act 1985 and s. 6 Company Directors Disqualification Act 1986.

Exercises

1. What advantages and disadvantages does the doctrine of the separate legal personality of a company have?

2. Is there any purpose in convicting a company of crimes?

3. Chimco plc makes fertilisers. It is a multinational company operating throughout the world with various subsidiaries. In particular it has three subsidiaries which are the subject of litigation. In South Africa, Genetic is a wholly owned subsidiary of Chimco which is being sued by a group of employees who claim that their health has been damaged by working with dangerous chemicals. Genetic is also being prosecuted by the South African authorities for polluting the river next to the factory. The prosecution could

lead to a fine of over $2 million. Chimco decides to take all the assets of Genetic and put it into liquidation.

In Portugal Launder is a subsidiary of Chimco, with Chimco owning 75 per cent of the shares. It has been involved in banking transactions which are contrary to the Money Laundering Regulations but has made a profit of £345,000, which Chimco transfers to its own account in London.

In Bristol a new subsidiary of Chimco has recently been incorporated. Before incorporation an agent of Chimco arranged a lease of an office building and ordered £75,000 worth of furniture.

Discuss the legal implications of the transactions. Assume that the laws of all countries are the same as English law.

Chapter 4

The memorandum of association

Key words

> ▶ **Objects** – the list of activities which a company is authorised to undertake.
> ▶ **Ultra vires** – acts done by a company which are not authorised by its
> constitution as set out in its memorandum of association.

The contents of the memorandum of association were discussed in Chapter 2. Before the Companies Act 2006 the memorandum of association was regarded as the most important part of the constitution of the company. This is no longer the case. One problem which caused extensive debate over many years was an issue arising from the setting out of the objects of association in the memorandum. The courts held that the company was unable to create legally binding contracts or act outside the scope of the objects of association as they were set out in the memorandum. The law has now been changed to eliminate this problem altogether. By s. 39 of the Companies Act 2006 a company has unlimited capacity to act. Section 31 Companies Act 2006 states that:

'Unless a company's articles specifically restrict the objects of the company, its objects are unrestricted.'

And s. 39 reads:

'The validity of an act done by a company shall not be called into question on the ground of lack of capacity by reason of anything in the company's constitution.'

Charities are excepted from this provision s. 39(2). However directors still have a duty to act in accordance with the company's constitution and by s. 40(4) a shareholder can obtain an injunction to prevent a director acting outside the constitution provided the act is challenged before a legal obligation has arisen. Further, if the act in question involves a director of the company or its holding company or a person connected with such a director the act is voidable by the company. In these circumstances the company can ask the court to set the act aside. The company's capacity might also be relevant where it seeks to set aside an act alleging that the third party was not acting in 'good faith' (see discussion of s. 40, below). It is only in these rare circumstances that any limitations to a company's 'objects' will be of relevance. It should be noted that the objects of the company will be found in the articles of association and any resolutions which form part of the constitution, not in the memorandum which has been downgraded to a simple statement of intent to form a company. In these new circumstances only a brief discussion of the intricacies of the old law is necessary as the issues could only arise in the limited circumstances set out above, and then only if the company has adopted a restricted list of objects.

4.1 Ultra vires – the old law

By s. 2(1)(c) Companies Act 1985, the memorandum of a company was required to 'state the objects of a company'. This simple requirement has been the object of much heart-searching in the past and gave rise to an enormous body of law. This law needs to be briefly examined in order to form a proper understanding of the present law. It also affords an interesting example of the way in which case law can develop.

It was first apparent that the requirement to state objects would cause problems when the courts held that if a company did an act which was outside the scope of the objects as described in the memorandum, that act would be wholly without legal effect (void). This so-called doctrine of 'ultra vires' is similar to the law concerning public bodies. They are unable to act outside the statutory powers given to them. It was felt that the same should be true of companies. Unfortunately, the law that developed had unhappy results. This is partly because the reason that public bodies should be restricted to the powers given to them by Parliament is in order to safeguard democracy. If a public body takes to itself more power than the elected representatives of the people have chosen to give it, it is setting itself up as more important than the electorate. Similar considerations do not apply when companies are considered. Companies need to respond with a considerable degree of flexibility to changing markets and it is difficult to see who has ever benefited from this doctrine.

4.2 Constructive notice

The doctrine of *ultra vires* only worked in conjunction with the doctrine of constructive notice. By this doctrine everyone is deemed to know the contents of the memorandum of association of the company with which they are dealing because it is a public document. (This doctrine disappeared on the implementation of Companies Act 1989 and has no equivalent in the Companies Act 2006.)

4.3 Justification of the doctrine

The original justification for the existence of the doctrine was that it would serve as a protection for shareholders and creditors. A company formed for one purpose should not be permitted to pursue other ends which did not have the blessing of the shareholders and creditors, who stood to lose their money if the company indulged in unprofitable adventures. However, as will be seen, the element of protection was lost the moment that the court accepted memoranda with objects clauses so widely drafted that they covered almost every activity. After that the doctrine was only of use if a party sought to avoid a contract. The determination of where the loss caused by the application of the doctrine should fall appears to have been a matter of mere chance of circumstances.

Apart from providing an expensive parlour game for lawyers, there appeared to be very little point to this doctrine. Reform was attempted on accession to the European Community but it was badly done. The relevant provision of the EC Directive 68/151/EEC is Article 9 which reads:

'Acts done by the organs of the company shall be binding upon it even if those acts are not within the objects of the company, unless such acts exceed the powers that the law confers or allows to be conferred on those organs. However, Member States may provide that the company shall not be bound where such acts are outside the objects of the company if it proves that the third party knew that the act was outside those objects or could not in view of the circumstances be unaware thereof; disclosure of the statutes shall not of itself be sufficient proof thereof.'

4.4 How to determine whether an act is *ultra vires*

If the validity of a particular act by a company director is being considered, the act must be measured against the company's constitution as follows, bearing in mind that if the statement of objects is too wide the company's main object will be deduced from the name of the company. Thus a very widely drawn clause is in danger of being read in the light of the 'main objects' rule as ancillary to the main objects of the company.

(1) Is the act within the express objects in the light of any possible restrictive interpretation? If so it binds the company; if not:
(2) Is the act within the validly stated ancillary objects or powers which are 'converted' into objects by an independent objects clause? If so the act binds the company; if not:
(3) Is the act within a 'subjective' clause and the directors *bona fide* believe that the business can be carried on with the other businesses of the company? If so the act is binding on the company; if not:

(4) Is the act done in accordance with an express power of the company and not done *mala fide* with the knowledge of the outsider? If so it binds the company; if not:

(5) Is the act done in accordance with implied powers of the company and done to further the objects of the company? If so it binds the company; if none of the above applies, the act is *ultra vires*.

4.5   The new law

This chapter deals only with the rules regarding the capacity of the directors to bind the company where they may be acting outside their powers or the powers of the company. Slightly different issues may arise where someone is acting as if they were a validly appointed director. These issues overlap and the other aspect of this will be discussed in Chapter 6. Section 40 Companies Act 2006 reads:

'(1) In favour of a person dealing with a company in good faith, the power of the directors to bind the company, or authorise others to do so, is deemed to be free of any limitation under the company's constitution.

(2) For this purpose –

(a) a person "deals with" a company if he is a party to any transaction or other act to which the company is a party,

(b) a person dealing with a company –

(i)   is not bound to enquire as to any limitation on the powers of the directors to bind the company or authorise others to do so,

(ii)   is presumed to have acted in good faith unless the contrary is proved, and

(iii) is not to be regarded as acting in bad faith by reason only of his knowing that an act is beyond the powers of the directors under the company's constitution.'

Note that the exception for acts involving directors or connected persons is in s. 41.

These provisions, which almost completely abolish *ultra vires*, have the effect that once an act has been done by a company, that act can only very rarely be challenged on the *ultra vires* basis so as to upset the rights of third parties. The only two situations where third party rights could be called into question are where a director or connected person is involved or where the third party is proved to have acted in bad faith. The only other time the issue could arise is where there is a challenge to directors' acts either to gain an injunction in advance of the act or to allege a breach of duty after the event. However, these remaining provisions mean that in very rare circumstances the old complicated case law might be argued.

4.6 Ratification

Under the 1985 Act special resolutions were required to ratify the acts of directors which were allegedly *ultra vires*. Section 239 Companies Act 2006 requires only an ordinary resolution for ratification of breaches of duty by directors but does provide that the votes of any director whose breach is the subject of the resolution and any connected persons do not count in calculating the simple majority which is enough to pass the ordinary resolution. In the case of a transaction involving a director or connected person, the director or connected person involved and any director who authorised the transaction remain liable under s. 41(3):

'(a) to account to the company for any gain which he has made directly or indirectly by the transaction, and

(b) to indemnify the company for any loss or damage resulting from the transaction.'

The contract will also cease to be voidable if:

'(a) restitution of any money or other asset which was the subject-matter of the transaction is no longer possible, or

(b) the company is indemnified for any loss or damage resulting from the transaction, or

(c) rights acquired *bona fide* and for value and without actual notice of the directors' exceeding their powers by a person who is not a party to the transaction would be affected by the avoidance, or

(d) the transaction is affirmed by the company.'

It is noteworthy that directors are caught by this section whether or not they know they are exceeding their powers. Others are not affected unless they know that the directors are exceeding their powers (s. 41(5)). If someone other than a director of the company or of its holding company or persons or companies connected or associated with that director enters into a contract with a company, the contract would normally be fully enforceable even if the directors were acting *ultra vires* according to the old law.

4.7 The old case law

In the limited circumstances where the case law is still relevant, all the old complications may need to be examined by the court. The following is a brief consideration of those difficulties.

One of the early cases was *Ashbury Railway Carriage and Iron Co.* (1875) LR 7 HL 653. The memorandum gave the company the power to make and sell railway carriages. The company purported to buy a concession for constructing a railway in Belgium. Later the directors repudiated the contract and were sued. Their defence was that the contract was *ultra vires*, outside the memorandum and had been of no effect from the first. The court held that a contract made by the directors of such a company on a matter not included in the memorandum of association was not binding on the company. Indeed, the court went further than this and decided that such a contract could not be rendered binding on the company even though it was expressly assented to by all the shareholders. This was because of a principle of agency law that an agent (in this case a director) cannot have more power than the principal (in this case the company). It is possible that this part of the decision would not have been laid down in such absolute terms if it were not for the fact that it was in those days impossible to alter the memorandum of association. Such an alteration was possible after 1890 but was made easier after 1948. However, *Ashbury* and cases like it laid the foundation stones of the doctrine of *ultra vires*, these being that a contract made in an area not covered by the objects is of no legal effect and that such a contract cannot be made effective by a vote of the shareholders. Although the doctrine could be advantageous to a company where it was used to avoid a contract which had become onerous, it could also be a burden. For example, banks or other companies might be reluctant to deal with a company where the objects of that company were unknown to the contracting partner, where they were narrowly drawn or of uncertain ambit. The courts had decided in *Re Crown Bank* (1890) 44 Ch D 634, that a proper statement of objects had not been made where the objects of the company were expressed in such wide terms as to be (in the words of North J):

'So wide that it might be said to warrant the company in giving up banking business and embarking in a business with the object of establishing a line of balloons between the earth and the moon.'

The courts did, however, determine that it was permissible to achieve a similar effect by listing every imaginable kind of business. In *Cotman* v. *Brougham* [1918] AC 514 the company's memorandum had 30 sub-clauses enabling the company to carry on almost any kind of business, and the objects clause concluded with a declaration that every sub-clause should be construed as a substantive clause and not limited or restricted by reference to any other sub-clause or by the name of the company and that none of such sub-clauses or the objects specified therein should be deemed subsidiary or auxiliary merely to the objects mentioned in the first sub-clause.

The last part of this statement of objects was there to avoid a restriction which the courts had been prone to place on statements of objects. They had construed them according to a 'main objects' rule. This meant that the main object of the company could be determined either from the name of the company or from the first named object on the list of objects. All subsequent statements in the objects clause would then be considered to be powers of the company which could only be validly exercised for the purpose of furthering the 'main' object. In *Cotman* v. *Brougham*, the draftsman had drafted the statement of objects to avoid this rule and also sought to avoid the *Re Crown Bank* restriction by the long list of 30 objects. His attempt was successful. It was held that the memorandum must be construed according to its literal meaning, although the practice of drafting memoranda in this way was criticised.

A further extension of the liberty given to companies came with the acceptance of the 'subjective clause' in *Bell Houses Ltd* v. *City Wall Properties Ltd* [1966] 2 QB 656. In that case the company's memorandum of association contained the following clause:

> '3(c) To carry on any other trade or business whatsoever which can, in the opinion of the board of directors, be advantageously carried on by [the plaintiff company] in connection with or as ancillary to any of the above businesses or the general business [of the company].'

It must be noted that this clause is more restricted than the one found to be an improper statement of objects in *Re Crown Bank*, particularly because it refers to the business already being carried on by the company and requires that the business justified under this clause must be compatible with business permitted by other clauses in the memorandum. If objects as wide as those in *Re Crown Bank* were accepted, the company would be permitted to carry on two competing businesses.

The subjective element in the *Bell Houses* case comes in the reference to the 'opinion of the directors'. With reference to this clause, Danckwerts LJ said in *Bell Houses*:

> 'On the balance of the authorities it would appear that the opinion of the directors if *bona fide* can dispose of the matter; and why should it not decide the matter? The shareholders subscribe their money on the basis of the memorandum of association and if that confers the power on the directors to decide whether in their opinion it is proper to undertake particular business in the circumstances specified, why should not their decision be binding?'

4.8 Objects and powers

We have seen that the memorandum should contain a statement of *objects*. We have also seen that sometimes the statement of objects would be construed so as to discern a 'main' object and ancillary objects which could only be exercised in order to further the company's main objects.

There are two further complications to this picture. One is that the 'long list' *Cotman* v. *Brougham* approach may list objects and also ancillary objects or powers necessary for the attainment of those objects. The memorandum may then contain a clause that all the clauses and sub-clauses are 'independent objects' and none of them subsidiary to the others. This raises the question as to whether there is any essential distinction between objects and powers, and if so, what it is and how each may be identified.

The second complication is that all companies are covered by the doctrine of 'implied powers' whereby the law will assume that all powers necessary for the attainment of a lawful objective are possessed by the body seeking to achieve the objective.

In view of these numerous complications it is perhaps unsurprising that the courts seem to have occasionally lost their way in the maze and confused objects and powers.

4.9 *Ultra vires* and objects

Strictly speaking, the doctrine of *ultra vires* should apply only to objects. However, on numerous occasions the courts have found that the company has acted outside its powers and held the act to be *ultra vires*. Many examples of this confusion concerned cases which either involved the company borrowing money in excess of its powers to do so or giving money away. An example of the latter is *Hutton* v. *West Cork Railway Company* (1883) 23 Ch D 654. In that case the company was about to be dissolved. A resolution was passed to the effect that money would be paid by the company to its officials as compensation for loss of office and to other directors who had never received remuneration for their work. The Court of Appeal held that payments of this sort would be invalid. Bowen LJ said:

> 'Most businesses require liberal dealings. The test . . . is not whether it is *bona fide*, but whether, as well as being done *bona fide*, it is done within the ordinary scope of the company's business, and whether it is reasonable incidental to the carrying on of the company's business for the company's benefit . . . a company which always treated its employees with Draconian severity, and never allowed them a single inch more than the strict letter of the bond, would soon find itself deserted – at all events, unless labour was very much more easy to obtain in the market than it often is. The law does not say that there are to be no cakes and ale, but that there are to be no cakes and ale except such as are required for the benefit of the company.'

It must be noted that this discussion related to the exercise of a *power* of the company; giving away money was something which the company had the power to do, but the Court of Appeal suggested in this case that such a gift would be invalid if it were not exercised *bona fide* for the benefit of the company. Similar restrictions were placed on the exercise of a power to give a gift for the furtherance of scientific education in *Evans* v. *Brunner Mond* [1921] 1 Ch 359. It is noteworthy that in that case the 'power' in question was no different from the implied powers a company would be assumed to have, but in this instance they had been enshrined in the memorandum.

Although accepting restrictions similar to those in *Hutton,* in this case the court held that it would be for the benefit of the company to increase the 'reservoir' of trained experts by making a gift which would benefit scientific education.

4.10 Knowledge by an outsider that a transaction is outside objects or powers

The *ultra vires* problem has also frequently arisen where borrowing powers are at issue. In *Re David Payne & Co. Ltd* [1904] 2 Ch 608 the court held that where borrowing was for an *ultra vires* purpose but this was unknown to the lender, the loan could be recovered. In that case the loan money could have been applied by the directors for *intra* or *ultra vires* purposes. The fact that the directors chose to apply the money to *ultra vires* purposes was a matter for which the directors could be called to account by the shareholders, as being a breach of their duties. It was not a matter which ought to affect the rights of the lender. It would have been different if the lender had notice that the money would be applied for *ultra vires* purposes. That was the situation in *Re Jon Beauforte (London) Ltd* [1953] Ch 131. The company's memorandum authorised the business of dressmaking. However, at the relevant time the business carried on was that of veneered panel manufacture. On notepaper which clearly indicated that this was the current business of the company, a supply of coke was ordered. The court held that as the coke supplier had had notice of the fact that the current business of the company was *ultra vires* business, the contract for the supply of coke was void and he would therefore not be paid. The validity of the contract in this case depends on the knowledge of the outsider. If he knows that the transaction is outside the powers of the company, the transaction will be unenforceable. We have to remember that the outsider was deemed to have constructive knowledge of the objects of the company under the doctrine of constructive notice (see 4.2 above), which has now been abolished.

4.11 Can borrowing ever be an object?

We have seen that one of the ploys used by draftsmen in order to ensure that a memorandum is as widely drafted as possible, is to insert a clause elevating the long list of clauses to the status of objects. This is added in an attempt to avoid the 'main objects' rule of construction. Despite the finding in *Cotman v. Brougham* (see p. 52) that a memorandum should be read literally, the court held that such an 'elevation' clause was ineffective in the case of borrowing. In *Introductions Ltd* v. *National Provincial Bank Ltd* [1970] Ch 199 there was a provision in the objects clause that the company could 'borrow or raise money in such manner as the company shall think fit'.

There was also a clause which expressly declared 'that each of the preceding sub-clauses shall be construed independently of and shall be in no way limited by reference to any other sub-clause and that the objects set out in each sub-clause are independent objects of the company'. Harman LJ said:

> 'you cannot convert a power into an object merely by saying so . . . I agree with the judge that it is a necessarily implied addition to a power to borrow whether express or implied, that you should add "for the purposes of the company".'

The reason for this restriction is that it makes no commercial sense to have a company with the sole object of 'borrowing'. The judges reasoned from this that borrowing could not be an object or objective but only a power exercised in order to achieve another object.

In that case the judge found that the borrowing was *ultra vires* and consequently the contract involved in that borrowing could not be relied on. As we have seen, this goes beyond the original doctrine which held that only actions outside the *objects* would be void.

4.12 1980s cases

Cases decided in the 1980s limited the *ultra vires* doctrine to a considerable extent. In *Re Halt Garage (1964) Ltd* [1982] 3 All ER 1016, Oliver J was faced with the task of deciding whether payments made to directors just prior to the liquidation of the company were valid, or whether the money could be recovered by the liquidator. There was a *power* to make payments but the company had been in some financial difficulty at the time when the payments had been made. Oliver J held that if the power to make payments had genuinely been exercised and the payments were not some other transaction in disguise, then they could not be challenged on the grounds that they were *ultra vires*. The judge refused to accept tests which had been put forward in older authorities which would have resulted in the payments being held to be *ultra vires* if they were not made in good faith and for the benefit of the company.

Similarly in *Re Horsley & Weight Ltd* [1982] Ch 442, the question was the validity of a pension which had been purchased by the company for a retiring director. The court held that the grant of the pension could fall within a clause of the memorandum which was capable of describing objects and if that were the case no question of deciding whether or not the action benefited the company arose – it was valid. The judgment of Buckley LJ contains some interesting observations on what can be considered objects and what can only ever be powers no matter that the memorandum contains an 'elevation' clause. He said:

> 'It has now long been a common practice to set out in memoranda of association a great number and variety of "objects", so called, some of which (for example, to

borrow money, to promote the company's interest by advertising its products or services, or to do acts or things conducive to the company's objects) are by their very nature incapable of standing as independent objects which can be pursued in isolation as the sole activity of the company. Such "objects" must, by reason of their very nature, be interpreted merely as powers incidental to the true objects of the company and must be so treated notwithstanding the presence of a separate objects clause . . . *ex hypothesi* an implied power can only legitimately be used in a way which is ancillary or incidental to the pursuit of an authorised object of the company, for it is the practical need to imply the power in order to enable the company effectively to pursue its authorised objects which justifies the implication of the power. So an exercise of an implied power can only be *intra vires* the company if it is ancillary or incidental to the pursuit of an authorised object. So, also, in the case of express "objects" which upon construction of the memorandum or by their very nature are ancillary to the dominant or main objects of the company, an exercise of any such powers can only be *intra vires* if it is in fact ancillary or incidental to the pursuit of some such dominant or main object.

On the other hand, the doing of an act which is expressed to be, and capable of being, an independent object of the company cannot be *ultra vires*, for it is by definition something which the company is formed to do and so must be *intra vires* . . . [counsel] submits that . . . a capacity to grant pensions to directors or ex-directors, is of its nature a power enabling the company to act as a good employer in the course of carrying on its business, and as such is an incidental power which must be treated as though it were expressly subject to a limitation that it can only be exercised in circumstances in which the grant of a pension will benefit the company's business. I do not feel able to accept this contention. Paragraph (o) must be read as a whole. In includes not only pensions and other disbursements which will benefit directors, employees and their dependants, but also making grants for charitable, benevolent or public purposes or objects. The objects of a company do not need to be commercial; they can be charitable or philanthropic; indeed they can be whatever the original incorporators wish, provided that they are legal. Nor is there any reason why a company should not part with its funds gratuitously or for non-commercial reasons if to do so is within its declared objects.'

This case was affirmed in *Rolled Steel Products* v. *British Steel Corporation* [1985] Ch 246 where Slade LJ, after an extensive review of the authorities, set out the following conclusions:

'(1) The basic rule is that a company incorporated under the Companies Acts only has the capacity to do those acts which fall within its objects as set out in its memorandum of association or are reasonably incidental to the attainment or pursuit of those objects. Ultimately, therefore, the question whether a particular transaction is within or outside its capacity must depend on the true construction of the memorandum.
(2) Nevertheless, if a particular act . . . is of a category which, on the true construction of the company's memorandum, is capable of being performed as reasonably incidental to the attainment or pursuit of its objects, it will not be rendered *ultra vires* the company merely because in a particular instance its directors, in performing the act in its name, are in truth doing so for purposes other than those set out in its memorandum. Subject to any express restrictions on the

relevant power which may be construed in the memorandum, the state of mind or knowledge of the persons managing the company's affairs or of the persons dealing with it is irrelevant in considering questions of corporate capacity.

(3) While due regard must be paid to any express conditions attached to or limitations on powers contained in a company's memorandum (e.g. a power to borrow only up to a specified amount), the court will not ordinarily construe a statement in a memorandum that a particular power is exercisable "for the purposes of the company" as a condition limiting the company's corporate capacity to exercise the power; it will regard it as simply imposing a limit on the authority of the directors: see the *Re David Payne* case.

(4) At least in default of the unanimous consent of all the shareholders ... the directors of a company will not have *actual* authority from the company to exercise any express or implied power other than for the purposes of the company as set out in its memorandum of association.

(5) A company holds out its directors as having *ostensible* authority [for a discussion of actual and ostensible authority, see Chapter 6] to bind the company to any transaction which falls within the powers expressly or impliedly conferred on it by its memorandum of association. Unless he is put on notice to the contrary, a person dealing in good faith with a company which is carrying on an *intra vires* business is entitled to assume that its directors are properly exercising such powers for the purposes of the company as set out in the memorandum. Correspondingly, such a person in such circumstances can hold the company to any transactions of this nature.

(6) If, however, a person dealing with a company is on notice that the directors are exercising the relevant power for purposes other than the purposes of the company, he cannot rely on the ostensible authority of the directors and, on ordinary principles of agency, cannot hold the company to the transaction.'

The practical effect of these decisions seems to be that if an act could be justified by reference to an object of the company, the transaction could not be challenged. If the act could be justified by reference to a power of the company then the transaction would be valid unless the power was being used as a disguise for another purpose and the outsider was on notice of this. An action may also be valid if it can be justified by reference to an implied power, that is, that it was done *bona fide* in furthering the objects of a company. This interpretation is supported by *Halifax Building Society* v. *Meridian Housing Association* [1994] 2 BCLC 540 which also makes plain a further area in which the complex case law will still be relevant. Many companies in the 'regulated sector', that is, insurance companies, building societies and friendly societies, have their objects restricted by statute as well as their rules. This case makes it plain that the old rules will be used to determine the validity of acts of such companies, and this will still be the case for charitable companies. In that case Mrs Arden J held that a development of mixed offices and residential accommodation was 'reasonably incidental to the pursuit' of the objects of Meridian, which were 'to carry on the industry, business or trade of providing housing or any associated amenities'.

Summary

1. Under the common law, if an act of a company was not authorised by the objects clause in the memorandum it was *ultra vires* the company and of no effect.

2. The Companies Act 2006 imperfectly abolishes the doctrine, leaving it open to (a) a shareholder who discovers in advance that an *ultra vires* action is planned and seeks an injunction, and (b) a member who alleges that there is a breach of duty by a director because he is acting *ultra vires*, to raise the issue of *ultra vires*, whereupon the whole of the old case law may become relevant.

3. Under the older law the doctrine of constructive notice applied and everyone was held to know the contents of the memorandum and articles of a company.

4. Various drafting devices were adopted to avoid the difficulties of the doctrine. Many clauses were inserted, a clause 'elevating' all the other clauses to the status of independent objects was included, and a subjective clause referring to the opinion of the directors was inserted.

5. These drafting devices were mostly effective but the courts held that some activities could not be sensible commercial objectives (for example, borrowing) and therefore refused to afford them any higher status than powers.

6. Even before the statutory reform, cases showed a tendency to equate objects and powers and to limit the effect of the doctrine.

Exercises

1. Does s. 31 Companies Act 2006 mean that a company has the same powers as a natural person?

2. Is the power which remains with shareholders to challenge *ultra vires* actions of directors sufficiently useful to justify the retention of the old case law?

3. Identify the situations when the old law is still relevant.

Chapter 5

The articles of association

The articles of association have replaced the memorandum of association as
the key document in the company's constitution (s. 18 Companies Act 2006,
which requires that a company must have articles of association 'prescribing
regulations for the company'). However, their contents are not compulsorily
laid down by the Companies Act, and by s. 20 a limited company may
register no articles, in which case the model articles drawn up by the
Secretary of State will apply. If articles are registered they will prevail over
the model articles but only 'in so far as they do not exclude or modify' the
model articles (s. 20(1)(b)).

The articles will be the chief instrument for regulating the relationship
between a shareholder and the company and the balance of power among
shareholders themselves. The voting rights attached to various classes of
shares will be one of the most important things set out in most articles of
association. Other important matters will be: the powers exercisable by the
board (or boards) of directors, payment of dividends, and alteration of the
capital structure of the company. A central feature of UK company law is
that members are free, subject to legal restraints, to make their own rules
about the internal affairs of the company, which will form a key part of the
company's constitution. The commentary on the Company Law Reform Bill
said that drafting the articles in the form of Table A, a mid-19th century
invention, is no longer an appropriate form of drafting articles. The
Company Law Reform Bill 2005 underlines the 'one size fits all' function of
Table A, expressly doubting its relevance to today's companies. In the Bill,
Table A is criticised as 'unintelligible' to non-specialists, remote from the
concerns of small companies, and difficult to adapt so as to incorporate
recent changes in company law such as the introduction of single member
companies in addition to further reform promoted by the government in the
relevant field. As the latter judges Table A as 'unfit' for modern company
law demands, it promotes a radically simplified set of articles for private
companies limited by shares reflecting the way small companies operate, a

separate set of model articles for public companies limited by shares, a full set of articles for private companies limited by guarantee, and comprehensive, clear and concise guidance for small companies that are using or thinking of using model articles. Some of the model article provisions under the 1985 Act are set out in the Case notes, and new ones are awaited.

One of the most difficult questions that arises concerning the articles of association, is the degree to which they form an enforceable agreement between the shareholders and the company itself, and among shareholders. If the articles were too rigidly binding, management would be restricted in their actions for fear that their decisions would be challenged as having contravened a small (and perhaps relatively unimportant) provision contained in the articles. On the other hand, the articles are part of the constitution of the company and stand between the shareholders and the otherwise practically unrestricted powers of the management.

The potential misuse of the power to alter articles was well put in the Australian case of *Re Peter's American Delicacy Company Ltd* (High Court of Australia) (1939) 61 CLR 457. In that case Dixon CJ said:

'If no restraint were laid upon the power of altering articles of association, it would be possible for a shareholder controlling the necessary voting power so to mould the regulations of a company that its operations would be conducted or its property used so that he would profit either in some other capacity than that of member of the company or, if as member, in a special or peculiar way inconsistent with conceptions of honesty so widely held or professed that departure from them is described, without further analysis, as fraud. For example, it would be possible to adopt articles requiring that the company should supply him with goods below cost or pay him 99 per cent of its profits for some real or imaginary services or submit to his own determination the question whether he was liable to account to the company for secret profits as a director.'

How has the law held the balance between the various power groups whose privileges and duties are governed by the articles?

5.1 The articles as a contract

Section 14 Companies Act 1985 reads as follows:

'(1) Subject to the provisions of this Act, the memorandum and articles, when registered, bind the company and its members to the same extent as if they respectively had been signed and sealed by each member, and contained covenants on the part of each member to observe all the provisions of the memorandum and articles.'

The precise effect of this provision was always most unclear. First of all, it is a peculiarly drafted provision as it provides that the members shall be bound as if they had signed and sealed the articles. It makes no mention of the company being bound by the same fiction. This appears to ignore the fact that the company is said to be a legal person separate and distinct from its members. The courts have ignored this apparent omission. In *Wood* v. *Odessa Waterworks* (1889) 42 Ch D 636 Stirling J said:

> 'The articles of association constitute a contract not merely between the shareholders and the company, but between each individual shareholder and every other.'

A further uncertainty is caused by the fact that, unlike an ordinary contract, the 'section 14' contract can be altered without the consent of one of the parties to it. By s. 9 Companies Act 1985 a company could alter its articles by special resolution. Thus, if 75 per cent of shareholders present and voting at a meeting determine that the articles are to be altered, that alteration will normally be effective and thus the 'contract' will be altered, as much for the objectors as for those in favour of the alteration. The ambit of the 2006 reforms are also somewhat unclear. Section 33 Companies Act 2006 provides:

> '(1) The provisions of a company's constitution bind the company and its members to the same extent as if there were covenants on the part of the company and of each member to observe those provisions.'

This effectively enacts the decision in *Wood* v. *Odessa Waterworks* but it does not seem to solve other difficulties which arose with the 'contract' in old s. 14.

5.2 What rights are governed by the contract in the articles?

Under the common law, the courts made it clear that the only relationship between members which is governed by this 'contract' in the articles is the dealings which they have with each other because they are shareholders in the company. No contractual relationship outside those confines is created by s. 14. This can be illustrated by *London Sack and Bag* v. *Dixon* [1943] 2 All ER 763.

This case concerned a dispute between two members of the UK Jute Association. The dispute had arisen out of trading transactions between them, and not as a result of shareholders' rights. It was argued by the appellants that there was a binding submission to arbitration by virtue of the fact that both disputants were members of the association. The articles of the association provided for arbitration in the event of a dispute between members. The court held that the appellants had failed to prove that there had been a binding submission to arbitration. Scott LJ said that the contract, which was created between the members under the predecessor to s. 14, did not constitute a contract between them 'about rights of action created entirely outside the company relationship such as trading transactions between members'.

An example from the other side of the line, where shareholders were bound to abide by the articles, was *Rayfield* v. *Hands* [1960] Ch 1. In that case the plaintiff was a shareholder in a company. Article 11 of the articles required him to inform the directors of an intention to transfer shares in the company. The same article provided that the directors 'will take the said shares equally between them at fair value'. The plaintiff notified his intention of selling the shares but they refused to buy. The plaintiff's claim for the determination of the fair value of the shares and for an order that the directors should purchase the shares at a fair price succeeded. Vaisey J said: 'the articles of association are simply a contract as between the shareholders *inter se* in respect of their rights as shareholders.' Vaisey J also relied on the fact that in this case a small company, somewhat akin to a partnership, had been involved. If he was right to believe that this strengthened the s. 14 contract we can see that this alleged contract affects the 'constitutional' rights of shareholders that are affected by the articles. The contract may be more readily enforced where there are few shareholders.

5.3   Outsiders

This issue does not appear to be reformed by the new wording in the Companies Act 2006 with the exception of 'entrenched provision' (see discussion of s. 22, below). Because shareholders are affected by the 'contract' only in their capacity as shareholders, it is clear that outsiders (non-shareholders) cannot be affected by the contract in the articles. Strangely, however, the rights of such outsiders are often set out in the articles. This may be partly because of the special definition of 'outsiders' in these circumstances. The practice has led to a number of cases. A good illustration of the point is *Eley* v. *Positive Government Security Life Association* (1876) 1 Ex D 88. There the articles of association contained a clause in which it was stated that the plaintiff should be solicitor to the company and should transact all the legal business. The articles were signed by seven members of the company and duly registered. Later the company employed another solicitor and the plaintiff brought an action for breach of contract. This action did not succeed. The court held that the articles were a matter between the shareholders among themselves or the shareholders and the directors (as representing the company). They did not create any contract between a solicitor and the company. This was so even though the solicitor had become a member of the company some time after the articles had been signed.

ambiguity?

This means that there is a subtlety in the definition of an 'outsider' in these circumstances. He is a person unable to enforce the articles or be affected by the contract in the articles. When the person seeking to enforce the articles has effectively two relationships with the company he may be both an 'outsider' in the sense discussed in *Eley*, but at the same time be a shareholder of the company. This problem was discussed in *Hickman* v. *Kent and Romney Marsh Sheepbreeders* [1915] 1 Ch 881. In that case, the articles contained a clause which provided for a reference to arbitration of any disputes between the company and its members concerning the construction of the articles or regarding any action to be taken in pursuance of those articles. When the plaintiff issued a writ claiming an injunction to prevent his expulsion from the company, the defendant company asked that the dispute be referred to arbitration. Astbury J cited a number of cases (*Prichard's Case* (1873) LR 8 Ch 956; *Melhado* v. *Porto Alegre Ry Co.* (1874) LR 9 CP 503; *Eley* v. *Positive Government Security Life Association* (1876) 1 Ex D 88; and *Browne* v. *La Trinidad* (1888) 37 Ch D 1), and went on to say:

claimed

'Now in these four cases the article relied upon purported to give specific contractual rights to persons in some capacity other than that of shareholder, and in none of them were members seeking to enforce or protect rights given to them as members, in common with the other corporators. The actual decisions amount to this. An outsider to whom rights purport to be given by the articles in his capacity as outsider, whether he is or subsequently becomes a member, cannot sue on those articles treating them as contracts between himself and the company to enforce those rights. Those rights are not part of the general regulations of the company applicable alike to all shareholders and can only exist by virtue of some contract between such person and the company, and the subsequent allotment of shares to an outsider in whose favour such an article is inserted does not enable him to sue the company on such article to enforce rights which are . . . not part of the general rights of the corporators as such.'

Having examined a number of other cases (including *Wood* v. *Odessa Waterworks* (1889) 42 Ch D 636; *Salmon* v. *Quinn & Axtens* [1909] AC 442; and *Welton* v. *Saffery* [1987] AC 299), Astbury J found the law clear on the following points:

'first, that no article can constitute a contract between the company and a third person; secondly, that no right merely purporting to be given by an article to a person, whether a member or not, in a capacity other than that of member, as, for instance, as solicitor, promoter, director, can be enforced against the company; and thirdly, that articles regulating the rights and obligations of the members generally as such do create rights and obligations between them and the company respectively.'

The conclusion arrived at by Astbury J was reached after consideration of the case of *Salmon* v. *Quinn & Axtens*. In that case the articles of association gave a veto to Joseph Salmon which could prevent the board of directors from validly making certain decisions. On the occasion in question in this case, Salmon had used his power of veto. Salmon was a managing director and yet he was able to enforce his right of veto by way of the contract in the articles despite the fact that there was only one other shareholder who held a similar right. This case can be reconciled with *Hickman* on the grounds that every shareholder has the right to enforce the articles of the company and it is irrelevant and coincidental that the article sought to be enforced in any one case stands to benefit the shareholder bringing the action more than others. In other words, a shareholder who also holds a position as outsider (such as managing director, solicitor, etc.) can, wearing his shareholder hat, enforce the contract in the articles, even if the direct result of that enforcement is of benefit to him wearing his outsider hat.

This approach was rejected in *Beattie* v. *Beattie* [1938] Ch 708 (see Case note 1, p. 73). Sir Wilfred Greene MR said:

> 'It is to be observed that the real matter which is here being litigated is a dispute between the company and the appellant in his capacity as a director, and when the appellant, relying on this clause, seeks to have that dispute referred to arbitration, it is that dispute and none other which he is seeking to have referred, and by seeking to have it referred he is not, in my judgment, seeking to enforce a right which is common to himself and all other members . . . He is not seeking to enforce a right to call on the company to arbitrate a dispute which is only accidentally a dispute with himself. He is asking, as a disputant, to have the dispute to which he is a party referred. That is sufficient to differentiate it from the right which is common to all the other members of the company under this article.'

The line between shareholders' rights and outsiders' rights remains, despite the anomalous decision in *Salmon* v. *Quinn & Axtens*.

Section 14 (with other issues) was the subject of a study by the Law Commission. In *Shareholder Remedies* (Law Commission Report No. 246, which is available on the Law Commission website **http://www.lawcom. gov.uk/library**) the Commission sets out the current law, acknowledges that the law is unclear but recommends against providing a statutory list of situations which fall within the scope of the section. The Law Commission does not suggest an approach which abandons seeing s. 14 as a type of contract, and making it clear that it is present to protect constitutional rights which belong to a substantial body of shareholders. It does however suggest adding further regulations in Table A with the aim of providing dispute resolution provisions and a means of 'exit' for shareholders in small companies. The Companies Act 2006 seems to have followed this recommendation, leaving us with opposing authorities. The only case above which might be construed as involving an 'entrenched provision' was *Salmon* v. *Quinn & Axtens* and it does not come squarely within that definition (see below), as the veto right in that case enabled vetoing certain decisions of the board of directors; it did not involve vetoing a change in articles.

established firmly

5.4 Entrenched provisions

What the 2006 Act has done is provide new law on provisions which are entrenched in the articles. It also provides that where provisions were in a company's memorandum because the company was formed under the 1985 Act or one of its predecessors, it will now be considered to be in the company's articles and thus subject to the new regime concerning change and entrenchment.

Section 22 provides that

'(1) A company's articles may contain provision ("Provision for entrenchment") to the effect that specified provisions of the articles may be amended or repealed only if conditions are met, or procedures complied with, that are more restrictive than those applicable in the case of a special resolution.

(2) Provision for entrenchment may only be made –
   (a) in the company's articles on formation, or
   (b) by an amendment of the company's articles agreed to by all members of the company.'

The section provides that an agreement of all members is sufficient for alteration even if there is an entrenched provision. A court or other relevant authority may also alter articles where it has power to do so.

5.5 The articles as evidence of a contract

Whereas an 'outsider' may not enforce rights which are in the articles by invoking s. 33 Companies Act 2006 and its predecessor, s. 14 Companies Act 1985, he may be able to show that he has a contract with the company apart from the articles, but the articles may provide or be evidence of some of the terms of that contract. An example of this is *Re New British Iron Company* Ex Parte *Beckwith* [1898] 1 Ch 324. In that case the articles provided (by article 62) that: 'The remuneration of the board shall be an annual sum of £1000 to be paid out of the funds of the company, which sum shall be divided in such manner as the board from time to time determine.' Wright J said:

'That article is not in itself a contract between the company and the directors; it is only part of the contract constituted by the articles of association between the members of the company *inter se*. But where on the footing of that article the directors are employed by the company and accept office the terms of article 62 are embodied in and form part of the contract between the company and the directors. Under the articles as thus embodied the directors obtain a contractual right to an annual sum of £1000 as remuneration.'

The same reasoning proved detrimental to the plaintiff in *Read* v. *Astoria Garage (Streatham) Ltd* [1952] 2 All ER 292. The company had adopted the standard form of articles of association set out in the Companies Act in force at the time. The article at the centre of the dispute provided that managing directors could be appointed by a resolution of the directors and for that appointment to be terminated by a resolution of the general meeting. The plaintiff was appointed and dismissed by those procedures. He claimed unfair dismissal, arguing that there was a contract between him and the company, one of the terms of which was that his employment should not be terminated without reasonable notice. The Court of Appeal could find no evidence of a contract between the company and the plaintiff, still less evidence of a contract which contradicted the terms of the articles, so the plaintiff failed.

Still more unfortunate was the plaintiff in *Re Richmond Gate Property Co. Ltd* [1965] 1 WLR 335. In that case the court held that the defendant had been employed by the company as managing director. The court looked to the articles to find what remuneration was due since there was no evidence of a contract term about pay elsewhere. The articles provided that he should be paid such amount 'as the directors may determine'. In fact the directors had made no determination so nothing was due to him. Furthermore because he had a contract with the company he could not recover any money on a '*quantum meruit*' claim, which is a claim for money when work has been done without any formal agreement as to the amount that will be paid in respect of that work. It is, in effect, a claim for a 'reasonable amount' for work done.

The facts of the previous two cases considered lead to the question: what would be the situation if a contract had existed and that contract and the articles contained contradictory clauses? In *Read v. Astoria Garage* (see above), Jenkins LJ said:

> 'a managing director whose appointment is determined by the company in general meeting . . . cannot claim to have been wrongfully dismissed unless he can show that an agreement has been entered into between himself and the company, the terms of which are inconsistent with the exercise by the company of the power conferred on it by the article . . .'

From this it follows that the company can exercise whatever powers the articles specify, but if a contractual right is breached by this exercise of powers, damages must be paid. This was what occurred in *Nelson v. James Nelson & Sons Ltd* [1914] 2 KB 770. In that case, the directors tried to terminate the employment of the plaintiff as managing director. He had been appointed as managing director for life provided that he complied with a number of conditions. It was not alleged that he had broken any of the conditions. The articles gave to the directors power to appoint managing directors and power to 'revoke' such appointments. The court held that the power to revoke appointments did not mean that the directors could do so in such a way that contracts entered into by the company would be broken. That was what had happened here and therefore the termination of the plaintiff's employment was unlawful and the company was liable in damages for breach of contract.

5.6   Alteration of the articles of association

Section 21 Companies Act 2006 reads as follows:

'(1) A company may amend its articles by special resolution.'

By s. 25 of the Act a member will not be bound by alterations made after he has joined the company in so far as they make him liable to pay extra money to the company, unless he has agreed in writing to take more shares than he was obliged to before the alteration. There are special provisions which apply when the rights attached to classes of shares are to be varied (see s. 630 *et seq.* and Chapter 14). This cannot be done simply by special resolution. The general rule concerning non-variation alterations is that articles may be altered by a special (75 per cent majority) resolution. This rule can put very considerable power in the hands of the majority. The number of shareholders making up such a majority may be very small, perhaps only one person. Because of this the court has found it necessary to control this power. The rule that has been formulated is that an alteration of articles is valid only if it is in good faith (*bona fide*) and for the benefit of the company as a whole. At first sight this would seem to be a stringent control, but closer examination of the cases shows a considerable reluctance to intervene in favour of an aggrieved minority, and great confusion as to what is actually meant by '*bona fide* for the benefit of the company as a whole'. These cases pre-date the Companies Act 2006 but there is no reason to doubt their applicability.

In *Allen* v. *Gold Reefs of West Africa Ltd* [1900] 1 Ch 656 (see Case note 2, p. 73), Lindley MR said:

'the power conferred by [what is now s. 9 of the Act] must, like all other powers, be exercised subject to those general principles of law and equity which are applicable to all powers conferred on majorities and enabling them to bind minorities. It must be exercised, not only in the manner required by law, but also *bona fide* for the benefit of the company as a whole, and it must not be exceeded. These conditions are always implied, and are seldom, if ever, expressed. But if they are complied with I can discover no ground for judicially putting any other restrictions on the power conferred by the section than those contained in it . . .'

The judge went on to say that shares were taken on the basis that articles were subject to alteration. It would therefore require very clear evidence of an undertaking by the company to treat a particular shareholder differently – an undertaking that a particular article would not be altered. However, where there was an agreement that would be broken by the alteration of the articles of association, the company would be liable for a breach of contract brought about by the change of article (Lindley MR in *Allen* v. *Gold Reefs of West Africa Ltd*):

> 'A company cannot break its contracts by altering its articles, but, when dealing with contracts referring to revocable articles, and especially with contracts between a member of the company and the company respecting his shares, care must be taken not to assume that the contract involves as one of its terms an article which is not to be altered.'

5.7   *Bona fide* for the benefit of the company

Given that a resolution to alter articles will be regarded as valid if it is passed '*bona fide* for the benefit of the company', and invalid if this can be shown not to be the case, do the cases throw light on what is meant by that phrase?

In *Brown* v. *British Abrasive Wheel* [1919] 1 Ch 290, the company needed to raise further capital. The 98 per cent majority were willing to provide this capital if they could buy up the 2 per cent minority. Having failed to effect this by agreement, the 98 per cent proposed to change the articles of association to give them power to purchase the shares of the minority. The proposed article provided for the compulsory purchase of the minority's shares on certain terms. However, the majority were prepared to insert any provision as to price which the court thought was fair. Despite this, the court held that the proposed alteration could not be made. Astbury J held that the alteration was not for the benefit of the company as a whole. One reason for this was that there was no direct link between the provision of the extra capital and the alteration of the articles. Although the whole scheme had been to provide the capital after removing the dissentient shareholders, it would in fact have been possible to remove the shareholders and then refuse to provide the capital. Astbury J's judgment seems to determine that two separate criteria must be met: the judgment must be 'within the ordinary principles of justice' and it must be 'for the benefit of the company as a whole'. So far as the latter requirement was concerned, the company seems to have been identified with the shareholders and the reality of the whole plan seems to have been overlooked, for the judge ignored the plan to provide capital on the grounds that there was no formal link between this and the alteration. He also said that the alteration would benefit the majority and not the company as a whole, thus ignoring the company's separate existence as a commercial entity in need of further funding.

Brown v. *British Abrasive Wheel* was not followed in the later case of *Sidebottom* v. *Kershaw, Leese & Co. Ltd* [1919] 1 Ch 290, and the approach taken by the judge in the *Brown* case was criticised. In *Sidebottom*, an alteration was approved although it provided for the compulsory purchase of shares. One difference between this case and *Brown* is that the ability to purchase the shares was limited to a situation where the shareholder in question was carrying on business in direct competition with the company. The relationship between this article and the benefit of the company was therefore much clearer. In *Sidebottom* two of the Court of Appeal judges made it clear that they believed that in *Brown*, Astbury J had been wrong to regard good faith and the company's benefit as two separate ideas. The important question was: Was the alteration for the benefit of the company as a whole?

Settling the important question and determining its meaning proved to be two different things. In *Dafen Tinplate Co. Ltd v. Llanelly Steel Co. (1907) Ltd* [1920] 2 Ch 124, the plaintiff company was a member of the defendant company. The defendants realised that the plaintiffs were conducting business in a manner detrimental to their interests. In fact they were buying steel from an alternative source of supply. There was an attempt to buy the plaintiff's shares by agreement but this failed. The defendant company then altered its articles by special resolution to include a power to compulsorily purchase the shares of any member requested to transfer them. It was this alteration which was the subject of the action. The court held that the alteration was too wide to be valid. The altered article would confer too much power on the majority. It went much further than was necessary for the protection of the company. The judge seemed to be using the '*bona fide* for the benefit of the company' test in an objective sense, that is, he was judging the situation from the court's point of view.

A different view of the meaning of this important question was taken in *Shuttleworth* v. *Cox Bros & Co. (Maidenhead) Ltd* [1927] 2 KB 9. In that case the company had a board of directors appointed for life. The alteration to the articles provided that any one of the board of directors should lose office if his fellow directors requested in writing that he should resign. The alteration was directed at a particular director whose conduct had not been satisfactory. Again the words '*bona fide* for the benefit of the company' were interpreted as one condition. This time, however, the court approached the question from the point of view of the subjective belief of the shareholders. Scrutton LJ said: 'the shareholders must act honestly having regard to and endeavouring to act for the benefit of the company.' Bankes LJ agreed and added:

'By what criterion is the court to ascertain the opinion of the shareholders on this question? The alteration may be so oppressive as to cast suspicion on the honesty of the persons responsible for it, or so extravagant that no reasonable man could really consider it for the benefit of the company. In such cases the court is, I think, entitled to treat the conduct of shareholders as it does the verdict of a jury and to say that the alteration of a company's articles shall not stand if it is such that no reasonable man could consider it for the benefit of the company . . . I cannot agree with what seems to have been the view of Peterson J in *Dafen Tinplate Co. v. Llanelly*

Steel Co. [see above] . . . that whenever the Court and the shareholders may differ in opinion upon what is for the benefit of the company, the view of the court must prevail.'

If this passage is right, the court will only intervene in the most extreme cases – when no reasonable man could believe that the alteration could be good for the company. One of the considerations which caused the courts to withdraw from their more interventionist stand is the fact that shares and the right to vote attached to shares are regarded as property rights. It would be unrealistic, in the words of Dixon CJ in *Peter's* (see p. 60):

'[to] suppose that in voting each shareholder is to assume an inhuman altruism and consider only the intangible notion of the benefit of the vague abstraction . . . "the company as an institution".'

A further difficulty is that the alteration of the articles presupposes that there will be conflicting interests to be adjusted. It is therefore very difficult for anyone to determine what will be for the positive benefit of the whole company. It may be that two conflicting rights have been confused. It can be argued that a shareholder has two rights. (This theory is based on the work of Professor S. Leader – see 'Private Property and Corporate Governance, Part 1: Defining the Interests', in F. Patfield (ed.), *Perspectives in Company Law I*, Kluwer, 1995.) One is the right to uphold the value of his shareholding. In defence of this right the shareholder may vote selfishly without any regard to the benefit of the company. If, despite so voting, the right is unfairly damaged the shareholder will be entitled to compensation (probably as a result of an action under s. 459 Companies Act 1985) for unfair prejudice. A shareholder defending such a right would not be entitled to set aside a decision of the management or company on such grounds.

However, a decision by the company or the management may be struck down if it is not taken *bona fide* in the interests of the company. This is because decisions which affect the interests of the company must be taken for the benefit of the company as a whole even if some shareholders are damaged in the process. A decision not taken for the benefit of the company as a whole should be challengeable by shareholders seeking to protect the value of the interests they hold in the company rather than the value of the interest they hold in their shares.

The courts have taken a cautious view and retained their power to prevent manifest abuses while fighting shy of interference in the internal affairs of the company. This caution can be seen as part of the whole approach of the law to the principle of majority rule (see Chapter 1).

Two other cases show the reluctance of the court to intervene. In *Greenhalgh* v. *Arderne Cinemas Ltd* [1951] Ch 286 (see Case note **3**, pp. 73–4), a change in articles which effectively removed the plaintiff's pre-emption rights was approved, despite the reference in the judgment to the factor of discrimination as a factor which would cause a resolution to be disallowed by the courts. It must be clear that *any* discrimination between majority and minority shareholders would not be sufficient to cause a resolution to fail the *bona fide* test, since many alterations of articles will cause adjustments between classes of shareholders from which some will emerge better off than others. An example of this is to be found in *Rights and Issue Investment Trust Ltd* v. *Stylo Shoes Ltd* [1965] Ch 250. In that case the effect of the alteration was (among other things) to halve the voting rights of a number of ordinary shareholders as against the rights held by management. Despite this the resolution was upheld. The management shares had not been voted and the resolution had been passed by the requisite majority. The court refused to interfere. It seems that if discrimination is to be a ground for interference it will have to be some very clear, perhaps vindictive, discrimination that is alleged before the court will be moved to upset the normal voting patterns of the company and declare a resolution invalid.

5.8   Remedies

The remedies that are available to a successful challenger when an alteration to the articles has been or is about to be made include the following.

Injunction

An injunction will be available where the alteration does not pass the *bona fide* test but it is doubtful whether it will be available where the objection to the alteration is that it will cause the company to break a contract. In *British Murac Syndicate* v. *Alperton Rubber Co.* [1915] 2 Ch 186 there was an agreement separate from the articles, by which the defendant company was obliged to accept two directors nominated by the plaintiff syndicate. Two directors were nominated but their appointment was not acceptable to the defendants. The defendant company proposed to delete the regulation that was in the same terms as the external contract. It was held that the company had no power to alter its articles of association for the purpose of committing a breach of contract and that therefore an injunction would be granted to restrain the holding of the meeting which was to be convened for that purpose.

This case must be contrasted with *Southern Foundries Ltd* v. *Shirlaw* [1940] AC 701. In that case the House of Lords held that the company could alter its articles so as to put itself in a position in which it could break a contract. When such powers were used, however, there would be a breach and the other party to that contract would be entitled to damages. Where there was a contract made in the expectation that a state of affairs would continue, it was not open to the company, by using its power to change articles, so to undermine that contract that it became worthless. While leaving a plaintiff a remedy in damages this case throws some doubt on the *British Murac* case, since it implies that the change in the articles could not be restrained by injunction. It was only misuse of the new powers inserted by the alteration that could be questioned. Damages were the remedy asked for, so that it is still uncertain if the use of the new powers could have been restrained in respect of this particular member. It may be that in *British Murac* the injunction should not have been aimed at preventing the meeting to alter the regulation, but at a future use of the altered regulation in order to break the contract that existed independently of the articles. The exact significance of these two cases is still somewhat uncertain.

Damages

There is no doubt that where alteration of the articles, or even use of a power contained in the articles, causes a contract with an outsider to be broken, damages will be awarded. In *Shindler* v. *Northern Raincoat Co. Ltd* [1960] 1 WLR 1038, the defendant company agreed to employ the plaintiff as its managing director for ten years. By using a power in the articles, the plaintiff was dismissed in the first year. He was entitled to damages.

Where the complaint is a breach of the contract in the articles (the s. 14 contract), matters are not so clear. In the old case of *Moffatt* v. *Farquhar* (1878) 7 Ch D 591 a challenger was awarded damages, but where the plaintiff is a member of the company at the time of bringing his action his right to damages might be blocked by the decision in the later case of *Houldsworth* v. *City of Glasgow Bank* (1880) 5 App Cas 317 (see Chapter 7), where it was laid down as a general principle that a member of a company could not recover damages from the company since this would involve a return of capital to the members of the company in contravention of the maintenance of capital provisions. This rule was abolished by Companies Act 1989 inserting s. 111A into Companies Act 1985.

Rectification

This would involve an order of the court altering the document (in this case the articles) so that it will read in the way that was originally intended. In the case of articles of association, the courts have held that this is out of the question because the Registrar approved the document in its original form. It is in that form and no other that the articles become the constitution of the company binding on the members, so it cannot be subsequently altered by the court (see *Scott* v. *Frank F. Scott (London) Ltd* [1940] Ch 794).

Summary

1. The articles of association regulate the relationship between the shareholders and the company, and the balance of power among shareholders.

2. It is difficult to assess the contractual binding force of the articles as a contract.

3. Some authorities require the right sought to be enforced under s. 33 Companies Act 2006 and the articles to be a 'member's right' and not a 'special right'. *Salmon* v. *Quinn & Axtens* appears to contradict this.

4. An alteration of the articles can be effected by a 75 per cent majority of the shareholders but can be challenged on the ground that the alteration was not '*bona fide* for the benefit of the company'.

Case notes

1. *Beattie* v. *Beattie* [1938] Ch 708

The articles of association contained an arbitration clause. An allegation was made by a shareholder who stated that the defendant had, in his capacity as director, paid himself unjustified remuneration. Sir Wilfred Greene said:

> 'It is to be observed that the real matter which is here being litigated is a dispute between the company and the appellant in his capacity as a director, and when the appellant, relying on this clause, seeks to have that dispute referred to arbitration, it is that dispute and none other which he is seeking to have referred, and by seeking to have it referred he is not, in my judgment, seeking to enforce a right which is common to himself and all other members.'

2. *Allen* v. *Gold Reefs of West Africa Ltd* [1900] 1 Ch 656

The case concerned an attempted alteration of the articles of association which would have retrospective effect and alter the obligations of a shareholder towards the company. The court held that, provided the alteration could be seen as '*bona fide* for the benefit of the company', the power to alter articles was otherwise unfettered.

3. *Greenhalgh* v. *Arderne Cinemas Ltd* [1951] Ch 286

Eveshed MR said:

> 'Certain principles can be safely stated as emerging from [the] authorities. In the first place, I think it is now plain that '*bona fide* for the benefit of the company as a whole' means not two things but one thing. It means that the shareholder must proceed upon what, in his honest opinion, is for the benefit of the company as a whole. The second thing is that the phrase 'the company as a whole' does not (at any rate in such a case as the present) mean the company as a commercial entity, distinct from the corporators as a general body. That is to say, the case may be taken of an individual hypothetical member and it may be asked whether what is proposed is, in the honest

opinion of those who voted in its favour, for that person's benefit.

I think that the matter can, in practice, be more accurately and precisely stated by looking at the converse and by saying that a special resolution of this kind would be liable to be impeached if the effect of it were to discriminate between the majority shareholders and the minority shareholders, so as to give to the former an advantage of which the latter were deprived.'

Exercises

1. What are the policy factors behind the decisions on enforcement of the articles of association as a contract?

2. What is meant by '*bona fide* for the benefit of the company'?

Chapter 6

Power to represent the company

Key words

▶ **Actual authority** – the 'real' authority which agents of the company have, enabling them to make the company liable for contracts they conclude.

▶ **Ostensible and usual authority** – the authority which a reasonable third party would expect company representatives to have, enabling them to make the company liable for contracts they conclude (see Figure 6.1, p. 76).

▶ **Pre-incorporation contract** – a contract supposedly made on behalf of a company but made before it has any legal existence.

6.1 Power of directors to bind the company

Even if an action is within the capacity of the company, it may be outside the powers of the individuals who are involved in the transaction. Rules have been formulated, therefore, to determine in what circumstances a company will be bound, notwithstanding that the individual does not have the power to carry out the transaction in question. A diagrammatic way through these complicated provisions (Figure 6.1) is to be found on p. 76. There are two regimes, under the common law and under the Companies Act 2006. These overlap to a considerable extent. Under the common law, persons outside a company are entitled to assume that internal procedures have been complied with. This is a consequence of *Royal British Bank* v. *Turquand* (1856) 6 E&B 327. That case involved an action for the return of money borrowed from the plaintiff by the official manager of a company. The company argued that it was not bound by the actions of the official manager in this case. This was because the company's deed of settlement contained the following clause:

'That the Board of Directors may borrow on mortgage, bond or bill in the name of, and if necessary under the common seal of, the Company such sum or sums of money as shall from time to time, by a resolution passed at a general meeting of the Company, be authorised to be borrowed: provided that the total amount of the sum or sums of money so borrowed shall not at any time exceed two thirds of the total amount on the instalments on the capital of the Company paid up or called for, and actually due and payable at the time of, the passing of such resolution.'

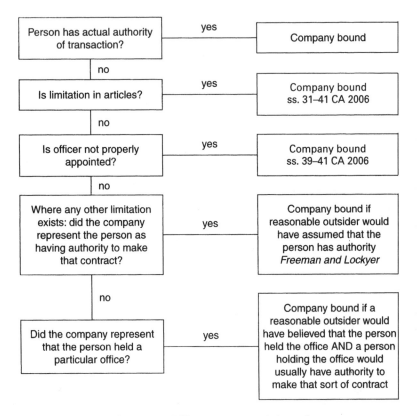

Figure 6.1 When a company is bound

No resolution as required by this clause had been passed. The court held that the plaintiffs had no knowledge that the resolution had not been passed, that it did not appear from the face of the public document (the contents of which the plaintiffs were deemed to know) that the borrowing was invalid. The company was therefore bound.

Outsiders are therefore entitled to assume that internal procedures such as the passing of the resolution in *Turquand*'s case have been complied with. This is now confirmed by ss. 40 and 161 Companies Act 2006. Section 40 reads:

'(1) In favour of a person dealing with a company in good faith, the power of the directors to bind the company, or authorise others to do so, is deemed to be free of any limitation under the company's constitution.

(2) For this purpose –

(a) a person "deals with" a company if he is a party to any transaction or other act to which the company is a party,

(b) a person dealing with a company –

    (i)   is not bound to enquire as to any limitation on the powers of the directors to bind the company or authorise others to do so,

    (ii) is presumed to have acted in good faith unless the contrary is proved, and

    (iii) is not to be regarded as acting in bad faith by reason only of his knowing that an act is beyond the powers of the directors under the company's constitution.'

Note that the exception for acts involving directors or connected persons is in s. 41.

Section 161 reads: → in spite of

'(1) The acts of a person acting as a director are valid notwithstanding that it is afterwards discovered –

(a) that there was a defect in his appointment,

(b) that he was disqualified from holding office,

(c) that he had ceased to hold office,

(d) that he was not entitled to vote on the matter in question.'

For almost all company law disputes this new legislation will form comprehensive protection for third parties dealing with a company. The exceptions are three: where the third party can be proved to be in bad faith; where the transaction involves a director or connected person and where the dealing is not with a 'person acting as director' or a person authorised by an acting director but with some other actor; and where there is scope for argument about the 'usual authority' of any party (see *Panorama Developments* v. *Fidelis Furnishing*, below).

Section 41 provides the exception to the general rule where the parties to a transaction include the company and either (i) a director of that company or of its holding company, or (ii) a person connected with such a director or a company with whom such a director is associated (see later in the chapter for an explanation of these terms). If the parties *include* such persons (there may be other parties as well), then the situation is as follows:

(a) the transaction is voidable at the instance of the company in respect of persons in categories (i) and (ii) above;

(b) each of the persons within categories (i) and (ii) above and any director who authorised the transaction is liable to account to the company for any gain made, or indemnify the company for any loss it suffers as a result of the transaction;

(c) as regards parties to the transaction other than those in categories (i) and (ii), they remain protected by the provisions of s. 40 Companies Act 2006, but in that case the court may, if such a person or the company applies, make an order affirming, severing or setting aside the transaction on such terms as appear to the court to be just.

6.2 Protection

One thing that is quite clear from s. 40 is that it is *only* intended to benefit an outsider dealing with the company in question. It cannot be used in any way by the company whose action is in question in order to save a transaction. The section could, of course, be used by a company dealing with another company, but only in order to benefit the company whose action is not questionable on constitutional grounds.

6.3 Transaction and dealing

The previous law contained an uncertainty about the ambit of the reference to 'transaction' and 'dealing'. There was some doubt about whether a gift would be included. This is covered by s. 40(2)(a): '(a) a person "deals with" a company if he is party to any transaction or other act to which the company is a party.'

6.4 Decided on by the directors

The law used to require a transaction 'decided on by the directors'. It was not clear what degree of delegation was permissible before a transaction became one which was decided on by someone other than 'the directors'. For example, if the directors decided that as a matter of policy they would attempt to move towards making the company environmentally friendly, was it a transaction 'decided on by the directors' when an expensive piece of de-polluting equipment was ordered by a plant manager? A similar problem arose if decisions were taken by a single director. If there was no express delegation of power to him to take decisions in that area, were his acts in pursuance of decisions by the directors? This delegation point is also covered by s. 40(1) which reads:

'In favour of a person dealing with a company in good faith, the power of the board of directors to bind the company, or authorise others to do so, shall be deemed to be free of any limitation under the company's constitution.'

6.5 Good faith

Section 40 applies if the third party is 'dealing with a company in good faith'. The outsider is presumed to be in good faith unless the contrary is proved (s. 40(2)(b)(ii)). This means that a company has to prove the absence of good faith if it wishes to avoid being bound. The meaning of the phrase 'good faith' is not clear. In *International Sales and Agencies* v. *Marcus* [1982] 3

All ER 551 Lawson J, referring to the First European Company Law Directive for guidance, came to the conclusion that:

> 'the defendants had actual knowledge that the payments to them were in breach of duty and trust and were *ultra vires* the companies . . . alternatively, at the lowest, that the defendants could not in all the circumstances have been unaware of the unlawful nature of the payments that they received.'

In these circumstances the allegation that the defendants were not in good faith had been proved. However, this finding did not help where the lack of good faith was less clear. Could behaviour less blameworthy qualify as bad faith? Did the bad faith relate solely to issues of constitutional irregularity or would an unconnected allegation be sufficient to prevent recovery? The only guidance we have is that a third party 'is not to be regarded as acting in bad faith by reason only of his knowledge that an act is beyond the powers of the directors under the company's constitution' (s. 40(2)(b)(iii)). Thus the dealings in *International Sales* v. *Marcus* could be impugned only on the breach of duty and trust ground, not on the ground that they were outside the powers of directors. Presumably the allegation of bad faith would need to show that the directors were breaching their duties in ways which were merely going beyond their powers. Maybe an allegation such as conflict of interest and duty will be necessary.

The following case was decided under the 1985 Act but, in view of the similarity of the wording with the Companies Act 2006, may well still be relevant. In *EIC Services Ltd & Another* v. *Phipps & Others* [2004] EWCA Civ 1069 the court of Appeal clarified the exact scope of s. 35A Companies Act 1985. According to paragraph 37 of the ruling: 'in the context of the company the term "third parties" naturally refers to persons other than the company and its members.' The controversy had been raised after the court ruling in *Smith* v. *Henniker-Major & Co.* [2002] EWCA Civ 762. In this case a director was assigned a right of action by an inquorate board. A quorum of two directors was required by the articles of association of the company in question but only one director attended. Thus, since the assignment was not valid the director did not have the standing to engage in the relevant action. The interesting point in this case is that the particular director sought to resort to s. 35A. According to s. 35A(2)(b): 'a person shall not be regarded as acting in bad faith by reason of only his knowing that an act is beyond the powers of directors under the company's constitution.' The particularity of this case was that the person who should not be regarded in bad faith because he was aware that the director was acting beyond the powers vested to him by the constitution was the director himself. He also sought to resort to s. 35A(2)(c) which states that a person, here the director himself, should be presumed to have acted in good faith unless the opposite is proved. On appeal the decision was taken by a majority supporting Rimer J's argumentation and with Robert Walker LJ dissenting on the s. 35A argument. The basic question in accordance with paragraph 118 of the judgment was: does s. 35A enable a director who has made an honest mistake as to the meaning of a provision in the articles of the company of which he is a director, himself to rely on his own mistake in order to give validity to something which would lack validity were it not for that mistake? To that question Robert Walker LJ gave an affirmative and Carnwath LJ and Rimer J a negative answer. Robert Walker LJ believed that a director in such a case could justifiably resort to s. 35A, but he supported that the validity of the agreement could still be challenged on the basis of s. 322A (predecessor to s. 41 Companies Act 2006), which however was not the case in *Smith*. Carnwath and Schiemann LJJ accepted that the word 'person' in the framework of s. 35A is wide enough to include a director of a company, however they both agreed that s. 35A inhibits a director who is the author of his own misfortune from profiting *vis-à-vis* third parties from his own mistake. In contrast, s. 322A was found to deal with a different problem, namely with what a company can do *vis-à-vis* its own director who has overstepped the mark. In practice s. 322A prevailed. This case revealed a confusion over the application of the two aforementioned sections and the relevant concepts.

From the interpretation of s. 35A it is revealed that a validly convened and constituted board of directors can confer authority to a given director to act in a certain way. But this authority is not vested to the director just because he is incorrectly convinced he is in possession of it. The fact that a director can still bind the company into an agreement with a third party even if he does not have the actual authority to enter such an agreement but only the ostensible one is a different issue to be dealt under the following section on unauthorised agents.

6.6   Unauthorised agents

Despite the reform of the law, a problem remains in that a person purporting to act for a company may actually have no connection whatsoever with that company. In those circumstances it would be wholly unfair to hold the company to a contract purportedly made on its behalf by someone who may be no more than a confidence trickster. If X purports to sell Tower Bridge to Y, should the Tower Bridge Company Ltd (supposing that they own the bridge) be bound? Obviously if there is no connection between X and the Tower Bridge Company Ltd, that course would be wholly unfair. However, if Y reasonably believes that X is authorised, because of the actions of the Tower Bridge Company Ltd, then the company ought to be bound. Although much complicated terminology is used in the cases, the law seems to achieve this result.

In *Freeman & Lockyer* v. *Buckhurst Park Properties Ltd* [1964] 2 QB 480, the plaintiff was a firm of architects and surveyors. The firm was engaged by a person acting as the defendant's managing director. The claim for fees was repudiated on the grounds that the apparent managing director had not been validly appointed. The Court of Appeal upheld the plaintiff's claim. Diplock LJ said:

'It is necessary at the outset to distinguish between an "actual" authority of an agent on the one hand, and an "apparent" or "ostensible" authority on the other. Actual authority and apparent authority are quite independent of one another. Generally they co-exist and coincide, but either may exist without the other and their respective scopes may be different. As I shall endeavour to show, it is on the apparent authority of the agent that the contractor normally relies in the ordinary course of business when entering into contracts.

An actual authority is a legal relationship between principal and agent created by a consensual agreement to which they alone are parties. Its scope is to be ascertained by applying ordinary principles of construction of contracts, including any proper implications from the express words used, the usages of the trade, or the course of business between the parties. To this agreement the contractor is a stranger; he may be totally ignorant of the existence of any authority on the part of the agent. Nevertheless, if the agent does enter into a contract pursuant to the "actual" authority, it does create contractual rights and liabilities between the principal and the contractor . . .

An "apparent" or "ostensible" authority, on the other hand, is a legal relationship between the principal and the contractor created by a representation, made by the principal to the contractor, intended to be and in fact acted on by the contractor, that the agent has authority to enter on behalf of the principal into a contract of a kind within the scope of the "apparent" authority, so as to render the principal liable to perform any obligations imposed on him by such a contract . . . The representation, when acted on by the contractor, by entering into a contract with the agent, operates as an estoppel, preventing the principal from asserting that he is not bound by the contract. It is irrelevant whether the agent had actual authority to enter into the contract.

In ordinary business dealings the contractor at the time of entering into the contract can in the nature of things hardly ever rely on the "actual" authority of the agent. His information as to the authority must be derived either from the principal or from the agent or from both, for they alone know what the agent's actual authority is. All that the contractor can know is what they tell him, which may or may not be true . . . The representation which creates "apparent" authority may take a variety of forms of which the commonest is representation by conduct, i.e. by permitting the agent to act in some way in the conduct of the principal's business with other persons. By doing so the principal represents to anyone who becomes aware that the agent is so acting that the agent has authority to enter on behalf of the principal into contracts with other persons of the kind which an agent so acting in the conduct of his principal's business has normally "actual" authority to enter into . . . unlike a natural person [a company] can only make a representation through an agent, [this] has the consequence that, in order to create an estoppel between the corporation and the contractor, the representation as to the authority of the agent which creates his "apparent" authority must be made by some person or persons who have "actual" authority from the corporation to make the representation . . . the contractor cannot rely on the agent's own representation as to his actual authority. He can rely only on a representation by a person or persons who have actual authority to manage or conduct that part of the business of the corporation to which the contract relates . . . If the foregoing analysis of the relevant law is correct, it can be summarised by stating four conditions which must be fulfilled to entitle a contractor to enforce against a company a contract entered into on behalf of the company by an agent who had no actual authority to do so. It must be shown: (a) that a representation that the agent had authority to enter on behalf of the company into a contract of the kind sought to be enforced was made to the contractor; (b) that such representation was made by a person or persons who had "actual" authority to manage the business of the company either generally or in respect of those matters to which the contract relates; (c) that he (the contractor) was induced by such representation to enter into the contract, i.e. that he in fact relied on it; and (d) that under its memorandum or articles of association the company was not deprived of the capacity either to enter into a contract of the kind sought to be enforced or to delegate authority to enter into a contract of that kind to the agent.'

As we have seen above, the advent of the Companies Act 1989 has almost certainly caused condition (d) to disappear. The outsider will need to show that the other party to the contract appeared, because of some actions by those actually entitled to represent the company, to be empowered to bind the company to the particular transaction in question. This may be because the company in some way represents that he has authority to enter into the particular transaction in question, or because the company make it appear that he holds a particular position or job within the company (often that of managing director). In the latter case, it is necessary for the outsider to go one step further and show that an officer of that kind 'usually' may bind the company to the type of transaction in question, that is, that the company's alleged agent has 'usual' authority. Where a transaction is questioned on the grounds that the company's representative has no power to enter into it (other than because of limitations under the constitution, unless the outsider was acting in bad faith), the relevant questions are:

(i) Did the person apparently representing the company have the authority to do so? If so, the contract is enforceable. If not:

(ii) Did the company lead the outsider to believe that the person apparently representing the company had the power to complete this particular transaction? If so, the contract is enforceable. If not:

(iii) Did the company lead the outsider to believe that the person apparently representing the company held a particular position in the company? If so *and* if a person validly appointed to that position would usually be able to complete the type of transaction in question, then the contract is enforceable.

6.7   Usual authority

An illustration of the last point made above is to be found in *Panorama Developments Ltd* v. *Fidelis Furnishing Fabrics* [1971] 3 WLR 440. In that case, the secretary of the company hired cars from the plaintiff pretending that they were for the use of the defendant, but in fact they were for his own use. The Court of Appeal held that the defendant was bound by the contracts. Lord Denning MR said:

> 'Mr Hames' second point is this: he says that the company is not bound by the letters which were signed by Mr Bayne as "Company Secretary". He says that, on the authorities, a company secretary fulfils a very humble role: and that he has no authority to make any contracts or representations on behalf of the company. He refers to *Barnett, Hoares & Co.* v. *South London Tramways Co.* (1887) 18 QBD 815, where Esher MR said:
>
>> "A secretary is a mere servant; his position is that he is to do what he is told, and no person can assume that he has any authority to represent anything at all."
>
> But times have changed. A company secretary is a much more important person nowadays than he was in 1887. He is an officer of the company with extensive duties and responsibilities. This appears not only in the modern Companies Acts, but also by the role which he plays in the day-to-day business of companies. He is no longer a mere clerk. He regularly makes representations on behalf of the company and enters into contracts on its behalf which come within the day-to-day running of the company's business. So much so that he may be regarded as held out as having authority to do such things on behalf of the company. He is certainly entitled to sign contracts connected with the administrative side of the company's affairs, such as employing staff, and ordering cars, and so forth.'

6.8   Promoters

One of the problems caused by the separate legal identity of the company is that prior to registration it has no existence at all. The persons who are responsible for the company coming into existence are known as 'promoters'. The law imposes duties on them not unlike those owed by directors. This is because the company can be badly cheated at the outset, particularly by those who sell it the assets on which it will found its business. The importance of the law on promoters has been much diminished by the controls exercised over public companies by the Financial Services Authority (see Chapter 8). It is now very rare for a new company to seek money from the public. However the rules remain valid.

6.9   Who are promoters?

In *Twycross* v. *Grant* (1877) 2 CPD 469, Cockburn CJ said:

'A promoter, I apprehend, is one who undertakes to form a company with reference to a given project and to set it going and who takes the necessary steps to accomplish that purpose. That the defendants were promoters of the company from the beginning can admit of no doubt. They framed the scheme; they not only provisionally framed the company but were, in fact to the end its creators, they found the directors and qualified them, they prepared the prospectus; they paid for printing and advertising and the expenses incidental to bringing the undertaking before the world. In all these respects the directors were passive; without saying that they were in a legal sense the agents of the defendants, they were certainly their instruments.'

This passage gives a clear indication of the actions which will be considered important by the courts when they are determining who was and who was not a promoter of a company. No stricter definition of a 'promoter' has been attempted because the situation can vary so widely. Investment of time or money in the enterprise will always be considered important. However, it is possible for a promoter not to have been obviously active. If he is the real 'power behind the throne' he will be held to have been a promoter. This is one case in which the court is committed to looking at the reality of the situation. Promoters of the type found in the cases are extinct. It is unusual for a newly formed company to make an issue of shares to the public, and impossible to obtain a stock market listing without having been in business for some time. There is also an enormous body of law and regulation (see Chapter 8) aimed at preventing the abuses that in the nineteenth century only the courts could prevent. Private companies do not issue shares to the public. Although they still have promoters in the sense described in the cases, the fact that they are unable to defraud the public makes control of their activities of less importance. Despite the obsolescence of this body of law it is still valid law, so the present tense will be used throughout to describe it.

6.10 Duties of promoters

Promoters are not trustees or agents of the company but they do stand in a special position in relation to the company. This is called a 'fiduciary' relationship and means that some of the same duties that trustees owe to their beneficiaries will also be owed by promoters to their company.

Promoters are most likely to defraud the company and its future shareholders by selling to the company property that they have previously bought. Because they are usually in control of the company at the outset they are able to determine the price that is paid. The temptation is to overvalue the property and fail to make disclosure of the overvaluation to an independent person. If that occurs, then the company can reverse (rescind) the contract, that is, give back the property and get back the money.

Situation 1 – If property is acquired before promotion commences (see *Erlanger* v. *New Sombrero Phosphate Co.* (1878) 3 App Cas 1218; and *Omnium Electric Palace* v. *Baines* [1914] 1 Ch 332)

If someone who subsequently becomes a promoter acquires property that is resold to the company, he may retain any profit that is made on that property provided he has made the correct disclosures (see p. 86). This is so even if the property was acquired with the idea that at some time in the future a company would be formed and the property would be sold to it. The vital factor which needs to be identified is the time at which the promotion commences because different rules apply thereafter.

Situation 2 – If property is acquired after promotion commences

If property is acquired by someone who has already become a promoter and that property is subsequently resold to the company, the courts will assume that the property was acquired for the company. Unless it can be proved that this was not the case the promoter will be unable to make a profit out of that property and the company will have the option of rescinding the contract or keeping the property and requiring the promoter to account for any profit he has made. This latter option is not open to the company in Situation 1 above. It was held in *Omnium Electric Palace* v. *Baines* [1914] 1 Ch 332 that proof that the property was not acquired on the company's behalf could consist of proof that the scheme had throughout been that the property should be bought and then resold to the company. The strange result of this seems to be that a profit may be kept if throughout the promoter had mercenary intentions. This is, of course, provided that the proper disclosures are made (as in Situation 1).

6.11   Disclosure

The general rule is that no promoter, whether in Situation 1 or 2, can make a *secret* profit. Thus if any property belonging to a promoter is sold to a company, or if a promoter makes a profit on a transaction connected with the company's formation (see *Gluckstein* v. *Barnes* [1900] AC 240), he will not in any event be permitted to keep that profit unless proper disclosure is made of the transaction. The difficulty is that frequently in this situation the same people are the promoters and the first directors. In *Gluckstein* v. *Barnes* and *Erlanger* v. *New Sombrero Phosphate Co.* (1878) 3 App Cas 1218 it was suggested that the transaction must have the blessing of an independent board of directors before a promoter would be permitted to keep his profit. This would seem to be far too sweeping since it would invalidate all '*Salomon* v. *Salomon*-type' transactions. Nevertheless the court was vehement in *Erlanger*. Lord Cairns said:

'I do not say that the owner of property may not promote and form a joint stock company and then sell his property to it, but I do say that if he does he is bound to take care that he sells it to the company through the medium of a board of directors who can and do exercise an independent and intelligent judgment on the transaction.'

This strict approach was not followed in *Lagunas Nitrate* v. *Lagunas Syndicate* [1899] 2 Ch 392. In that case the company was formed and directed by a syndicate. The company was specifically formed to purchase part of the property of the syndicate which consisted of nitrate works. The syndicate and the board of directors were composed of the same people. The court held that the company was not entitled to recission or damages in respect of the contract to purchase the property of the syndicate. Among the reasons given were:

(1) At the date of the contract the company knew, because it appeared in its memorandum and articles, that its directors were also the vendors or agents of the vendor syndicate. The mere fact that the directors did not constitute an independent board was not a sufficient ground for setting aside the contract.
(2) That there had been no misrepresentation made to, or any material fact concealed from, any of the persons who were members of the company at the date of the contract, those persons being the directors themselves.
(3) The defendants as directors had not been guilty of such negligence or breach of trust as would render them liable to the company.

It would seem, then, that disclosure to an independent board *or* to the present and future shareholders via the memorandum and articles will be sufficient disclosure. If this is done and the property was acquired before the buyer became a promoter, or was not acquired on behalf of the company, then the profit may be kept by the promoter.

Two other issues are relevant to this discussion: the loss of the right to recission and the possibility of a remedy in damages.

6.12 The loss of the right to recission

Another reason that was given by the court for the decision in *Lagunas* was that the alteration of the position of the parties as a result of the working of the land had so altered the position of the parties as to make recission impossible. The remedy of recission was not available because the contract could not be reversed. The parties could never be put back into the position that they were in before the contract was made. The loss of the remedy is particularly serious in Situation 1 above (see p. 85). It has been held that where the right to recission is lost, a company has not available the alternative remedy of demanding that the promoter pay his profits to the company, nor is there a right to damages (see *Gover's Case* [1875] 1 Ch D 182; and *Re Cape Breton* (1885) 29 Ch D 795). In the second situation the company has that alternative.

6.13   Actions for damages

The leading case on damages for fraudulent misrepresentation is *Smith New Court Securities Ltd* v. *Citibank NA and Others* [1996] 4 All ER 769 where the House of Lords ruled that where a plaintiff has acquired shares in reliance on a fraudulent misrepresentation, he is entitled to recover the entire loss sustained as a direct consequence of the transaction even where the loss was not foreseeable. The court held that this would include the full price paid less any benefit received as a result of the transaction. As a general rule, the benefit received would include the market value of the property acquired at the date of its acquisition, unless (a) the misrepresentation continued to operate after the date of acquisition so as to induce the plaintiff to retain the asset or (b) the circumstances of the case are such that the plaintiff is, by reason of the fraud, locked into the property. Further, the plaintiff is entitled to receive consequential losses.

6.14   Remuneration of promoters

Promoters do not have a right to remuneration simply because such a right is included in the articles of association (see Chapter 5). Any contract purportedly made with the company before it was formed will equally not be binding on the company (see section 6.15). To receive either remuneration, or even recoup preliminary expenses, the promoter must prove the existence of a binding contract with the company (see *Re National Motor Mail Coach Co.* [1908] 2 Ch 515). Section 97 Companies Act 1985 is of relevance here but only permits a company to pay underwriting commission to a promoter if the articles so permit. To enforce a right to this and any other remuneration the promoter will need to show that the company is contractually bound to pay him.

6.15   Pre-incorporation contracts

Until a company is registered it has no existence of any kind. Sometimes promoters wish to enter into contracts which are intended to be for the benefit of the company and/or the liability under those contracts is intended to be the company's liability. This may be done in order for the public to see, when they are asked to subscribe for shares, that the company is more than just an 'empty shell'. This would be an unusual situation now, when shares are so rarely offered to the public immediately after a company is formed. It may be done simply to 'get things going'. In any event, the promoter must be careful since it is not possible to act for a non-existent person. The position at common law was confused, but s. 51 Companies Act 2006 now provides:

'Pre-incorporation contracts, deeds and obligations

(1) A contract that purports to be made by or on behalf of a company at a time when the company has not been formed has effect, subject to any agreement to the contrary, as one made with the person purporting to act for the company or as agent for it, and he is personally liable on the contract accordingly.

(2) Subsection (1) applies –

  (a) to the making of a deed under the law of England and Wales, and Nortern Ireland,

  (b) to the undertaking of an obligation under the law of Scotland, as it applies to the making of a contract.'

This is unchanged from s. 36C Companies Act 1985 so that cases under that section will still be valid.

The promoter is thus personally liable on any pre-incorporation contract. A wide interpretation of the section was adopted in *Phonogram* v. *Lane* [1981] 3 WLR 736. It was held that the company need not actually be in the process of formation for the section to apply and that there need be no representation that the company is already in existence. Further, it was held that the words in the section 'subject to an agreement to the contrary' would only prevent the operation of the section if there was an express agreement that the person who was signing was not to be liable.

However, in other situations a narrow interpretation of s. 36C has been favoured. In *Oshkosh B'Gosh Inc* v. *Dan Marbel Inc Ltd* [1989] BCLC 507 the Court of Appeal held that the section did not apply when the company was in existence at the time when the relevant contracts were made. The promoters were about to buy the company 'off the shelf'. This was held to be the case even though the company had since changed its name. Further, in *Cotronic (UK) Ltd* v. *Dezonie* [1991] BCLC 721 it was held (also by the Court of Appeal) that s. 36C does not apply when a person purports to make a contract for a company which once existed but has been dissolved.

Since the contract is said to have 'effect' as one entered into by the person purporting to act for the company, it would seem likely that the contract will be enforceable by him as well as against him.

An interesting question was raised in *Braymist Ltd & Others* v. *Wise Finance Company Ltd* [2002] EWCA Civ 127. In this case the solicitor of Braymist signed a contract for the sale of land. The principal point of attention is the fact that Braymist, the vendor, was not in existence at the time the agreement was signed. Later the other party to the contract refused to go on with it and the solicitors of Braymist, who also acted as its agents, sought to enforce the contract against the purchaser by virtue of s. 36C(1). Thus, the question was whether an agent is not only liable on the contract where his principal is a company in course of formation, but entitled to sue on it. The court of appeal decided that the agent, the solicitor in this case, was not only liable for the contract but could also sue for its breach. The enforcement of the pre-incorporation contract could therefore be pursued by the agent as well.

6.16 Liability of the company

It is unfortunate that the reform of this area of the law did not go so far as to permit the company to adopt the contract by passing a resolution to that effect in a general meeting. This 'ratification' procedure has been held not to make the company liable (see *Re Northumberland Avenue Hotel Co.* (1866) 33 Ch D 16). The company will still not be liable even though all persons concerned act as if the company is bound, and large sums of money are spent in the belief that the contract is binding on the company. In certain circumstances a new contract between the original non-promoter party and the company can be deduced from the circumstances, but this will be rare. It is a new contract that is necessary, either expressed or implied. In *Howard v. Patent Ivory Co.* (1888) 38 Ch D 156, the circumstances were such that a new contract could be inferred. In that case, the contract was made before the company was formed. After formation the contract was the subject of a resolution passed by the company at a meeting at which the other party to the contract was present. It is significant that the resolution altered the original terms of the agreement. In these circumstances the court could find that there had been a new contract (a novation) formed between the company and the party to the original contract. It is only in this sort of circumstance that a company could be sued on a contract made before its formation by its promoters. It is impossible for a company simply to adopt or ratify a pre-incorporation contract.

Summary

1. The power of any person to bind a company is governed by agency principles and *bona fide* outsiders will be protected by s. 40 Companies Act 2006.

2. Promoters are persons who undertake to form a company and take the necessary steps to set it going.

3. Promoters stand in a fiduciary relationship to the company.

4. If promoters purchase property on behalf of a company they are not permitted to make a profit on it.

Summary cont'd

5. If promoters make a secret profit they can be forced to disgorge it.

6. Contracts made prior to incorporation do not bind the company but will make those who enter into them personally liable.

7. A pre-incorporation contract will only bind the company if a novation (new contract) occurs.

Exercises

1. Distinguish the various types of authority which may equip a person to make a binding contract on behalf of a company.

2. Explain the situations in which a promoter may become liable to the company for activities prior to incorporation.

3. If an agreement is made by a person prior to incorporation of a company but the promoter making the contract expressly states that he is not to be liable on that contract, who are the contracting parties?

Chapter 7

Public issue of securities

Key words

> **Offer to the public** – only private limited companies may offer shares directly to the public, as defined at the beginning of this chapter.
>
> **Prospectus** – a document containing the information to be made available to those wishing to buy shares (investors).

By s. 755 Companies Act 2006 it is an offence for a private company to offer shares to the public. The result is that only private limited companies (plc) can offer shares to the public. Section 756 explains what is meant by offer to the public:

> '(2) An offer to the public includes an offer to any section of the public, however selected.
>
> (3) An offer is not regarded as an offer to the public if it can properly be regarded in all the circumstances, as –
>
>   (a) not being calculated to result, directly or indirectly, in securities of the company becoming available to persons other than those receiving the offer; or
>
>   (b) otherwise being a private concern of the person receiving it and the person making it.
>
> (4) An offer is to be regarded (unless the contrary is proved) as being a private concern of the person receiving it and the person making it if –
>
>   (a) it is made to a person already connected with the company and, where it is made on terms allowing that person to renounce his rights, the rights may only be renounced in favour of another person connected with the company; or
>
>   (b) it is an offer to subscribe for securities to be held under an employees' share scheme . . .'

Subsection (5) sets out the definition of a 'person already connected with a company', including family members, civil partners, debenture holders and trustees.

The offer must therefore be to persons within a very restricted range, most of whom will be known to each other.

Theoretically it is possible for a company to start life as a public company, but in fact a company is now always registered first as a private company. It will then be converted to a public company when more money than can be supplied by the members needs to be found to fund an expansion of the business. This will require the raising of money by issuing shares.

7.1 Shares

For a discussion of the nature of rights in shares, see Chapter 14. In this chapter we shall be concerned with the way in which shares come into the hands of the shareholders, and the rules governing issuing shares to the public. This chapter also contains an overview of the regulatory framework which now governs the carrying on of 'investment business'.

7.2 Direct offers, offers for sale, issuing houses

A direct offer of shares to the public is now an unusual method of proceeding, although still possible. If it were used, investors would subscribe for shares which would be allotted directly by the company.

A more common method of issuing shares is by an *offer for sale*. Here the whole of the shares are taken by an 'issuing house' which then offers the shares to the public for purchase. This means that the issuing house, and not the company, will take responsibility for the risk that all the shares may not be sold. It will therefore be the issuing house which will need to take out insurance against this risk.

7.3 The two regimes

There are two systems, one for public companies whose shares are listed on the Stock Exchange and the other for public companies which do not have such a listing. The latter companies may have their shares traded on the *Alternative Investment Market* (AIM).

The law relating to public offers of shares and listing is based on European Directives (see Chapter 18). In October 1999 the UK government decided to transfer responsibility for implementing the rules in these Directives from the London Stock Exchange to the new 'super regulator', the Financial Services Authority (FSA, see Chapter 8). The rules are now to be found in Part VI of the Financial Services and Markets Act 2000. On 1 May 2000 the London Stock Exchange ceased to be the United Kingdom's listing authority and was replaced by the FSA. The Stock Exchange's *Yellow Book* has become the *Listing Rules* issued by the FSA, although the content of the rules remained much the same. The public offer of unlisted securities is still regulated by the Public Offers of Securities Regulations 1995.

7.4 Rights offers and public offers

If a company wishes to raise money from existing shareholders it may seek to do so via a *restricted rights offer*. This is an offer of more shares made to existing shareholders and capable of acceptance only by existing shareholders. If the shareholder may pass the offer on to others the issue is described as a *rights issue*. In the case of a rights issue the shares will usually be offered in a renounceable letter of right. If the shareholder to whom it is addressed does not wish to avail himself of the offer, he may renounce his right to do so in favour of another person.

A public offer is an invitation to the public at large to buy the shares. When shares are bought for the first time it is said to be a *subscription*, the shares are *subscribed for* and the buyer is known as a *subscriber*.

7.5   Placing

An alternative way of disposing of the shares and raising the money is to sell (at the time of first sale of a share this is known as an *allotment*) the entire issue to an 'issuing house' who will find buyers other than by an offer to the public at large. They are said to 'place' the shares with their clients, hence this method is known as a 'placing' of shares. This type of placing is now also referred to (in the *Listing Rules*) as 'selective marketing'.

7.6   Pre-emption rights

Sections 560–577 Companies Act 2006 set out a procedure which must be followed if the company already has shareholders who own ordinary (equity) shares. Those shareholders have the right to be offered a proportion of the new securities which correspond to the proportion of 'relevant shares' (ordinary shares) already held by them. The shares must be offered on the same or more favourable terms than the eventual offer to the public. The definition of 'relevant shares' excludes shares which have a right to participate in a distribution only up to a specified amount (non-participating preference shares). (See Chapter 14 for a description of the different types of shares a company may issue.)

The offer may be made in hard or electronic form (s. 562). The shareholders then have at least 21 days (s. 562(5)) in which to accept the offer. This right applies to public and private companies but it may be excluded by the memorandum or articles of a private company (s. 567). Private companies must not contravene the ban on offering shares to the public. Private companies may thus make restricted rights offers only in respect of equity securities (ordinary shares) provided the offer is limited to its own shareholders or its employees.

In both a private and a public company pre-emptive rights may be overridden by a general authority given to directors under s. 551 Companies Act 2006 if confirmed by the articles or a special resolution (s. 570).

7.7 Authority to issue shares

Section 551 Companies Act 2006 requires directors who issue shares to have been authorised to do so either by the company's articles or by a resolution of the company. An authority may be given for a particular occasion or it may be a general power. The authority must state the maximum amount of shares which must be allotted under it. It must also state the date on which it will expire. This is to be not more than five years from the date of the incorporation when an authority was included in the articles. In any other case it is not more than five years from the date on which the authority is given by resolution. Where directors have a *general* authority under s. 551 they may be given power by the articles or by special resolution to allot shares as if the pre-emption rights granted by s. 561 did not exist. Pre-emption rights also do not apply where the shares are to be wholly or partly paid for otherwise than in cash. This provision makes a large hole in the idea of the protection of the existing shareholders since only a small part of the consideration need be otherwise than in cash.

7.8 Directors' duties

Directors must use their powers to issue shares *bona fide* for the benefit of the company (*Percival* v. *Wright* [1902] 2 Ch 421). The court will examine the reason for the issue and if the 'primary purpose' was not to raise capital the issue will be an abuse of the directors' powers (*Howard Smith Ltd* v. *Ampol Petroleum Ltd* [1974] AC 821). Directors may purchase shares from existing shareholders but must not do so on favourable terms (see *Alexander* v. *Automatic Telephone Co.* [1990] 2 Ch 56) unless the terms have been publicised.

7.9 The structure of the rules

The issue of shares in a company applying for Stock Exchange Listing is governed by the Financial Services and Markets Act 2000 (abbreviated to FSMA 2000) and by the FSA rules. The rules which apply to Listing Particulars and the rules in the Public Offers of Securities Regulations (POSR) 1995 which apply to prospectuses are very similar.

In the case of both an application for listing and an issue of a prospectus, there will be a very wide duty of disclosure (ss. 80(1) and 80(2) FSMA 2000; Reg. 9 POSR 1995). In both cases supplementary documents must be issued if there is a change of circumstances (s. 81 FSMA 2000; Reg. 10 POSR) and in both cases the provision for compensation for misleading information is very wide (ss. 82 and 90 FSMA 2000; Reg. 14(1) POSR 1995).

7.10 Admission to Stock Exchange Listing

Where the shares are to be listed on the Stock Exchange the company must comply with the Financial Services Authority which sets out a number of conditions to be fulfilled by an applicant.

Among the conditions are:

(i)   The applicant must be a public company.

(ii) The expected market value of securities for which listing is sought must be at least £700,000 in the case of shares. Securities of a lower value may be admitted provided that the Committee of the Stock Exchange is satisfied that adequate marketability can be expected. These limits do not apply where the issue is of more shares of a class already listed.

(iii) The securities must be freely transferable.

(iv) A company must have published or filed accounts in accordance with its national law for five years preceding its application for listing. The Committee has a discretion to accept a shorter period provided that it is satisfied (a) that it is desirable in the interests of the company or of investors and (b) investors will have the necessary information available to arrive at an informed judgment on the company and the securities for which listing is sought.

(v)   At least 25 per cent of any class of shares must at the time of admission be in the hands of the public (that is, persons who are not associated with the directors or major shareholders).

(vi) The Bank of England controls sterling issues in excess of one million pounds in value. In such cases application must be made to the government broker for a date known as 'impact day' when the size and terms of the issue are to be made known.

(vii) All offer documents (including listing particulars) must be lodged in final form forty-eight hours before the Committee is to hear the application.

(viii) No offer documents may be made public until they have received the approval of the Department of Trade and Industry.

7.11 Contents of listing particulars

The required contents for listing particulars is a long list. Included in the mandatory contents are:

(i)   details of the company and details of any group or company of which it is a part;

(ii) details of the shares which are to be issued;

(iii) considerable financial detail of the company and group including an accountant's report for the last five completed financial years;

(iv) details of the persons forming the management of the company;

(v) a description of the recent developments and prospects of the company and its group.

7.12 Continuing obligations

Companies that wish to obtain a listing on the Stock Exchange must comply with continuing obligations imposed by the Listing Rules. These require a listed company to notify to the Financial Services Authority any information necessary to enable holders of the company's listed securities and the public to assess the performance of the company. The obligation requires a company to make an announcement where, to the knowledge of the company directors, there is a change in the company's financial position, the performance of its business or in the company's expectation of its performance, where knowledge of that change is likely to lead to a substantial movement in the price of the company's listed securities. No guidance is given as to the meaning of 'substantial movement' which will therefore depend on the individual track record of the particular company.

7.13 Remedies for defective listing particulars

The remedies available where listing particulars are defective consist of remedies available under the common law (discussed under remedies for defective prospectuses on p. 99) and statutory remedies contained in ss. 90 and 91 FSMA 2000. The reason for reserving the discussion of the common law remedies until later is that the relevant statutory and common law remedies apply to defective prospectuses as well as to defective listing particulars. In both cases the remedies afforded by the FSMA 2000 are widely drafted so that it would only be in an unusual situation that a litigant would pursue a remedy under the common law rather than rely on the statute.

Section 80 FSMA 2000 contains a general duty of disclosure. It reads:

'(1) Listing particulars submitted to the competent authority under section 79 must contain all such information as investors and their professional advisers would reasonably require, and reasonably expect to find there, for the purpose of making an informed assessment of –

(a) the assets and liabilities, financial position, profits and losses, and prospects of the issuer of the securities; and

(b) the rights attaching to the securities.

(2) That information is required in addition to any information required by –

(a) listing rules, or

(b) the competent authority,

as a condition of the admission of the securities to the official list.'

The information must be within the knowledge of any person responsible for the preparation of the particulars or it must be information which 'it would be reasonable for him to obtain by making enquiries' (s. 80(3)(b)). In determining what information should be included, the type of investment and the type of persons likely to acquire such investments are to be taken into account (s. 80(4)). Presumably the more unsophisticated the potential purchasers of the securities, the more information should be included, although s. 80(4)(c) tends to limit the ambit of information to be made available by requiring that in determining the information to be included in listing particulars regard shall be had 'to the fact that certain matters may reasonably be expected to be within the knowledge of professional advisers of any kind which those persons may reasonably be expected to consult'. Section 81 FSMA 2000 requires any significant changes or new matter which would be relevant to be the subject of supplementary listing particulars.

Given the long list of matters which must be included and the general duty of disclosure, the remedy afforded by s. 90 FSMA 2000 is very wide. Section 90 reads:

'(1) Any person responsible for listing particulars is liable to pay compensation to a person who has –
  (a) acquired securities to which the particulars apply; and
  (b) suffered loss in respect of them as a result of –
    (i) any untrue or misleading statement in the particulars; or
    (ii) the omission from the particulars of any matter required to be included in section 80 or 81.
(2) Subsection (1) is subject to exemptions provided by Schedule 10.
(3) If listing particulars are required to include information about the absence of a particular matter, the omission from the particulars of that information is to be treated as a statement in the listing particulars that there is no such matter.
(4) Any person who fails to comply with section 81 is liable to pay compensation to any person who has –
  (a) acquired securities of the kind in question; and
  (b) suffered loss in respect of them as a result of the failure.
(5) Subsection (4) is subject to exemptions provided by Schedule 10.
(6) This section does not affect any liability which may be incurred apart from this section.
(7) References in this section to the acquisition by a person of securities include reference to his contracting to acquire them or any interest in them.
(8) No person shall, by reason of being a promoter of a company or otherwise, incur any liability for failing to disclose information which he would not be required to disclose in listing particulars in respect of a company's securities –
  (a) if he were responsible for those particulars; or
  (b) if he is responsible for them, which he is entitled to omit by virtue of section 82.

(9) The reference in subsection (8) to a person incurring liability includes a reference to any other person being entitled as against that person to be granted any civil remedy or to rescind or repudiate an agreement.

(10) "Listing particulars", in subsection (1) and Schedule 10, include supplementary listing particulars.'

Schedule 10 contains exemptions from liability if, at the time when the listing particulars were submitted the person responsible for the listing particulars believed, after making reasonable enquiries that the statement was true and not misleading or that the omission was proper and:

'(a) that he continued in that belief until the time when the securities were acquired; or

(b) that they were acquired before it was reasonably practicable to bring a correction to the attention of persons likely to acquire the securities in question; or

(c) before the securities were acquired he had taken all such steps as it was reasonable for him to have taken to secure that a correction was brought to the attention of those persons; or

(d) that he continued in that belief until after the commencement of dealings in the securities following their admission to the Official List and securities were acquired after such a lapse of time that they ought in the circumstances to be reasonably excused.'

It is important to note that it is for the 'person responsible' to satisfy the court of the exemptions – once a breach of the rules is established, that person bears the burden of proof.

Schedule 10 contains other exemptions, for example an exemption relating to statements made on the authority of an expert. A person responsible for particulars will not be liable if they believed on reasonable grounds that the expert was competent and had consented to the inclusion of the statement (Schedule 10, para. 2). Similarly there will be no responsibility for the accurate and fair reproduction of a statement made by an official person or contained in a public official document (Schedule 10, para. 5). The full list of exemptions in Schedule 10 is set out in the Case notes on pp. 103–5, together with the list of persons who are responsible for listing particulars.

Several points must be noted about this remedy:

(i) It applies to omissions as well as positive misstatements.

(ii) The plaintiff need only show that he has acquired the securities and suffered loss as a result of the untrue or misleading statement or omission. After that the burden lies on the persons responsible for listing particulars to exculpate themselves. This reversal of the usual burden of proof could assist a plaintiff considerably.

(iii) The remedy is available to first time purchasers of shares when they are initially issued (subscribers) and to later purchasers.

(iv) The remedy is available as well as the common law remedies discussed below in relation to liabilities for misleading prospectuses. In view of the width of the statutory remedy, however, it would be rarely if ever that the common law remedies would be more beneficial to a plaintiff.

7.14 Prospectus issues

Where the shares are not to be listed on the Stock Exchange, any advertisement of them for sale must be accompanied by a 'prospectus' complying with the requirements of the EC Prospectus Directive as implemented by the POSR 1995 amended by the Public Offers of Securities Amendment Regulations 1999 which implement the EC Prospectus Directive. A prospectus for unlisted shares must contain the information specified in Schedule 1 to the POSR (Reg. 8(1)) or equivalent information where Schedule 1 is inappropriate to the issuer's sphere of activity or legal form. Regulation 9 imposes a general duty of disclosure in the same terms as the duty imposed by Schedule 10 to FSMA. Regulation 93 follows Art. 11(2) of the Prospectus Directive and requires that the information in a prospectus for unlisted shares should be presented 'in as easily analysable and comprehensible form as possible'.

7.15 Remedies for defective prospectuses

Regulations 14 and 15 POSR are very similar to the equivalent provisions in FSMA 2000 regarding listing particulars, and impose the same duties and liabilities in respect of a prospectus for unlisted securities.

7.16 Liabilities for misstatements in prospectuses and listing particulars

As well as the remedies mentioned before in this chapter, the issue of a misleading prospectus could also give rise to actions by oppressed minority shareholders, either by way of ss. 459–461 Companies Act 1985 or a derivative action. Further, the directors may well be in breach of their duties to the company and be liable for such breaches. Criminal penalties under s. 91 FSMA 2000, ss. 1 and 2 Theft Act 1978, or under ss. 15 and 19 Theft Act 1968, might apply.

In the past a problem was caused by *Houldsworth* v. *City of Glasgow Bank* (1880) 5 App Cas 317. In that case, the question discussed was whether a person holding shares in a company is entitled to receive damages from that company. It was held that because of the shareholder's special relationship with the company it was not open to him to remain a member of the company and claim damages from the company for fraudulently inducing him to buy the stock.

Following that case it was clear that where the company is the defendant in an action for fraud no damages could be awarded to a member of the company. Recission was the only remedy available to him. Following the implementation of s. 131 Companies Act 1989, members have an unrestricted right to claim damages from a company. Section 131 of the 1989 Act introduced a new section (s. 111A) into the Companies Act 1985 which provides that a person is not to be debarred from obtaining damages or other compensation from a company simply because he holds or has held shares in the company or has any right to apply or subscribe for shares or to be included in the company's register in respect of shares. The measure of damages for intentional wrongdoing was determined recently by the House of Lords. In *Smith New Court Securities* v. *Scrimgeour Vickers (Asset Management) Ltd and Another* (1996) *The Times*, November 22nd, the House of Lords decided that an intentional wrongdoer in an action for fraudulent misrepresentation would be liable for all loss (including consequential loss) directly flowing from the fraudulent misrepresentation and could not benefit from any issues as to foreseeability. The plaintiff was entitled to be put into the position as if no misrepresentation had been made.

A number of actions claiming damages for negligence and deceit have left the law in some confusion. Thus in *Al-Nakib Investments (Jersey) Ltd* v. *Longcroft* [1990] 1 WLR 1390 a prospectus, which was issued specifically to enable shareholders to consider the rights offer, was held not to give rise to a duty of care between the issuers and people who subsequently purchased shares on the market. No duty would arise unless the person responsible for the prospectus was aware, or ought to have known, that the recipient would rely on it for the specific purpose of entering into a particular transaction. However, in *Possfund Custodian Trustee* v. *Diamond* [1996] 2 BCLC 665 Lightman J in the Chancery Court refused to strike out an action for deceit and negligence by purchasers subsequent to the original subscribers. He held that it was arguable that persons responsible for the issue of a company's share prospectus owed a duty of care to, and could be liable for damages to, subsequent purchasers of shares on the unlisted securities market provided that the purchaser could establish that he had reasonably relied on representations made in the prospectus and reasonably believed that the representor intended him to act on them, and that there existed a sufficient direct connection between the purchaser and the representor to render the imposition of such a duty fair, just and reasonable. He also felt that *Al-Nakib* should be reviewed by a higher court. That has not happened so the extent of the duty owed by issuers to subsequent purchasers remains uncertain.

7.17   The EC Prospectus Directive

This Directive (OJ 32 L124, 5 May 1989), pp. 8–15, was adopted on 17 April 1989 and has been implemented in the UK by the Public Offers of Securities Regulations 1995 (SI 1995 No. 1537), since amended by the Public Offers of Securities Amendment Regulations 1999.

The Public Offers of Securities Regulations 1995

The Public Offers of Securities Regulations 1995 implement the EC Prospectus Directive in the UK. These measures came into force on 19 June 1995. The major features of the regulations are that they:

(i)   alter the listing requirements where a UK public offer is to be made before the admission of the securities to the Official List of the London Stock Exchange;

(ii) create a new prospectus regime for public offers in the UK of securities which will not be listed;

(iii) introduce new provisions for the recognition of UK prospectuses in other Member States of the EEA by introducing an optional regime under which issuers can apply to the London Stock Exchange for the pre-vetting of prospectuses for unlisted and non-listed securities;

(iv) replace the existing provisions under which 'incoming' prospectuses from the EEA countries will qualify for mutual recognition in the UK.

The Regulations apply to offerings of defined classes of securities. Offers of securities outside the scope of the Regulations may still be covered by the general regime on investment advertisements and business in the Financial Services Act 1986.

One of the difficulties with the Directive is the lack of definition of 'offer to the public'. This part of the Directive was implemented by s. 144(2) Financial Services Act 1986 and is now covered by Part V FSMA 2000. Both written and oral offers are included. This is wider than the regime in the Companies Act 1985 which required a document before the regime was triggered. The offer must be one which is either an invitation to make a contractual offer or is capable of being accepted to form a contract for the sale or issue of securities. This will exclude much warm-up advertising. That type of activity will remain subject to the general advertising restrictions in the Financial Services and Markets Act 2000.

Offer to the public

An offer which is made to any section of the public (in the UK), whether selected as members or debenture-holders of a body corporate, or as clients of the person making the offer, or in any other manner, is to be regarded as made to the public (s. 84 and Schedule 11 FSMA 2000).

The rules require a prospectus where the offer is made to the public 'in the United Kingdom' – thus incoming offers may trigger a prospectus requirement. A prospectus is only required where the offer is being made 'for the first time' in the UK (s. 84 FSMA). This is the case even if the first offer was made before these regulations came into force.

There is a long list of exemptions, most notably in favour of securities which are offered to 'persons whose ordinary activities involve them in dealing in investments for the purposes of their business' or 'persons in the context of their trades, professions or occupations', and where the offer is made to no more than 50 persons, to members of a club or association who have a common interest, or the total consideration payable is less than €40,000 (Schedule 11 FSMA).

There are also exceptions for private companies, offers to public authorities, large-denomination offers, and exchange and employee share schemes, as well as the expected exemption for Eurosecurities.

Summary

1. At present there are two regimes. Where the shares of a company are to be listed on the Stock Exchange, an issue must be accompanied by Listing Particulars, and the contents and liabilities for omissions and misstatements are governed by FSMA 2000 and the Listing Rules issued by the FSA.

2. Where the shares are not to be listed, an issue must be accompanied by a prospectus. This is governed by very similar rules contained in the Public Offers of Securities Regulations 1995, which implement the EC Prospectus Directive.

3. The remedy for defective Listing Particulars contained in FSMA and the similar remedy for defective prospectuses in the POSR are wide and comprehensive. It is unlikely that a plaintiff would contemplate using the other remedies that are theoretically available to him unless he can benefit from an enhanced measure of damages following the House of Lords' decision in *Smith New Court Securities* v. *Scrimgeour*, where it held that an intentional wrongdoer in an action for fraudulent misrepresentation would be liable for all damage done by the representation regardless of foreseeability issues.

Case notes

FSMA 2000

SCHEDULE 10

COMPENSATION: EXEMPTIONS

Statements believed to be true

1 (1) In this paragraph 'statement' means –

(a) any untrue or misleading statement in listing particulars; or

(b) the omission from listing particulars of any matter required to be included by section 80 or 81.

(2) A person does not incur any liability under section 90(1) for loss caused by a statement if he satisfies the court that, at the time when the listing particulars were submitted to the competent authority, he reasonably believed (having made such enquiries, if any, as were reasonable) that –

(a) the statement was true and not misleading, or

(b) the matter whose omission caused the loss was properly omitted,

and that one or more of the conditions set out in sub-paragraph (3) are satisfied.

(3) The conditions are that –

(a) he continued in his belief until the time when the securities in question were acquired;

(b) they were acquired before it was reasonably practicable to bring a correction to the attention of persons likely to acquire them;

(c) before the securities were acquired, he had taken all such steps as it was reasonable for him to have taken to secure that a correction was brought to the attention of those persons;

(d) he continued in his belief until after the commencement of dealings in the securities following their admission to the official list and they were acquired after such

a lapse of time that he ought in the circumstances to be reasonably excused.

Statements by experts

2 (1) In this paragraph 'statement' means a statement included in listing particulars which –

(a) purports to be made by, or on the authority of, another person as an expert; and

(b) is stated to be included in the listing particulars with that other person's consent.

(2) A person does not incur any liability under section 90(1) for loss in respect of any securities caused by a statement if he satisfies the court that, at the time when the listing particulars were submitted to the competent authority, he reasonably believed that the other person –

(a) was competent to make or authorise the statement, and

(b) had consented to its inclusion in the form and context in which it was included,

and that one or more of the conditions set out in sub-paragraph (3) are satisfied.

(3) The conditions are that –

(a) he continued in his belief until the time when the securities were acquired;

(b) they were acquired before it was reasonably practicable to bring the fact that the expert was not competent, or had not consented, to the attention of persons likely to acquire the securities in question;

(c) before the securities were acquired he had taken all such steps as it was reasonable for him to have taken to secure that that fact was brought to the attention of those persons;

(d) he continued in his belief until after the commencement of dealings in the securities following their admission to the official list and they were acquired after such a lapse of time that he ought in the circumstances to be reasonably excused.

Corrections of statements

3 (1) In this paragraph 'statement' has the same meaning as in paragraph 1.
(2) A person does not incur liability under section 90(1) for loss caused by a statement if he satisfies the court –

(a) that before the securities in question were acquired, a correction had been published in a manner calculated to bring it to the attention of persons likely to acquire the securities; or

(b) that he took all such steps as it was reasonable for him to take to secure such publication and reasonably believed that it had taken place before the securities were acquired.

(3) Nothing in this paragraph is to be taken as affecting paragraph 1.

Corrections of statements by experts

4 (1) In this paragraph 'statement' has the same meaning as in paragraph 2.
(2) A person does not incur liability under section 90(1) for loss caused by a statement if he satisfies the court –

(a) that before the securities in question were acquired, the fact that the expert was not competent or had not consented had been published in a manner calculated to bring it to the attention of

persons likely to acquire the securities; or

(b) that he took all such steps as it was reasonable for him to take to secure such publication and reasonably believed that it had taken place before the securities were acquired.

(3) Nothing in this paragraph is to be taken as affecting paragraph 2.

Official statements

5 A person does not incur any liability under section 90(1) for loss resulting from –

(a) a statement made by an official person which is included in the listing particulars, or

(b) a statement contained in a public official document which is included in the listing particulars,

if he satisfies the court that the statement is accurately and fairly reproduced.

False or misleading information known about

6 A person does not incur any liability under section 90(1) or (4) if he satisfies the court that the person suffering the loss acquired the securities in question with knowledge –

(a) that the statement was false or misleading,

(b) of the omitted matter, or

(c) of the change or new matter,

as the case may be.

Belief that supplementary listing particulars not called for

7 A person does not incur any liability under section 90(4) if he

satisfies the court that he reasonably believed that the change or new matter in question was not such as to call for supplementary listing particulars.

Meaning of 'expert'

8 'Expert' includes any engineer, valuer, accountant or other person whose profession, qualifications or experience give authority to a statement made by him.

Exercises

1. Consider the range of remedies available to a person who suffers loss as a result of misstatements in Listing Particulars/prospectuses.

2. Find a prospectus in one of the broadsheet newspapers. Does the quantity of information that needs to be disclosed make it unreadable?

Chapter 8

The regulation of investment business

Key words

▶ **Authorised person** – person permitted to carry on investment business in the United Kingdom.
▶ **Regulated business** – business regulated by the Financial Services Authority.

There is now an enormous amount of regulation which affects the way that 'investment business' is carried on. As investment business includes dealing in shares and debentures, the regulatory framework has an effect not only on companies or firms which are involved in investment businesses but also on companies whose shares are being dealt with. The Financial Services Act 1986 provided a framework within which there was originally to be a degree of self-regulation. However, on 20 May 1997 the Chancellor of the Exchequer announced that a new regulator was to be established to regulate the whole financial services industry (including the banks). The new 'super regulator', the Financial Services Authority (FSA), is now fully operational under the Financial Services and Markets Act (FSMA) 2000 which is fully in force. Even before the legal framework was complete, the FSA acted quickly, agreeing with its predecessors to take over their staff and contracting them back until the regulators finally disappeared. In 1998 the Bank of England Act transferred banking supervision from the Bank of England to the FSA. The range of responsibilities of the FSA is enormous, regulating over 20,000 financial services firms and supervising about 3,000 listed companies (see Chapter 7). The FSA has a board, appointed by the Treasury, responsible for three divisions: (a) internal organisation; (b) authorisation and enforcement; and (c) supervision. Supervision is still divided into industry sectors, for example, banks are supervised separately from investment businesses. Although officially the FSA is a single body, there are still different regimes of supervision for different parts of the financial services industry. Sections 2–6 of the FSMA sets out four objectives: to maintain confidence in the financial system; to promote public understanding of that system; to secure 'the appropriate degree of protection for consumers'; and to reduce the extent to which it is possible for a financial services business to be used for a purpose connected with financial crime. The decisions of the FSA will be subject to judicial review following the case law which concerned its predecessor, the Securities and Investment Board, with regard to setting the limits of its powers (see *R* v. *SIB* [1995] 2 BCLC 76; [1996] 2 BCLC 342) but in *Melton Medes* v. *SIB* (1994) *The Times*, July 27th the Chancery Court held that no action for breach of statutory duty would lie against a regulatory body.

Section 19 FSMA contains the 'general prohibitions':

'(1) No person may carry on a regulated activity in the United Kingdom or purport to do so, unless he is –
(a) an authorised person; or
(b) an exempt person.'

Before considering in more detail the way a person becomes an 'authorised' or 'exempted' person it is useful to know what is meant by a regulated activity. These are described in Schedule 2 of FSMA. The definitions follow the same pattern as its predecessor, the Financial Services Act 1986. The approach adopted by that Act is to include an enormous range of activities within the scope of the restriction and then try to exempt from the Act operations which could be seen as 'commercial' rather than 'investment' transactions. Obviously there is a very fine line between the two and considerable difficulty has been experienced in drawing the line. An example of this can be seen in the treatment of 'futures' contracts. Essentially these are contracts to buy a commodity at some time in the future. At one end of the scale these contracts are clearly investment contracts. This is when there is never any intention for one of the parties to the contract to deliver to the other any of the actual commodity involved, while at the same time it is clear that the right to the quantity of the commodity acquired will be sold on to another buyer quickly, perhaps even before the commodity exists or has been extracted from the ground (for example, wheat before it has grown, oil before extraction). At the other end of the scale, the Financial Services Act was never meant to regulate a contract between two parties to buy and sell a quantity of a commodity. There are many shades in between. If a cargo of oil is purchased with the buyer intending to take delivery, but the buyer's circumstances change and he resells that cargo, has this become an investment rather than a commercial contract? The treatment of futures in the statute is important, not because it will be of wide importance in company law, but because it is indicative of the whole approach of the statute which embraces all and then seeks to exclude.

8.1 Financial Services and Markets Act 2000 – 'regulated business'

Something of the immense complexity of the system should be apparent from the foregoing discussion. Under the FSMA the matters of most immediate concern to all companies are Schedule 2, para. 11.

Further elaboration is contained in the Act, for so far only the definition of 'investment' has been examined. What s. 19 prohibits is the carrying on of regulated business. This is defined by Schedule 2, Part 1 FSMA. It is defined in terms of certain activities carried on in relation to 'investments' as already defined. The activities are:

(1) dealing in investments;
(2) arranging deals in investments;
(3) managing investments;
(4) advising on investments;
(5) deposit taking;
(6) establishing collective investment schemes;
(7) using computer-based systems for giving investment instructions.

Of course the boundaries of each of these activities are uncertain, but the exemptions under the Act repeat those of the Financial Services Act, Schedule 1. The following are 'excluded activities':

(i) The act only applied to a person buying shares for himself or otherwise dealing in investments if it was done by way of a regular business. This excluded people buying shares from time to time as personal investments rather than to further a career. The difficulty of distinguishing between these two types of activity shows what fine lines have to be drawn.

(ii) There was an exemption for dealing in investments which takes place among members of a group of companies or joint enterprises.

(iii) There was a general exemption where the true nature of the contract was the supply of goods or services or the sale of goods.

There were also exemptions for employees' share schemes, where shares in private companies are sold, where a trustee was making investments on behalf of a beneficiary, where advice was given in the course of exercising a profession or non-investment business and where advice was given in a newspaper or other publication 'if the principal purpose of the publication, taken as a whole and including any advertisements contained in it, is not to lead persons to invest in any particular investment'.

To explain the way in which it will seek to achieve its statutory objectives, the Financial Services Authority issued a document entitled *A New Regulator for the New Millennium* in January 2000. The authority argues that: 'Market confidence is fundamental to any successful financial system; only if it is maintained will participants and users be willing to trade in financial markets and use the services of financial institutions.' The key is: 'Preserving . . . actual stability in the financial system and the reasonable expectation that it will remain stable.' Two strategies are to be adopted to achieve this stability: 'preventing material damage to the soundness of the UK financial system caused by the conduct of, or collapse of firms, markets or financial infrastructure' but also 'stating explicitly what the regulator can and cannot achieve.' It is important that people should not be too complacent about the regulation of the market, as this leads to the sort of 'moral hazard' referred to by Alistair Alcock in his book explaining *The Financial Services and Markets Act 2000* (see Bibliography at end of book). He argues that: 'standardised regulation and generous compensation schemes can encourage customers to ignore risks and seek the highest return. This in turn encourages reckless behaviour by the suppliers of financial services.' Thus, the FSA takes care to emphasise that: 'Market confidence does not imply zero failure . . . Given the nature of financial markets, which are inherently volatile, achieving a "zero failure" regime is impossible and would in any case be undesirable.' To try to do so would 'damage the economy as a whole . . . [and] stifle innovation and competition'. However, in order to maintain a desirable stability, the FSA will work with the Treasury and the Bank of England on financial stability issues. In pursuit of the aim of raising public awareness of financial issues, the FSA pledges to develop and improve information available to consumers through mechanisms such as their consumer helpline. It also wishes to promote 'financial education as an integral part of the educational system'. The statutory aim in s. 5 of the FSMA is 'protection of consumers'. Here again it is noticeable that the aim of zero risk is clearly not the intention of the legislation, which charges the FSA with the task of 'securing the *appropriate* degree of protection for consumers' (italics added). The FSA has identified four main types of risk:

(1) prudential risk – the risk of the collapse of a firm 'because of incompetent management or a lack of capital';
(2) bad faith risk – fraudulent or negligent conduct on the part of the selling firms;
(3) complexity/unsuitability risk – that consumers end up with an unsuitable or impossible-to-understand product;
(4) performance risk – 'the risk that the investments do not deliver hoped-for returns'.

The FSA does not believe that it is part of its role to protect consumers against performance risk, other than to raise awareness that it is inherent in the market. On the other risks, it makes a distinction between *consumers* and *counterparties*. Counterparties are professionals who can be assumed to be much more aware of the workings of the financial markets. Consumers will therefore need higher levels of protection. Regulatory objective (4), contained in s. 6 FSMA, is the reduction of financial crime. The FSA identifies as its particular targets: money laundering, fraud and dishonesty, in particular 'financial e-crime and fraudulent marketing of investments', and criminal market misconduct including insider dealing. The FSA will also work closely with the police and the Serious Fraud Office on other financial crimes, for example credit card fraud. To push these statutory aims forward, the FSA has put in place a new operating framework. It will:

(a) identify the risks to the statutory objectives;
(b) assess and prioritise the risks.

The first stage is described as an information-gathering exercise whereby the FSA will use information provided by firms as well as whole industry reviews and consultations with consumers and other market participants. The second stage is much more complex and involves the development of a risk assessment process. The risk will be scored taking into account *probability* and *impact* factors (see Figure 8.1). Probability factors take into consideration the likelihood of the risk happening. Impact

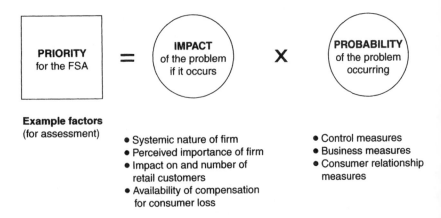

Figure 8.1 Risk assessment and prioritisation: firm-specific approach

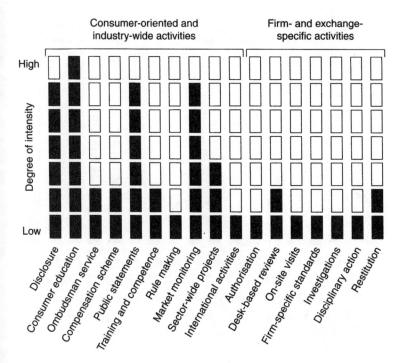

Figure 8.2   Response to risks arising from a new product being
marketed direct to the public

factors assess the 'scale and significance' of the harm done should the risk
occur. There is a more detailed explanation of the scheme in the Case notes
(pp. 117–18).

The FSA proposes a spectrum of supervision from maintaining a
continuous relationship with firms that have a high-impact risk rating to
'remote monitoring' of low-impact firms. Firms in the latter category 'would
not have a regular relationship with the FSA, but would be expected to
submit periodic returns for automated analysis, and to inform the FSA of
any major strategic developments'.

Having assessed the risks, the FSA proposes to deploy its 'regulatory
toolkit' to counter the risks. Figures 8.2 and 8.3 set out the contents of the
regulatory toolkit. Most of these tools are self-explanatory. However, one
needs further elucidation. Authorisation is one of the key firm-specific tools.
As we have seen, any firm wishing to carry on a regulated activity must be
authorised by the FSA.

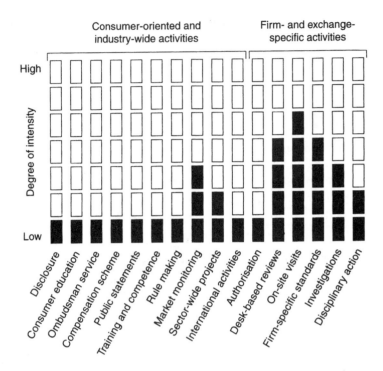

Figure 8.3 Choice of regulatory response: firm-specific approach

8.2 How the range of regulatory tools is used in practice

Figures 8.2 and 8.3 illustrate how the FSA might use this range of tools in response to particular situations. Figure 8.2 shows the ways in which the FSA might expect to act where risks have arisen as a result of a new product being marketed direct to the public. This approach might be appropriate, for example, in the early stages of the introduction of stakeholder pensions. The figure illustrates how in this case the emphasis is on consumer-oriented and industry-wide activities (such as consumer education, disclosure and market monitoring) rather than on firm-specific activities.

Figure 8.3 shows how the FSA might use a different range of tools in response to a particular problem within a specific firm or group. It takes as an example a major bank with a significant capital markets operation, which includes trading for its own account in derivative products. As a result of identified control and management weaknesses, the bank is vulnerable to major trading losses through errors, mismarking etc. The example shows how the FSA's response in such situations is likely to focus on the tools which are directed at individual firms, rather than those which are directed at consumers, at all banks, or at all firms engaged in proprietary trading.

The tools listed at the bottom of Figures 8.2 and 8.3 are illustrative only and do not represent the full range available to the FSA. For example, in the situation described in Figure 8.3, the FSA might well wish to commission work from the firm's external auditors, in addition to using the tools illustrated. Moreover, in both examples some of the tools are described in fairly high-level terms, whereas in practice careful consideration would need to be given, for example, to whether disciplinary action might be appropriate or precisely which issues are to be addressed in the course of a visit to a firm.

8.3   Financial Services Authority: authorisation provisions

Authorisation is to carry out specific activities. It can be obtained:

(i)   by permission directly from the FSA to carry out one or more regulated activities in the UK (s. 31 FSMA);
(ii) by obtaining authorisation from the European Economic Area state in which it has its headquarters (s. 31 FSMA);
(iii) by using its authorisation under the previous regime (ss. 426 and 427 FSMA).

An authorised person carrying on a regulated activity outside the terms of the permission does not make that person guilty of an offence or the transaction void or unenforceable (s. 20) but does make that person subject to a wide range of disciplinary procedures available to the FSA (ss. 20 and 66). A person breaching the general prohibition, that is, an unauthorised person carrying on regulated activity, is guilty of a criminal offence (s. 23). Similarly a false claim to be authorised or exempt is a criminal offence (s. 24). The FSA has the power to withdraw authorisation (s. 33). Clearly this is a very drastic remedy and both this action and the use of disciplinary powers will be subject to the provisions of the Human Rights Act 1998 (see below). Challenges to these procedures can be expected. Section 41 and Schedule 6 set out the 'threshold conditions' for authorisation: the applicant must have an appropriate legal status, carry on business in the UK, not have 'close links' with an entity which would prevent effective supervision by the FSA (for example, be a subsidiary of a parent outside the EEA), have adequate resources and 'be a fit and proper person'. In *High Standards for Firms and Individuals* (FSA, June 2000), the authority indicated that three factors will be important in assessing fitness and propriety:

(1) honesty, integrity and reputation;
(2) competence and capability;
(3) financial soundness.

The applicant must show that those in senior positions within the firm fulfil those criteria and will abide by the Statements of Principle for Approved Persons and the Associated Code of Practice. The Principles require that:

(1) individuals must act with integrity;
(2) individuals must act with due skill, care and diligence;
(3) individuals must deal with FSA and other regulators in an open and co-operative way and disclose all information which regulators might reasonably expect.

In addition to this, those in a senior position in a firm must take reasonable steps to ensure that proper systems of control are in place in the firms for which they are responsible. 'Senior managers' are those 'performing significant influence functions' within the firm.

8.4 Complaints

The Financial Services and Markets Tribunal

The tribunal, set up by s. 132 FSMA, is an important part of the new regulatory scheme. Many decisions of the FSA will come under its scrutiny, including decisions to authorise (or not), to vary or withdraw authorisation, disciplinary measures and the imposition of financial penalties for market abuse. An appeal from a final decision of the Tribunal may be made, with leave, to the Court of Appeal and ultimately the House of Lords, but only on a point of law (s. 137 FSMA).

The Financial Ombudsman

The rather complex provisions that have emerged from the consultations carried out by the FSA on this topic have created voluntary and compulsory schemes for access to the Ombudsman. The compulsory scheme is confined to authorised firms whereas the voluntary scheme may be joined by regulated or unregulated firms. Under the compulsory scheme, the Ombudsman must determine the case as he thinks 'fair and reasonable in all the circumstances' and is not confined to finding breaches of rules or Codes of Conduct. He must provide a written statement of his decision. If the complainant accepts it, the determination becomes final and binding. If not, he may take the matter to court. The respondent firm has no right of appeal even on a matter of law (s. 228 FSMA). It is likely that this arrangement will need to be altered in order to provide a firm with some redress other than resort to judicial review in order to comply with the provisions of the Human Rights Act 1998 which require a fair hearing (see below). The Ombudsman scheme is separate from the compensation scheme which is required in the event of the insolvency of a firm. This scheme is run by the *Financial Services Compensation Scheme* (FSCS). The FSA must make rules enabling the FSCS to assess and pay compensation for claims in respect of regulated activities of defaulting authorised firms and raise levies on authorised persons to create the fund to make this possible.

The Market Code

The legislators accepted that law is insufficient for defining conduct which is undesirable in the marketplace. It is inflexible and cannot change easily as new financial instruments are invented, with the opportunities for fraud which they represent. Section 119 FSMA therefore requires the FSA to issue a Code of Market Conduct which will be continuously reviewed. The exact contents of the Code are still being formulated and its status remains unclear. It is likely that it will create a presumption that behaviour condemned in it is a 'market abuse' and the firm involved in such behaviour will be subject to disciplinary action. At present, discussions centre around the definitions of three concepts: the misuse of information; giving a false or misleading impression; and 'distortion' of the market. All these are complex concepts and the eventual Code is likely to be a controversial document.

The Human Rights Act 1998

The UK government implemented the European Convention on Human Rights into the law of the UK by the Human Rights Act 1998. The UK courts are now bound to construe legislation so far as possible in compliance with the Convention and will make a public declaration of non-compliance where the legislation contravenes the Convention. The European Court of Human Rights (ECHR), in interpreting the Convention, has insisted that the protection of the Convention will be extended to those undertaking private commercial activities (*Pudas* v. *Sweden* (1988) 10 ECHR 380). Most importantly, this includes the right to a fair and public hearing within a reasonable time by an independent tribunal established by law (Art. 6(1) of the Convention, applying to civil and criminal proceedings). More extensive rights apply to criminal proceedings and the ECHR does not accept that states can escape from those obligations by merely defining punitive procedures as civil proceedings (*Engel* v. *Netherlands* (1976) 1 ECHR 647). The disciplinary regimes of the FSA are likely to be challenged under this jurisprudence, particularly the regime of the imposition of fines for market abuse (see the discussion of the Code of Conduct, above) and the Ombudsman provisions.

8.5 The Investment Services Directive

The Investment Services Directive was implemented in the UK by the Investment Services Regulations 1995, the Financial Services Act 1986 (Investment Services) (Extension of Scope) Order 1995 and the Financial Services Act 1986 (EEA Regulated Market) (Exemption) Order 1995, which came into effect on 1 January 1996. It is now reflected in the provisions of the Financial Services and Markets Act 2000. The adoption of the Directive made it easier for UK firms to offer investment services abroad and eases the entry into the UK market of firms from other EU Member States.

Introduction

The Investment Services Directive was adopted in July 1993. The idea was that 'investment firms' should gain authorisation from their 'home' state. This authorisation would then act as a 'passport' to enable them to carry on that investment business in other Member States (Arts. 1 and 4). The service in question could be provided on a cross-border basis within the Community or the investment firm in question will be permitted to set up branches in the other Member States without needing to be authorised again. This regime has been strengthened and extended by Directive 2001/34/EC and the new prospectus Directive (see Chapter 7).

The Directive provides for the monitoring of the financial soundness of the investment firm and its compliance with major conduct of business rules.

Summary

1. No investment business may be carried on in the UK unless the person conducting the business is an exempt or authorised person under the Financial Services and Markets Act 2000.

2. The Financial Services Authority is the sole regulator, regulating all investment business and the conduct of banks. It is also responsible for the Listing Rules (see Chapter 7).

3. The EC Investment Services Directive seeks to provide firms with a 'passport' permitting them to operate throughout the Community.

Case notes

Assessing firm-specific risks: impact and probability factors

IMPACT FACTORS

For firm-specific risks, the first step is to assess the impact were a particular event to occur.

Impact relates to the damage that a regulatory problem within a firm (collapse or lapse of conduct) would cause to the FSA's objectives. While a firm may have a high probability of a regulatory problem, if it is low impact (for example, a small firm conducting little retail business) the overall risk posed to the objectives is likely to be low.

The impact of an event will be assessed by reference to the following criteria:

- Systemic significance of the firm (that is, the impact which the collapse of the firm would have on the industry as a whole);
- Perceived importance of the firm (impact of the firm's collapse on public perception of the market and thereby on market confidence);
- Retail customer base (number and nature of customers, nature of customers' exposure to firm);
- Availability of compensation or redress for consumer loss.

In assessing impact, we will also take into account the cumulative effect of problems in a number of similar firms, even though, considered individually, the firms concerned might be graded low-impact.

PROBABILITY FACTORS

For firm-specific risks, the probability of a problem occurring is assessed under three headings:

1 *Business risk*
The risk arising from the underlying nature of the industry, the external context and the firm's business decisions and strategy. High business risk on its own may not pose a threat to the stability of a firm, if the controls are sound. However, the firm could collapse if its capital or controls are inadequate for the business risks it faces. Business risk relates to:

- Capital adequacy (ability to absorb volatility/loss);
- Volatility of balance sheet (risk of portfolio of assets and liabilities, exposure to external risks);
- Volatility and growth of earnings (historical trends and patterns, mix of business, sources of income);
- Strategy (change in business, sustainability of earnings).

2 *Control risk*
The risk that a firm cannot or will not assess, understand, and respond appropriately to the risks it faces. High control risk means that the firm's controls are not adequate in the light of its business risk. Control risk subdivides into consideration of:

- Internal systems and controls (information flow, decision-making processes, risk management, etc.);
- Board, management and staff (skill, competence, fitness and propriety, etc.);
- Controls culture (adherence to internal controls, compliance record, etc.).

3 *Consumer relationship risk*
The risk that the firm will cause damage to consumers by failing to provide suitable products and services. In this respect firms operating exclusively in wholesale

markets will typically be lower risk. A medium/high impact firm with a medium/high risk grading could constitute a threat to the consumer protection objective. A substantial problem of this nature could also affect market confidence. This risk is assessed by reference to:

- Nature of customers and products (focusing on any mismatch between customer sophistication and product sold);
- Marketing, selling and advice practices (focusing on sales force incentives, compliance culture, record-keeping).

Exercises

1. Under its risk assessment scheme, how would the FSA regulate a small investment bank operating in the City of London but with high-risk business outside the European Economic Area?

2. Why is it important to devote so much energy to regulating Financial Services?

Chapter 9

Maintenance of capital

Key word

> ▶ **Dividends** – payments out of company profits made to shareholders at the discretion of directors.

The principal concern of the law in this area is that the company should get full value for the shares it issues and that having received the money, that money should be kept within the company. Because the members of a company are in control of it, they could make the company transfer all its assets to them. In particular, therefore, money should not be returned to the members of the company, leaving the creditors with an empty shell to rely on when their bills are due to be paid. In this area the original common law rules have, to a considerable extent, been overtaken by statutory rules, many of them introduced by the Companies Acts 1980 and 1981 as a direct result of the European Community's company law harmonisation programme. These rules are now part of the Companies Act 2006.

9.1 Fundamental rule

The basic common law rule was that it was illegal for a company to acquire its own shares. The reasoning was that the capital of a company could be discovered by adding up the amounts paid for the shares it had issued. If those shares had been purchased by the company itself, no money in respect of those shares had flowed into the company's coffers. Thus, a creditor would be relying on illusory prosperity if he relied on the value of shares issued when giving credit to the company. The rule was established in the case of *Trevor* v. *Whitworth* (1887) 12 App Cas 409 and is therefore often referred to as the rule in *Trevor* v. *Whitworth*. In that case Lord Watson said:

> 'It is inconsistent with the essential nature of a company that it should become a member of itself. It cannot be registered as a shareholder to the effect of becoming a debtor to itself for calls ....'

This passage emphasises the difficulties that would arise if a company were able to buy its own shares. If they were not fully paid for, the company itself would be liable to pay itself money when the 'call' to pay the outstanding amount was made.

However, this 'blanket' prohibition was felt to be too restrictive. Resultant attempts to modify the rules and to define when it is permissible to pay money out to the shareholders have led to a very complex system of rules. We will deal first with the basis on which payment of money to members is permitted, since understanding this will help to make sense of the rules governing prohibited payments.

9.2 Payment of money to members

One of the difficulties of understanding these rules is that the law tends to treat the capital of a company as a fixed amount kept in a piggy bank. The reality is quite different – the money contributed by the shareholders is used in the business and used to buy a continually changing set of assets. These will go up or down in value. It is unlikely that their value will remain static. Consequently the rules designed to draw a sharp distinction between the capital of a company and profits available for distribution to members are based on a false view of the way companies work. The distinction is particularly false where the company is a small private company and the members are all directors or employees. Payments to such people are not governed by the rules on 'distributions' to members and count as ordinary trading debts. If not otherwise controlled it would be open to the members of such companies to pay the assets of the company to themselves by way of remuneration. If the company has resolved to pay such salaries the court will not usually enquire as to whether such a payment was reasonable, that is, the size of the payment will not normally invalidate it in civil proceedings (see *Re Halt Garage (1964) Ltd* [1982] 3 All ER 1016). However, it has been held that unreasonable payments of this nature can amount to theft of the company's property even when the alleged thieves are the sole owners and directors of the company (see the House of Lords' decision in *R* v. *Gomez* [1992] 3 WLR 1067).

Other controls on such practices are contained in the Insolvency Act 1986. Section 238 of that Act gives a liquidator of a company a power to apply to the court for an order cancelling the effect of a gift of the company's property made in the two years preceding commencement of the winding-up, if the company was insolvent (see Chapter 17 for the definition of 'insolvent') at the time of the gift or if the gift made the company insolvent. The provision also applies to a transaction with a person in which the consideration given by the person was significantly less valuable than the consideration provided by the company.

As well as this, large payments to member-directors while the company is struggling have been considered as one reason, with others, for issuing a disqualification order against a director, preventing him from acting as a director. This power is given to the court by the Company Directors Disqualification Act 1986 (see Chapter 12).

9.3 Distributions

By far the majority of companies exist to make profits for their shareholders. There must therefore be a system by which those profits can be distributed to the shareholders. As explained above, the law seeks to permit distribution of profits alone, leaving intact a quantity of assets, known as 'capital', which is to be kept in the company as a source to which creditors can look for payment of their bills and, at the end of the company's life, as the fund out of which the shareholders will be repaid the amount they put into the company when they bought their shares. Thus, although the power to distribute money to the shareholders is implied, there need not be a specific clause in the articles permitting a distribution. The rule is that the distributions of a company should not exceed its realised profits. Capital, which includes amounts held in the share premium and capital redemption reserve, must remain intact.

9.4 Rules governing distributions

By s. 829 Companies Act 2006 the statutory rules governing distributions apply to 'every description of distribution of a company's assets to its members, whether in cash or otherwise', with the following exceptions (s. 829(2):

(a) an issue of shares as fully or partly paid bonus shares;
(b) the reduction of share capital –
   (i) by extinguishing or reducing the liability of any of the members on any of the company's shares in respect of share capital not paid up, or
   (ii) by repaying paid-up share capital;
(c) the redemption or purchase of any of the company's own shares out of capital . . . or out of unrealized profits [in accordance with the Act, see below];
(d) a distribution of assets to member of the company on its winding-up.

The exceptions will be examined in more detail later. The next step is to examine the rules surrounding the most common method of distribution of profits to the members of a company, which is by paying a dividend to members.

9.5   Dividends

Profits available for the purpose

The company's profits available for this purpose are set out in s. 830(2):

> 'its accumulated, realised profits, so far as not previously utilised by distribution or capitalisation, less its accumulated, realised losses, so far as not previously written off in a reduction or reorganisation of capital duly made.'

Realised and unrealised profits

The notion of restricting the amount available for distributions to realised profits was introduced into UK law by the Companies Act 1980 in accordance with the provisions of the EC Fourth Directive. It means that companies must examine their accounts and separate out any amounts that appear which are due to the revaluation of assets. Before this provision came to be in the law it was considered permissible to pay a dividend where assets had increased in value even when that asset had not been sold so that the value had not been 'realised'. Realisation means turning an asset into cash. The realised profits of a company for a financial year is the profit on its sales of assets – that is, the amount by which income from the sale of its assets exceeds associated expenses. An unrealised profit will occur when assets have risen in value: when, for example, the buildings owned by the company have increased in value, but those buildings have not been sold. Similarly a realised loss occurs when expenses associated with sales for a particular year exceed revenue derived from those sales, while an unrealised loss will occur where assets fall in value but they have not yet been sold at a loss. As a general rule expenses must be recorded in accounts when they are incurred, not when they are actually paid for. Similarly, income from sales of goods or supply of services must generally be recorded at the time of sale or supply rather than when the money is actually received, provided that there is an amount fixed at that time and provided also that there is a reasonable possibility of eventual collection of the debt. It is interesting to note that one of the ways in which the Enron company inflated its 'profits' was to record as income money which it would only receive over a long period (sometimes as much as 20 years). This, of course, did not give a 'true and fair view' of the company's assets (see below). At the end of the year some money appearing in the income side of the accounts will not have been received by the company. These bad debts must be reflected in the accounts. This is done by calculating the percentage of the total trade debts which the company's past experience shows will not be paid. In a new concern, the pattern of business in the industry would provide first estimates.

Realised and unrealised losses

If a company is about to incur a future liability which cannot be precisely quantified it can set aside a fund called a 'provision'. The definition of what is to be a provision will be set out in Regulations yet to be made under the new Act. They will certainly require an amount estimated to be sufficient to cover the future liability. This liability has not yet been incurred so that it is not a 'realised' loss. However, the Regulations will require such a fund to be treated as a realised loss, thus preventing the company from counting the assets in the fund from being available for a distribution to the members.

9.6 Public companies

As well as the restrictions discussed above, public companies are subject to the further restrictions contained in s. 831 Companies Act 2006. By that section a distribution may not exceed the amount arrived at by the application of the formula: 'net assets less (the called up share capital plus the undistributable reserves)'. The undistributable reserves are:

(a) the share premium account – this contains any amount paid for a share over and above its par or face value;
(b) the capital redemption reserve – this contains an amount equivalent to the value of shares legally redeemed (see below);
(c) accumulated unrealised profits less accumulated unrealised losses; and
(d) any other reserve which the company is forbidden to distribute under its memorandum and articles or any rule of law.

One of the important differences between public and private companies is contained in this formula, in that a public company must write off its unrealised losses against realised and unrealised profits before it can make a distribution out of the balance of its realised profits. A private company need not do this.

9.7 Members' liability

Section 847 Companies Act 2006 makes a member liable to repay a distribution he has received if, at the time of the distribution, he knew or had reasonable grounds for knowing, that it was being paid in contravention of the Act.

9.8 Other permitted payments to members

We saw earlier that the rules concerning distributions do not apply to certain other payments to members. These are (s. 829 Companies Act 2006):

(a) return of capital or distribution of surplus assets on winding-up;
(b) return of capital to members in a properly authorised reduction of capital (including the cancellation or reduction of liability on partly paid shares);
(c) issue of fully or partly paid bonus shares;
(d) purchase or redemption of the company's own shares.

The return of capital and assets on a winding-up are covered by rules explained in Chapter 17. The rules relating to the other types of payment out are discussed below.

9.9　Reductions of capital

The provisions regarding the reduction of capital are set out in ss. 641–657 Companies Act 2006. The reduction of a company's capital was traditionally regarded as a matter to be strictly controlled since it reduced the fund available for creditors.

Reduction by special resolution and confirmation by the court

Section 641 sets out the framework for reduction of capital:

(1) A limited company having a share capital may reduce its share capital –
    (a) in the case of a private company limited by shares, by special resolution supported by a solvency statement;
    (b) in any case by special resolution confirmed by the court.
(2) A company may not reduce its capital under subsection 1(a) if as a result of the reduction there would no longer be any member of the company holding shares other than redeemable shares.
(3) Subject to that, a company may reduce its share capital under this section in any way.

Section 641(4) sets out particular situations where the power may be used. They are: to reduce members' liability to pay uncalled capital or to reflect a diminution of the company's assets. In a private company, a reduction of capital and the return of capital to a member or members may be necessary when a company changes hands on the death or retirement of a person who was chiefly concerned in the running of the business. Until 1981 this could only be done by special resolution and confirmation by the court. Now private companies in particular have other choices (see below). In *Carruth v. Imperial Chemical Industries Ltd* [1937] AC 707 it was held that it was proper to reduce the nominal value of one class of the company's shares so as to reflect the low price at which they were traded on the Stock Exchange.

Confirmation by the court

This regime is available to both public and private companies, although private companies will try to steer clear of it because of the expense. The court has refused to determine whether a reduction of capital is commercially sensible. However, the court will attempt to ensure that the reduction is not unfair. In *British and American Trustee & Finance Corporation Ltd* v. *Couper* [1894] AC 229, Lord Herschell LC said:

> 'There can be no doubt that any scheme which does not provide for uniform treatment of shareholders whose rights are similar, would be most narrowly scrutinised by the Court, and that no such scheme ought to be confirmed unless the Court be satisfied that it will not work unjustly or inequitably.'

In that case, the court had already ascertained that no interests of creditors would be affected by the reduction. It is clear, then, that two important considerations which will influence the court when deciding whether to sanction a reduction are:

(i) whether and to what extent the interests of creditors will be affected; and

(ii) whether the reduction deals with different classes of shareholders fairly and equitably.

A third consideration referred to by the House of Lords' judges in Ex Parte *Westburn Sugar Refiners Ltd* [1951] AC 625 was 'the public interest'. This was not very clearly defined but the concern seems to have been to ensure that sufficient capital was retained in the company to safeguard the interests of those 'who may in future form connections with the company as creditors or shareholders'. Political considerations such as whether the reduction was in response to and likely to defeat the purpose behind nationalisation of an industry were held to be irrelevant. It seems, then, that in this case a vague third requirement applied:

(iii) that the reduction should not be contrary to the public interest.

The validity of this consideration was doubted by Harman J, in *Re Jupiter House Investments (Cambridge) Ltd* [1985] BCLC 222, who considered it of more importance that:

> '(iv) the causes of the reduction should have been properly put to shareholders so that they were able to exercise an informed choice and that the reason for the reduction is supported by evidence before the court.'

Despite these requirements it has been held that it is permissible to carry out a reduction of capital by extinguishing entirely a class of members. This was done in *British and American Trustee & Finance Corporation Ltd* v. *Couper* [1894] AC 229 and in *Re Saltdean Estate Co. Ltd* [1968] 1 WLR 1844. In *Re Saltdean Estate Co. Ltd* the company's preference shareholders were eliminated by returning the capital paid by them plus a premium of 50 per cent. It was further held in that case that the expulsion of the preference shareholders did not amount to a variation of their rights. In these circumstances 'variation' of rights is a very technical concept (explained in Chapter 14). Where a reduction of capital *does* involve a variation of the rights of one or more classes of shareholders, the special procedures explained in Chapter 14 must be followed as well as the approval by the court of the reduction of capital.

9.10 Interests of creditors

The Companies Act 2006 provides a special procedure where the interests of creditors are likely to be adversely affected by a reduction of capital. If the reduction involves either a diminution of a member's liability to pay future calls on shares or repayment of capital to members, the special procedure comes into operation, subject to a discretion which the court has to dispense with it (ss. 645 and 646). By s. 645(4) the court may direct that this special procedure should be adopted in the case of any other type of reduction, but it was held in *Re Meux's Brewery Co. Ltd* [1919] 1 Ch 28 that where a company is not parting with a means of paying its creditors, the creditors must show a very strong reason why they should be heard in objection to the company's petition seeking approval for the reduction.

The special procedure involves drawing up a list of the creditors of the company. Section 647 makes it an offence to conceal the company's creditors or misrepresent their claims. The creditors that must be included are those who could prove for their claims if the company went into liquidation as at a date fixed by the court. The court may make an order confirming the reduction only when it is satisfied that every creditor on the list has either been paid in full or has positively consented to the reduction (s. 648(2)). The court may dispense with the consent of a creditor if it is satisfied that the company has made provision for paying him. In the case of a disputed claim the court must be satisfied that adequate provision has been made (s. 646(5)). Any creditor on the list is entitled to be heard by the court in opposition to the proposed reduction.

9.11 Procedure

If the court sanctions the reduction, the order approving the reduction must be registered with the Registrar. The reduction does not take effect until the registration has been carried out. The Registrar then certifies the registration and his certificate is conclusive evidence that all the requirements of the Act have been complied with (s. 649).

9.12 Bonus shares

These are shares which are issued with the value paid out of the profits of the company. Because they are wholly paid for by the company (s. 582 Companies Act 2006) rather than the member, and yet they confer a right on the member to participate in a shareout of capital in the event of the liquidation of the company, they represent a transfer of capital from the company to the member. This transfer would be prohibited by the rule against return of capital to members were it not permitted by the Companies Act 2006. Bonus shares are allotted to existing members of a company. Under the 1985 regime, unless the articles of association of the particular company exclude the relevant provisions of Table A, Article 110 of Table A will govern a bonus share issue. This article provides that the number of bonus shares to be allotted to a particular member is to be determined in the same way as his entitlement to dividend, that is, the number of bonus shares received by each member should be in proportion to the number of shares he holds, for example one bonus share for every ten shares held. A decision to issue bonus shares paid for by capital (a capitalisation issue) is to be taken by the directors on the authority of an ordinary resolution of its members. Regulations under the 2006 Act are awaited.

9.13 Redeemable shares

The final permitted methods of the transfer of capital from the company to its members are by way of redeemable shares and the forfeiture of shares.

By s. 684 Companies Act 2006 a company may issue shares which are redeemable. For a public company this is permitted only if authorisation for such a class of shares is contained in the articles. By s. 685 the directors may determine the terms of redemption if so authorised by the articles or by a resolution of the company. Where they are not authorised, the terms of redemption must be stated in the company's articles. A private company may pay for redeemable shares out of capital. Public companies may only use distributable profits or the proceeds of a share issue made for the purposes of the redemption. When the temporary membership of the company conferred as a result of issue of these shares comes to an end, the shares are cancelled and the nominal value of the shares is repaid to the member. Sometimes a redemption bonus will be paid as well as the nominal value of the shares.

Implications for the capital of the company

Normally the company is obliged to maintain a fund which must not be diminished by the repayment of redeemable shares. In the case of a public company the repayment to a member on the redemption of a redeemable share will not represent a reduction of this core capital fund, as it can only redeem redeemable shares out of profits or the proceeds of a further issue of shares. However, a private company can, by adopting the procedure set out in the Act, redeem shares out of existing capital. The members of a private company may adopt a special resolution to enable its shares to be redeemed without the capital accounts being increased in exact proportion to the payments out. This could be of great value to a private company, particularly where the head of a small company was hoping to take his capital out of the company and retire. However, the legislature has hedged about the ability to reduce capital in this way with so many restrictions that the procedure is not as valuable as it otherwise could be.

Only a fully paid up share may be redeemed (s. 686(1) Companies Act 2006). When a redeemable share is redeemed it must be cancelled. The nominal value of the share is deducted from the share capital account. In a public company this reduction would be compensated by the transfer from the profit and loss account of an amount equivalent to the amount written off the share capital account. An alternative would be to issue new shares. However, the members of a *private* company may use the redemption of shares to reduce capital by adopting a resolution not to make up the amount in this way. There is a limit set to the extent to which a reduction in this way may be made. The amount set is called the 'permissible capital payment' (s. 710 Companies Act 2006). This is calculated so that a company must transfer the proceeds of new issues of shares and all distributable profits to the capital account which is to be reduced. The payment out of capital must be approved by special resolution of the company (s. 716). The persons holding the shares proposed for redemption may not vote in favour of the resolution to redeem the shares (s. 717). There are complex rules relating to the calculation of available profits (s. 712) and the directors' statement (s. 714).

Not more than a week before a resolution to make a payment out of capital is adopted by a company, the directors must make a statutory declaration of the size of the permissible capital payment (s. 714 Companies Act 2006). The directors' declaration must state:

(a) that the company will be able to pay its other debts immediately after the redemption is made; and

(b) the company will continue in business for the whole of the year following the redemption and for the whole of that year will be able to pay its debts.

A director who makes such a declaration without reasonable grounds for the opinion expressed in the declaration will be liable to a criminal penalty (s. 715). If the company goes into insolvent liquidation within a year of making a redemption out of capital, the member whose shares were redeemed and the directors who made the declaration are liable to repay the amount paid out of capital in so far as this is necessary to pay the company's debts. There are extensive provisions requiring an auditor's report and requiring publicity of the redemption. Indeed these are so extensive that it prompted Dr Sealy to call for the replacement of the twenty sections involved in the 1985 Act with the single section used to achieve the same result in Canada (see Sealy, *Company Law and Commercial Reality* (Sweet & Maxwell, 1986)). Sadly, the opportunity to streamline the system in the 2006 Act has not been taken.

9.14 Purchase of own shares

Having seen at the outset of this chapter that there was a general rule which prohibits the purchase by a company of its own shares we now have to look at the exceptions which statutes have made to this rule. These exceptions are now so wide that it could be said that there is a general rule that a company *may* purchase its own shares; it is in the exceptional case that this manoeuvre is forbidden. However, although there are many situations in which it is permissible to purchase its own shares, the correct procedure must be followed otherwise the purchase will be illegal. The strictness of the rules, and the prohibition of using this method to reduce the capital of a *public* company, support the traditional view that the general prohibition still stands; it is only in exceptional cases that such a purchase is permitted.

The general prohibition is now contained in s. 658 Companies Act 2006 backed by criminal penalties both for the company and any individual involved. This is immediately followed by a list of exceptions in s. 659:

(1) A limited company may acquire any of its own fully paid shares otherwise than for valuable consideration.
(2) Section 658 does not prohibit
    (a) the acquisition of shares in a reduction of capital duly made;
    (b) the purchase of shares in pursuance of a court order;
    (c) the forfeiture of shares . . .

Essentially the scheme is that the rules on reduction of capital must be followed as the purchase of shares is just one way this can be achieved. However, things get really complex when we come to the issue of financial assistance for the purchase of shares.

9.15 Illegal transactions

The procedures discussed in this chapter so far are the legal methods by which a company can come to own its own shares. We now have to consider transactions which fall on the other side of the line and are prohibited.

Financial assistance for the purchase of shares

Section 678 Companies Act 2006 prohibits a public company or its subsidiary from giving financial assistance, either directly or indirectly, for the purpose of the acquisition of its shares. The significant change brought in by the 2006 Act is that s. 678 applies to public companies only. Section 679 extends the prohibition to assistance by a public company for the acquisition of shares in its private holding company but private companies escape the provisions.

Financial assistance is defined by s. 677 and includes the widest imaginable range of transactions.

One problem that the courts have encountered concerns the involvement of the company in the illegal transaction. It is a general principle of English law that a plaintiff must not base a claim for compensation on an illegal act in which he was involved: 'no person should profit from his own wrong.' In the case of illegal payments being made out of company funds for the purchase of shares in that company, the company, as a separate legal person, is in law involved. The rules could therefore lead to the conclusion that the company (which in fact was the victim of this transaction) could not recover compensation because in law it was a party to the wrongful transaction. This difficulty was solved in the case of *Selangor United Rubber Estates* v. *Craddock* [1968] 1 WLR 1555. In that case, Craddock made a bid for the shares of the plaintiff company. The bid was made through an agent. Craddock got the money from a bank. Money from the plaintiff company was then transferred to the bank and lent to Craddock, who used it to repay the bank. The company sought to recover the money from Craddock, claiming that because he had wrongfully been in possession of money which in fact belonged to the company, he held that money on trust for the company. Between themselves, that would make Craddock a trustee and the company the person entitled to benefit, 'the beneficiary', who could call for payment of the money in trust at any time. Ungoed Thomas J said:

> 'I appreciate that, in the ordinary case of a claim by a beneficiary against a trustee for an illegal breach of trust, the beneficiary is not a party to the illegality; but that, when directors act for a company in an illegal act with a stranger [in this case Craddock], the company is itself a party to the transaction and therefore the illegality. The company, therefore, could not rely on the transaction as "the source of civil rights" and, therefore, for example, it could not successfully sue the

stranger with regard to rights which it was claimed the transaction conferred . . . The plaintiff's claim, however, for breach of trust is not made by it as a party to that transaction, or in reliance on any right which that transaction is alleged to confer, but against the directors and constructive trustees for perpetrating that transaction and making the plaintiff company party to it in breach of trust owing to the plaintiff company.'

The essence of the passage is that the company, being more sinned against than sinning, can recover the money. The wrong has been done to the company by its directors and their cronies and not by the company, even though it was perforce a party to the illegal transaction.

The major difficulty in this area in the past has not been the legal problems involved so much as the immense complexity of the arrangements that must be unravelled to discover if they contravene the section. The exclusion of private companies from the prohibition is a great step forward, as cases such as the following will only have relevance where a public company is involved and they are assumed to have sophisticated legal advice. In *Belmont Finance Corporation v. Williams Furniture Ltd (No. 2)* [1980] 1 All ER 393, the Court of Appeal accepted previous authority to the effect that a purchase of property at an inflated price in order to put the seller in funds to buy shares would contravene the predecessor section to s. 151 Companies Act 1985. In the *Belmont* case itself, the judgments went further. Buckley LJ accepted that both parties to the transaction in question had honestly believed that they were entering into commercial transactions in which they were getting value for money. However, he went on to say:

'but it was certainly not a transaction in the ordinary course of Belmont's business or for the purposes of that business as it subsisted at the date of the agreement. It was an exceptional and artificial transaction and not in any sense an ordinary commercial transaction entered into for its own sake in the commercial interests of Belmont. It was part of a comparatively complex scheme for enabling Mr Grosscurth and his associates to acquire Belmont at no cash cost to themselves.'

The transaction was therefore caught by the prohibition against providing assistance even though both parties believed that it was a transaction for full value. It was significant to Buckley LJ that: 'It was not a transaction whereby Belmont acquired anything which Belmont genuinely needed or wanted for its own purposes.'

This decision was difficult to apply to complex transactions since the legality of those transactions depended wholly on whether the property which one party believed was being bought or sold was in the judgment of the court something which the company would have found of equal value if the share deal had not been related.

Section 54 Companies Act 1948, under which the above cases were decided, was repealed by Companies Act 1981 and replaced by s. 151

Companies Act 1985. Section 153 Companies Act 1985 sought to exempt transactions such as that in *Belmont* from the ambit of the section. The provisions of this section are repeated in the Companies Act 2006 but the *Belmont* transactions would not be caught by the 2006 regime as they concerned a private company. Section 678 exempts from its ambit those transactions which in fact give assistance if:

(a) the company's principal purpose in giving the assistance is not to give it for the purpose of any such acquisition, or
(b) the giving of the assistance for that purpose is but an incidental part of some larger purpose of the company; and the assistance is given in good faith in the interests of the company.

This provision was discussed at length in *Brady* v. *Brady* [1989] 1 AC 755. That case arose from a complicated scheme to divide a business between two brothers who were unable to agree to work together amicably. Because the businesses had assets of unequal value, some complicated moves were made in order to achieve a fair distribution between the two brothers of the assets of what had been a family firm. In the course of this a transaction occurred which undoubtedly resulted in the original company (Brady) giving assistance to one of the new companies, Motoreal Ltd, in the acquisition by Motoreal of the shares in Brady. It was admitted that the assistance had been given but it was argued that the transaction was saved by the exceptions set out in s. 153.

Lord Oliver found that the first part of s. 153 could not apply. In this case the sole purpose and therefore the principal purpose of the assistance had been to enable the acquisition of shares. Consequently the company could not come within the 'principal purpose' exception. The company could only escape if it could show that the assistance was part of 'some larger purpose' of the company and that it had been given in good faith and in the interests of the company. Lord Oliver confessed that he found the concept of 'larger purpose' difficult to grasp but was anxious not to give it too wide a meaning as this would enable wholesale evasion of the rule in s. 151. He went on to say:

'there has always to be borne in mind the mischief against which s. 151 is aimed. In particular, if the section is not, effectively, to be deprived of any useful application, it is important to distinguish between a purpose and the reason why a purpose is formed. The ultimate reason for forming the purpose of financing an acquisition may, and in most cases probably will, be more important to those making the decision than the immediate transaction itself. But "larger" is not the same thing as "more important" nor is "reason" the same as "purpose". If one postulates the case of a bidder for control of a public company financing his bid from the company's own funds – the obvious mischief at which the section is aimed – the immediate purpose which it is sought to achieve is that of completing the purchase and vesting control of the company in the bidder. The reasons why that course is considered desirable may be many and varied. The company may have fallen on hard times so that a change of management is considered necessary to avert disaster. It may merely be thought, and no doubt would be thought by the purchaser and the directors whom he nominates once he has control, that the business of the company will be more profitable under his management than it was heretofore. These may be excellent reasons but they cannot, in my judgment, constitute a "larger purpose" of which the provision of assistance is merely an incident. The purpose and the only purpose of the financial assistance is and remains that of enabling the shares to be acquired and the financial or commercial advantages flowing from the acquisition, whilst they may form the reason for forming the purpose of providing the assistance are a by-product of it rather than an independent purpose of which the assistance can properly be considered to be an incident.'

The problem with this approach is that in seeking to avoid a construction which would permit wholesale evasion of the prohibition in s. 151, such a narrow view of the exception was taken that it is difficult to envisage a deliberate scheme which would escape prohibition. If the financial assistance were provided by accident it might perhaps escape, but that seems an unlikely scenario. So long as the provision of assistance is deliberately with a view to the purchase of shares it will have been given for that 'purpose' according to Lord Oliver's formulation. The reason driving the whole arrangement would not be regarded as a larger purpose.

In *Brady* the scheme was held to have contravened s. 151 but was saved by virtue of the fact that it could be validly carried out under other sections of the 1985 Act. A fairly liberal approach to construction seems to have been adopted in *Acatos and Hutcheson plc* v. *Watson* [1995] 1 BCLC 218; [1995] BCC 441 where the court held that the purchase of another company whose sole asset was a substantial holding of shares in the first company was not precluded by the rules against a company acquiring its own shares. Note that these transcactions would be exempt from the 2006 regime as they involved private companies. The interpretation of the courts will still be valid if public companies are involved in similar transactions.

Exceptions

In this chapter we have already examined some of the exceptions to the rule in some detail. A complete list may, however, be of value. Section 681 Companies Act 2006 contains a list of transactions wholly outside the operation of s. 678. They are:

(a) a distribution of a company's assets by way of a dividend lawfully made including a distribution made in the course of winding up the company;

(b) the allotment of bonus shares;

(c) any reduction of capital made under the Act;

(d) a redemption or purchase of any shares made in accordance with the relevant sections of the Act;

(e) anything done by way of a court-approved compromise or arrangement with members or creditors;

(f) anything done under an arrangement made in pursuance of s. 110 of the Insolvency Act 1986, that is a reconstruction linked to a voluntary winding-up (see Chapter 17);

(g) anything done under an arrangement made between a company and its creditors which is binding on the creditors by virtue of Part I of the Insolvency Act 1986 (see Chapter 17).

More exceptions appear in s. 682 but a public company is only permitted to take advantage of these if the transaction does not reduce the company's net assets, or if it does so, then the assistance is provided out of distributable profits.

Three exceptions concern employee share schemes (see Chapter 1). The other exempts the lending of money in the ordinary course of its business by a company whose ordinary business includes moneylending.

9.16 Serious loss of capital by a public company

Section 656 Companies Act 2006 contains a measure first introduced into UK law as a supposed implementation of the EC Second Directive on company law. The Directive requires a meeting to be convened in the situation that the net assets of a public company are half or less of its called-up share capital 'to consider whether any, and if so what, steps should be taken to deal with the situation. The meeting must be convened not less than 28 days after the day on which a director learns that the company has lost capital to this extent. It must take place within 56 days of that day. The section is silent as to what happens if the meeting decides to do nothing. The section seems to have no other purpose than notifying the shareholders of the situation. Criminal sanctions attach to the failure of a director to call the meeting but no civil consequences flow from contravention of the section.

9.17 Accounts

The amount that a company has available for distribution must in principle be determined from its most recent accounts that have been laid before a general meeting. The directors must state in the balance sheet the total amount they recommend should be distributed as dividend (Schedule 4, para. 51(3) Companies Act 1985). This will only happen after consideration of accounts drawn up according to strict rules.

9.18 Company accounts

It is a fundamental principle of both European and UK company law that annual accounts should be provided and circulated to members. The accounts are useful for members so that they can judge the state of the enterprise in which they have invested, and assess the performance of its directors. It may also be useful to creditors seeking reassurance that their debts will be paid.

Much legislative energy has been expended in attempting to compel companies to paint as accurate a picture as possible in their accounts. It is now a fundamental principle that, overall, the accounts must give a 'true and fair view' of the economic state of the company. A major difficulty is the valuation of the fixed assets of a company. If the value that is entered into the accounts is the value at the time of acquisition this could have been radically altered by inflation over a number of years. On the other hand, if a current valuation is entered, this will vary according to the method used in arriving at the valuation and also according to whether the asset is valued at the sum it would raise if sold, or valued as part of the company as a going concern.

9.19 FRSs and FREDs

The Accounting Standards Board is a body which issues documents called Financial Reporting Standards (FRSs) with the object of working towards a uniform approach to problems of providing a true and fair view of a company's financial state. The first consultation drafts are called Financial Reporting Exposure Drafts (FREDs). The final standards have a legal effect in that they may be considered by courts as providing a standard method of preparing accounts. Any departure from the standard will require explanation before the court will accept that the accounts in question have been properly drawn up.

Increasingly, accounting standards are being developed at an international level. The international accounting standards board has an excellent website at **www.iasb.org** where latest developments are posted. Companies listed on the Stock Exchange must comply with FRS requirements (Admission of Securities to Listing (continuing obligations for companies) Ch. 5, para. 21(a)).

9.20 The obligation to prepare accounts

The Companies Act 2006 amends the law concerning company accounts. Section 386 provides:

'(1) Every company must keep adequate accounting records.
(2) Adequate accounting records means records that are sufficient –
    (a) to show and explain the company's transactions,
    (b) to disclose with reasonable accuracy, at any time, the financial position of the company at that time, and
    (c) to enable the directors to ensure that any accounts required to be prepared comply with the requirements of this Act [and relevant regulations].
(3) Accounting records must, in particular, contain –
    (a) entries from day to day of all sums of money received and expended by the company, and the matters in respect of which the receipt and expenditure takes place,
    (b) a record of the assets and liabilities of the company.'

The section also provides that a company dealing in goods must keep records of stock. A failure to keep accounting records amounts to an offence (s. 387).

9.21 Keeping the records

By s. 388 the accounting records must be kept at a company's registered office or 'such other place as the directors think fit'. There are safeguards which require records to be available in the UK. The records must be open to inspection by the company's officers at all times. Private companies must keep their records for three years from the date at which they are made; public companies for six years.

9.22 Duty to prepare individual company accounts and 'true and fair view'

A key section in the statute is s. 393 which continues the obligation on directors to approve accounts only if they give a 'true and fair view' of the assets of the company or group of companies. Sections 394–396 require the directors of every company to prepare for each financial year a balance sheet and profit and loss account, giving a a true and fair view of the state of affairs of the company.

Small companies and small groups

Small companies and small groups are identified by ss. 381–385 Companies Act 2006. Only private companies qualify. In the case of an individual company, a small company is one which satisfies two or more of the following requirements (s. 382(3)):

(1) Aggregate turnover not more that £5.6 million net or £6.72 million gross.
(2) Aggregate balance sheet total not more than £2.8 million net or £3.36 million gross.
(3) Aggregate number of employees not more than 50.

A parent of a group qualifies as a small company if the group meets the same requirements (s. 383(4)). By section 477 such companies are excluded from the obligation to have an audit of their accounts.

Medium-sized companies

A medium-sized company is not exempted from audit but has fewer filing requirements for its accounts. By s. 465 a medium-sized company exists if in any year it meets two or more of the 'following requirements' (s. 465(3)):

(1) Turnover not more than £22.8 million.
(2) Balance sheet total not more than £11.4 million.
(3) Number of employees not more than 250.

9.23 Group accounts

Where companies are operating together, a fairer picture of the financial health of the enterprise as a whole will be given by 'consolidated' or 'group' accounts. Small companies are exempt from this requirement (s. 398). Accordingly, s. 399 Companies Act 2006 provides that if at the end of a financial year a company is a parent company, the directors have an additional duty to prepare group accounts, which must give a true and fair view of the state of affairs of the parent and its subsidiaries at the end of the year and also a true and fair view of the profit and loss of the undertakings included in the consolidation during that year.

Considerable difficulty has been experienced in devising a law which adequately requires consolidation of accounts. The problem is partly one of devising a satisfactory definition of parent and subsidiary. By s. 1159 Companies Act 2006:

(1) A company is a 'subsidiary' of another company, its 'holding company', if that other company –
  (a) holds a majority of the voting rights in it, or
  (b) is a member of it and has the right to appoint or remove a majority of its board of directors, or
  (c) is a member of it and controls alone, pursuant to an agreement with other members, a majority of the voting rights in it,
  or if it is a subsidiary of a company that is itself a subsidiary of that other company.

The duty extends also to groups which may include a partnership or unincorporated association carrying on a business, which are known as 'undertakings' (s. 1161).

By s. 1162 (2) an undertaking is a parent undertaking in relation to another undertaking, a subsidiary undertaking, if:

(a) it holds a majority of the voting rights in the undertaking, or
(b) it is a member of the undertaking and has the right to appoint or remove a majority of its board of directors, or
(c) it has the right to exercise a dominant influence over the undertaking –
    (i) by virtue of provisions contained in the undertaking's memorandum or articles, or
    (ii) by virtue of a control contract, or
(d) it is a member of the undertaking and controls alone, pursuant to an agreement with other shareholders or members, a majority of the voting rights in the undertaking.

In the accounts of both single companies and groups, information about employee numbers and costs must be given (s. 411) as well as information about directors' benefits (ss. 412 and 413).

The company's auditors must have reported on the accounts and before a distribution can lawfully be made. By ss. 475–484, if the report of the auditors contains any qualification concerning the way in which profits, losses, assets, liabilities, provisions, share capital or reserves have been dealt with in the accounts they must state whether or not, in their opinion, the legality of the proposed distribution would be affected by the matters stated in the qualification. Their statement on this point must be presented to the members with the accounts.

An alternative justification for a distribution is on the basis of interim accounts more recent than the last annual accounts available. In the case of a private company no rules concerning the method of preparation of those accounts appear in the statute. So far as public companies are concerned, such interim accounts must be prepared as nearly as possible in the manner in which annual accounts are prepared. No auditor's report is required but such accounts must be filed with the Registrar.

Directors' report

By s. 415 the directors must prepare a directors' report for each financial year of the company. Section 416 states the general contents which include the names of the directors and the principal activities of the company. Section 417 contains much more detail, requiring a 'business review'. By s. 417(2) the purpose of the business review is to inform members of the company and help them assess how the directors have performed their duty under s. 172. To that end it must be:

(3)(a) a fair review of the company's business and
    (b) the position of the company's business at the end of that year, consistent with the size and complexity of the business.

Quoted companies alone are required, 'to the extent necessary for an understanding of the development, performance or position of the company', to include –

(a) the main trends and factors likely to affect the future development, performance and position of the company's business; and
(b) information about
    (i)   environmental matters (including the impact of the company's business on the environment),
    (ii) the company's employees, and
    (iii) social and community issues,
    including information about any policies of the company in relation to those matters and the effectiveness of those policies.

This is the remnants of the Operating and Financial Review (see *Hot Topic*, p. 42) from which so much was expected. It appears in this much diluted form and relates only to quoted companies.

9.24 Conclusion

We have seen the immensely elaborate attempts that the law makes with the purpose of trying to preserve a fund in order to protect the interests of creditors. The necessity for such an elaborate scheme must be a matter of some doubt, particularly in view of the extent of directors' duties which would also prohibit unreasonable use of capital. For a discussion of this area of law see M. J. Sterling, 'Financial assistance by a company for the purchase of its shares' (1987) 8 Co. Law 99 and note that the reform of this area of the law is under active discussion. However, the UK has limited room for reform as it is obliged to conform with its obligations under the EC Second Directive (see Chapter 18). These obligations include a duty to prohibit the purchase by a company of its own shares and the provision of financial assistance for such a purchase.

Summary

1. The law seeks to ensure that companies get full value for their shares and that a fund of money remains in the company so that creditors have something to rely on.

2. A basic rule is that a company cannot acquire its own shares. This is subject to a number of exceptions.

3. Money may be returned to members by way of an authorised distribution.

4. Dividends are paid out of profits available for the purpose.

5. If a company wishes to reduce its capital it must comply with strict controls.

6. In very restricted circumstances redeemable shares may be issued and a company permitted to purchase its own shares.

7. The rules about maintenance of capital are reinforced by the rule that a company may not provide financial assistance for the purchase of its own shares. This rule is also subject to exceptions.

Exercises

1. Are the above rules instrumental in ensuring a fund is available for creditors of the company?

2. Are the rules unnecessarily complicated?

3. Are there more exceptions than rules in this area?

4. In a world where millions of pounds, dollars or euros can be transmitted (and won or lost) within seconds, are the complex accounting rules a method of shutting the stable door after the horse may have bolted?

Chapter 10

The balance of power inside the company: corporate governance

Key words

▶ **Corporate governance** – no-one knows what this means and it is used in a wide variety of contexts; some people use it to identify all controls over company decision-making (the widest meaning); probably its narrowest meaning is used by accountants and auditors who use it to denote the control that they exercise through financial reporting.

A great deal has been written about 'corporate governance'. The debate ranges over many of the issues covered in this book because it concerns all issues about the best way to run a company. People have been debating what is the best model of company to adopt (see Chapters 1 and 2), the best way to control directors (see Chapter 11), whether or not EC dual board pattern should be adopted (see Chapter 18), and whether and to what extent the company owes 'social duties' to employees, the environment and the state generally. One of the issues is the proper balance of power between the factions within the company structure, and it is this issue which concerns us throughout this chapter. In it we examine some situations where the balance of power in a company is determined by the law and practice surrounding the procedures by which a company is managed. Many things may influence this balance, including matters not immediately governing the relationships between the various factions. For example, fears have been expressed that the system of electronic transmission of shares operated by the Stock Exchange (CREST) diminishes the already small influence of the small investor by exacerbating the tendency to apathy. This is because most small investors have to join with others and nominate someone to deal with the shares for them when asked to do so. A side-effect of this is that information from the company will only be sent directly to the investor if it is specifically requested. It is felt that this distancing can only decrease any sense of involvement by the small investor in the affairs of the company. The issue of 'corporate governance' was a key feature of the exercise carried out by the Department of Trade and Industry in their consultation process:

Modern Company Law for a Competitive Economy (DTI Company Law Review Committee, 2000–2001). The approach adopted by the group was 'to argue that the overall objective of wealth generation and competitiveness for the benefit of all' is to be achieved by what is called an 'inclusive approach', that is, the directors are to consider 'all the relationships on which the company depends' as well as long- and short-term interests, but are to act 'with a view to achieving company success for the benefit of shareholders as a whole'. The group also called for 'wider public accountability' including the publication of a broad operating financial review. The legislation which has resulted from this review includes the Companies Act 2006. This will be in force by 2008. In the meantime we are awaiting implementation orders and regulations which will be drafted to implement some issues, including model articles of association. This chapter updates the references to the relevant sections of the Companies Act 2006 but draws on the regulations drafted under the 1985 Act as at the time of writing (2007) new regulations had not been drafted.

The difficulty with an 'inclusive approach' is that it includes contradictory aims. Broader public accountability is flawed because it is difficult for the public to do anything about companies – and shareholders have little power for the various reasons discussed below.

Theoretically, the general meeting of the body of shareholders has considerable power to make decisions which affect the management of the company by using the vote attached to their shares. This apparently independent power is subject to a number of practical qualifications. Others will appear throughout the chapter. First, a qualification of considerable importance is the right of shareholders to appoint a proxy.

10.1 Proxy voting

Section 324 Companies Act 2006 confers a right on a shareholder to appoint a proxy to attend meetings and vote instead of him at those meetings. The proxy need not be a member. In the case of a private company the proxy has the same right to speak at the meeting as the member would have had. The articles of association will normally have regulations governing the form in which proxies may be made (see the sample form of proxy set out on p. 174).

Section 324 Companies Act 2006 also provides that a proxy may exercise all or any of the member's rights.

10.2 Solicitation of proxies

Two important elements which affect the balance of power between management and shareholders are (i) the management may themselves

↑ requesting

hold a considerable number of the shares, and (ii) the directors may employ the company's money in soliciting proxies on behalf of its policies. In *Peel* v. *London and North Western Rly Co.* [1907] 1 Ch 5, the court held that the company was bound to explain its policy to shareholders, and was entitled to solicit votes in support of that policy at the company's expense. If an officer of the company issues invitations to appoint a proxy, those invitations must go to all members entitled to notice of the meeting or a criminal offence will be committed by him.

The ability of the directors to issue reasoned circulars accompanied by proxy forms mean that many issues affecting a company will be determined before the meeting is held and determined in favour of the management.

10.3   Formality of procedure

It has been established for some time that agreement of all the members to a course of conduct was sufficient to bind the company, even when no formal meeting had been held. In *Cane* v. *Jones* [1981] 1 WLR 1451, this principle applied even in the case where the articles had in effect been altered. The informality principle now has statutory force: s. 288 Companies Act 2006 provides that, in the case of a private company, a written resolution which is passed (s. 296(4)) by the required majority signifying consent is as effective as a resolution passed at a meeting. There are two exceptions to this general power. Resolutions under s. 168 removing a director before his term of office has expired and resolutions under s. 510 Companies Act 2006 to remove an auditor before the expiration of his term of office.

10.4   Meetings

Private companies are not required to hold an annual general meeting since the requirement to hold such a meeting is imposed by s. 336 only on public companies. Instead ss. 302 and 303 permit directors to call general meetings (s. 302). Section 303 permits members to require directors to hold a general meeting if those members represent 10 per cent of the paid-up capital of the company or, if there is no share capital, 10 per cent of the voting rights, unless the last meeting was held more than a year ago, in which case the required percentage is 5 per cent. If the members require the directors to call a meeting, this must happen within 21 days. The meeting must be convened ⇒ *called* within that time limit, not necessarily held within it (see *Re Windward Islands (Enterprises) UK Ltd* [1983] BCLC 293). If the directors fail to convene a meeting within the 21 days, those requesting the meeting may do so. The expense will fall on the company (ss. 305 and 306).

By s. 371 Companies Act 1985, the court has a reserve power to call a meeting if 'for any reason it is impracticable' to call the meeting otherwise.

An application to the court to order a meeting under this section can be made by any director or any member entitled to vote at the meeting. In *Re El Sombrero Ltd* [1958] Ch 900 the court held that to decide when the holding of a meeting was 'impracticable' the court must, in the words of Wynn-Parry J:

> 'examine the circumstances of the particular case and answer the question whether, as a practical matter, the desired meeting of the company can be conducted, there being no doubt, of course, that it can be convened and held.'

In that case the order was granted, the facts of the case being an illustration of the circumstances in which the power to order a meeting to be held is very useful. In *Re El Sombero Ltd* there were three shareholders, two of these being directors. A quorum of three was required for a meeting. The non-director shareholder, who held a majority of the shares, wished to convene a meeting to remove the directors. They refused to attend a meeting, thus preventing a quorum from being achieved. However, the Court of Appeal held that it would be wrong to use the power in s. 371 Companies Act 1985 to call a meeting and determine its quorum if the effect of that would be to override class rights which were embedded in a shareholder agreement. In *Harman and Another* v. *BML Group Ltd* [1994] 2 BCLC 674 the capital of the company was divided into A and B shares, the B shares being registered in the name of B. H and M held a majority of the A shares. Under an agreement signed by all the shareholders it was provided that a meeting of shareholders would not be quorate unless a B shareholder or proxy were present. H and M applied for an order under s. 371 that a meeting of the company be summoned. The judge ordered that a meeting be summoned, ruling that any two members of the company would constitute a quorum. The Court of Appeal held that this was not a proper use of s. 371.

Annual general meeting

A public company must hold an annual general meeting (s. 336 Companies Act 2006). This must be held in addition to any other meetings that are convened. Section 336 provides that: 'Every public company must hold a general meeting as its annual general meeting in each period of 6 months from the date when its annual accounts are dated.' Sections 336(3) and 336(4) provide criminal penalties for all officers in default if the meeting is not held. The Act does not specify in any detail the business to be transacted by the annual general meeting. This usually consists of:

(i) the adoption of the annual accounts;

(ii) the reading of the auditor's report and the appointment of auditors for the future;

  (iii) the directors' report which will include the directors' recommendation of the dividend to be paid to shareholders – a resolution will be proposed that the amount recommended be paid by way of dividend;

  (iv) appointment of directors where some are retiring;

  (v) a resolution to pay the auditors;

  (vi) a resolution to pay the directors.

Notice of meetings

The information disclosed in notices of meetings must be sufficient to enable the shareholder to exercise an informed judgment. The courts will require full disclosure of any benefits which directors will reap from proposed resolutions. In *Baillie* v. *Oriental Telephone and Electric Company Ltd* [1915] 1 Ch 503, the notice did not disclose the fact that the directors stood to gain substantially from the passing of certain resolutions. Lord Cozens-Hardy MR said:

> 'I feel no difficulty in saying that special resolutions obtained by means of a notice which did not substantially put the shareholders in the position to know what they were voting about cannot be supported, and in so far as these special resolutions were passed on the faith and footing of such a notice the defendants cannot act upon them.'

Class meetings

If there is a reason to convene a meeting of a particular class of shareholder, for example to consider the variation of share rights (see Chapter 14), only the holders of the shares of the particular class should be present. In *Carruth* v. *Imperial Chemical Industries Ltd* [1937] AC 707, Lord Russell of Killowen said:

> '*Prima facie* a separate meeting of a class should be a meeting attended only by members of the class, in order that the discussion of the matters which the meeting has to consider may be carried on unhampered by the presence of others who are not interested to view those matters from the same angle as that of the class; and if the presence of outsiders was retained in spite of the ascertained wish of the constituents of the meeting for their exclusion, it would not, I think, be possible to say that a separate meeting of the class had been duly held.'

Quorum

Section 318 Companies Act 2006 provides that a single member is sufficient for a valid meeting in the case of a single member company. In all other cases two members are sufficient unless they both represent the same person as a proxy or they represent the same corporation. However, the section is expressly subject to contrary provision in the articles. The quorum of meetings may also be contained in shareholder agreements (see *Harman and Another* v. *BML Group Ltd* [1994] 2 BCLC 674 – see p. 144).

Except in the case of a single member company, no single member can constitute a quorum, even if representing several shareholders (see *Re M. J. Shanley Contracting Ltd* (1979) 124 SJ 239). This rule is displaced when the meeting is called by the court or the DTI.

Resolutions

The decisions in a company are made either by voting on resolutions at a meeting or by voting on written resolutions. Public companies have only the option of passing resolutions at meetings (s. 281(2) Companies Act 2006). The usual decision-making process is by ordinary resolution which requires a simple majority of votes to pass (s. 282). The company's articles may require a higher majority and the Companies Act 2006 imposes a higher majority in certain cases, such as amendment of the articles (s. 21).

Special resolutions

These are more often required. Alteration of articles by special resolution is dealt with in Chapter 5. Section 283 provides:

> 'A special resolution of the members (or of a class of the members) of a company means a resolution passed by a majority of not less than 75 per cent.'

In the case of a written resolution, it must have been proposed as a special resolution.

Unanimous consent

The members do not have to meet if they all agree to a particular course of conduct unless the course of conduct is illegal or there is a provision in the articles forbidding this method of proceeding. In the latter case it would seem that the unanimous consent of the shareholders can effect an alteration in the articles so that the effectiveness of such a prohibition must be in some doubt (see *Cane* v. *Jones* [1981] 1 WLR 1451).

Voting

The voting rights of the shareholders will normally be set out in the articles. The usual method of voting is to take a show of hands. In this case, each member will have one vote. However, in some circumstances a member, dissatisfied with the outcome of a show of hands, may call for a 'poll'. The standard article provides that on a poll 'every member shall have one vote for every share of which he is the holder'.

It can clearly be seen that the outcome of a vote on a poll may radically differ from that on a show of hands. The right to demand a poll is therefore of considerable importance. The circumstances in which a poll may be demanded may appear in the articles. However, the Companies Act 2006 provides a 'minimum standard' for the articles. It reads (s. 321):

'(1) A provision contained in a company's articles is void in so far as it would have the effect of excluding the right to demand a poll at a general meeting on any question other than –
   (a) the election of the chairman of the meeting; or
   (b) the adjournment of the meeting.
(2) A provision of a company's articles is void in so far as it would have the effect of making ineffective a demand for a poll on any such question which is made –
   (a) by not less than 5 members having the right to vote on the resolution; or
   (b) by a member or members representing not less than 10 per cent of the total voting rights of all the members having the right to vote on the resolution (excluding any voting rights attached to any shares in the company held as treasury shares); or
   (c) by a member or members holding shares in the company conferring a right to vote on the resolution, being shares on which an aggregate sum has been paid up equal to not less than 10 per cent of the total sum paid up on all the shares conferring that right (excluding shares in the company conferring a right to vote on the resolution which are held as treasury shares).'

Exercise of voting rights

There is considerable weight of authority to support the proposition that a shareholder may exercise his right to vote as he pleases and does not have any duty to take into account the interests of others or of the company. In *Pender* v. *Lushington* (1877) 6 Ch D 70, Jessel MR said:

'[A] man may be actuated in giving his vote by interests entirely adverse to the interests of the company as a whole. He may think it more for his particular interest that a certain course may be taken which may be in the opinion of others very adverse to the interests of the company as a whole, but he cannot be restrained from giving his vote in what way he pleases because he is influenced by that motive.'

(See also *North West Transportation* v. *Beatty* (1887) 12 App Cas 589.)

An inroad into this principle appeared to be made by the judgment in the case of *Clemens* v. *Clemens Bros Ltd* [1976] 2 All ER 268. In that case a challenge was made to a resolution to issue further shares to directors. This would have had the effect of substantially reducing (from 45 per cent to below 25 per cent) the voting power of the plaintiff. Foster J said:

'I think that one thing which emerges from the cases to which I have referred is that in such a case as the present Miss Clemens is not entitled to exercise her majority vote in whatever way she pleases. The difficulty is in finding a principle, and obviously expressions such as *"bona fide* for the benefit of the company as a whole", "fraud on a minority" and "oppressive" do not assist in formulating such a principle.

I have come to the conclusion that it would be unwise to try to produce a principle, since the circumstances of each case are infinitely varied. It would not, I think, assist to say more than that in my judgment Miss Clemens is not entitled as of right to exercise her votes as an ordinary shareholder in any way she pleases . . . I cannot escape the conclusion that the resolutions have been framed so as to put into the hands of Miss Clemens and her fellow directors complete control of the company and to deprive the plaintiff of her existing rights as a shareholder with more than 25 per cent of the votes . . . They are specifically and carefully designed to ensure not only that the plaintiff can never get control of the company but to deprive her of what has been called her negative control. Whether I say that these proposals are oppressive to the plaintiff or that no one could honestly believe that they are for her benefit matters not. A court of equity will in my judgment regard these considerations as sufficient to prevent the consequences arising from Miss Clemens using her legal right to vote in the way she has and it would be right for a court of equity to prevent such consequences taking effect.'

This passage is clearly irreconcilable with the traditional view above. The right to vote as a shareholder pleases derives from the idea that the right to vote is a property right which should not be subject to equitable restraints. It is possible to reconcile the two cases by arguing that a shareholder has the right to vote to protect the value of shares in any way they wish, but the best interests of the company can override that right and a decision contrary to these best interests will not be upheld.

Adjournments

Article 45 of Table A under the 1985 Act provides that the chairman shall adjourn the meeting if so directed by the meeting. Article 51 provides that a poll demanded on the question of adjournment shall be taken forthwith. If the articles give the power of adjournment to the chairman, the majority cannot compel an adjournment (see *Salisbury Gold Mining Co.* v. *Hathorn* [1897] AC 268). An adjourned meeting is a continuation of the original meeting (see *Will* v. *Murray* (1850) 4 Ex 843).

Shareholder agreements

Shareholders are free to agree among themselves how they will vote on particular issues. These agreements may be enforced by mandatory injunction (*Puddephatt* v. *Leith* [1916] 1 Ch 200). Such agreements can substantially affect the balance of power among the various groups of shareholders and anyone seeking to understand how any particular company functions would need to know of the existence and content of such agreements. The agreements may supplement the articles of association and contain quite fundamental rights (see discussion of *Harman and Another* v. *BML Group Ltd* [1994] 2 BCLC 674 – pp. 144 and 146).

In *Russell* v. *Northern Bank Development Corporation Ltd* [1992] BCLC 1016, the House of Lords held that an agreement between four shareholders of a private company not to vote in favour of an increase in share capital unless they had first agreed to do so in writing was valid and enforceable. However the part of the agreement which purported to bind the company was void because it was an attempt to fetter the company's statutory power to alter its articles.

10.5 Management of the company

We saw in Chapter 1 that one of the advantages of incorporation was to create a legal being separate from its members which could operate at a distance from those members. Used properly this enables (though not obliges) companies to be run by specialists. The members may simply regard the company as an investment for their money. The persons actually concerned in the running of the company are known as the directors. Even if they have not been appointed officially, the law will in many instances treat them in the same way as directors because they will qualify as 'shadow directors' (this term is discussed more fully on p. 152). If they wish one person to be particularly concerned with the everyday running of the business, that person should be appointed as managing director. If the shareholders are not content to have their money managed on their behalf by the directors, but wish to have a say in the way that the company is run, the chances are quite high that they will come into conflict with the 'professional' management in the form of the directors. Berle and Means found (*The Modern Corporation and Private Property* (New York, 1932); see also P. S. Florence, *Ownership, Control and Success of Large Companies* (New York, 1961)) that where ownership of shares in large American corporations was widely dispersed, no individual or group was in a position to control the corporation; instead management was in control. Large institutional investors such as pension funds and insurance companies are in a position to exercise control over management. However, such control seems usually to be exercised in an informal way rather than through the formal mechanisms of meetings, which is where, according to the company's constitution, decisions will be taken. Most meetings of public companies are poorly attended. The UK government's policy of encouraging small shareholdings (in, for example, privatised industries) would seem likely to exacerbate this problem, as the difficulty and expense of attending a meeting when the shareholder has only a small sum at stake will not be undertaken. In large public companies the management are in control of business decisions and are out of control in the sense that they are not effectively accountable to other organs of the company. This perception may have fuelled the debate about the benefits of a two-tier structure of management, with a supervisory board of directors overseeing the directors involved in day-to-day business decisions. Such a system is an option that a company could adopt under the EC proposals for a Fifth Directive and for a European Company Statute (see Chapter 18). In any event, under those proposals there would be a 'supervisory' element to the board structure. It was also instrumental in starting the committee enquiry which eventually reported as the Cadbury Committee on the Financial Aspects of Corporate Governance. This produced a Code, which relied heavily on the appointment of non-executive directors. This body was followed by the Hampel Committee on Corporate Governance and eventually by the issue of a 'Combined Code' which is embedded in the rules of the London Stock Exchange. All listed companies are obliged to comply with the Combined Code or give reasons for not doing so. An important part of the Combined Code is the requirement of a 'sound system of internal control' to manage 'significant risks'. The board must consider:

(1) the nature and extent of the risks facing the company;
(2) the likelihood of the risks materialising;
(3) the company's ability to reduce the impact of such risks if they do materialise;
(4) costs relative to benefits.

The Code is now supplemented by the Companies Act 2006 provision on directors' duties (see Chapter 11).

In the case of small companies, the system of agreement at formal meetings may also be unreal. Decisions may well be made by the few people who actually run the business, meeting informally day by day. If there are any other shareholders they may take no interest in the business at all.

Others are interested in the way that the company is run as well. Employees have a very considerable interest in the decisions that are made in the course of managing the business. Creditors are also concerned, particularly when the company has fallen upon hard times. Each of these groups has some claim to be consulted or at least have their interests considered when management decisions are made. In this chapter we shall examine the way that each of these interest groups can influence decisions about the way that the company is managed.

With the reservations expressed above in mind, we turn to examination of the rules governing the appointment and removal of officers of the company, managing directors and shadow directors, directors' meetings, the general meeting, the relationship between managers and shareholders, and the influence of employees and creditors.

10.6 Appointment of directors

Section 154 Companies Act 2006 provides that every company must have at least one director. The term director is not fully defined, s. 250 merely stating that a director is a person acting as director whatever label is attached to them (but see s. 251 Companies Act 2006 and discussion of 'shadow directors' on p. 152), nor is there anywhere in the legislation much positive guidance as to how a director should act. There is a considerable body of both statute and case law which will show directors what they must not do but, except in general terms (see the following chapter), there is little guidance on how the company should be managed. Much of the structure of management will appear in the articles of association which will often adopt at least parts of the regulation which will replace Table A, Companies Act 1985 (see Case notes, pp. 166–84), although modifications may be made to accommodate peculiarities relating to the particular company.

The first directors of any company are the directors named in a statement signed by all the subscribers and delivered with the memorandum and articles of association of the company to the Registrar of Companies when the company is formed.

Until the subscribers to the memorandum have made appointments the company cannot act except by a decision of the general meeting (which is made by a majority at a meeting of subscribers or in writing by all the subscribers without a meeting: *John Morley Building Co.* v. *Barras* [1891] 2 Ch 386; and *Re Great Northern Salt and Chemical Works Co.* (1890) 44 Ch D 472). Articles 64–98 of Table A are relevant to all aspects of procedure relating to directors. These articles to Table A appear in the Case notes at the end of this chapter (pp. 175–81). A company need not adopt articles which follow these provisions, but in practice they often do so. Thus Art. 70 provides that 'the business of the company shall be managed by the directors who may exercise all the powers of the company'. Article 84 permits the appointment of a managing director who is not subject to the practice, enshrined in these model articles, whereby the directors retire by rotation. All the first directors retire at the first annual general meeting, and at every subsequent meeting one-third of the directors retire (Art. 73). These provisions may be excluded from the articles of a private company.

Number

Section 154(2) Companies Act 2006 requires public companies to have at least two directors. A private company must have at least one director. By

s. 155 a company must have at least one director who is a natural person. Article 64 of Table A requires there to be at least two directors unless the company determines otherwise by ordinary resolution.

Definition

Section 250 Companies Act 1985 has a partial definition of director and s. 251 defines 'shadow director'. The latter is a term used in the statute where there is a possibility that someone responsible for misfeasance could escape liability where he had not officially been appointed as a director, but was really in charge of the business. Section 251 reads:

'(1) In the Companies Acts "shadow director", in relation to a company, means a person in accordance with whose directions or instructions the directors of the company are accustomed to act.

(2) A person is not to be regarded as a shadow director by reason only that the directors act on advice given by him in a professional capacity.'

This latter exception prevents a person who is only giving advice as, for example, a solicitor to the company, from being regarded as a shadow director and thus sharing some of the responsibilities of true directors, merely because the directors usually act on his advice. Shadow directors are creatures of statute and so will only be under a duty to the company where such a duty is specifically imposed by statute. This is done where responsibilities would easily be evaded by someone who was the real 'power behind the throne' but was not officially a director. Examples of the imposition of duties on shadow directors can be found in the chapters concerning the statutory liability of directors (Chapter 12) and the insolvency of a company (Chapter 17). The definition of shadow director has now been considered by the courts. In *Re Hydrodan (Corby) Ltd* [1994] BCC 161, Millett J made it clear that a shadow director is different from a *de facto* director, that is, a person acting as a director without valid appointment. He said that there are four steps to establishing that someone was a shadow director. These are: (i) the identity of the appointed and acting directors must be established; (ii) it must be established that the alleged shadow director directed those directors as to their actions in relation to the company; (iii) it must be established that the directors followed those directions; and (iv) it must be established that the directors were accustomed to follow directions from the alleged shadow director. Those factors were not established in *Re Unisoft Group Ltd (No. 2)* [1994] BCC 766 where it was held that compliance by one of a number of directors with the directions of an outsider could not make that outsider a shadow director. Only if the whole board or a governing majority were accustomed to act on the directions of the outsider would he become a shadow director.

In order to prevent evasion of duties by the use of members of a director's family or a company controlled by a director, statute often extends a prohibition relating to a transaction to 'connected persons' or 'associated companies'. By s. 252 Companies Act 2006, the persons 'connected with' a director are:

(a) Members of the director's family.
(b) A body corporate with which the director is connected.
(c) A person acting in his capacity as trustee of a trust –
    (i) the beneficiaries of which include the director or a person [connected] with him, or
    (ii) the terms of which confer a power on the trustees that may be exercised for the benefit of the director or any such person.
(d) A person acting in his capacity as partner
    (i) of the director, or
    (ii) of a person [connected} with the director.
(e) A firm which is a legal person under the law by which it is governed and in which
    (i) the director is a partner,
    (ii) a partner is a [connected person], or
    (iii) a partner is a firm in which the director is a partner or in which there is a partner who [is a connected person].

Of these perhaps the most interesting is the definition of the members of a director's family which appears at s. 253 and lists:

- the director's spouse or civil partner;
- any person (whether of a different sex or the same sex) with whom the director lives as a partner in an enduring family relationship;
- the director's children or step-children;
- any children or step-children of a partner who live with the director and are under 18;
- the director's parents.

Age

Section 157 Companies Act 2006 sets 16 as the minimum age for a director.

Remuneration

Directors are in a curious position, as their appointment to a directorship does not entitle them to be paid, even if they in fact do work for the company (see *Re George Newman and Co.* [1895] 1 Ch 674). However, the articles of association may provide for directors' pay (as in Art. 82 of Table A). This will not benefit the director unless he is in a position to enforce any provision in his favour in the articles by using s. 33 Companies Act 2006 (see Chapter 5). Usually the right to be paid will arise from a contract of employment made with the company. Some of the terms of that contract may be discoverable by looking at the articles where, for example, the amount that directors are to be paid may be specified. The situation which arises then is clearly set out in *Re New British Iron Company* Ex Parte *Beckwith* [1898] 1 Ch 324 where the articles of association contained the following provision:

> '62: The remuneration of the board shall be an annual sum of £1000 to be paid out of the funds of the company, which sum shall be divided in such manner as the board shall from time to time determine.'

Wright J said:

> 'Article 62 fixes the remuneration of the directors at the annual sum of £1000. That article is not in itself a contract between the company and the directors; it is only part of the contract constituted by the articles of association between the members of the company *inter se*. But where on the footing of that article the directors are employed by the company and accept office the terms of article 62 are embodied in and form part of the contract between the company and the directors. Under the article as thus embodied the directors obtain a contractual right to an annual sum of £1000 as remuneration.'

In *Re Richmond Gate Property Co. Ltd* [1965] 1 WLR 335, the articles provided that the directors were to be paid such remuneration as the board of directors determined by resolution. The company was wound up before a resolution settling the amount to be paid had been passed. The directors were entitled to nothing under the employment contract. Plowman J said:

> 'a contract exists between [the applicant] and the company for payment to him of remuneration as managing director, and that remuneration depends on Article 108 of Table A [equivalent article is Article 84 of Table A to Companies Act 1985], and is to be such amount "as the directors may determine"; in other words, the managing director is at the mercy of the board, he gets what they determine to pay him, and if they do not determine to pay him anything he does not get anything. That is his contract with the company, and those are the terms on which he accepts office.'

It was argued in that case that the directors should be entitled to be paid for work which they had actually done under a claim known as a '*quantum meruit*' claim. It was held, however, that because there was a contract of employment, such a claim was excluded.

Considerable public disquiet concerning large pay rises awarded to directors of public companies led the Confederation of British Industry to set up a committee chaired by Sir Richard Greenbury to consider the remuneration of directors. The committee drew up a Code of Best Practice (contained in its 1995 report) which was subsequently echoed in the combined Code. A company listed on the Stock Exchange must state in its annual report and accounts whether it has complied with the Code. The best-practice provisions require the directors of a listed company to set up a remuneration committee, consisting exclusively of non-executive directors, to determine the company's policy on executive directors' pay and specific packages for each executive director. This attempt to inject some objectivity into the level of pay does not seem to have had a significant impact. Nor does the 'advisory vote' which shareholders are now entitled to exercise on directors' pay although there is some evidence of withdrawal of huge pay rises where the company has been doing particularly badly.

10.7 Removal of a director

Section 168 Companies Act 2006 provides: / special notice

> '(1) A company may, by ordinary resolution remove a director before the expiration of his period of office, notwithstanding anything in any agreement between it and him.'

This replaces s. 303 Companies Act 1985 which included 'notwithstanding anything in its articles'.

This sweeping power apparently given to the general meeting to remove a director is, however, subject to two very significant qualifications. One appears in statutory form in s. 168(5) Companies Act 2006 which expressly preserves the right of a director dismissed in accordance with s. 168 to damages for any breach of contract of employment that has occurred. The rule is that the director may be dismissed, but because he has been dismissed by the company that is also the other party to his employment contract, he will be entitled to damages on the principle expressed in *Stirling v. Maitland* (1864) 5 B&S 840, where Cockburn LJ said:

> 'if a party enters into an arrangement which can only take effect by the continuance of a certain existing set of circumstances, there is an implied engagement on his part that he shall do nothing of his own motion to put an end to that state of circumstances under which alone the arrangement can be operative.'

Thus, a director's employment contract can only continue to operate when the company refrains from dismissing him by passing a resolution under s. 303 Companies Act 1985. If such a resolution is passed, it is effective to dismiss him, but it is at the same time a breach of contract and damages for that breach must be paid. The same principle applies where the company is in breach of such a contract by alteration of its articles. See *Southern Foundries Ltd v. Shirlaw* [1940] AC 701; *Shindler v. Northern Raincoat Co. Ltd* [1960] 1 WLR 1038; *Nelson v. James Nelson & Sons Ltd* [1914] 2 KB 770;

and *Read* v. *Astoria Garage (Streatham) Ltd* [1952] 2 All ER 292 (see Chapter 5). A provision which may in some cases alleviate this liability is to be found at s. 188 Companies Act 2006. This provides that a director may not be employed for a period exceeding two years unless there is prior approval of the contract by the general meeting. Any term included in a director's employment contract which contravenes this prohibition is void to the extent that two years are exceeded. Unless the general meeting so approve, this will limit the damages payable to the amount payable to the director for what remains of the two-year period at the time of his dismissal. The director will also be under a duty to 'mitigate' the damage, that is, to take any reasonable steps available to him to limit the amount payable to him. Whatever the length of the contract, it is common practice for directors to have 'rolling' contracts which renew themselves daily. Thus each day the contract stretches two years into the future.

The second qualification to the power to remove a director by using s. 188 arises because of the strange decision in *Bushell* v. *Faith* [1970] AC 1099. In that case, the articles of a private company provided that: 'in the event of a resolution being proposed at any general meeting for the removal from office of any director any shares held by that director shall on a poll in respect of such resolution carry the right of three votes per share.' Since only three persons were involved (a brother and two sisters), the situation was that if an ordinary resolution was passed under the predecessor section to s. 303 Companies Act 1985 the sisters outvoted the brother by two to one, and he was removed as a director. If his special voting right was taken into account the same resolution was defeated by 3:2. This meant that the director in question was effectively irremovable. It was argued that such a 'weighted voting provision' was inconsistent with s. 303, since that section had been intended to prevent entrenchment of directors by inserting provisions in the articles. The relevant section (s. 303) therefore contained the words 'notwithstanding anything in the articles'. Lord Upjohn said:

> 'My Lords, when construing an Act of Parliament it is a canon of construction that its provisions must be construed in the light of the mischief which the Act was designed to meet. In this case the mischief was well known; it was a common practice, especially in the case of private companies, to provide in the articles that a director should be irremovable or only removable by an extraordinary resolution; in the former case the articles would have to be altered by special resolution before the director could be removed and of course in either case a three-quarters' majority would be required. In many cases this would be impossible, so the Act provided that notwithstanding anything in the articles an ordinary resolution would suffice to remove a director.'

Despite the identification of the 'mischief' at which the section was aimed, and the admission that the device used in the case made the director irremovable, the House of Lords came to the conclusion that it was permissible to have this type of weighted voting provision and that it was not in conflict with the predecessor to s. 303. This was said to be because no restriction had been placed on the company's right to specify the voting rights of particular shares. There is much to be said for the dissenting judgment of Lord Morris of Borth-y-Gest:

> 'Some shares may, however, carry a greater voting power than others. On a resolution to remove a director shares will therefore carry the voting power that they possess. But this does not, in my view, warrant a device such as Article 9 introduces. Its unconcealed effect is to make a director irremovable. If the question is posed whether the shares of the respondent possess any added voting weight the answer must be that they possess none whatever beyond, if valid, an *ad hoc* weight for the special purpose of circumventing [now s. 303]. If Article 9 were writ large it would set out that a director is not to be removed against his will and that in order to achieve this and to thwart the express provision of [now s. 303] the voting power of any director threatened with removal is to be deemed to be greater than it actually is. The learned judge thought that to sanction this would be to make a mockery of the law. I think so too.'

Note that a similar effect to that of *Bushell* v. *Faith* can be achieved using shareholder agreements (discussed at 10.4). The application of *Bushell* v. *Faith* is in doubt following the omission of 'notwithstanding anything in the articles' from s. 168. However this will depend on the interpretation of s. 33 as to whether the constitution is an 'agreement' between the director and the company. Under s. 169 a director has the right to protest against removal and he is entitled to be heard at the meeting called to remove him.

10.8 Validity of directors' acts

Section 161 provides that the acts of a person acting as director are valid even if it is subsequently discovered that there is a defect in his appointment, that he was disqualified from holding office or that he was not entitled to vote on the matter in question.

10.9 Disqualification

A person subject to a disqualification order made under the Company Directors Disqualification Act 1986 may not act as a director (see Chapter 12). The articles may contain other situations which will require a director to vacate office (see Table A, Article 81; also see Case notes, pp. 177–8).

10.10 Directors' meetings

The rules governing directors' meetings are usually to be found in the articles of association (see Table A, Articles 88–98 in Case notes, pp. 179–81). However, the Companies Act 2006 requires a director (including a director of a single member company) to declare transactions in which he has an interest (s. 182) and provides that it is a criminal offence not to do so (s. 183).

One clear rule is that notice must be given to all directors of a meeting (see *Re Portuguese Copper Mines* (1889) 42 Ch D 160) unless he is abroad and unable to be reached by notice (see *Halifax Sugar Refining Co. v. Franklyn* (1890) 59 LJ Ch 591). Sections 248 and 249 provide that minutes of directors' meetings must be taken and may be used as evidence of the proceedings at those meetings.

10.11 Managing director

It is usual to include in the articles of association a power for the directors to appoint one or more of their number to be managing director or directors and permitting the delegation of such powers as are necessary for him or them to manage the business. It will be the business of such an appointee to be closely involved in the day-to-day running of the business. He will be an 'executive' director. Others on the board may consider themselves to be 'non-executive' directors and to be chiefly concerned with matters of policy rather than the nitty-gritty of the management of the company.

Article 84 of Table A (see Case notes, p. 178) allows the directors to appoint a managing director (and other executive directors) on such terms as they determine and, by Art. 72, to delegate such of their powers as they consider desirable. This delegation may be altered or revoked. However, if the managing director is removed from office before his contract of employment expires, this will entitle him to damages for breach of contract (see *Nelson v. James Nelson & Sons Ltd* [1914] 2 KB 770) under the doctrine discussed above in relation to s. 168, that the one party to a contract must not do anything which prevents the other party from completing his side of the bargain. There is thus some difficulty between the rule often to be found in the articles that the delegation of powers by the board may be revoked, and the commission of a breach of contract by the company, who may, by such a revocation, be preventing the managing director from continuing to carry out his employment. A case in which the relationship between these two rules arose is *Harold Houldsworth & Co. (Wakefield) Ltd v. Caddies* [1955] 1 WLR 352. The case is of limited use as a precedent for the future, as it is generally considered to have turned on the construction of the particular contract of employment in that case. Under that contract, Caddies had been appointed managing director of Houldsworth (the parent company). The contract provided that he should perform the duties and exercise the powers in relation to the business of the company and the business of its existing subsidiaries 'which may from time to time be assigned to or vested in him by the board of directors of the company'.

At first Caddies managed Houldsworth and a subsidiary. However, a dispute arose between Caddies and his fellow directors. The board of directors instructed Caddies to thereafter confine his attentions to the subsidiary alone. The House of Lords held that this was not a breach of the contract of employment. If the contract had not contained the clause giving such wide discretion to the board to define Caddies' job from time to time, the action would have been a breach of contract.

The powers of a managing director were considered in *Mitchell & Hobbs (UK)* v. *Mill* [1996] 2 BCLC 102 where it was held that the proper construction of Table A, Reg. 70 (see the next section for a further discussion of this regulation) led to the result that a managing director did not have the power to commence legal proceedings on behalf of the company without reference to the other directors or shareholders. The regulation provided that the power to manage the company could be exercised by the board of directors, but not by a single director. The court also held that Table A, Reg. 72 did not give any powers to a managing director over and above those held by the other directors unless such powers had been delegated by the board.

10.12 Relationship between the board of directors and the general meeting

For companies registered prior to 1 July 1985, the relationship between these two organs was usually governed by an article similar or identical to Art. 80 of Table A annexed to the Companies Act 1948. This read:

> 'The business of the company shall be managed by the directors who may pay all expenses incurred in promoting and registering the company, and may exercise all such powers of the company as are not, by the Act, or by these regulations, required to be exercised by the company in general meeting, subject, nevertheless, to any of these regulations, to the provisions of the Act and to such regulations, being not inconsistent with the aforesaid regulations or provisions as may be prescribed by the company in general meeting; but no regulations made by the company in general meeting shall invalidate any prior act of the directors which would have been valid if that regulation had not been made.'

This appeared to reserve to the general meeting a power to make regulations to govern the conduct of directors. The scope of this power was most uncertain until the judges determined the balance of power issue firmly in favour of the directors to the detriment of the powers of the general meeting. Thus in *Automatic Self Cleansing Filter Syndicate Company Ltd* v. *Cunningham* [1906] 2 Ch 34, the Court of Appeal held that a resolution passed by a simple majority of shareholders (an ordinary resolution) was not effective. The resolution purported to order the directors to go ahead with an agreement to sell the whole of the assets of the company. The directors believed that this was an unwise course. Warrington J said:

'The effect of this resolution, if acted upon, would be to compel the directors to sell the whole of the assets of the company, not on such terms and conditions as they think fit, but upon such terms and conditions as a simple majority of the shareholders think fit. But it does not rest there. Article 96 [this was very similar to Article 80 of Table A to the 1948 Act above] provides that the management of the business and control of the company are to be vested in the directors. Now that article, which is for the protection of a minority of the shareholders, can only be altered by a special resolution, that is to say, by a resolution passed by a three-fourths' majority, at a meeting called for the purpose, and confirmed at a subsequent meeting. If that provision could be revoked by a resolution of the shareholders passed by a simple majority, I can see no reason for the provision which is to be found in Article 81 that the directors can only be removed by a special resolution. It seems to me that if a majority of shareholders can, on a matter which is vested in the directors, overrule the discretion of the directors, there might just as well be no provision at all in the articles as to the removal of directors by special resolution. Moreover, pressed to its logical conclusion, the result would be that when a majority of the shareholders disagree with the policy of the directors, though they cannot remove the directors except by special resolution, they might carry on the whole of the business of the company as they pleased, and thus, though not able to remove the directors, overrule every act which the board might otherwise do. It seems to me on the true construction of these articles that the management of the business and control of the company are vested in the directors, and consequently that the control of the company as to any particular matter, or the management of any particular transaction or any particular part of the business of the company, can only be removed from the board by an alteration of the articles, such alteration, of course, requiring a special resolution.'

This approach was adopted in *Breckland Group Holdings Ltd* v. *London and Suffolk Properties Ltd* [1989] BCLC 100, where the court held that since the company's articles of association adopted Art. 80 of Table A, Schedule 1 Companies Act 1948, the conduct of the business of the company was vested in the board of directors, and the shareholders in general meeting could not intervene to adopt unauthorised proceedings.

It seems to have been the case that the general meeting could not interfere in management decisions by way of an ordinary resolution, even under the 1948 Companies Act. The 1985 equivalent is Art. 70, Table A attached to the Companies Act 1985 (by the Companies (Tables A to F) Regulations 1985, SI 1985 No. 805 (as amended by SI 1985 No. 1052)). This reads:

'Subject to the provisions of the Act, the memorandum and the articles and to any directions given by special resolution, the business of the company shall be managed by the directors who may exercise all the powers of the company. No alteration of the memorandum or articles and no such direction shall invalidate any prior act of the directors which would have been valid if that alteration had not been made or that direction had not been given. The powers given by this regulation shall not be limited by any special power given to the directors by the articles and a meeting of directors at which a quorum is present may exercise all powers exercisable by the directors.'

The justification for the insistence that there should be no interference in director-control save by a special resolution was well expressed in *Gramophone and Typewriter Ltd* v. *Stanley* [1908] 2 KB 89. Buckley LJ said:

'The directors are not servants to obey directions given by the shareholders as individuals; they are agents appointed by and bound to serve the shareholders as their principals. They are persons who may by the regulations be entrusted with the control of the business, and if so entrusted they can be dispossessed from that control only by the statutory majority which can alter the articles.'

When coupled with the knowledge that a very few persons can hold a large number of the shares in a company, that directors can be entrenched by *Bushell* v. *Faith* clauses, and that shareholders with small stakes in a company rarely take an interest in meetings, it can be seen that 'shareholder democracy' is an extremely hollow concept and the directors will often have complete freedom from control in managing the business. We await the provisions of model articles under Companies Act 2006.

10.13 Where the board of directors ceases to function

The above analysis holds good for the situation where the board of directors is a functioning organ of the company. If for some reason the directors are unable or unwilling to exercise their powers of management, those powers revert to and are exercisable by the company in general meeting. In *Alexander Ward & Co. Ltd* v. *Samyang Navigation Co. Ltd* [1975] 2 All ER 424, the House of Lords held that the company could act through its two shareholders to recover its debts. This was possible despite an article in the company's constitution which read as follows:

'The business of the Company shall be managed by the Directors, who . . . may exercise all such powers of the company as are not by the [Hong Kong] Ordinance or by these Articles required to be exercised by the Company in General Meeting.'

The company had no directors at the relevant time. Lord Hailsham said:

'In my opinion, at the relevant time the company was fully competent either to lay attestments or to raise proceedings in the Scottish courts. The company could have done so either by appointing directors, or, as I think, by authorising proceedings in general meeting, which in the absence of an effective board, has a residual authority to use the company's powers. It had not taken, and did not take the steps necessary to give authority to perform the necessary actions. But it was competent to have done so, and in my view it was therefore a competent principal . . . So far as regards the powers of general meeting, in Gower, *Modern Company Law* (3rd edn, 1969), pp. 136–37 it is stated:

"It seems that if for some reason the board cannot or will not exercise the powers vested in them, the general meeting has been held effective where there was a deadlock on the board, where an effective quorum could not be obtained, where the directors are disqualified from voting, or, more obviously, where the directors have purported to borrow in excess of the amount authorised by the articles."

Moreover, although the general meeting cannot restrain the directors from conducting actions in the name of the company, it still seems to be the law (as laid down in *Marshall's Valve Gear Co.* v. *Manning Wardle & Co.* [1909] 1 Ch 267, that the general meeting can commence proceedings on behalf of the company if the directors fail to do so. In that case counsel attempted to draw a distinction between the cases supposed in this passage, where the directors were for some reason unable or unwilling to act, and the instant case where there were no directors. I see no difference in the distinction . . .'

10.14 The secretary

Sections 270 and 271 Companies Act 2006 provide that private companies need not have a secretary but that public companies must have a secretary. The increased importance of the company secretary was recognised by Lord Denning in *Panorama Developments Ltd* v. *Fidelis Furnishing Fabrics* (see Chapter 6). In that case, it was held that a company secretary had the power to make certain contracts on behalf of the company. Contracts to hire cars were held to be binding on the company, despite the fact that the company secretary in question had hired the cars ostensibly for the company, but in fact for his own use. The increased importance of company secretaries is also recognised by s. 273 Companies Act 2006. This applies only to public companies and imposes a duty on the directors of such companies to 'take all reasonable steps to secure that the secretary (or each joint secretary) of the company is a person who appears to them to have the requisite knowledge and experience to discharge the functions of secretary of the company'. There follows a list of acceptable qualifications for the post which include membership of a number of accountants' professional organisations and legal qualifications. However, these qualifications are not exclusive, as s. 273 also provides that the secretary may be: 'a person who, by virtue of his holding or having held any other position or his being a member of any other body, appears to the directors to be capable of discharging those functions.'

The secretary is responsible for making sure that the documents that a company must send to the Registrar are accurate and are sent on time. With the increasing complexity of requirements to make disclosure of company affairs in this way, the role has become considerably more complex and important.

10.15 Employees

By s. 309 Companies Act 1985:

'(1) The matters to which the directors of a company are to have regard in the performance of their functions include the interests of a company's employees in general, as well as the interests of its members.'

This has been replaced in s. 172 Companies Act 2006 by:

'A director of a company must act in the way he considers, in good faith, would be most likely to promote the success of the company for the benefit of its members as a whole, and in doing so have regard (amongst other matters) to – . . . (b) the interests of the company's employees.'

The effect of this replacement is completely unclear and directors' duties generally are discussed in Chapter 11. However, it is arguable that the new version represents a dilution of the rights of employees to be considered, firstly because they are included in a list of other matters to be considered and secondly because the duty comes explicitly with a 'filter' which promotes the interests of the members as of paramount consideration. This is an enactment of the understanding at common law but it nevertheless is a clear and explicit statement that employees interests are only relevant in so far as considering their interests promotes the interests of the shareholders.

In both Acts, duty imposed on directors has no effective enforcement mechanism. If there was an alleged failure to take account of employees' interests the failure would theoretically have to be enforced by the company voting in general meeting to bring an action against the directors. It seems unlikely that there would be enough employee shareholders or a sufficient number of altruistic shareholders in order to achieve the necessary majority. Even if it were possible, proof that employees' interests had not been considered might be extremely difficult to determine.

The status of employees in company law is a matter of considerable concern to the EC legislators. All the Member States of the EC, with the exception of Ireland and the UK, have in place some form of compulsory system for ensuring worker participation in the running of companies. The basic source for the comparison which follows is a working document of the European Parliament dated 13/12/89, PE136.297, rapporteur: Christine Oddy. It appears only for a general comparison of approaches and further research is necessary if it is used to indicate the current position in any of the jurisdictions. It must be understood that many countries adopt a 'two-tier' structure of boards of directors: an administrative board which usually consists of executive directors, and a 'supervisory board' on which sit non-executive directors.

Hot Topic . . .

INTERNATIONAL DEBATE ON CORPORATE SOCIAL RESPONSIBILITY

The debate is now international. In May 1999 the Organisation for Economic Co-operation and Development (OECD) published a set of corporate governance principles. These concentrate on the rights of shareholders and their equitable treatment. There is an endorsement for the takeover market. The role of 'stakeholders' is addressed: 'The corporate governance framework should recognise the rights of stakeholders as established by law.' It is interesting to consider whether s. 309 Companies Act 1985 complies with this statement, especially in view of a sub-rule: 'where stakeholder interests are protected by law, stakeholders should have the opportunity to obtain effective redress for the violations of their rights.' The full statement is available at **http://www.oecd.org**

The UN has also launched its 'Global Compact Initiative'. According to the UN's Global Compact:

'The Global Compact is not a regulatory instrument or code of conduct, but a value-based platform designed to promote institutional learning. It utilizes the power of transparency and dialogue to identify and disseminate good practices based on universal principles.'

The Compact encompasses nine such principles, drawn from the Universal Declaration of Human Rights, the ILO's Fundamental Principles on Rights at Work and the Rio Principles on Environment and Development (see Annex I for complete listing). And it asks companies to act on these principles in their own corporate domains. Thus, the Compact 'promotes good practices by corporations; it does not endorse companies'.

The nine principles are:

Human Rights
The Secretary-General asked world business to:

Principle 1: support and respect the protection of international human rights within their sphere of influence; and
Principle 2: make sure their own corporations are not complicit in human rights' abuses.

Labour
The Secretary-General asked world business to uphold:

Principle 3: freedom of association and the effective recognition of the right to collective bargaining;
Principle 4: the elimination of all forms of forced and compulsory labour;
Principle 5: the effective abolition of child labour; and
Principle 6: the elimination of discrimination in respect of employment and occupation.

Environment
The Secretary-General asked world business to:

Principle 7: support a precautionary approach to environmental challenges;

Principle 8: undertake initiatives to promote greater environmental responsibility; and
Principle 9: encourage the development and diffusion of environmentally friendly technologies.

'Why should business participate in this initiative? Because as markets have gone global, so, too, must the principle and practice of corporate citizenship. In this new global economy, it makes good business sense for firms to internalize these principles as integral elements of corporate strategies and practice.' **(www.un.org)**

For the EU Commission 'Corporate Social Responsibility [CSR] is essentially a concept whereby companies decide voluntarily to contribute to a better society and a cleaner environment' **(http://europa.eu.int)**. The European Commission Green Paper *Promoting a European Framework for Corporate Social Responsibility* considers as its first substantive issue, Human Resources Management:

'Responsible recruitment practices, involving in particular non-discriminatory practices, could facilitate the recruitment of people from ethnic minorities, older workers, women and the long-term unemployed and people at a disadvantage.' (COM (2001) 366 final, Brussels, 18.7.2001)

The UK government prefers to define the 'behaviour of a responsible organisation':

(1) it recognises that its activities have a wider impact on the society in which it operates;

(2) in response, it takes account of the economic, social, environmental and human rights' impact of its activities across the world; and

(3) it seeks to achieve benefits by 'working in partnership with other groups and organisations' (*Business and Society: Corporate Social Responsibility Report*, Department of Trade and Industry, 2002).

Note that the 'benefit' accrues to 'it', the corporation, since 'CSR can help to build brand value, foster customer loyalty, motivate their staff, and contribute to a good reputation among a wide range of stakeholders'. For CISCO systems it is 'outreach' which provides education for the disadvantaged (*Corporate Citizenship*, The Smith Institute, 2000). For Hopkins it means 'ethical behaviour of business towards its constituencies or stakeholders. I define stakeholders as consisting of seven azimuths or major groups' which are

- owners/investors (share or stock holders)
- management
- employees
- customers
- natural environment
- the wider community
- contractors/suppliers.

(M. Hopkins, *The Planetary Bargain*, Basingstoke, Palgrave Macmillan, 1999)

The UK *Corporate and Social Responsibility Report* states that '[t]he fundamentals of equal opportunities are a central plank of CSR' (Department of Trade and Industry, 2002). It should be noted, however, that the whole concept of CSR is not without its opponents. A comprehensive attack on 'global salvationism' and CSR in particular can be found in *Misguided Virtue* (D. Henderson, Institute of Economic Affairs, 2001) where it is argued that:

'CSR embodies the notion that progress in relation to environmental and social issues lies in making norms and standards more stringent and more uniform, in part by corporations acting on their own initiative. This approach takes too little account of costs and benefits at extending regulation in ways that would reduce welfare. The effects of enforced uniformity are especially damaging in labour markets. The greatest potential for harm of this kind arises from attempts, whether by government or businesses, in the name of CSR and 'Global Corporate Citizenship' to regulate the world as a whole. Imposing common international standards, despite the fact that circumstances may be widely different across countries, restricts the scope for mutually beneficial trade and investment flows. It is liable to hold back the development of poor countries through the suppression of employment opportunities within them.'

However, these initiatives can only be of use if they are implemented by the relevant decision-making body within the company. It is vital to identify where power lies.

Summary

1. The voting power of shareholders may be more apparent than real. One limitation in practice is the power of management to solicit proxy votes.

2. Ordinary resolutions passed at meetings of shareholders require a simple majority. Special resolutions require a 75 per cent majority.

3. There are a number of technical rules concerning the conduct of meetings but it is doubtful if there is a general principle that a shareholder must use his vote otherwise than in his own selfish interest except in the case of a director who may not vote to ratify his own actions.

Summary cont'd

4. The power of shareholders over management is probably less than it would appear from the legal framework.

5. A public company must have at least two directors.

6. Appointment as a director does not as such entitle the appointee to payment.

7. Section 168 Companies Act 2006 provides for the removal of directors but this power does not prevent the director from gaining compensation for loss of office if he is dismissed in breach of contract.

8. A managing director may be appointed to manage the day-to-day affairs of the company.

9. The general meeting may not interfere in the general conduct of business by the directors unless the board of directors is unable or unwilling to exercise its usual functions.

10. The secretary of a company, particularly of a public company, is to be regarded as 'more than a mere clerk' and as being capable of committing the company to binding contracts in his sphere of competence.

11. The directors must have regard to the interests of employees but there is no effective method of enforcing this obligation.

Case notes

These model articles are from Regulations made under Companies Act 1985. At the time of writing (2007) the new Regulations under Companies Act 2006 were awaited.

SCHEDULE

TABLE A

REGULATIONS FOR MANAGEMENT OF A COMPANY LIMITED BY SHARES

INTERPRETATION

1. In these regulations –

'the Act' means the Companies Act 1985 including any statutory modifications or re-enactment for the time being in force.
'the article' means the articles of the company.
'clear days' in relation to the period of a notice means that period excluding the day when the notice is given or deemed to be given and the day for which it is given or on which it is to take effect.
'executed' includes any mode of execution.
'office' means the registered office of the company.
'the holder' in relation to shares means the member whose name is entered in the register of members as the holder of the shares.
'the seal' means the common seal of the company.
'secretary' means the secretary of the company or any other person appointed to perform the duties of the secretary of the company,

including a joint, assistant or deputy secretary.

'the United Kingdom' means Great Britain and Northern Ireland.

Unless the context otherwise requires, words or expressions contained in these regulations bear the same meanings as in the Act but excluding any statutory modification thereof not in force when these regulations become binding on the company.

SHARE CAPITAL

2. Subject to the provisions of the Act and without prejudice to any rights attached to any existing shares, any share may be issued with such rights or restrictions as the company may by ordinary resolution determine.

3. Subject to the provision of the Act, shares may be issued which are to be redeemed or are to be liable to be redeemed at the option of the company or the holder on such terms and in such manner as may be provided by the articles.

4. The company may exercise the powers of paying commissions conferred by the Act. Subject to the [provisions] of the Act, any such commission may be satisfied by the payment of cash or by the allotment of fully or partly paid shares or partly in one way and partly in the other.

5. Except as required by law, no person shall be recognised by the company as holding any share upon any trust and (except as otherwise provided by the articles or by law) the company shall not be bound by or recognise any interest in any share except an absolute right to the entirety thereof in the holder.

SHARE CERTIFICATES

6. Every member, upon becoming the holder of any shares, shall be entitled without payment to one certificate for all the shares of each class held by him (and, upon transferring a part of his holding of shares of any class, to a certificate for the balance of such holding) or several certificates each one for one or more of his shares upon payment for every certificate after the first of such reasonable sum as the directors may determine. Every certificate shall be sealed with the seal and shall specify the number, class and distinguishing numbers (if any) of the shares to which it relates and the amount or respective amounts paid up thereon. The company shall not be bound to issue more than one certificate for shares held jointly by several persons and delivery of a certificate to one joint holder shall be a sufficient delivery to all of them.

7. If a share certificate is defaced, worn-out, lost or destroyed, it may be renewed on such terms (if any) as to evidence and indemnity and payment of the expenses reasonably incurred by the company in investigating evidence as the directors may determine but otherwise free of charge, and (in the case of defacement or wearing-out) on delivery up of the old certificate.

LIEN

8. The company shall have a first and paramount lien on every share (not being a fully paid share) for all moneys (whether presently payable or not) payable at a fixed time or called in respect of that share. The directors may at any time declare any share to be wholly or in part exempt from the provisions of this regulation. The company's lien on a share shall extend to any amount payable in respect of it.

9. The company may sell in such manner as the directors determine any shares on which the company

has a lien if a sum in respect of which the lien exists is presently payable and is not paid within fourteen clear days after notice has been given to the holder of the share or to the person entitled to it in consequence of the death or bankruptcy of the holder, demanding payment and stating that if the notice is not complied with the shares may be sold.

10. To give effect to a sale the directors may authorise some person to execute an instrument of transfer of the shares sold to, or in accordance with the directions of, the purchaser. The title of the transferee to the share shall not be affected by any irregularity in or invalidity of the proceedings in reference to the sale.

11. The net proceeds of the sales, after payment of the costs, shall be applied in payment of so much of the sum for which the lien exists as is presently payable, and any residue shall (upon surrender to the company for cancellation of the certificate for the shares sold and subject to a like lien for any moneys not presently payable as existed upon the shares before the sale) be paid to the person entitled to the shares at the date of the sale.

CALLS ON SHARES AND FORFEITURE

12. Subject to the terms of allotment, the directors may make calls upon the members in respect of any moneys unpaid on the shares (whether in respect of nominal value or premium) and each member shall (subject to receiving at least fourteen clear days' notice specifying when and where payment is to be made) pay to the company as required by the notice the amount called on his shares. A call may be required to be paid by instalments. A call may, before receipt by the company of any sum due thereunder, be revoked in whole or part and payment of a call may be postponed in whole or in part. A

person upon whom a call is made shall remain liable for calls made upon him notwithstanding the subsequent transfer of the shares in respect whereof the call was made.

13. A call shall be deemed to have been made at the time when the resolution of the directors authorising the call was passed.

14. The joint holders of a share shall be jointly and severally liable to pay all calls in respect thereof.

15. If a call remains unpaid after it has become due and payable the person from whom it is due and payable shall pay interest on the amount unpaid from the day it became due and payable until it is paid at the rate fixed by the terms of allotment of the share or in the notice of the call or, if no rate is fixed, at the appropriate rate (as defined by the Act) but the directors may waive payment of the interest wholly or in part.

16. An amount payable in respect of a share on allotment or at any fixed date, whether in respect of nominal value or premium or as an instalment of a call, shall be deemed to be a call and if it is not paid the provisions of the articles shall apply as if that amount had become due and payable by virtue of a call.

17. Subject to the terms of allotment, the directors may make arrangements on the issue of shares for a difference between the holders in the amounts and the times of payment of calls on their shares.

18. If a call remains unpaid after it has become due and payable the directors may give to the person from whom it is due not less than fourteen clear days' notice requiring payment of the amount unpaid together with any interest which may have accrued. The notice shall name the place where payment is to be made and shall state that if the notice is not complied with the shares in respect of which the call was made will be liable to be forfeited.

19. If the notice is not complied with any share in respect of which it was given may, before the payment required by the notice has been made, be forfeited by a resolution of the directors and the forfeiture shall include all dividends or other moneys payable in respect of the forfeited shares and not paid before the forfeiture.

20. Subject to the provisions of the Act, a forfeited share may be sold, re-allocated or otherwise disposed of on such terms and in such manner as the directors determine either to the person who was before the forfeiture the holder or to any other person and at any time before the sale, re-allotment or other disposition, the forfeiture may be cancelled on such terms as the directors think fit. Where for the purposes of its disposal a forfeited share is to be transferred to any person the directors may authorise some person to execute an instrument of transfer of the share to that person.

21. A person any of whose shares have been forfeited shall cease to be a member in respect of them and shall surrender to the company for cancellation the certificate for the shares forfeited but shall remain liable to the company for all moneys which at the date of forfeiture were presently payable by him to the company in respect of those shares with interest at the rate at which interest was payable on those moneys before the forfeiture or, if no interest was so payable, at the appropriate rate (as defined in the Act) from the date of forfeiture until payment but the directors may waive payment wholly or in part or enforce payment without any allowance for the value of the shares at the time of forfeiture or for any consideration received on their disposal.

22. A statutory declaration by a director or the secretary that a share has been forfeited on a specified date shall be conclusive evidence of the facts stated in it as against all persons claiming to be entitled to the share and the declaration shall (subject to the execution of an instrument of transfer if necessary) constitute a good title to the share and the person to whom the share is disposed of shall not be bound to see to the application of the consideration, if any, nor shall his title to the share be affected by any irregularity in or invalidity of the proceedings in reference to the forfeiture or disposal of the share.

TRANSFER OF SHARES

23. The instrument of transfer of a share may be in any usual form or in any other form which the directors may approve and shall be executed by or on behalf of the transferor and, unless the share is fully paid, by or on behalf of the transferee.

24. The directors may refuse to register the transfer of a share which is not fully paid to a person of whom they do not approve and they may refuse to register the transfer of a share on which the company has a lien. They may also refuse to register a transfer unless –

(*a*) it is lodged at the office or at such other place as the directors may appoint and is accompanied by the certificate for the shares to which it relates and such other evidence as the directors may reasonably require to show the right of the transferor to make the transfer;

(*b*) it is in respect of only one class of shares; and

(c) it is in favour of not more than four transferees.

25. If the directors refuse to register a transfer of a share, they shall within two months after the date on which the transfer was lodged with the company send to the transferee notice of the refusal.

26. The registration of transfers of shares or of transfers of any class of shares may be suspended at such times and for such periods (not exceeding thirty days in any year) as the directors may determine.

27. No fee shall be charged for the registration of any instrument of transfer or other document relating to or affecting the title to any share.

28. The company shall be entitled to retain any instrument of transfer which is registered, but any instrument of transfer which the directors refuse to register shall be returned to the person lodging it when notice of the refusal is given.

TRANSMISSION OF SHARES

29. If a member dies the survivor or survivors where he was a joint holder, and his personal representatives where he was a sole holder or the only survivor of joint holders, shall be the only person recognised by the company as having any title to his interest; but nothing herein contained shall release the estate of a deceased member from any liability in respect of any share which had been jointly held by him.

30. A person becoming entitled to a share in consequence of the death or bankruptcy of a member may, upon such evidence being produced as the directors may properly require, elect either to become the holder of the share or to have some person nominated by him registered as the transferee. If he elects to become the holder he shall give notice to the company to that effect. If he elects to

have another person registered he shall execute an instrument of transfer of the share to that person. All the articles relating to the transfer of shares shall apply to the notice or instrument of transfer as if it were an instrument of transfer executed by the member and the death or bankruptcy of the member had not occurred.

31. A person becoming entitled to a share in consequence of the death or bankruptcy of a member shall have the rights to which he would be entitled if he were the holder of the share, except that he shall not, before being registered as the holder of the share, be entitled in respect of it to attend or vote at any meeting of the company or at any separate meeting of the holders of any class of shares in the company.

ALTERATION OF SHARE CAPITAL

32. The company may by ordinary resolution –

(a) increase its share capital by new shares of such amount as the resolution prescribes;

(b) consolidate and divide all or any of its share capital into shares of larger amount than its existing shares;

(c) subject to the provisions of the Act, subdivide its shares, or any of them, into shares of a smaller amount and the resolution may determine that, as between the shares resulting from the subdivision, any of them may have any preference or advantage as compared with the others; and

(d) cancel shares which, at the date of the passing of the resolution, have not been taken or agreed to be taken by any person and diminish the amount of its share capital by the amount of the shares so cancelled.

33. Whenever as a result of a consolidation of shares any members would become entitled to fractions of a share, the directors may, on behalf of those members, sell the shares representing the fractions for the best price reasonably obtainable to any person (including, subject to the provisions of the Act, the company) and distribute the net proceeds of sale in due proportion among those members, and the directors may authorise some person to execute an instrument of transfer of the shares to, or in accordance with the directions of, the purchaser. The transferee shall not be bound to see to the application of the purchase money nor shall his title to the shares be affected by any irregularity in or invalidity of the proceedings in reference to the sale.

34. Subject to the provisions of the Act, the company may by special resolution reduce its share capital, any capital redemption reserve and any share premium account in any way.

PURCHASE OF OWN SHARES

35. Subject to the provisions of the Act, the company may purchase its own shares (including any redeemable shares) and, if it is a private company, make a payment in respect of the redemption or purchase of its own shares otherwise than out of distributable profits of the company or the proceeds of a fresh issue of shares.

GENERAL MEETINGS

36. All general meetings other than annual general meetings shall be called extraordinary general meetings.

37. The directors may call general meetings and, on the requisition of members pursuant to the provisions of the Act, shall forthwith proceed to convene an extraordinary general meeting for a date not later than eight weeks after receipt of the requisition. If there are not within the United Kingdom sufficient directors to call a general meeting, any director or any member of the company may call a general meeting.

NOTICE OF GENERAL MEETINGS

38. An annual general meeting and an extraordinary general meeting called for the passing of a special resolution or a resolution appointing a person as a director shall be called by at least twenty-one clear days' notice. All other extraordinary general meetings shall be called by at least fourteen days' notice but a general meeting may be called by shorter notice if it is so agreed –

(a) in the case of an annual general meeting, by all the members entitled to attend and vote thereat; and

(b) in the case of any other meeting by a majority in number of the members having a right to attend and vote being a majority together holding not less than ninety-five per cent in nominal value of the shares giving that right.

The notice shall specify the time and place of the meeting and the general nature of the business to be transacted and, in the case of an annual general meeting, shall specify the meeting as such. Subject to the provisions of the articles and to any restrictions imposed on any shares, the notice shall be given to all the members, to all persons entitled to a share in consequence of the death or bankruptcy of a member and to the directors and auditors.

39. The accidental omission to give notice of a meeting to, or the non-receipt of notice of a meeting by, any person entitled to receive notice shall not invalidate the proceedings at that meeting.

PROCEEDINGS AT GENERAL MEETINGS

40. No business shall be transacted at any meeting unless a quorum is present. Two persons entitled to vote upon the business to be transacted, each being a member or a proxy for a member or a duly authorised representative of a corporation, shall be a quorum.

41. If such a quorum is not present within half an hour from the time appointed for the meeting, or if during a meeting such a quorum ceases to be present, the meeting shall stand adjourned to the same day in the next week at the same time and place or [to] such time and place as the directors may determine.

42. The chairman, if any, of the board of directors or in his absence some other director nominated by the directors shall preside as chairman of the meeting, but if neither the chairman nor such other director (if any) be present within fifteen minutes after the time appointed for holding the meeting and willing to act, the directors present shall elect one of their number to be chairman and, if there is only one director present and willing to act, he shall be chairman.

43. If no director is willing to act as chairman, or if no director is present within fifteen minutes after the time appointed for holding the meeting, the members present and entitled to vote shall choose one of their number to be chairman.

44. A director shall, notwithstanding that he is not a member, be entitled to attend and speak at any general meeting

and at any separate meeting of the holders of any class of shares in the company.

45. The chairman may, with the consent of a meeting at which a quorum is present (and shall if so directed by the meeting), adjourn the meeting from time to time and from place to place, but no business shall be transacted at an adjourned meeting other than business which might properly have been transacted at the meeting had the adjournment not taken place. When a meeting is adjourned for fourteen days or more, at least seven clear days' notice shall be given specifying the time and place of the adjourned meeting and the general nature of the business to be transacted. Otherwise it shall not be necessary to give any such notice.

46. A resolution put to the vote of a meeting shall be decided on a show of hands unless before, or on the declaration of the result of, the show of hands a poll is duly demanded. Subject to the provisions of the Act, a poll may be demanded –

(*a*) by the chairman; or

(*b*) by at least two members having the right to vote at the meeting; or

(*c*) by a member or members representing not less than one-tenth of the total voting rights of all members having the right to vote at the meeting; or

(*d*) by a member or members holding shares conferring a right to vote at the meeting being shares on which an aggregate sum has been paid up equal to not less than one-tenth of the total sum paid up on all the shares conferring that right;

and a demand by a person as proxy

for a member shall be the same as a demand by the member.

47. Unless a poll is duly demanded a declaration by the chairman that a resolution has been carried or carried unanimously, or by a particular majority, or lost, or not carried by a particular majority and an entry to that effect in the minutes of the meeting shall be conclusive evidence of the fact without proof of the number or proportion of the votes recorded in favour of or against the resolution.

48. The demand for a poll may, before the poll is taken, be withdrawn, but only with the consent of the chairman and a demand so withdrawn shall not be taken to have invalidated the result of a show of hands declared before the demand was made.

49. A poll shall be taken as the chairman directs and he may appoint scrutineers (who need not be members) and fix a time and place for declaring the result of the poll. The result of the poll shall be deemed to be the resolution of the meeting at which the poll was demanded.

50. In the case of an equality of votes, whether on a show of hands or on a poll, the chairman shall be entitled to a casting vote in addition to any other vote he may have.

51. A poll demanded on the election of a chairman or on a question of adjournment shall be taken forthwith. A poll demanded on any other question shall be taken either forthwith or at such time and place as the chairman directs not being more than thirty days after the poll is demanded. The demand for a poll shall not prevent the continuance of a meeting for the transaction of any business other than the question on which the poll was demanded. If a poll is demanded before the declaration of the result of a show of hands and the demand is duly withdrawn, the meeting

shall continue as if the demand had not been made.

52. No notice need be given of a poll not taken forthwith if the time and place at which it is to be taken are announced at the meeting at which it is demanded. In any other case at least seven clear days' notice shall be given specifying the time and place at which the poll is to be taken.

53. A resolution in writing executed by or on behalf of each member who would have been entitled to vote upon it if it had been proposed at a general meeting at which he was present shall be as effectual as if it had been passed at a general meeting duly convened and held and may consist of several instruments in the like form each executed by or on behalf of one or more members.

VOTES OF MEMBERS

54. Subject to any rights or restrictions attached to any shares, on a show of hands every member who (being an individual) is present in person or (being a corporation) is present by a duly authorised representative, not being himself a member entitled to vote, shall have one vote and on a poll every member shall have one vote for every share of which he is the holder.

55. In the case of joint holders the vote of the senior whether in person or by proxy, shall be accepted to the exclusion of the votes of the other joint holders; and seniority shall be determined by the order in which the names of the holders stand in the register of members.

56. A member in respect of whom an order had been made by any court having jurisdiction (whether in the United Kingdom or elsewhere) in matters concerning mental disorder may vote, whether on a show of hands or on a poll, by his receiver, *curator bonis* or other person authorised in that behalf appointed by that court, and any such receiver, *curator bonis* or other person may, on a poll, vote by proxy. Evidence to the satisfaction of the directors of the authority of the person claiming to exercise the right to vote shall be deposited at the office, or at such other place as is specified in accordance with the articles for the deposit of instruments of proxy, not less than 48 hours before the time appointed for holding the meeting or adjourned meeting at which the right to vote is to be exercised and in default the right to vote shall not be exercisable.

57. No member shall vote at any general meeting or at any separate meeting of the holders of any class of shares in the company, either in person or by proxy, in respect of any share held by him unless all moneys presently payable by him in respect of that share have been paid.

58. No objection shall be raised to the qualification of any voter except at the meeting or adjourned meeting at which the vote objected to is tendered, and every vote not disallowed at the meeting shall be valid. Any objection made in due time shall be referred to the chairman whose decision shall be final and conclusive.

59. On a poll votes may be given either personally or by proxy. A member may appoint more than one proxy to attend on the same occasion.

60. An instrument appointing a proxy shall be in writing, executed by or on behalf of the appointor and shall be in the following form (or in a form as near thereto as circumstances allow or in any other form which is usual or which the directors may approve) –

"   PLC/Limited
          I/We,   , of
                    , being a
member/members of the above-named company, hereby appoint
          of
          , or failing him,
of   , as my/our proxy to vote in my/our name[s] and on my/our behalf at the annual/extraordinary general meeting of the company to be held on 20   , and at any adjournment thereof.
Signed on   20   ."

61. Where it is desired to afford members an opportunity of instructing the proxy how he shall act the instrument appointing a proxy shall be in the following form (or in a form as near thereto as circumstances allow or in any other form which is usual or which the directors may approve) –

"   PLC/Limited
          I/We,   , of
                    , being a
member/members of the above-named company, hereby appoint
          of
          , or failing him,
of   , as my/our proxy to vote in my/our name[s] and on my/our behalf at the annual/extraordinary general meeting of the company to be held on 20   , and at any adjournment thereof. This form is to be used in respect of the resolutions mentioned below as follows:
     Resolution No 1 *for *against.
     Resolution No 2 *for *against.
*Strike out whichever is not desired.
     Unless otherwise instructed, the proxy may vote as he thinks fit or abstain from voting.
Signed this   day of   20 ."

62. The instrument appointing a proxy and any authority under

which it is executed or a copy of such authority certified notarially or in some other way approved by the directors may –

(a) be deposited at the office or at such other place within the United Kingdom as is specified in the notice convening the meeting or in any instrument of proxy sent out by the company in relation to the meeting not less than 48 hours before the time for holding the meeting or adjourned meeting at which the person named in the instrument proposes to vote; or

(b) in the case of a poll taken more than 48 hours after it is demanded, be deposited as aforesaid after the poll has been demanded and not less than 24 hours before the time appointed for the taking of the poll; or

(c) where the poll is not taken forthwith but is taken not more than 48 hours after it was demanded, be delivered at the next meeting at which the poll was demanded to the chairman or to the secretary or to any director;

and an instrument of proxy which is not deposited or delivered in a manner so permitted shall be invalid.

63. A vote given or poll demanded by proxy or by the duly authorised representative of a corporation shall be valid notwithstanding the previous determination of the authority of the person voting or demanding a poll unless notice of the determination was received by the company at the office or at such other place at which the instrument of proxy was duly deposited before the commencement of the meeting or adjourned meeting at which the vote is given or the poll demanded or (in the case of a poll taken otherwise than on the same day as the meeting or adjourned meeting) the time appointed for taking the poll.

NUMBER OF DIRECTORS

64. Unless otherwise determined by ordinary resolution, the number of directors (other than alternate directors) shall not be subject to any maximum but shall be not less than two.

ALTERNATE DIRECTORS

65. Any director (other than an alternate director) may appoint any other director, or any other person approved by resolution of the directors and willing to act, to be an alternate director and may remove from office an alternate director so appointed by him.

66. An alternate director shall be entitled to receive notice of all meetings of directors and of all meetings of committees of directors of which his appointor is a member, to attend and vote at any such meeting at which the director appointing him is not personally present, and generally to perform all the functions of his appointor as a director in his absence but shall not be entitled to receive any remuneration from the company for his services as an alternate director. But it shall not be necessary to give notice of such a meeting to an alternate director who is absent from the United Kingdom.

67. An alternate director shall cease to be an alternate director if his appointor ceases to be a director; but, if a director retires by rotation or otherwise but is reappointed or deemed to have been reappointed at the meeting at which he retires, any appointment of an alternate director made by him which was in force immediately prior to his retirement shall continue after his reappointment.

68. Any appointment or removal of an alternate director shall be by notice to the company signed by the director making or revoking the appointment or in any other manner approved by the directors.

69. Save as otherwise provided in the articles, an alternate director shall be deemed for all purposes to be a director and shall alone be responsible for his own acts and defaults and he shall not be deemed to be the agent of the director appointing him.

POWERS OF DIRECTORS

70. Subject to the provisions of the Act, the memorandum and the articles and to any directions given by special resolution, the business of the company shall be managed by the directors who may exercise all the powers of the company. No alteration of the memorandum or articles and no such direction shall invalidate any prior act of the directors which would have been valid if that alteration had not been made or that direction had not been given. The powers given by this regulation shall not be limited by any special power given to the directors by the articles and a meeting of directors at which a quorum is present may exercise all powers exercisable by the directors.

71. The directors may, by power of attorney or otherwise, appoint any person to be the agent of the company for such purposes and on such conditions as they determine, including authority for the agent to delegate all or any of his powers.

DELEGATION OF DIRECTORS' POWERS

72. The directors may delegate any of their powers to any committee consisting of one or more directors. They may also delegate to any managing director or any director holding any other executive office such of their powers as they consider desirable to be exercised by

him. Any such delegation may be made subject to any conditions the directors may impose, and either collaterally with or to the exclusion of their own powers and may be revoked or altered. Subject to any such conditions, the proceedings of a committee with two or more members shall be governed by the articles regulating the proceedings of directors so far as they are capable of applying.

APPOINTMENT AND RETIREMENT OF DIRECTORS

73. At the first annual general meeting all the directors shall retire from office, and at every subsequent annual general meeting one-third of the directors who are subject to retirement by rotation or, if their number is not three or a multiple of three, the number nearest to one-third shall retire from office; but, if there is only one director who is subject to retirement by rotation, he shall retire.

74. Subject to the provisions of the Act, the directors to retire by rotation shall be those who have been longest in office since their last appointment or reappointment, but as between persons who became or were last reappointed directors on the same day those to retire shall (unless they otherwise agree among themselves) be determined by lot.

75. If the company, at the meeting at which a director retires by rotation, does not fill the vacancy the retiring director shall, if willing to act, be deemed to have been reappointed unless at the meeting it is resolved not to fill the vacancy or unless a resolution for the reappointment of the director is put to the meeting and lost.

76. No person other than a director retiring by rotation shall be appointed or reappointed a director at any general meeting unless –

(a) he is recommended by the directors; or

(b) not less than fourteen nor more than thirty-five clear days before the date appointed for the meeting, notice executed by a member qualified to vote at the meeting has been given to the company of the intention to propose that person for appointment or reappointment stating the particulars which would, if he were so appointed, be required to be included in the company's register of directors together with notice executed by that person of his willingness to be appointed or reappointed.

77. Not less than seven nor more than twenty-eight clear days before the date appointed for holding a general meeting notice shall be given to all who are entitled to receive notice of the meeting of any person (other than a director retiring by rotation at the meeting) who is recommended by the directors for appointment or reappointment as a director at the meeting or in respect of whom notice has been duly given to the company of the intention to propose him at the meeting for appointment or reappointment as a director. The notice shall give the particulars of that person which would, if he were so appointed or reappointed, be required to be included in the company's register of directors.

78. Subject as aforesaid, the company may by ordinary resolution appoint a person who is willing to act to be a director either to fill a vacancy or as an additional director and may also determine the rotation in which any additional directors are to retire.

79. The directors may appoint a person who is willing to act to be a director, either to fill a vacancy or as an additional

director, provided that the appointment does not cause the number of directors to exceed any number fixed by or in accordance with the articles as the maximum number of directors. A director so appointed shall hold office only until the next following annual general meeting and shall not be taken into account in determining the directors who are to retire by rotation at the meeting. If not reappointed at such annual general meeting, he shall vacate office at the conclusion thereof.

80. Subject as aforesaid, a director who retires at an annual general meeting may, if willing to act, be reappointed. If he is not reappointed, he shall retain office until the meeting appoints someone in his place, or if it does not do so, until the end of the meeting.

DISQUALIFICATION AND REMOVAL OF DIRECTORS

81. The office of a director shall be vacated if –

(a) he ceases to be a director by virtue of any provision of the Act or he becomes prohibited by law from being a director; or

(b) he becomes bankrupt or makes any arrangement or composition with his creditors generally; or

(c) he is, or may be, suffering from mental disorder and either –

   (i) he is admitted to hospital in pursuance of an application for admission for treatment under the Mental Health Act 1983 or, in Scotland, an application for admission under the Mental Health (Scotland) Act 1960, or

   (ii) an order is made by a court having jurisdiction (whether in the United Kingdom or elsewhere) in matters concerning mental disorder for his detention or for the appointment of a receiver, *curator bonis* or other person to exercise powers with respect to his property or affairs; or

(d) he resigns his office by notice to the company; or

(e) he shall for more than six consecutive months have been absent without permission of the directors from meetings of directors held during that period and the directors resolve that his office be vacated.

REMUNERATION OF DIRECTORS

82. The directors shall be entitled to such remuneration as the company may by ordinary resolution determine and, unless the resolution provides otherwise, the remuneration shall be deemed to accrue from day to day.

DIRECTORS' EXPENSES

83. The directors may be paid all travelling, hotel and other expenses properly incurred by them in connection with their attendance at meetings of directors or committees of directors or general meetings or separate meetings of the holders of any class of shares or of debentures of the company or otherwise in connection with the discharge of their duties.

DIRECTORS' APPOINTMENTS AND INTERESTS

84. Subject to the provisions of the Act, the directors may appoint one or more of their number to the office of managing director or to any other executive office under the company and may enter into an agreement or arrangement with any director for his employment by the company or for the provision by him of any services outside the scope of the ordinary duties of a director. Any such appointment, agreement or arrangement may be made upon such terms as the directors determine and they may remunerate any such director for his services as they think fit. Any appointment of a director to an executive office shall terminate if he ceases to be a director but without prejudice to any claim to damages for breach of the contract of service between the director and the company. A managing director and a director holding any other executive office shall not be subject to retirement by rotation.

85. Subject to the provisions of the Act, and provided that he has disclosed to the directors the nature and extent of any material interest of his, a director notwithstanding his office –

(a) may be a party to, or otherwise interested in, any transaction or arrangement with the company or in which the company is otherwise interested;

(b) may be a director or other officer of, or employed by, or a party to any transaction or arrangement with, or otherwise interested in, any body corporate promoted by the company or in which the company is otherwise interested; and

(c) shall not, by reason of his office, be accountable to the company for any benefit which he derives from any such office or employment or from any such transaction or arrangement or from any interest in any such body corporate and no such transaction or arrangement shall be liable to be avoided on the ground of any such interest or benefit.

86. For the purposes of regulation 85 –

(*a*) a general notice given to the directors that a director is to be regarded as having an interest of the nature and extent specified in the notice in any transaction or arrangement in which a specified person or class of persons is interested shall be deemed to be a disclosure that the director has an interest in any such transaction of the nature and extent so specified; and

(*b*) an interest of which the director has no knowledge and of which it is unreasonable to expect him to have knowledge shall not be treated as an interest of his.

DIRECTORS' GRATUITIES AND PENSIONS

87. The directors may provide benefits, whether by the payment of gratuities or pensions or by insurance or otherwise, for any director who has held but no longer holds any executive office or employment with the company or with any body corporate which is or has been a subsidiary of the company or a predecessor in business of the company or of any such subsidiary, and for any member of his family (including a spouse and a former spouse) or any person who is or was dependent on him, and may (as well before as after he ceases to hold such office or employment) contribute to any fund and pay premiums for the purchase or provision of any such benefit.

PROCEEDINGS OF DIRECTORS

88. Subject to the provisions of the articles, the directors may regulate their proceedings as they think fit. A director may, and the secretary at the request of a director shall, call a meeting of the directors. It shall not be necessary to give notice of a meeting to a director who is absent from the United Kingdom. Questions arising at a meeting shall be decided by a majority of votes. In the case of an equality of votes, the chairman shall have a second or casting vote. A director who is also an alternate director shall be entitled in the absence of his appointor to a separate vote on behalf of his appointor in addition to his own vote.

89. The quorum for the transaction of the business of the directors may be fixed by the directors and unless so fixed at any other number shall be two. A person who holds office only as an alternate director shall, if his appointor is not present, be counted in the quorum.

90. The continuing directors or a sole continuing director may act notwithstanding any vacancies in their number, but, if the number of directors is less than the number fixed as the quorum, the continuing directors or director may act only for the purpose of filling vacancies or of calling a general meeting.

91. The directors may appoint one of their number to be the chairman of the board of directors and may at any time remove him from that office. Unless he is unwilling to do so, the director so appointed shall preside at every meeting of directors at which he is present. But if there is no director holding that office, or if the director holding it is unwilling to preside or is not present within five minutes after the time appointed for the meeting, the directors present may appoint one of their number to be chairman of the meeting.

92. All acts done by a meeting of directors, or of a committee of directors, or by a person acting as a director shall, notwithstanding that it be afterwards discovered that there was a defect in the appointment of any director or that any of them were disqualified from holding office, or had vacated office, or were not entitled to vote, be as valid as if every such person had been duly appointed and was qualified and had continued to be a director and had been entitled to vote.

93. A resolution in writing signed by all the directors entitled to receive notice of a meeting of directors or of a committee of directors shall be as valid and effectual as if it had been passed at a meeting of directors or (as the case may be) a committee of directors duly convened and held and may consist of several documents in the like form each signed by one or more directors; but a resolution signed by an alternate director need not also be signed by his appointor and, if it is signed by a director who has appointed an alternate director, it need not be signed by the alternate director in that capacity.

94. Save as otherwise provided by the articles, a director shall not vote at a meeting of directors or of a committee of directors on any resolution concerning a matter in which he has, directly or indirectly, an interest or duty which is material and which conflicts or may conflict with the interests of the company unless his interest or duty arises only because the case falls within one or more of the following paragraphs –

(a) the resolution relates to the giving to him of a guarantee, security, or indemnity in respect of money lent to, or an obligation incurred by him for the benefit of, the company or any of its subsidiaries;

(b) the resolution relates to the giving to a third party of a guarantee, security, or indemnity in respect of an obligation of the company or any of its subsidiaries for which the director has assumed responsibility in whole or part and whether alone or jointly with others under a guarantee or indemnity or by the giving of security;

(c) his interest arises by virtue of his subscribing or agreeing to subscribe for any shares, debentures or other securities of the company or any of its subsidiaries or by virtue of his being, or intending to become, a participant in the underwriting or sub-underwriting of an offer of any such shares, debentures, or other securities by the company or any of its subsidiaries for subscription, purchase or exchange;

(d) the resolution relates in any way to a retirement benefits scheme which has been approved, or is conditional upon approval, by the Board of Inland Revenue for taxation purposes.

For the purposes of this regulation, an interest of a person who is, for any purpose of the Act (excluding any statutory modification thereof not in force when this regulation becomes binding on the company), connected with a director shall be treated as an interest of the director and, in relation to an alternate director, an interest of his appointor shall be treated as an interest of the alternate director without prejudice to any interest which the alternate director has otherwise.

95. A director shall not be counted in the quorum present at a meeting in relation to a resolution on which he is not entitled to vote.

96. The company may by ordinary resolution suspend or relax to any extent, either generally or in respect of any particular matter, any provision of the articles

prohibiting a director from voting at a meeting of directors or of a committee of directors.

97. Where proposals are under consideration concerning the appointment of two or more directors to offices or employments with the company or any body corporate in which the company is interested the proposals may be divided and considered in relation to each director separately and (provided he is not for another reason precluded from voting) each of the directors concerned shall be entitled to vote and be counted in the quorum in respect of each resolution except that concerning his own appointment.

98. If a question arises at a meeting of directors or of a committee of directors as to the right of a director to vote, the question may, before the conclusion of the meeting, be referred to the chairman of the meeting and his ruling in relation to any director other than himself shall be final and conclusive.

SECRETARY

99. Subject to the provisions of the Act, the secretary shall be appointed by the directors for such a term, at such remuneration and upon such conditions as they may think fit; and any secretary so appointed may be removed by them.

MINUTES

100. The directors shall cause minutes to be made in books kept for the purpose –

(a) of all appointments of officers made by the directors; and

(b) of all proceedings at meetings of the company, of the holders of any class of shares in the company, and of the directors, and of committees of directors, including the names of the directors present at each such meeting.

THE SEAL

101. The seal shall only be used by the authority of the directors or of a committee of directors authorised by the directors. The directors may determine who shall sign any instrument to which the seal is affixed and unless otherwise so determined it shall be signed by a director and by the secretary or by second director.

DIVIDENDS

102. Subject to the provisions of the Act, the company may by ordinary resolution declare dividends in accordance with the respective rights of the members, but no dividend shall exceed the amount recommended by the directors.

103. Subject to the provisions of the Act, the directors may pay interim dividends if it appears to them that they are justified by the profits of the company available for distribution. If the share capital is divided into different classes, the directors may pay interim dividends on shares which confer deferred or non-preferred rights with regard to dividend as well as on shares which confer preferential rights with regard to dividend, but no interim dividend shall be paid on shares carrying deferred or non-preferred rights if, at the time of payment, any preferential dividend is in arrear. The directors may also pay at intervals settled by them any dividend payable at a fixed rate if it appears to them that the profits available for distribution justify the payment. Provided the directors act in good faith they shall not incur any liability to the holders of shares conferring preferred rights for any loss they may suffer by the lawful payment of an interim dividend on any shares having deferred or non-preferred rights.

104. Except as otherwise provided by the rights attached to shares, all dividends shall be declared and paid according to the amounts paid up on the shares on which the dividend is paid. All dividends shall be apportioned and paid proportionately to the amounts paid up on the shares during any portion or portions of the period in respect of which the dividend is paid; but, if any share is issued on terms providing that it shall rank for dividend as from a particular date, that share shall rank for dividend accordingly.

105. A general meeting declaring a dividend may, upon the recommendation of the directors, direct that it shall be satisfied wholly or partly by the distribution of assets and, where any difficulty arises in regard to the distribution, the directors may settle the same and in particular may issue fractional certificates and fix the value for distribution of any assets and may determine that cash shall be paid to any member upon the footing of the value so fixed in order to adjust the rights of members and may vest any assets in trustees.

106. Any dividend or other moneys payable in respect of a share may be paid by cheque sent by post to the registered address of the person entitled or, if two or more persons are the holders of the share or are jointly entitled to it by reason of the death or bankruptcy of the holder, to the registered address of that one of those persons who is first named in the register of members or to such person and to such address as the person or persons entitled may in writing direct. Every cheque shall be made payable to the order of the person or persons entitled or to such other person as the person or persons entitled may in writing direct and payment of the cheque shall be a good discharge to the company. Any joint holder or other person jointly entitled to a share as aforesaid may give receipts for any dividend or other moneys payable in respect of the share.

107. No dividend or other moneys payable in respect of a share shall bear interest against the company unless otherwise provided by the rights attached to the share.

108. Any dividend which has remained unclaimed for twelve years from the date when it became due for payment shall, if the directors so resolve, be forfeited and cease to remain owing by the company.

ACCOUNTS

109. No member shall (as such) have any right of inspecting any accounting records or other book or document of the company except as conferred by statute or authorised by the directors or by ordinary resolution of the company.

CAPITALISATION OF PROFITS

110. The directors may with the authority of an ordinary resolution of the company –

(a) subject as hereinafter provided, resolve to capitalise any undivided profits of the company not required for paying any preferential dividend (whether or not they are available for distribution) or any sum standing to the credit of the company's share premium account or capital redemption reserve;

(b) appropriate the sum resolved to be capitalised to the members who would have been entitled to it if it were distributed by way of dividend and in the same proportions and apply such sum on their behalf either in or towards paying up the amounts, if any, for the time being unpaid on any shares held by them respectively, or in paying up in full unissued shares or debentures of the company of a nominal amount equal to that sum, and allot the shares or debentures credited as fully paid to those members, or as they may direct, in those proportions, or partly in one way and partly in the other: but the share premium account, the capital redemption reserve, and any profits which are not available for distribution may, for the purposes of this regulation, only be applied in paying up unissued shares to be allotted to members credited as fully paid;

(c) make such provision by the issue of fractional certificates or by payment in cash or otherwise as they determine in the case of shares or debentures becoming distributable under this regulation in fractions; and

(d) authorise any person to enter on behalf of all the members concerned into an agreement with the company providing for the allotment to them respectively, credited as fully paid, of any shares or debentures to which they are entitled upon such capitalisation, any agreement made under such authority being binding on all such members.

NOTICES

111. Any notice to be given to or by any person pursuant to the articles shall be in writing except that a notice calling a meeting of the directors need not be in writing.

112. The company may give any notice to a member either personally or by sending it by post in a prepaid envelope addressed to the member at his registered address or by leaving it at that address. In the case of joint holders of a share, all notices shall be given to the joint holder whose name stands first in the register of members in respect of the joint holding and notice so given shall be sufficient notice to all the joint holders. A member whose registered address is not within the United Kingdom and who gives to the company an address within the United Kingdom at which notices may be given to him shall be entitled to have notices given to him at that address, but otherwise no such member shall be entitled to receive any notice from the company.

113. A member present, either in person or by proxy, at any meeting of the company or of the holders of any class of shares in the company shall be deemed to have received notice of the meeting and, where requisite, of the purposes for which it was called.

114. Every person who becomes entitled to a share shall be bound by any notice in respect of that share which, before his name is entered in the register of members, has been duly given to a person from whom he derives his title.

115. Proof that an envelope containing a notice was properly addressed, prepaid and posted shall be conclusive evidence that the notice was given. A notice shall, . . . be deemed to be given at the expiration of 48 hours after the envelope containing it was posted.

116. A notice may be given by the company to the persons entitled to a share in consequence of the death or bankruptcy of a member by sending or delivering it, in any manner authorised by the articles for the giving of notice to a member, addressed to them by name, or by the title of representatives of the deceased, or trustee of the bankrupt or by any like description at the address, if any, within the United Kingdom supplied for that purpose by the persons claiming to be so entitled. Until such an address has been supplied, a notice may be given in any manner in which it might have been given if the death or bankruptcy had not occurred.

WINDING-UP

117. If the company is wound up, the liquidator may, with the sanction of an extraordinary resolution of the company and any other sanction required by the Act, divide among the members *in specie* the whole or any part of the assets of the company and may, for that purpose, value any assets and determine how the division shall be carried out as between the members or different classes of members. The liquidator may, with the like sanction, vest the whole or any part of the assets in trustees upon such trusts for the benefit of the members as he with the like sanction determines, but no member shall be compelled to accept any assets upon which there is a liability.

INDEMNITY

118. Subject to the provisions of the Act but without prejudice to any indemnity to which a director may otherwise be entitled, every director or other officer or auditor of the company shall be indemnified out of the assets of the company against any liability incurred by him in defending any proceedings, whether civil or criminal, in which judgment is given in his favour or in which he is acquitted or in connection with any application in which relief is granted to him by the court from liability for negligence, default, breach of duty or breach of trust in relation to the affairs of the company.

Exercises

1. Which legal provisions assist shareholders to gain control over the management and which militate against this?

2. Should employees have a say in the running of a company?

Chapter 11

Directors' duties:
the general duties

Key words

> ▶ **Fiduciary duties** – duties which are strict because they reflect the powerful position of directors who have full legal powers to deal with other people's property.

A director of a company will often be dealing with other people's property, not only in the legal sense in that he will be in charge of the property of the company, but also the company may have shareholders who have put money into the company by buying shares but have little or no control over what the directors do. Their investment will be lost if the company becomes insolvent. Also, if goods or services are supplied to a company on credit, the directors will be dealing with money to which the creditors have a claim until they are paid in full. It is obviously necessary to control the behaviour of someone in such a position of power and to impose upon him a standard of conduct which will protect people who stand to lose if the director is either incompetent or dishonest. There are three major difficulties in imposing such a standard.

1. Directors vary very considerably in the extent of their involvement with a company. It is now becoming recognised practice to separate the members of a board of directors into 'executive' and 'non-executive' members. The executive directors will be very closely involved with the day-to-day affairs of the company and the amount of knowledge that they might be expected to have about the internal affairs of the company will far exceed that of the non-executive members, whose job is to take an overall view of the running of the company, lend what expertise they have to the making of policy decisions, and sound warning bells if anything suspicious comes to their notice. This separation was not common practice in the past and is by no means universal now. The law has sought to impose a standard of conduct on all directors regardless of their degree of involvement with the company. To formulate a standard of conduct which would be fair to all types of director has proved difficult.

2. Not only are there different types of director, there are also different types of company. Companies vary from huge multinational giants such as ICI to small family businesses run by one person (though they must have two shareholders unless they are a designated 'single member company', see Chapter 1) which have decided that the business could be best managed in corporate form. This huge difference in the size and complexity of companies has also caused difficulty in formulating a standard by which the performance of all company directors can be judged. There has been considerable reluctance, until recent legislation (much of it EC Directive-driven), to attempt to impose different director's duties depending on the type of his company. Now, in statutes, the distinction is often drawn between directors of public companies and directors of private companies. This distinction is sometimes criticised because there can be large and complex private companies as well as small and relatively simple public companies. Nevertheless, if a distinction is to be made, no distinction would ever be wholly satisfactory and the public/private distinction seems to work as well as any would.

The case law in this area is still very important. In the case law on directors' duties no formal distinction is normally made between different types of companies. Rather, the cases impose a sliding scale of responsibility which depends on what can reasonably be expected of someone in that position. A complex body of both case and statute law has grown up. Not all of it is satisfactory, as we will see.

3. The third difficulty in formulating a standard of behaviour for directors is to be found in the nature of the decisions that they make. Most of these decisions will be business decisions about which contracts it would be best for the company to enter into. It is very difficult for a court of law looking at events with hindsight to judge whether that decision was commercially foolish at the time it was made. It may have turned out badly for the company but that may be because of factors which could not be foreseen by the directors when the decision was made. The courts do not wish to encourage directors to become too cautious by imposing too high a duty of care. They must therefore respect decisions which they believe were made in good faith even though they may have been commercially disastrous for the company as things turned out. The difference in the sizes and complexity of companies and the differences in the degree of involvement of the directors in question, coupled with the unique economic circumstances surrounding each decision, make it difficult for the court to build up a body of precedents. This is unlike judging the performance of other professions where often similarly qualified persons have had similar decisions to make.

11.1 The Cadbury, Hampel and Combined Code initiatives

In response to a number of financial scandals a committee chaired by Sir Adrian Cadbury was set up in May 1991. Its function was to make recommendations aimed at tightening corporate control mechanisms. The Committee focused on financial control mechanisms, particularly the Board of Directors, auditing and shareholder responsibility. The Committee published its final report in December 1992. The Committee's central recommendation was that the Boards of all listed companies registered in the UK should comply with a Code of Best Practice. Smaller listed companies, who could not comply with the Code immediately, would have to give their reasons for non-compliance as an alternative (p. 19, para. 3.15).

The Committee were of the opinion that compliance with the Code as a listing requirement would ensure an open approach to the disclosure of information, contribute to the efficient working of the market economy, prompt boards to take effective action and allow shareholders to scrutinise companies more thoroughly (p. 19, para. 3.15). The make-up and function of the Board was by far the most controversial area. The Committee emphasised that tests of a Board's effectiveness included the way in which members as a whole work together (p. 20, para. 4.2). They also felt that executive and non-executive directors were likely to contribute in different and complementary ways. Non-executive directors could make two particularly important contributions which would not conflict with the unitary nature of the board (p. 20, para. 4.5). These were the role of 'reviewing' the performance of the board and executive (p. 20, para. 4.5) and taking the lead 'where potential conflicts of interest arise' (p. 21, para. 4.6).

The Committee emphasised the need for the financial audit of companies to be tighter but made no very radical recommendations as to how this should be achieved. The proper scope of auditor liability is clearly a nettle which the Cadbury Committee failed to grasp and should continue to be the subject of lively debate.

The Committee had very little to say about private individual shareholders and focused on the perceived power of institutional shareholders to ensure that the company complied with the Code. In response to the draft report issued by the Cadbury Committee for comment, the Institutional Shareholders Committee submitted a paper addressing 'The Responsibilities of Institutional Shareholders'. This was not a specific response to the Cadbury proposals but dealt with some of the issues raised in the draft report. The Institutional Shareholders Committee acknowledged that: 'Because of the size of their shareholdings, institutional investors, as part proprietors of a company, are under a strong obligation to exercise their influence in a responsible manner.' The paper (published in December 1991) examined ways in which this responsibility should be fulfilled including 'regular, systematic contact at senior executive level to exchange views and information on strategy, performance, Board Membership and quality of management'. The Commission also felt that institutional investors 'should support Boards by a positive use of voting rights, unless they have good reason for doing otherwise' and:

'should take a positive interest in the composition of Boards of Directors with particular reference to:
(i) concentrations of decision-making power not formally constrained by checks and balances appropriate to the particular company,
(ii) the appointment of a core of non-executives of appropriate calibre, experience and independence.'

The Cadbury Committee clearly accepted these views and placed heavy reliance on the power of institutional shareholders within a company.

The Cadbury Committee's recommendations have drawn considerable criticism. The voluntary nature of the Code has been attacked, but so too has the Stock Exchange's attempt to give the Code some teeth. The major criticism that has surfaced is that the reliance on non-executive directors leads to a type of two-tier board with different directors fulfilling different functions. This criticism must be viewed in the light of a proper understanding of the two-tier board system as it operates elsewhere in Europe. It often includes provision for a supervisory board which has the power to dismiss the executive board. The Cadbury proposals do not go very far towards that system; there is no suggestion that appointment and dismissal of all directors should be removed from shareholder control.

A follow-up committee, the Hampel Committee, considered wider issues of corporate governance and, despite some alarm at the 'box-ticking' approach to compliance with the Cadbury recommendations, was widely in agreement with its proposals. Following the Hampel report, a 'Combined Code' has been implemented by the London Stock Exchange. All listed companies are obliged to comply with the Combined Code or give reasons for not doing so. An important part of the Combined Code is the requirement of a 'sound system of internal control' to manage 'significant risks'. The board must consider:

(1) the nature and extent of the risks facing the company;
(2) the likelihood of the risks materialising;
(3) the company's ability to reduce the impact of such risks if they do materialise;
(4) costs relative to benefits.

The Code also contains rules relating to directors' remuneration and the way in which it is calculated. Companies must state that they have complied with the Combined Code or give reasons for divergences from it.

11.2   Duty owed to the company

It is important to remember that directors owe their duties to that legal person 'the company' rather than to shareholders or potential shareholders. This is particularly significant where the enforcement of those duties is in question, because the general rule is that directors' duties can only be enforced by the company suing directors (see further discussion on the effect of this rule in Chapter 13). The principle can be illustrated by the facts of *Percival v. Wright* [1902] 2 Ch 421. In that case, shareholders wrote to the secretary of a company asking if he knew anyone likely to buy their shares. The chairman and two other directors purchased the shares at £2 10s [£2.50p] per share. The shareholders subsequently discovered that prior to the negotiations for the sale of the shares the chairman and directors had been approached by a third party. The third party wished to purchase the company and was offering a price which would mean that each share would be valued at well over £2 10s. The shareholders asked for the sale of the shares to be set aside by the court on the grounds that the chairman and directors had been in breach of a duty to the shareholders.

Swinfen-Eady J refused to set aside the sale and firmly rejected the idea that there was any duty owed by the chairman and directors to the shareholders. Their duties were owed to the company. This situation may well now be caught by the s. 459 remedy (see Chapter 13). However, the fundamental principle that directors owe their duty to the company is unchanged. This principle may cause difficulties where there are several companies acting as a group. Normally one company is seen as the 'parent' company and will hold a majority of the shares in its subsidiary companies. The exact relationship between parent and subsidiary is discussed elsewhere (see Chapters 1 and 10). In these circumstances directors may be appointed to the board of the subsidiary by the parent company. It is very tempting for them to look after the interests of the parent company and ignore the interests of the subsidiary. That they must not do so is clearly illustrated by the case of *Scottish Co-operative Wholesale Society Ltd* v. *Meyer* [1959] AC 324 where Lord Denning emphasised that the duty of directors was owed to the particular company which had appointed them (see Case note 1, p. 213).

This is another area of law where reform is being actively considered. Many companies do act with group interests in mind and it seems sensible to bring the law more into accord with commercial practice.

11.3 What is the company?

In Chapters 2 and 3 various different models of companies were described. The model chosen makes a difference to the way in which directors exercise their duties to the company, because the interests which are seen as making up the company vary with the model chosen. To say that the directors owe a duty to the company is clear, but it makes no sense if the company is regarded as a legal personality or piece of paper alone. The directors must take note of the interests of the human beings who are actively involved in the company's affairs. Which persons are entitled to have their interests regarded?

1. Members

Clearly the members' interests are of very considerable importance although that also raises the problem of whether a dissenting minority of members have a right to have their interests considered. This question is considered in more detail in the chapter concerning shareholders' rights (Chapter 13) and in the chapter where alteration of the articles of association and the 'bona fide' test are considered (Chapter 5).

2. Employees

By s. 172 Companies Act 2006, company directors are 'to have regard' to the interests of employees as well as the interests of members. However, this duty to have regard to employees' interests is expressed to be part of the general duty owed by directors to the company. It can only therefore be enforced by the company. The employees would have no standing to complain to the court that their interests had not been considered. This duty has no enforcing teeth and can be seen as mere 'window dressing'.

3. Creditors

Creditors also have their money tied up in the company. It is logical to expect their interests to be important to the directors in making a decision and s. 172 Companies Act 2006 does so. In *Lonrho* v. *Shell Petroleum* [1980] 1 WLR 627 this factor was acknowledged by Lord Diplock, who said: 'it is the duty of the board to consider . . . the best interests of the company. These are not exclusively those of its shareholders but may include those of its creditors' (p. 634).

The Court of Appeal confirmed this view in *The Liquidator of the Property of West Mercia Safetywear Ltd* v. *Dodd and Another* [1988] BCLC 250. However, in that case the interests of the company were said to include the interests of creditors because the company was insolvent at the relevant time. In *Lonrho* insolvency was not an issue. Nor was insolvency an issue in

Winkworth v. *Edward Baron* [1987] BCLC 193 where Lord Templeman referred to a duty owed directly to creditors. In *Brady* v. *Brady* [1989] 1 AC 755, Nourse LJ regarded the interests of the company as synonymous with the interests of the creditors where the company was insolvent or 'doubtfully solvent'. It seems clear:

(1) Where the company is insolvent the interests of creditors and the interests of the company coincide to a considerable degree (see *Standard Charted Bank* v. *Walker* [1992] 1 WLR 561).

(2) Where a company is approaching insolvency the interests of the creditors are important where an assessment is made of whether the directors acted in the interests of the company. (What is not clear is precisely at what stage in the slide into insolvency the creditors' interests become paramount or what test is to be applied to determine the directors' appreciation of the insolvency. If they ought to have known of the insolvency but did not, are they still liable? The cases provide no clear answer. See further on this, Vanessa Finch, *Company Lawyer*, vol. 10, no. 1, p. 23.)

(3) In the case of a solvent company the interests of creditors should still be considered but it is unclear what weight the directors should give to consideration of those interests.

In *Modern Company Law for a Competitive Economy: Developing the Framework* (March 2000), the DTI Company Law Review Committee proposed an 'inclusive approach' to the issue 'in whose interests should the company be run?', arguing that 'the overall objective of wealth generation and competitiveness for the benefit of all' can best be achieved through a duty on directors requiring them to have regard to the long- and short-term interests of the company and 'all the relationships on which the company depends'. This formula contains unworkable contradictions which are only partly solved by the fact that the aim is stated as 'achieving company success for the benefit of shareholders as a whole'. It seems clear that shareholders are still to be viewed as the paramount interest but, as we have discussed, long- and short-term interests may well be wholly at odds with each other; there is no such thing as 'shareholders as a whole'.

Nevertheless this approach was enacted. The Companies Act 2006 also contains a somewhat mysterious reference to the pre-existing law. Thus ss. 170(3) and 170(4) read as follows:

'(3) The general duties are based on certain common law rules and equitable principles as they apply in relation to directors and have effect in place of those rules and principles as regards the duties owed to a company by a director.

(4) The general duties shall be interpreted and applied in the same way as common law rules or equitable principles, and regard shall be had to the corresponding common law rules and equitable principles in interpreting and applying the general duties.'

These subsections indicate that the common law rules developed by the courts will be of considerable significance in interpreting the statutory rules. However, the extent to which the statutory rules change the common law is less clear and will need to be developed by the courts on a case-by-case basis. The text of this chapter looks at the statute and the common law rules together to try and give an indication of likely interpretations. The common law duties were divided into 'fiduciary' duties, which reflected the position of the director as a guardian of the interests of the company and those concerned in it (principally the shareholders), and duties of care and skill. The statute follows a similar layout with a separate section setting out the 'duty to act with reasonable care, skill and diligence'. As this is perhaps the easiest to understand we will start with this duty.

More specific duties of directors are covered in Chapter 12.

11.4 Duties of care and skill

The difference in the degree of involvement of directors can be well illustrated by the facts of the old case known as *The Marquis of Bute's Case* [1892] 2 Ch 100.

The Marquis of Bute became president of the Cardiff Savings Bank when he was six months old, having inherited the office from his father. He attended only one board meeting of the bank in 38 years. However, he was held not liable for irregularities which occurred in the lending operations of the bank. The judge held that he could not be considered liable as he knew nothing about what was going on. There was no hint that he ought to have kept himself informed.

Similarly, in *Dovey* v. *Cory* [1901] AC 477 the director was able to escape liability for malpractice which had occurred, on the grounds that he had relied on information given to him by the chairman and general manager of the company. The standard applied here seems to be somewhat stricter than that in *The Marquis of Bute's Case* since the court held that the reliance on the chairman and general manager was *reasonable* and that the director had not been *negligent*. The standard in this case was one of negligence, that is, the director must have acted as a reasonable man. If a reasonable man would have been suspicious of the information that was given and would have investigated further, a director who failed to do so could well have been liable for the loss caused by the irregularity. This may well be a higher standard than that imposed in the previous case where there seems to be no suggestion that a 'reasonable man' test should be used to judge the Marquis's inaction.

A case in which these issues were fully explored is *Re City Equitable Fire Insurance* [1925] Ch 407. That case is still generally regarded as important in this area although the courts have moved away from the subjective standards imposed in *Re City Equitable Fire Insurance* to a more objective standard (see below).

In *Re City Equitable Fire Insurance* the judge set out three important rules:

(1) A director need not exhibit in the performance of his duties a greater degree of skill than may reasonably be expected from a person of his knowledge and experience.
(2) A director is not bound to give continuous attention to the affairs of his company. His duties are of an intermittent nature to be performed at periodical board meetings and at meetings of any committee of the board on which he happens to be placed. He is not, however, bound to attend all such meetings, though he ought to attend whenever in the circumstances he is reasonably able to do so.
(3) In respect of all duties that, having regard to the exigencies of business and the articles of association, may properly be left to some other official, a director is, in the absence of grounds for suspicion, justified in trusting that official to perform such duties honestly.

These rules were affirmed in *Dorchester Finance Co. Ltd* v. *Stebbing* [1989] BCLC 498 where it was also held that there was no difference in the duties owed by executive and non-executive directors.

Notable aspects of these rules are:

Rule 1

The standard is not a 'reasonable professional director' standard but refers to the reasonable man with the skill and experience actually possessed by the particular director in question. This has two effects. If someone like the baby Marquis of Bute is appointed to the board of a company he will presumably be held not liable for irregularities, as a small baby has extremely limited skill and experience. This may be fair from the baby's point of view but the standard does little to protect the public. However, leaving such extreme examples aside, the standard is capable of working quite well and of having sufficient flexibility to be valuable in different types of companies for judging the behaviour of different types of directors. Larger and more complex businesses are more likely to employ highly qualified and experienced directors to run affairs. Under the test in Rule 1 such people will have a higher standard of skill expected of them. Thus the more complex the operation, the more the interests of those with money at stake will be protected. The test is therefore only seriously inadequate where a very inappropriate appointment has been made, whether the operation is large or small.

Rule 2

Similar considerations apply to Rule 2, since the duty is to attend meetings and give attention to company affairs 'whenever in the circumstances [the director] is reasonably able to do so'. In the case of a full-time salaried director of a large company it is obviously reasonable to expect his working life to be devoted to the affairs of the company. The standard will vary to take into account different types of director so that a non-executive director will not be bound to give the affairs of the company so much of his time as would an executive director.

Rule 3

At first sight this seems to benefit a director who absents himself or who fails to keep himself informed on company matters so that he will not be aware of any 'grounds for suspicion' and so can safely leave the running of the company to others. However, if this rule is taken in conjunction with the other two rules, it will be seen that the director is obliged (by Rules 1 and 2) to take proper part in the affairs of the company so that unless his appointment has been manifestly foolish (as in the case of the baby Marquis), the rules will work together to provide a sliding scale of responsibility which will weigh heaviest on those most able to do the job, and whose expectations of reward from the job are probably highest.

In extreme cases, however, the rules will not protect those with money at stake. For many years there has been a call for an objective standard of competence to be imposed so that directors could not do the job if they were dishonest or foolish (or six months old). The DTI Company Law Review Committee accepted that an objective standard has been adopted into the general law by analogy with s. 214 Insolvency Act 1986 (see *Modern Company Law for a Competitive Economy: Developing the Framework*, March 2000). In *Re D'Jan of London Ltd* [1993] BCC 646 Hoffman LJ stated that the common law duty of care owed by directors was accurately stated in s. 214 Insolvency Act 1986. The 2006 Companies Act adopts this objective standard. Section 174 reads:

'**Duty to exercise reasonable care, skill and diligence**
(1) A director of a company must exercise reasonable care, skill and diligence.
(2) This means the care, skill and diligence that would be exercised by a reasonably diligent person with –

(a) the general knowledge, skill and experience that may reasonably be expected of a person carrying out the functions carried out by the director in relation to the company, and

(b) the general knowledge, skill and experience that the director has.'

This means that there is a base level of reasonable expectation which appears to be related to the type of company in which the director finds himself and so imports some of the flexibility of *Re City Equitable Fire Insurance* but, where the director is particularly experienced, he will not be permitted to perform to a lower standard. An example might be if an executive director of a large Plc retires and takes a directorship in a small family firm. He would be expected to perform to a high standard because of his past experience.

The statute strikes a good balance, as imposition of too high a standard might pose the same problems as have been experienced in the USA, where the imposition of huge liabilities on the board of directors for negligence (see *Smith* v. *Van Gorkom* [1985] 488 A.2d 858 (Supreme Court of Delaware 1985) – see Case note **2**, pp. 213–4) has led to the adoption by a number of States of legislation permitting the elimination of the liability of directors for various breaches of duty. The imposition of liability for negligence proved too strict in view of the huge sums of money involved and led to a distinct reluctance to join boards as non-executive (outside) directors.

An example of such a law is Delaware Corporation Law s. 102(b)(7) which was adopted on 1 July 1986 and reads:

'the certificate of incorporation may also contain any or all of the following matters:

(7) A provision eliminating or limiting the personal liability of a director to the corporation or its stockholders for monetary damages for breach of fiduciary duty as director, provided that such provision shall not eliminate or limit the liability of a director, (i) for any breach of the director's duty of loyalty to the corporation or its stockholders; (ii) for acts or omissions not in good faith or which involve intentional misconduct or knowing violation of the law; (iii) under s. 174 of this title [relating to limitations on distributions to stockholders]; or (iv) for any transaction from which the directors derived an improper personal benefit. No such provision shall eliminate or limit the liability of a director for any act or omission occurring prior to the date when such provision became effective . . .'

In English law the excuse of incompetence is clearly unavailable, however one aspect of company law that always influences the standard imposed on directors in practice is the means of enforcing the duties that are owed. More will be said on this matter in Chapter 13, but it should always be borne in mind that there is no point in imposing a duty on someone if there are no effective means of enforcing that duty.

Hot Topic . . .

PERFORMANCE OF COMPANIES AND GOVERNMENT DEPARTMENTS (REPORTING) BILL 2004 (2)

Section 172 Companies Act 2006:

'Duty to promote the success of the company

(1) A director of a company must act in the way he considers, in good faith, would be most likely to promote the success of the company for the benefit of its members as a whole, and in doing so have regard (amongst other matters) to –

(a) the likely consequences of any decision in the long term,

(b) the interests of the company's employees,

(c) the need to foster the company's business relationships with suppliers, customers and others,

(d) the impact of the company's operations on the community and the environment,

(e) the desirability of the company maintaining a reputation for high standards of business conduct, and

(f) the need to act fairly as between members of the company.

(2) Where or to the extent that the purposes of the company consist of or include purposes other than

the benefit of its members, subsection (1) has effect as if the reference to promoting the success of the company for the benefit of its members were to achieving those purposes.

(3) The duty imposed by this section has effect subject to any enactment or rule of law requiring directors, in certain circumstances, to consider or act in the interests of creditors of the company.'

Compare this with the provisions of a Bill which preceded the Companies Act 2006 but which was never passed. Which do you think is the better approach?

As a result of the DTI Review a Performance of Companies and Government Departments (Reporting) Bill 2004 was presented to Parliament.

Directors' duties

Section 8 requires that:

'A director of a company must act in accordance with –

(a) the company's constitution, and

(b) decisions taken under the constitution (or by the company, or any class of members, under any enactment or rule of law as to means of taking company or class decisions),

and must exercise his powers for their proper purpose.'

Section 9 reads:

'Promotion of company's objectives

(1) A director of a company must in any given case –

(a) act in the way he decides, in good faith, would be most likely to promote the success of the company for the benefit of its members as a whole (excluding anything which would breach his duty under section 8);

(b) in deciding what would be most likely to promote that success, take account in good faith of all the material factors that it is practicable in the circumstances for him to identify; and

(c) take all reasonable steps to minimise the impact of the company's impact on the communities it affects and on the environment.

(2) In this section 'the material factors' means –

(a) the likely consequences (short and long term) of the actions open to the director, so far as a person of care and skill would consider relevant; and

(b) all such other factors as a person of care and skill would consider relevant, including such of the matters in subsection (3) below as he would consider so.

(3) Those matters are –
  (a) the company's need to foster its business relationships, including those with its employees and suppliers and the customers for its products or services;
  (b) its need to have regard to the impact of its operations on the communities affected and on the environment;
  (c) its need to maintain a reputation for high standards of business conduct; and
  (d) its need to achieve outcomes that are fair as between its members.

(4) In subsection (2) a 'person of care and skill' means a person exercising the care, skill and diligence required by section 11. (See p. 212.)

(5) A director's decision as to what constitutes the success of the company for the benefit of its members as a whole must accord with the constitution and any decision mentioned in section 8.'

11.5 Fiduciary duties

It was traditional under the common law to give a list of the breaches of fiduciary duties of directors under headings such as: misappropriation of company property; exercise of powers for an improper purpose; fettering discretion; and permitting interest and duty to conflict. While no one would dispute that these are all areas where directors have been found to be in breach of duty, the listing of the duties in this way tended to obscure the fundamental point that a director is under one overriding duty and that is to act *bona fide* in the interests of the company. The list of duties that grew out of the case law was in fact a list of situations where a director is most likely to be in breach of his fundamental duty. Thus, for example, if a director finds himself in a position where he has a conflict of interests he is in dire peril of being found to be in breach of his overriding duty to act *bona fide* for the benefit of the company. The Companies Act 2006 seems to partially accept this reasoning by articulating a general duty to promote the success of the company. However, the statute also sets out a list of other duties which are formulations of the pre-existing case law. The duty to promote the interests of the company is not separate from the list of duties, nor is it the first duty to be mentioned. Although it appears to be an overriding duty it is not obviously identified as such. It will be interesting to discover what the courts make of the legislation in this respect. Regarding all duties as on the same level tends to obscure the debate about the possibility that behaviour that does come under one of these headings can be excused by the company voting to that effect in general meeting. It is difficult to accept the ratification (excusing) of something which is the breach of a fundamental duty. It is easier to see how, if a director places himself in one of the perilous situations, but his behaviour has not breached the fundamental duty of *bona fides*, such behaviour may be regarded as acceptable by the company. Behaviour which is not *bona fide* for the benefit of the company cannot be condoned unless 'the company' (in the wide sense explained above – members, creditors and possibly employees) agree. Thus, where sole shareholders and directors took money from a company, this was nevertheless held to be theft despite the fact that they clearly had the agreement of all the members (themselves) to do so (*Re Attorney-General's Reference (No. 2 of 1982)* [1984] 2 WLR 447; and *R v. Phillipou* [1989] Crim LR 559 and 585). These cases were affirmed by the House of Lords in *R v. Gomez* [1992] 3 WLR 1067. The distinction between the overriding duty of good faith and the effect of putting oneself in one of the perilous situations varies with the seriousness with which the particular behaviour is viewed. Thus, it will be a most unusual situation where there has been a 'misappropriation of company property' but the directors can nevertheless be held to have acted *bona fide* for the benefit of the company and therefore can be excused by a majority of shareholders against the wishes of the minority. As we have seen, where dishonesty is proved, not even the unanimous consent of the shareholders will suffice to excuse the behaviour. However, where there is much more equivocal behaviour, such as using powers given for one purpose to achieve a different object, it is much easier for the court to accept that the directors are acting *bona fide* and thus may be excused by the company. The duty which appears to be a fundamental one appears at s. 172:

'Duty to promote the success of the company
(1) A director of a company must act in the way he considers, in good faith, would be most likely to promote the success of the company for the benefit of its members as a whole and in doing so have regard (amongst other matters) to –
(a) the likely consequences of any decision in the long term,
(b) the interests of the company's employees,
(c) the need to foster the company's business relationships with suppliers, customers and others,
(d) the impact of the company's operations on the community and the environment,
(e) the desirability of the company maintaining a reputation for high standards of business conduct, and
(f) the need to act fairly as between members of the company.
(2) Where or to the extent that the purposes of the company consist of or include purposes other than the benefit of the members, subsection (1) has effect as if the reference to promoting the success of the company for the benefit of its members were to achieving those purposes.
(3) The duty imposed by this section has effect subject to any enactment or rule of law requiring directors, in certain circumstances, to consider or act in the interests of creditors of the company.'

The purport of subsection (3) is to save the law explained above at p. 190. The impact of the remainder of the section is unclear. It was argued in

Chapter 10 that the new formulation in relation to employees may be weaker than that provided by s. 309 Companies Act 1985 because of the explicit primacy of members' interests. What is very clear is that this is not a 'stakeholder' or 'pluralist' formulation of the company. Directors are required only to consider the listed matters in so far as they benefit the shareholders.

11.6 Are the prohibitions absolute?

We have seen already that the answer to this question is 'no'. The behaviour may be forgiven by the company with a varying degree of ease depending on how serious a view the court takes of it. The behaviour can be ratified under s. 239 Companies Act 2006 and the statutory statement regarding ratification retains the common law uncertainty about the limits of ratification. Section 239(7) states that:

> 'This section does not affect any other enactment or rule of law imposing additional requirements for valid ratification or any rule of law as to acts that are incapable of being ratified by the company.'

At common law, breaches such as use of powers for an improper purpose were regarded as unlikely to breach the *bona fide* rule and could normally be condoned by a majority of the general meeting. At the other end of the scale, theft or fraud could not be condoned unless all those affected agreed to the behaviour.

A further point to note under this head is that the prohibitions may themselves be redefined by the company in advance. This clearly points to the difference between the fundamental duty and the prohibitions or disabilities as they were called in one case (*Movitex Ltd* v. *Bulfield and Others* [1988] BCLC 104). It would be unthinkable for the court to permit an insertion in the articles of a clause allowing the directors to act in bad faith against the interests of the company. The courts have, however, permitted the articles of association to remove or redefine what would otherwise be disabilities or prohibitions.

An example of the way the system works is to be found in *Movitex Ltd* v. *Bulfield and Others* [1988] BCLC 104. There it was held that the true explanation of what was urged by counsel for the company to be the 'self-dealing' duty, or in other words the duty not to allow oneself to be in a position where duty and interest conflict, was that a director was, because of his position, unable (under a disability) to act in certain ways, because it was likely that his behaviour would be seen as a breach of his fundamental duty of good faith. The company could agree in advance that certain types of behaviour would not automatically be regarded as breach of the fundamental duty. Thus the articles (which allowed self-dealing transactions in certain circumstances) had not exempted the directors from a duty, they had relieved the director from a prohibition or disability he would normally be under. This rule is variously reflected in the statute in relation to each of the listed duties.

11.7 The categories of duties

The other duties listed in Companies Act 2006 (see Case note 5, pp. 215–18) are:

(1) Duty to act within powers
(2) Duty to exercise independent judgment
(3) Duty to avoid conflicts of interest
(4) Duty to declare interest in proposed transaction or arrangement
(5) Duty not to accept benefits from third parties.

(1) Duty to act within powers

This has two aspects. Section 171 states:

'A director of a company must –
(a) act in accordance with the company's constitution, and
(b) only exercise powers for the purpose for which they are conferred.'

We have seen that the consequence of acting outside the constitution will not affect third parties (see Chapter 6). The courts also decided that certain of the powers of directors were given to them for a particular purpose. If the directors use them to achieve a different object the court will intervene to prevent this, if they are requested to do so. This is one area, however, where the courts are very often happy to permit the majority to excuse the action of the directors, so that this is perhaps an area where a director is in the least danger of being found to be in breach of his fundamental duty. A good example is the power to issue shares. The courts have determined that where directors have this power the purpose for which it was bestowed was to raise capital. It is a power which can easily be used to fend off a takeover or to prevent themselves from being removed from office. This can be done by diluting the voting capacity of a hostile element of shareholders by the issue of new shares. *Punt* v. *Symonds & Co.* [1903] 2 Ch 506 and *Piercy* v. *S. Mills & Co. Ltd* [1920] 1 Ch 77 (see Case notes 3 and 4, pp. 214–15) are good examples of this type of manoeuvring. A slightly more complicated problem arose in the case of *Howard Smith Ltd* v. *Ampol Petroleum Ltd* [1974] AC 821. In that case a company was threatened with a takeover by two associates who between them held 55 per cent of the company's shares. The company needed more capital but proposed to obtain it by issuing over four million shares to members other than the takeover bidders. This allotment would have reduced the takeover bidders to a minority in the company and was held to be a misuse of the directors' powers. The case was complicated by the fact that the issue had been made for two purposes: to raise capital (the proper purpose) and to defeat the takeover (an improper purpose). The court reached the conclusion that directors would be acting within their powers if the dominant or substantial purpose of the exercise of those powers was proper. Lord Wilberforce, giving the advice of the Privy Council, said:

'In their Lordship's opinion it is necessary to start with a consideration of the powers whose exercise is in question . . . Having ascertained, on a fair view, the nature of this power, and having defined as can best be done in the light of modern conditions the, or some, limits within which it may be exercised, it is then necessary for the court, if a particular exercise of it is challenged, to examine the substantial purpose for which it was exercised, and to reach a conclusion whether that purpose was proper or not. In doing so it will be necessary to give credit to the *bona fide* opinion of the directors, if such is found to exist, and will respect their judgment as to matters of management; having done this, the ultimate conclusion has to be as to the side of a fairly broad line on which the case falls.' (p. 835)

Lord Wilberforce also emphasised that the court would not simply accept a statement by directors that they acted for a particular purpose. He said:

'[When] a dispute arises whether directors of a company made a particular decision for one purpose or another, or whether, there being more than one purpose, one or another purpose was the substantial or primary purpose, the court, in their Lordships' opinion, is entitled to look at the situation objectively in order to estimate how critical or pressing, or substantial or, *per contra*, insubstantial an alleged requirement may have been. If it finds that a particular requirement, though real, was not urgent, or critical, at the relevant time, it may have reason to doubt, or discount, the assertions of individuals that they acted solely in order to deal with it, particularly when the action they took was unusual or even extreme.' (p. 832)

In *Criterion Properties Plc* v. *Stratford UK Properties LLC* [2004] UKHL 28, two companies were parties to a joint venture, which was governed by a partnership agreement. This agreement was accepted as valid and enforceable. In 2000 a supplementary agreement was signed aimed at amending the initial one. The effect of the new supplementary agreement was to protect Stratford UK Properties LLC against a potential takeover and change of management by the introduction of a 'poison pill' device. The second supplementary agreement was signed on behalf of Stratford UK Properties LLC by one of its directors without the approval of the entire board of directors. That managing director had come to an agreement with an important shareholder within the company context that required the company to buy out his shareholding at a high price if there was a change of control in the company or a removal of a director from the board. In April 2001 the managing director was dismissed because the board of directors had learnt for the first time about the existence of the second supplementary agreement. The company also asked the court to set the agreement aside because it was signed for an improper purpose. The agreement according to the claims had not been a proper use of directors' powers and could not be enforced against the company. The agreement had as a result that Stratford UK Properties LLC would have to endure a heavy financial burden in the case of a breach of its terms (that is, in the case of a potential takeover or a removal of a director from the board). Thus, a potential bidder would have been discouraged from trying to acquire it. The House of Lords in this case chose to view the case from a different angle from that of the 'proper purpose' argument and focused more on the argument related to the nature of the authority of the managing director in question who had entered into the agreement on behalf of the company. The agreement would be set aside and the company would not be found bound to that only if the director was not under any authority (actual or ostensible) to sign the agreement. The House stated that in order to resolve this issue the principles relevant to consider are those of agency. The House further recommended that the relevant 'authority' issues should be dealt with at a separate trial, especially in the light of the fact that they were not addressed during the proceedings in the lower courts.

In *Re Looe Fish Ltd* [1993] BCC 368 the failure by a director to exercise the power of allotment of shares for the purpose for which it was conferred led to disqualification under s. 8 Company Directors Disqualification Act 1986. See also *Bishopgate Investment Management (in liquidation)* v. *Maxwell* [1993] BCC 120.

(2) Duty to exercise independent judgment

Section 173 Companies Act 2006 reads:

'(1) A director of a company must exercise independent judgment.
(2) This duty is not infringed by his acting –
   (a) in accordance with an agreement duly entered into by the company that restricts the future exercise of discretion by its directors, or
   (b) in a way authorised by the company's constitution.'

This is a statutory restatement of the common law which prevented a director from 'fettering his discretion', which was probably merely another way in which directors have an interest in conflict with their duty to the company. If they bind themselves by agreement to act in a particular way they have a personal interest in fulfilling that engagement. This is in conflict with their duty to be able to act always in the best interests of the company. The issue was discussed in *Fulham Football Club and Others* v. *Cabra Estates Plc* [1994] 1 BCLC 363. In that case the directors of Fulham Football Club (the company) agreed with the respondents to support planning applications for the development of land leased by the company and oppose different plans proposed by the local council. Large sums of money were paid to the company as a result of that agreement. A number of planning applications failed and enquiries were held, and the issue in the case was whether the undertakings by the directors applied to new planning applications by the respondents and others, whether the undertakings had been improper in fettering the discretion of the directors and whether the agreement was subject to an implied term that the directors would not be required to do anything contrary to their fiduciary duties. The Court of Appeal held that the agreement was valid, was not an improper fettering of discretion and was not subject to the suggested implied term. The company had gained substantially from the agreement. The test to be applied was: 'was the contract as a whole *bona fide* for the benefit of the company?' If it was, then the directors were entitled to bind themselves to do anything necessary to carry it out.

(3) Duty to avoid conflicts of interest

Here the Companies Act 2006 has taken a new approach to two situations which were dealt with together under the case law. Section 175 provides:

'(1) A director of a company must avoid a situation in which he has, or can have, a direct or indirect interest that conflicts, or possibly may conflict, with the interests of the company.

(2) This applies in particular to the exploitation of any property, information or opportunity (and it is immaterial whether the company could take advantage of the property, information or opportunity).

(3) This duty does not apply to a conflict of interest arising in relation to a transaction or arrangement with the company.

(4) This duty is not infringed –
   (a) if the situation cannot reasonably be regarded as likely to give rise to a conflict of interest; or
   (b) if the matter has been authorised by the directors.'

The matter can be authorised by the directors if it is possible under the constitution and the interested director does not vote on the matter.

(4) Duty to declare interest in proposed transaction or arrangement

This covers the situation where the transaction is made between the director and the company before the transaction is made. The declaration must be made to the directors. Note that both duties now continue after a director ceases to hold office.

Section 170 extends the duty:

'(2) A person who ceases to be a director continues to be subject –
   (a) to the duty in section 175 . . . as regards the exploitation of any property, information or opportunity of which he became aware at a time when he was a director, and

(b) to the duty in section 176 . . . as regards things done or omitted to be done by him before he ceased to be a director,

to the extent those duties apply to a former director as to a director, subject to any necessary adaptations.'

This is one area where it is unclear if the statute changes the (already uncertain) case law.

The preceding case law covered various situations where benefits were siphoned away from the company by directors. This may happen in a more sophisticated way than merely taking money from the company. An example is *Menier* v. *Hooper's Telegraph Works* [1874] LR 9 Ch D 350. In that case, Hooper's company was a substantial shareholder in the European Telegraph company and had contracted with it to make and lay a cable to South America under certain concessions granted to the European company by the foreign governments concerned. Menier, a minority shareholder in the European company, claimed that Hooper's company had used its votes to procure the diversion of this business to a third company, to cause the abandonment of proceedings brought by the European company to assert its right to the concessions, and to have the European company wound up. James LJ said:

'Hooper's company have obtained certain advantages by dealing with something which was the property of the whole company. The minority of the shareholders say in effect that the majority has divided the assets of the company, more or less, between themselves, to the exclusion of the minority. I think it would be a shocking thing if that could be done, because if so the majority might divide the whole assets of the company, and pass a resolution that everything must be given to them, and that the minority should have nothing to do with it.'

The court upheld Menier's claim (p. 353).

Similarly, in *Cook* v. *Deeks* [1916] 1 AC 554 the directors of a company were involved in negotiating a series of construction contracts with the Canadian Pacific Railway. The last of the series of contracts was negotiated in the same way as the others, but when the negotiations were complete, the directors took the contracts in their own names. It was held that, because the directors were acting for the company at the time of the negotiations, the benefit of the contracts belonged to the company. The directors could not therefore take the benefit of those contracts for themselves.

Where there is a conflict of interest and duty there is clearly a breach of duty but it remains unclear when such breaches can be ratified. The more serious the courts judge the conflict to be, the less likely are they to permit a majority of the company to ratify the actions of the directors, particularly where there is a dissenting minority.

An example of a situation in which duty and interest can be in conflict is *Scottish Co-operative Wholesale Society Ltd* v. *Meyer* [1959] AC 324 (see Case note 1, p. 213) where three directors were both directors of a parent company and directors of a subsidiary of that parent. As soon as the interests of these two companies conflicted, the directors were unable to fulfil their duty to both companies.

Under case law, the situation where a director contracts with his company was dealt with under the same heading. It is now separate, under s. 176, but the general rule remains, that a director is in peril of being in breach of his overriding duty if he makes a contract in which he has a personal interest with his company. In *Aberdeen Railway Co.* v. *Blaikie Bros* (1854) 1 Macq 461 (HL) Lord Cranworth said:

> 'it is a rule of universal application that no one, having [fiduciary] duties to discharge, shall be allowed to enter into engagements in which he has or can have a personal interest conflicting or which possibly may conflict with the interests of those whom he is bound to protect.'

This rule has been referred to as the 'self-dealing' rule (see *Movitex Ltd* v. *Bulfield and Others* on p. 199). It is by no means absolute and this is an area where the company will readily be able to ratify acts done in breach of the general rule provided there has been sufficient disclosure and the directors are apparently acting honestly. This is also an area where the duty itself can be modified in advance of any action by directors. This can be done by redefining the duties in the articles of association (see *Movitex*, above).

The most difficult area where interest and duty often conflict is where a director is alleged to have profited personally from an opportunity or information which came to him in his capacity as director. A famous case where this type of situation was in issue was *Regal (Hastings) Ltd* v. *Gulliver* [1942] 1 All ER 378.

In that case the directors of the appellant company, which owned a cinema, were anxious to acquire two other cinemas. A subsidiary company was formed for the purpose of acquiring the additional cinemas. Its capital was 5,000 shares with a par value of £1. A lease of two cinemas was offered provided that the subsidiary company's capital was paid up. It was the directors' intention that the appellant company should own all the shares in the subsidiary company. However, the appellant company could only afford to invest £2,000. Accordingly, the directors and the company solicitor each took 500 shares, and three investors found by the chairman also took 500 shares each. Subsequently the shares in the company and the subsidiary were sold, and the new shareholders of the company sought to make the directors, the solicitor and the chairman liable to account to the company for the profit made in respect of the subsidiary company's shares. The House of Lords held that the directors were liable to account to the company for their profit.

It is notable that this is a case where the company was unable to make use of the opportunity, which was then taken advantage of by the directors.

A case in which the principle in *Regal (Hastings)* was applied is *Industrial Developments* v. *Cooley* [1972] 1 WLR 443. In that case the defendant was managing director of the plaintiff company. While serving in that capacity he became aware of information that would have been valuable to the company, but instead of passing it on to the company he kept it to himself. He also obtained his release from the company by dishonest representations and for the purpose of obtaining a lucrative contract for himself. The plaintiff company could not have obtained the contract because the other party to the contract was opposed to the 'set-up' of the plaintiff company and the group of which it was a part. Despite this, and despite the fact that the defendant had made it clear to the other party to the contract that he was dealing with him on a personal basis and not in the capacity of managing director of the plaintiffs, the court held that the defendant must account to the plaintiff company for the profits that had been made from the contract.

Consistent with this line of reasoning the court ruled in *Gencor ACP Ltd* v. *Dalby* [2000] 2 BCLC 734, that a director cannot escape liability on the basis of a defence that his company would not have taken advantage of a particular business opportunity. However, he can escape liability if he manages to obtain the consent of the company's shareholders for his actions.

Similarly, in *CMS Dolphin Ltd* v. *Simonet* [2002] BCC 600, an advertising company claimed that its former managing director was in breach of his fiduciary duty to act *bona fide* for the benefit of the company as a whole and his fidelity duty stemming from his employment contract. The rationale behind the company's claims stemmed from the fact that the director resigned from the company and created a new one to which he transferred the principal clients and business from the company. The court held that the power of the director to resign was not a fiduciary power and that a fiduciary obligation towards the company does not continue to exist and operate beyond the end of the relationship which gave rise to it. The former director of a company is not precluded to release himself from the company and use his personal skill and knowledge to compete with the company. However, the exploitation on the part of the director of a maturing business opportunity of the company was regarded as a misuse of the company's property, in relation to which a fiduciary duty does exist. The director took advantage of information he had access to because of his previous position and status in the company, which he chose to misuse. He, thus, breached his duty to act *bona fide* for the benefit of the company and was personally liable towards the company for the profits he made. In addition to that the director in question was found to be in breach of contract and he gave no notice of his resignation. Therefore, the duties stemming from his contract had continued to exist and the diversion of clients and business to his own company was found to be a breach of them. He was found liable for damages towards the company.

In *Bhullar* v. *Bhullar* [2003] EWCA Civ 424, following a breakdown in the relations of the two families who comprised the company in question, it was decided that no further properties should be bought by the company. One of the directors had subsequently bought property situated next to the company's existing investment properties on his own behalf at a quite advantageous price. The judge found him in breach of his fiduciary duty, although the company did not, because of the circumstances, seek to take advantage of property opportunities at that point. According to the court, the director had brought himself to a situation where his personal interest had conflicted with the duty he owed to the company. By buying this property he had gained a personal interest which can potentially come into conflict with the interests of the company. Thus, interestingly enough, the director was found in breach of duty even if the company could not or would not benefit from the opportunity in question. The latter was found as irrelevant. The issue was that the director had obtained access to information that was very useful from a commercial point of view. He was under a fiduciary duty to communicate it to the company. Whether the company would have acquired the property is irrelevant. What matters is that information relevant to the company was not passed to it by the director in question who was consequently found to be in breach of his duty towards the company and therefore liable to account for his profits. *Cooley* was applied in this case as well.

In *Item Software (UK)* v. *Fassihi* [2004] EWCA Civ 1244, the appellant appealed against a decision which found him to be in a breach of duty. He along with another person (C) were the only directors of a company (A) dealing with distributing software produced by another company (B). The two companies entered formal discussions for the renegotiating of the terms of their co-operation, but the director entered into private talks with B interested in creating his own company. He later encouraged C to change the terms of the contract and subsequently B assumed the decision to terminate it. The company sought damages for a breach of a fiduciary duty and the director was dismissed. The court found the director to be in breach of his duty because he failed to disclose his own wrongdoing. The court stated that the director was under a fiduciary duty to disclose his own wrongdoing to the company. This was found to be a part of the broad and well-established duty to act *bona fide* for the benefit of the company as a whole. And the director was not justified in believing that it was in the company's best interest to keep his actions secret from it, since the latter had such an adverse effect on the company's interests. Furthermore, as a director he was under this duty since he was not just an employee who would not be covered by such an obligation.

A contrasting case is *Island Export Finance Ltd* v. *Umunna and Another* [1986] BCLC 460. In that case the defendant was managing director of the plaintiff company. He secured for the company a contract for postal caller boxes in the Cameroons. He subsequently resigned from the company solely because of his dissatisfaction with it. At the time of his resignation the company was not seeking any further contracts for postal caller boxes. The defendant then procured two such contracts for his own company. The court held that there had been no breach of duty. It accepted that a duty could continue after resignation but the facts in this case pointed to there having been no breach. The facts singled out as particularly important in coming to this conclusion were:

(1) The company had only a vague hope of further contracts rather than an expectation and were not actively seeking new contracts at the time of the defendant's resignation. This would now appear to be irrelevant under s. 175(2).

(2) The resignation was not prompted or influenced by the desire to obtain the contracts for himself.

(3) The information about the contracts was not confidential information, since it merely amounted to knowledge of the existence of a particular market. To prevent directors using such information would conflict with public policy on the restraint of trade.

Another case which failed was *Framlington Group Plc and Another* v. *Anderson and Others* [1995] 1 BCLC 475. In that case the defendants were directors of and employees of the plaintiffs. The defendants were free, if they left the employment of the plaintiffs, to set up or join a competing business and to take with them the plaintiff's clients. They were all private client fund managers. R plc offered jobs to all three defendants. At the same time R plc negotiated a transfer of funds from the plaintiff company. This negotiation was carried out by other members of the plaintiff company and the defendants were told not to get involved. The defendants did not inform the plaintiff company of the employment packages they negotiated. The plaintiffs claimed that the benefits received by the defendants from R plc were secret profits and should be paid to the company. The court held in favour of the defendants. The fact of the negotiations on employment had been known to the plaintiff company, which had taken deliberate steps to keep the two negotiations separate and had told the defendants that they were not concerned with the detail of the employment package which was being negotiated. A case which throws some doubt on the continuance of directors' duties after resignation was *British Midland Tool Ltd* v. *Midland International Tooling Ltd* [2003] 2 BCLC 523. In that case there was a conspiracy by four directors to set up a new company and poach employees and business from the plaintiff company. One of the directors resigned but he was actively engaged in the conspiracy with the remaining directors for some months. The three directors who continued in office were found to be in breach of their duties but the director who resigned was held not to have breached his duty to the company he had left.

In *In Plus Group Ltd* v. *Pyke* [2002] EWCA Civ 370, judge Levy stated that: 'it is not a breach of a fiduciary duty of a director to work for a competing company in circumstances where he has been excluded effectively from the company of which he is a director' (para. 89 of the ruling). In this case, P and M founded a number of companies and held 50 per cent each as directors and shareholders. Their relationship broke down and the companies in question did not provide any further remuneration to P, who could not have any access to the companies' finances. A customer of one of the companies stopped placing any contracts with it and instead, six months after the relationship broke down, P started doing subcontract work for this customer. The company in question who lost the client and the related business supported that this was a clear breach of P's duty not to bring himself into a situation of conflict of interests. However, the appeal was dismissed on the grounds that while the duty to act *bona fide* for the benefit of the company as a whole in its specific application of the non-conflict rule is well established and generally accepted, a fact-specific analysis had to be made. While the court acknowledged that there was a well-established duty to act in a certain way, each case should be dealt on an individual basis on the grounds of the specific facts. P was not found in breach of duty on this point although there remained the claim of bringing himself into a situation of conflicting interests. However, since he was found to be effectively expelled from the everyday life and functions of the companies involved, he could not have made use of any of the company's assets and did not obtain relevant information as a part of his post as a director of the companies in question. Therefore, he was not found to have breached the duty towards the company. 'The defendant's role as a director of the claimants was throughout the relevant period entirely nominal . . . in the concrete sense that he was entirely excluded from all decision making and all participation in the claimant company's affairs. For all the influence he had, he might as well have resigned' (para. 90 of the judgment). 'The unusual circumstances of the instant case seem to . . . lead inescapably to the conclusion that the claim based on fiduciary duty fails . . . had P resigned as a director in late 1996 or early 1997 his resignation would have done no more than reflect what has in practice already happened' (para. 94 of the judgment).

In *Thomas Marshall (Exports) Ltd* v. *Guinle* [1979] Ch 227, Megarry VC sought to identify the type of information which would be protected by the courts in that they would prevent the disclosure of it or prevent anyone owing a duty to the company who was entitled to the benefit of the information from profiting from it. He said:

'First, I think that the information must be information the release of which the owner believes would be injurious to him or of advantage to his rivals or others. Second, I think the owner must believe that the information is confidential or secret, i.e., that it is not already in the public domain. It may be that some or all of his rivals already have the information: but as long as the owner believes it to be confidential I think he is entitled to try and protect it. Third, I think that the owner's belief under the two previous heads must be reasonable. Fourth, I think that the information must be judged in the light of the usage and practices of the particular industry or trade concerned. It may be the information which does not satisfy all these requirements may be entitled to protection as confidential information or trade secrets: but I think that any information which does satisfy them must be of a type which is entitled to protection.' (p. 248)

From the statute and cases the following principles emerge:

(1) A director is in danger of being in breach of his fundamental duty to the company if he places himself in a position where one of his private interests comes into conflict with the company's interests.

(2) This duty continues after resignation.

(3) Use of information or opportunity which comes to the director because of his position in the company will be very likely to be a breach of his duty to the company even if he tries to disassociate himself from the company by: (a) saying he is acting in a private capacity on this occasion; or (b) resigning for the purpose of exploiting the information or opportunity.

Here the statute and case law may differ, although the statute refers to 'necessary adaptations' for directors who have left office and the ambit is therefore unclear.

(4) Confidential information includes those categories described by Megarry VC in *Thomas Marshall*, but that definition was not exclusive, so other information may be included.

As in other areas of 'duty' it must be remembered that breaches may be excused by the majority on the same principles as described briefly above and examined in more detail in Chapter 13.

(5) Duty not to accept benefits from third parties

Section 176 introduces a duty not to accept benefits in return for a particular action:

(1) A director of a company must not accept a benefit from a third party conferred by reason of –
   (a) his being a director, or
   (b) his doing (or not doing) anything as director.

This would seem to be a reflection of the general duty not to allow duty and interest to conflict.

11.8 Consequences of a breach

Section 178 Companies Act 2006 refers to the preceding common law concerning the consequences of a breach of duty. A director may be prevented from doing an action in breach of his duties by an injunction and if he has profited from the breach he will be obliged to pay the company any money that he has made because of the breach. A director may become a constructive trustee of money which has been mishandled. As well as these remedies, breach of directors' duties may be the foundation of actions open to shareholders or the company (see also Chapter 13). Section 183 makes it a criminal offence to fail to declare an interest in a transaction with the company.

Hot Topic . . .

PERFORMANCE OF COMPANIES AND GOVERNMENT DEPARTMENTS (REPORTING) BILL 2004 (3)

Compare this with provisions of a Bill which preceded the Companies Act 2006 but which was never passed. Which do you think is the better approach?

As a result of the DTI Review a Performance of Companies and Government Departments (Reporting) Bill 2004 was presented to Parliament.

Section 173 Companies Act 2006:

'Duty to exercise independent judgment
(1) A director of a company must exercise independent judgment.
(2) This duty is not infringed by his acting –

(a) in accordance with an agreement duly entered into by the company that restricts the future exercise of discretion by its directors, or
(b) in a way authorised by the company's constitution.'

'Section 10 Delegation and Independence of Judgment
(1) A director of a company must not, except where authorized to do so by the company's constitution or any decisions as mentioned in section 8 –

(a) delegate any of his powers; or
(b) fail to exercise his independent judgment in relation to any exercise of his powers.

(2) Where a director has, in accordance with this section, entered into an agreement which restricts his power to exercise independent judgment later, this section does not prevent him from acting as the agreement requires where (in his independent judgment, and according to the other provisions of this Act) he should do so.'

'Section 11 Care, Skill and Diligence
A director of a company must exercise the care, skill and diligence which would be exercised by a reasonably diligent person with both —

(a) the knowledge, skill and experience which may reasonably be expected of a director in his position; and
(b) any additional knowledge, skill and experience which he has.'

Summary

1. Directors' duties can be divided into a duty to act in the company's interests and with a certain degree of skill.

2. The duties of care and skill contain an objective and a subjective element.

3. Directors are under an equitable duty to act in good faith to promote the interests of the company. If they put themselves into certain positions they are in danger of breaching this duty.

4. Those positions are: where they act outside their powers, do not exercise independent judgment, do not act with appropriate care and skill, where their interests and duty conflict, and where they accept benefits from third parties or fail to declare an interest in a transaction with the company.

5. The courts may permit the company, acting by a majority in general meeting, to forgive directors who have acted in any of the ways described in 4. The ease with which this will be allowed depends on the view taken by the court of the seriousness of the behaviour. This topic is covered in more detail in Chapter 13.

6. The company may define in advance behaviour which will not be regarded as a breach of duty.

Case notes

1. Scottish Co-operative Wholesale Society Ltd v. Meyer [1959] AC 324

The appellant company formed a subsidiary company to manufacture rayon cloth at a time when manufacture of rayon was subject to a system of licensing. The appellant company was entitled to nominate three directors of the board of the subsidiary. It nominated three of its own directors with the result that three directors held office as directors of both the parent (appellant company) and the subsidiary company. When licensing of rayon ceased, the appellant company was able, because of the votes of those three directors, to transfer the rayon business to another part of its operation. This had the effect of causing the subsidiary's affairs to come to a standstill. It made no profits and the value of its shares fell greatly. The action was brought by shareholders who claimed the company's affairs had been conducted in an 'oppressive' manner. This was the language of s. 210 Companies Act 1948, the predecessor to ss. 459–461 Companies Act 1985 (see Chapter 13). The House of Lords found that the affairs of the subsidiary had been conducted in an oppressive manner, in particular because of the breach of duty of the directors nominated by the appellant company. Lord Denning said:

'What, then, is the position of the nominee directors here? Under the articles of association of the textile company the co-operative society was entitled to nominate three out of the five directors, and it did so. It nominated three of its own directors and they held office, as the articles said, "as nominees" of the co-operative society. These three were therefore at one and the same time directors of the co-operative society – being three out of twelve of that company – and also directors of the textile company – three out of five there. So long as the interests of all concerned were in harmony, there was no difficulty. The nominee directors could do their duty by both companies without embarrassment. But, so soon as the interests of the two companies were in conflict, the nominee directors were placed in an impossible position . . . It is plain that, in the circumstances, these three gentlemen could not do their duty by both companies, and they did not do so. They put their duty to the co-operative society above their duty to the textile company in the sense, at least, that they did nothing to defend the interests of the textile company against the conduct of the co-operative society. They probably thought that "as nominees" of the co-operative society their first duty was to the co-operative society. In this they were wrong. By subordinating the interests of the textile company to those of the co-operative society, they conducted the affairs of the textile company in a manner oppressive to the other shareholders.' (pp. 366–7)

2. Smith v. Van Gorkom [1985] 488 A.2d 858

Van Gorkom was the chief executive officer and chairman of the board of directors of Trans Union Corporation, a publicly-held corporation principally involved in the leasing of rail cars. He was nearly 65 years old and approaching retirement. Trans Union had a substantial cash flow but its taxable income was insufficient to permit it to take full advantage of tax benefits it was entitled to under the Internal Revenue Code. For several years, Trans Union had therefore tried to purchase income-producing businesses, apparently without great success. During discussions about strategy, the possibility of selling Trans Union to a larger corporation was raised, as was the possibility of a buy-out by management of the interests of the public shareholders. Studies showed that the cash flow would cover a management buy-out at $50 but $60 would be difficult to do. At a meeting, Van Gorkom vetoed the idea of a buy-out but stated that he would accept $55 for each of the 75,000 shares that he owned. (The price of the stock of Trans Union at this time was about $38 per share.) Following these discussions, Van Gorkom on his own decided to approach Jay Pritzker, a well-known takeover specialist, with a proposal that Pritzker should purchase the company at $55 per share. Pritzker was a personal acquaintance of Van Gorkom. Pritzker and Van Gorkom quickly worked out a proposed deal (though after some negotiation) under which: (1) Pritzker would be entitled to buy one million shares of Trans Union at $38 per share; (2) Pritzker's wholly owned corporation would agree to enter into a statutory merger with Trans Union pursuant to which each shareholder of Trans Union would receive $55 per share; and (3) the merger was subject to cancellation if a higher price was forthcoming from another bidder within ninety days. Approval of this deal required the approval of the Trans Union's board of directors and a majority of its shareholders. The board of directors of Trans Union consisted of five executive and five non-executive directors. The nine directors present at the meeting unanimously approved the deal despite the fact that there had been no independent valuation of the shares of Trans Union. Seventy per cent of the shareholders of Trans Union approved the deal. A suit was filed by a minority of Trans Union's shareholders alleging that the directors had failed to exercise due care in reviewing and recommending approval of the transaction. The Delaware Supreme Court rejected defences put forward by the defendant directors and the case was adjourned for determination of damages. It was then settled, by the plaintiff's accepting a payment of $23.5 million.

The massive liability incurred by the defendants was based on lack of due care, not fraud or breach of fiduciary duties. It led to a severe (but temporary) shortage of well-qualified persons willing to act as directors (see further, *Hamilton* [1988] 4 JIBL 152).

3. *Punt v. Symonds & Co.* [1903] 2 Ch 506

This was a case where friction had arisen between two factions of shareholders. The directors issued new shares. Byrne J said:

'It is argued on the evidence that but for the issue by the directors of the shares under their powers as directors, and, therefore, in their fiduciary character under the general power to issue shares, it would have been impossible to pass the resolution proposed; and that the shares were not issued *bona fide*, but with the sole object and intention of creating voting power to carry out the proposed alteration in the articles. On the evidence I am quite clear that these shares were not issued *bona fide* for the general advantage of the company, but that they were issued with the immediate object of controlling the holders of the greater number of shares in the company, and of obtaining the necessary statutory majority for passing a special resolution while, at the same time, not conferring upon the minority the power to demand a poll. I need not go through the affidavits. I am quite satisfied that the meaning, object, and intention of the issue of these shares was to enable the shareholders holding the smaller amount of shares to control the holders of a very considerable majority. A power of the kind exercised by the directors in this case, is one which must be exercised for the benefit of the company: primarily it is given them for the purpose of enabling them to raise capital when required for the purposes of the company. There may be occasions when the directors may fairly and properly issue shares in the case of a company constituted like the present for other reasons. For instance, it would not be at all an unreasonable thing to create a sufficient number of shareholders to enable statutory powers to be exercised; but when I find a limited issue of shares to persons who are obviously meant and intended to secure the necessary statutory majority in a particular interest, I do not think that is a fair and *bona fide* exercise of the power.' (pp. 515–16)

4. *Piercy* v. *S. Mills & Co. Ltd* [1920] 1 Ch 77

This also concerned a dispute between controllers of a company. Peterson J said:

'With the merits of the dispute as between the directors and the plaintiff I have no concern whatever. The plaintiff and his friends held a majority of shares in the company, and

they were entitled, so long as that majority remained, to have their views prevail in accordance with the regulations of the company; and it was not, in my opinion, open to the directors, for the sole purpose of converting a minority into a majority, and solely for the purpose of defeating the wishes of the existing majority, to issue the shares which are in dispute in the present action.' (pp. 84–5)

5. Sections 172–177 Companies Act 2006

172 Duty to promote the success of the company

(1) A director of a company must act in the way he considers, in good faith, would be most likely to promote the success of the company for the benefit of its members as a whole, and in doing so have regard (amongst other matters) to –

    (a) the likely consequences of any decision in the long term,

    (b) the interests of the company's employees,

    (c) the need to foster the company's business relationships with suppliers, customers and others,

    (d) the impact of the company's operations on the community and the environment,

    (e) the desirability of the company maintaining a reputation for high standards of business conduct, and

    (f) the need to act fairly as between members of the company.

(2) Where or to the extent that the purposes of the company consist of or include purposes other than the benefit of its members, subsection (1) has effect as if the reference to promoting the success of the company for the benefit of its members were to achieving those purposes.

(3) The duty imposed by this section has effect subject to any enactment or rule of law requiring directors, in certain circumstances, to consider or act in the interests of creditors of the company.

173 Duty to exercise independent judgment

(1) A director of a company must exercise independent judgment.

(2) This duty is not infringed by his acting –

(a) in accordance with an agreement duly entered into by the company that restricts the future exercise of discretion by its directors, or

(b) in a way authorised by the company's constitution.

174 Duty to exercise reasonable care, skill and diligence

(1) A director of a company must exercise reasonable care, skill and diligence.

(2) This means the care, skill and diligence that would be exercised by a reasonably diligent person with –

(a) the general knowledge, skill and experience that may reasonably be expected of a person carrying out the functions carried out by the director in relation to the company, and

(b) the general knowledge, skill and experience that the director has.

175 Duty to avoid conflicts of interest

(1) A director of a company must avoid a situation in which he has, or can have, a direct or indirect interest that conflicts, or possibly may conflict, with the interests of the company.

(2) This applies in particular to the exploitation of any property, information or opportunity (and it is immaterial whether the company could take advantage of the property, information or opportunity).

(3) This duty does not apply to a conflict of interest arising in relation to a transaction or arrangement with the company.

(4) This duty is not infringed –

(a) if the situation cannot reasonably be regarded as likely to give rise to a conflict of interest; or

(b) if the matter has been authorised by the directors.

(5) Authorisation may be given by the directors –

(a) where the company is a private company and nothing in the company's constitution invalidates such authorisation, by the matter being proposed to and authorised by the directors; or

(b) where the company is a public company and its constitution includes provision enabling the directors to authorise the matter, by the matter being proposed to and authorised by them in accordance with the constitution.

(6) The authorisation is effective only if –

   (a) any requirement as to the quorum at the meeting at which the matter is considered is met without counting the director in question or any other interested director, and

   (b) the matter was agreed to without their voting or would have been agreed to if their votes had not been counted.

(7) Any reference in this section to a conflict of interest includes a conflict of interest and duty and a conflict of duties.

176 Duty not to accept benefits from third parties

(1) A director of a company must not accept a benefit from a third party conferred by reason of –

   (a) his being a director, or

   (b) his doing (or not doing) anything as director.

(2) A 'third party' means a person other than the company, an associated body corporate or a person acting on behalf of the company or an associated body corporate.

(3) Benefits received by a director from a person by whom his services (as a director or otherwise) are provided to the company are not regarded as conferred by a third party.

(4) This duty is not infringed if the acceptance of the benefit cannot reasonably be regarded as likely to give rise to a conflict of interest.

(5) Any reference in this section to a conflict of interest includes a conflict of interest and duty and a conflict of duties.

177 Duty to declare interest in proposed transaction or arrangement

(1) If a director of a company is in any way, directly or indirectly, interested in a proposed transaction or arrangement with the company, he must declare the nature and extent of that interest to the other directors.

(2) The declaration may (but need not) be made –

   (a) at a meeting of the directors, or

   (b) by notice to the directors in accordance with –

      (i) section 184 (notice in writing), or

      (ii) section 185 (general notice).

(3) If a declaration of interest under this section proves to be, or becomes, inaccurate or incomplete, a further declaration must be made.

(4) Any declaration required by this section must be made before the company enters into the transaction or arrangement.

(5) This section does not require a declaration of an interest of which the director is not aware or where the director is not aware of the transaction or arrangement in question.

For this purpose a director is treated as being aware of matters of which he ought reasonably to be aware.

(6) A director need not declare an interest –

(a) if it cannot reasonably be regarded as likely to give rise to a conflict of interest;

(b) if, or to the extent that, the other directors are already aware of it (and for this purpose the other directors are treated as aware of anything of which they ought reasonably to be aware); or

(c) if, or to the extent that, it concerns terms of his service contract that have been or are to be considered –

(i) by a meeting of the directors, or

(ii) by a committee of the directors appointed for the purpose under the company's constitution.

Exercises

1. To whom does a director owe his duties?

2. What factors make it difficult to impose one standard on all directors?

3. Explain the effect of the ruling in *Re City Equitable Fire Insurance* on an executive director of a large company.

4. John and Mary are directors of Wash Ltd. They become suspicious of the behaviour of Joe, the third director of the company. He has recently bought a Porsche and has taken several foreign holidays. John and Mary know that his salary as director would not be sufficient to pay for these luxuries. John discovers that Joe has been buying raw materials for Wash Ltd from a company in which he, Joe, owns all but one of the shares. The price of these materials appears to be excessive. John tells Mary that she is better off knowing nothing about what is going on. She agrees. John then uses his powers under the articles to issue enough shares to friends to ensure that Joe is voted out of office. The company becomes insolvent. It has paid no VAT, PAYE or NIC for many months. What breaches of duty have been committed? Is it likely that any of the directors will be disqualified?

Chapter 12

Specific duties of directors

Key words

▶ **Phoenix companies** – new companies trading with the same personnel and a very similar name to a failed company. The ability to disqualify directors was introduced partly as a response to the misuse of companies by starting one company, defaulting on that company's debts, winding up the company, then duping the public by immediately beginning to trade using a similarly-named company.

▶ **Unfit** – one of the key disqualification provisions requires the disqualification of an 'unfit' director. The meaning of this term is still rather uncertain.

The general duties of directors (see Chapter 11) are reinforced by specific statutory duties spelt out in the Companies Act 2006 (see Case note **1**, on pp. 243–8). These replace very complicated provisions under the 1985 Act, many of which were introduced as a result of financial scandals. The government of the day wished to be seen to be 'doing something' to remedy the situation. Very few of the provisions in Part X of the Companies Act 1985 were enforced and abolition of this part of the Companies Act is very welcome. The provisions are based on *Modern Company Law for a Competitive Economy: Developing the Framework* (DTI Company Law Review, March 2000), building on the work of The Law Commission (Report No. 261 *Company Directors: Regulating Conflicts of Interest and Formulating a Statement of Duties*, September 1999). The scheme of the 2006 Act is to require members' approval of certain transactions with directors. These are:

▶ Directors' service contracts of more than two years (ss. 188 and 189);
▶ Substantial property transactions with directors (ss. 190–196);
▶ Loans, quasi-loans and credit transactions (ss. 197–214);
▶ Payments for loss of office (ss. 215–222).

The sections mentioned contain definitions of the transactions and exceptions, and set out the legal consequences if they are infringed. This simplification is very welcome and we await implementation of the provisions.

12.1 Disqualification of directors

(For a treatment of this subject in the context of the personal liability of directors, see L. S. Sealy, *Disqualification and the Personal Liability of Directors*, CCH, 5th edn, 2000).

Under the Company Directors Disqualification Act 1986 the courts must under s. 6 disqualify a director from managing a company if he has been a director of a company which has become insolvent (either while he was acting for it or later) and the court finds that his conduct 'makes him unfit to be concerned in the management of a company'. By s. 6(4) the minimum period of disqualification is two years and the maximum fifteen years. Although this legislation raises many questions the major issue relevant to the standard of directors' duties is what is meant by 'unfitness'. Unfitness also seems to have an objective content and this will be discussed in detail later. There are other grounds for disqualification which must also be examined. In *Official Receiver* v. *Brady and Others* [1999] BCLC 258 it was held that companies, as well as individuals, could be subject to disqualification orders.

Under ss. 2–5 Company Directors Disqualification Act 1986 a court may make a disqualification order against a person for the following reasons.

Conviction of indictable offence

He is convicted of an indictable offence in connection with the promotion, formation, management or liquidation of a company or with the receivership or management of a company's property (s. 2). The offence need only be capable of being prosecuted on indictment. The relevant conviction could be obtained in a magistrates' court. Actual misconduct of a company's affairs need not be proved. In *Re Georgiou* (1988) 4 BCC 322 the offence was carrying on an unauthorised insurance business. There was no allegation that it was a badly managed insurance business. In *R* v. *Goodman* [1994] BCLC 349 a chairman and major shareholder of a public company 'gave' his shares to a friend who sold them three days before it became public knowledge that the company was in trouble. He was later convicted of insider dealing and disqualified for 10 years under s. 2 of the Company Directors Disqualification Act 1986. He appealed on the grounds that the insider trading was not an offence committed in connection with the management of a company. It was held that it was. The correct test was whether the offence had some relevant factual connection with the management of the company, not whether it had been committed in the course of managing the company (such as not filing returns). Here there was a clear connection. There is no minimum period of disqualification under this section and disqualification is discretionary. If the offence is dealt with by a magistrates' court the maximum disqualification period is five years. If the offence is dealt with on indictment the maximum period is fifteen years.

Persistent default

He appears to the court to have been persistently in default in relation to any requirement under the companies' legislation for the filing, delivery or sending of any return, account or other document or the giving of any notice with or to the Registrar of Companies (s. 3). There is a presumption that a person has been 'persistently in default' if he has been convicted of a default, or has been required by court order to make good a default, three times in the preceding five years (ss. 3(2) and 3(3)). This does not prevent an application for an order being made under this section when neither of those matters can be shown. In *Re Arctic Engineering Ltd* [1986] 1 WLR 686 'persistently' was held to require some degree of continuance or repetition. There is no need to show a wilful disregard of statutory requirements, although the absence of fault will be important when the exercise of the discretion not to disqualify is in question. Under this section any court having jurisdiction to wind up the company has jurisdiction to make the order. Section 5 gives jurisdiction in precisely the same circumstances to a magistrates' court. This will usually be the court which actually convicts the director. Under both sections disqualification is discretionary and there is a maximum period of five years.

Fraud discovered in winding-up

He appears to the court in the course of winding-up the company:

(1) to have been guilty of an offence (whether convicted or not) of fraudulent trading;
(2) to have otherwise been guilty, while an officer or liquidator of the company or receiver or manager of its property, of any fraud in relation to the company or of any breach of his duty as such officer, liquidator, receiver or manager (s. 4).

This section applies to fraud, and so on, whenever it occurred. It is the revelation that must be in the course of the winding-up, not the fraud. The court with jurisdiction to make the order is 'any court having jurisdiction to wind up the company'. Disqualification is discretionary and the maximum period is fifteen years. It is not necessary for the purposes of s. 4 that the company should be insolvent. Under s. 4(1)(a) anyone guilty of fraudulent trading may be disqualified. This offence may be committed by any person who was knowingly a party to the carrying on of the fraudulent business. By contrast, those liable to be disqualified under s. 4(1)(b) are more uncertain. Sealy (*Disqualification and Personal Liability of Directors*, CCH, 5th edn, 2000) lists the officers caught and possibly caught under s. 4(1)(b). They are:

(i) certainly caught:
    a director
    a shadow director
    a secretary
    a 'manager' (see below)
    a liquidator
    a receiver.

There is a great deal of uncertainty surrounding the definition of a 'manager'. In *Re A Company No. 00996 of 1979* [1980] Ch 138, at p. 144, Shaw LJ said:

> 'any person who in the affairs of the company exercises a supervisory control which reflects the general policy of the company or which is related to the general administration of the company is in the sphere of management. He need not be a member of the board of directors. He need not be subject to specific instructions from the board.'

Those less certainly included (depending on the construction of the term 'officer') are:

(ii) an auditor
    the supervisor of a voluntary arrangement (made under ss. 1–7 Insolvency Act 1986)
    an administrator (appointed under s. 8 Insolvency Act 1986).

Note that the disqualification order under the above provisions is discretionary. The court does not have to make such an order even if the facts that would enable it to do so are proved.

Duty to disqualify

There is a duty to disqualify imposed on the court under s. 6 Company Directors Disqualification Act 1986, which reads as follows:

> 'The court shall make a disqualification order for a period of not less than two years nor more than fifteen years against a person if, on application by the Secretary of State or at his discretion by the Official Receiver where a company is being wound up by the court in England and Wales, the court is satisfied that –

(a) such person is or has been a director of a company which has at any time become insolvent (whether while he was a director or subsequently); and

(b) his conduct as a director of the company (taken alone or together with his conduct as a director of any other company or companies) makes him unfit to be concerned in the management of a company.'

Insolvency

This is defined by s. 6(2). A company becomes insolvent if:

(a) it goes into liquidation at a time when its assets are insufficient to pay its debts, liabilities and winding-up expenses; or

(b) an 'administration order' is made (irrespective of the solvency or otherwise of the company at any relevant time); or

(c) an 'administrative receiver' is appointed (irrespective of the company's financial state).

The net is spread wide as every liquidator (or administrator and so on) must report on the conduct of those possibly caught by the statute to a special enforcement unit which then takes the decision whether or not to ask the court for a disqualification order.

Probable effect on directors' duty of care

If the courts are expecting directors to live up to a high standard in order to escape being adjudged 'unfit' it is possible that this legislation will have the effect of raising the standards expected of directors generally. It would seem strange to the courts if a position is reached where a director has been found unfit and disqualified and yet is not liable to account for irregularities under the rule in that case. There may well be a tendency to adopt a similar standard by which to judge directors. What has been the standard to determine unfitness? There has been a considerable amount of case law on the subject but as yet no very clear conclusion can be drawn. The statute itself gives some guidance on matters which are to be considered by the court, but gives no further explanation of what is meant by 'unfit'. Thus by s. 6 the conduct that must be taken into account is conduct in relation to the company that has become insolvent and any other company. By s. 9 the matters referred to in Parts I and II of Schedule 1 must be considered to determine unfitness. The court is directed to have regard 'in particular' to those matters. It is clear that these are the matters considered important by Parliament when an assessment of a director's fitness is made. The matters include: breaches of duty by the director, misuse of company funds, responsibility for and/or misconduct in the insolvency of the company;

failure to comply with a number of administrative obligations, such as failing to keep proper accounts and other records required by the Companies Act 1985; and failure to communicate the contents of the accounts and records (where required to do so) to the Registrar of Companies.

Judging from the extensive case law on the subject, the courts have taken these matters into account. They have also had regard to other matters not on this list, some of which appear to have become important. There is also an unfortunate confusion as to the meaning of the final overall standard of unfitness. Some of the confusion is caused by the fact that a number of the relevant decisions were decided when s. 300 Companies Act 1985 was still in force. This was very similar to s. 6 Company Directors Disqualification Act 1986, but required the director's involvement in the insolvency of two companies. The disqualification under this section was discretionary. Under s. 6 the court *must* make a disqualification order for a minimum of two years if a relevant company has gone into liquidation and there is a finding of unfitness. However, this is apparently mitigated by the ability of the court to permit the disqualified director to act as a director during the period of disqualification (imposing terms if the court deems it appropriate (see p. 232). (Section 1 defines a disqualification order as an order that '[the defendant] shall not, *without leave of the court* be a director . . .' [emphasis added].)

Unfitness

Apart from the factors set out in the statute which the court is directed to take into account, other facts have been considered important in determining unfitness. In particular, there has been some debate as to the importance of the existence of outstanding debts for VAT, PAYE and NIC.

In *Re Dawson Print Group* [1987] BCLC 601 (see Case note **2**, p. 248) and *Re Stanford Services* [1987] BCLC 607 (see Case note **3**, pp. 248–9) different views were taken about the importance of using 'Crown debts' to finance the company. What was happening in both cases was that the directors had withheld VAT, National Insurance and PAYE money which ought to have been paid by the company to the government. This money was used in order for the company to continue trading. In *Stanford* the misuse of this money was seen as a clear indication of unfitness, whereas in *Dawson* similar misuse was not seen as being particularly significant. The Court of Appeal in *Re Sevenoaks Stationers* [1991] BCLC 325 made no distinction between 'Crown debts' and others unless especial suffering had been caused by non-payment of Crown debts.

In *Re Amaron Ltd* [1998] BCC 264 the court confirmed that issues not mentioned in Schedule 1 may, and indeed should, be taken into account in considering disqualification. That case concerned allowing the company to trade when it was insolvent.

Breach of what standard of care makes a director unfit?

As far as the overall standard is concerned, various alternatives have been considered by the courts. In *Dawson* and *Stanford* alone the following explanations of 'unfitness' appeared:

(i)   a breach of commercial morality;
(ii) really gross incompetence;
(iii) recklessness;
(iv) the director would be a danger to the public if he were allowed to continue to be involved in the management of companies.

Consideration (iv) seems now to be ruled out by the Court of Appeal's decision in *Secretary of State for Trade and Industry* v. *Gray and Another* [1995] 1 BCLC 276 where the court found that only the behaviour alleged to make the defendant unfit could be considered. The future protection of the public was not a relevant consideration. The Court of Appeal approved the decision of Vinelott J in *Re Pamstock Ltd* [1994] 1 BCLC 736 where a disqualification order was made even though: 'The respondent seemed to me . . . to be a man who today is capable of discharging his duties as director honestly and diligently.'

In *Re Bath Glass* [1988] BCLC 329 and *AB Trucking and BAW Commercials* Ch D, 3 June 1987, unreported, an objective standard was imposed. A director was unfit if his actions were very far from those of a reasonably competent director. Until a generally agreed interpretation of unfitness has emerged from the decisions it is impossible to tell whether this legislation will have an effect on the standard imposed on directors under *Re City Equitable Fire Insurance*. The willingness of the court to disqualify where the director is incapable of understanding his duties may indicate that the excuse of incompetence which is available under *Re City Equitable Fire Insurance* is ripe for review and may have a limited life. This willingness is illustrated by *AB Trucking and BAW Commercials*. The respondent was said to be 'incapable of understanding the commercial reality of accounts' and thus 'incapable of discharging his duty to the public'. Nevertheless Harman J imposed a disqualification order for four years.

A very high standard of behaviour seems to have been required by the court in *Re New Generation Engineers Ltd* [1993] BCLC 435. The factors said to merit disqualification were keeping inadequate accounting records so that it was not possible to monitor the financial position of the company and adopting a policy of only paying those creditors who pressed for payment or who needed to be paid in order to keep the company's business going. Each of these was said to provide grounds for disqualification, although the eventual order was only for three years.

Important factors in determining unfitness

1. *The amount of debts outstanding and the practice of not paying debts as a method of continuing to trade* – see *Secretary of State for Trade and Industry* v. *McTighe and Another (No. 2)* [1996] 2 BCLC 477, although Crown debts do not now seem to be particularly significant; see *Re Sevenoaks Stationers* [1991] BCLC 325.

2. *The number of companies that the director has been involved in* – in particular the number of liquidations that he has been concerned with.

3. *The way in which the companies have been managed* – in particular to what extent accounts have been kept up to date and returns made to the Companies' Registry.

4. *The personal circumstances of the director.* Here the cases are confusing. Sometimes the youth and inexperience of a director are held to mitigate against a disqualification. The idea of this presumably is that he is growing up. On the other hand in *Re Majestic Recording Studios Ltd* [1989] BCLC 1 the court was quite adamant that a person could be unfit when they were incompetent. Fraudulent behaviour did not need to be shown. What seems to be happening is that the court is assessing the degree of moral blame to be attached to the director for the company's failures. This will be less if incompetence was the cause of failure rather than fraud. This does not mean that there will be no finding of unfitness but it will be a factor which the court will take into account when deciding to exercise its discretion as to the length of disqualification.

5. *The state of mind of the defendant.* The relevance of this factor is closely tied to the debate as to the true nature of disqualification. There are two clearly opposed approaches. One is that the imposition of a disqualification order is a penal sanction which may well have the effect of removal of the livelihood of the director in question. The other approach regards disqualification as the removal of a licence to trade using limited liability. Passages in judgments can be found clearly supporting either approach. In *Re Civicia Investments Ltd* [1983] BCLC 456, Nourse J said:

> 'It might be thought that [consideration of the appropriate period of disqualification] is something which, like the passing of sentence in a criminal case, ought to be dealt with comparatively briefly and without elaborate reasoning . . . no doubt in this, as in other areas, it is possible that there will emerge a broad and undefined system of tariffs for defaults of varying degrees of blame . . . the

longer periods of disqualification are to be reserved for cases where the defaults and conduct of the person in question have been of a serious nature, for example, where defaults have been made for some dishonest purpose.'

The quasi-penal nature of disqualification under this section was clearly acknowledged in *Re Crestjoy Products Ltd* [1990] BCC 23; [1990] BCLC 677. In that case the judgment of Browne-Wilkinson VC in *Re Lo-Line Electric Motors Ltd* [1988] BCLC 698 was cited as a 'most useful encapsulation of the current authority'. The passage cited reads:

'The primary purpose of the section is not to punish the individual but to protect the public against the future conduct of companies by persons whose past records as directors of insolvent companies have shown them to be a danger to creditors and others. Therefore, the power is not fundamentally penal. But, if the power to disqualify is exercised . . . disqualification does involve a substantial interference with the freedom of the individual. It follows that the rights of the individual must be fully protected.'

The court went on to hold that:

'since the making of a disqualification order involves penal consequences for the director, it is necessary that he should know the substance of the charges that he has to meet.'

The judge in *Crestjoy* agreed with this analysis but nevertheless went on to say:

'It seems to me, however, that when I am faced with a mandatory two-year disqualification if facts are proved, the matter becomes more nearly penal, or, at least, more serious for the individual faced with it than under the former situation where a judge could, in the exercise of his discretion, say that although the conduct had been bad yet he was now convinced that a disqualification should not be made because, for example, the respondent had learnt his lesson.'

In view of the seriousness of the matter, an application to bring an action seeking a disqualification order out of time was refused.

The approach in *Crestjoy* has been disapproved by the Court of Appeal in *Secretary of State for Trade and Industry* v. *Gray and Another* where the Court held that only past behaviour could be considered. Mitigating factors which arose after the events alleged would not be relevant. However, both in that case (see further discussion below) and in subsequent cases the quasi-penal nature of the proceedings have been acknowledged. In *Re Living Images Ltd* [1996] 1 BCLC 348 the court determined that although the proceedings were civil proceedings and the standard of proof was therefore on a balance of probabilities, the seriousness of both the allegations and the consequences meant that the court would 'require cogent evidence as proof', thus presumably setting a higher standard than the 'more likely than not' test.

Although it seems that this reason for regarding the matter as serious is less convincing in view of the possibility of permitting the director to continue as such under licence (see p. 232), nevertheless it is still a significant interference with the freedom of the individual if that licence has to be obtained from the court. The disqualification remains mandatory, not discretionary.

The debate as to the nature of disqualification may be continued if challenges are mounted to the legislation under the Human Rights Act 1998. In *Hinchcliffe* v. *Secretary of State for Trade and Industry* [1999] BCC 226, the court refused to stay disqualification proceedings until the entry into force of the Human Rights Act 1998. The respondent intended to apply under the Act to have the disqualification proceedings dismissed. The court held that in disqualification proceedings it was in the public interest to impose the disqualification as soon as possible and, in any event, it would not stay proceedings pending the passage of a Bill which might never become law.

Objective (negligence) standard or subjective fault?

In *Re Bath Glass* [1988] BCLC 329 Peter Gibson J said:

> 'To reach a finding of unfitness the court must be satisfied that the director has been guilty of a serious failure or serious failures, whether deliberately or through incompetence, to perform those duties of a director which are attendant on the privilege of trading through companies with limited liability. Any misconduct of the respondent *qua* director may be relevant.'

Since the 'serious failure' could occur because of the incompetence of the director, this means that the test imposed is an objective one, in that the standard can be breached by someone, who through no fault of his own, is incapable of performing the duties of a director. This is a clear divergence from the *Re City Equitable Fire Insurance* approach.

A similar view was taken by Harman J in *AB Trucking and BAW Commercials* Ch D, 3 June 1987, unreported. The respondent was said to be 'incapable of understanding the commercial reality of accounts' and thus 'incapable of discharging his duty to the public'. Harman J imposed a disqualification order for four years.

It seems clear that an objective standard of 'fitness' is being imposed. The exact nature of the test is still unclear. As we have seen, various tests appear in the cases (see Dine, *Company Lawyer*, vol. 9, no. 10, p. 213 and the list set out on p. 225).

All or any of these could be at least partially objective in nature. Analysis of the standard has been poor. The view that 'incompetence' is sufficient seems to be growing, but in the absence of a definition of the ability to be expected of a 'reasonable director' such a standard is still necessarily vague.

The one thing that does seem clear is that this mythical creature can both understand and keep accounts. If he cannot, he is unfit. Even if he employs a professional who should be competent to deal with the necessary paperwork, this will only be a matter to take into consideration when determining the length of disqualification.

This approach was taken by Harman J in *Re Rolus Properties Ltd & Another* (1988) 4 BCC 446. He said:

'The privilege of limited liability is a valuable incentive to encourage entrepreneurs to take on risky ventures without inevitable personal total financial disaster. It is, however, a privilege which must be accorded upon terms and some of the most important terms that Parliament has imposed are that accounts be kept and returns made so that the world can, by referring to those, see what is happening. Thus, a total failure to keep statutory books and to make statutory returns is significant for the public at large and a matter which amounts to misconduct if not complied with and is a matter of which the court should take account in considering whether a man can properly be allowed to continue to operate as a director of companies, or whether the public at large is to be protected against him on the grounds that he is unfit, not because he is fraudulent but because he is incompetent and unable to comply with the statutory obligations attached to limited liability. In my view that is a correct approach and the jurisdiction does extend and should be exercised in cases where a man has by his conduct revealed that he is wholly unable to comply with the obligations that go with the privilege of limited liability.'

The disqualification order was reduced from a four-to-six-year period to two years because of the reliance by the director on professional advice. In *Re Continental Assurance Co. of London plc* [2001] BPIR 733 the court held that: 'the degree of competence required ... extended at least to a requirement that a director who was a corporate financier should be prepared to read and understand the statutory accounts of the holding company.'

One thing seems clear. An unfit director is worse than merely incompetent. He is guilty of 'gross negligence or total incompetence' (*Re Lo-Line Electric Motors Ltd* (1988) 4 BCC 415), or being 'wholly unable to comply with the obligations which go with the privilege of limited liability' (*Re Rolus Properties* – see above). The merely incompetent or those guilty of commercial misjudgment will not be considered unfit (*Re McNulty's Interchange Ltd & Another* (1988) 4 BCC 533). In *Secretary of State for Trade and Industry* v. *Hickling and Others* [1996] BCC 678 the court held that directors who had been guilty of naivety, over-optimism and misplaced trust should not, in the absence of dishonesty, commercial immorality or gross incompetence, be disqualified. There is, however, a rather opaque reference to disqualification being nearer to a 'negligence' standard than a determination of 'reasonable financial provision' in *Secretary of State for Trade and Industry* v. *Gray and Another* [1995] 1 BCLC 276. However the reference was in the context not of setting the standard for disqualification but of determining whether or not the Court of Appeal should interfere with the judge's findings. It seems to indicate that there is a discoverable standard for disqualification which the Court of Appeal can impose rather than set that standard, which remains obscure. Until the courts have settled the standard of competence of a 'reasonable' director, it will continue to be uncertain whether a particular director has been incompetent. Further uncertainty is added by the requirement that the director should have been totally or wholly incompetent. It would be helpful if the courts addressed the definition of the degree of competence required of a 'fit' director. However, discussion of the meaning of 'unfitness' may be discouraged by the Court of Appeal's *dicta* in *Re Sevenoaks Stationers* [1991] BCLC 325, where it was held that such 'judicial paraphrases should not be construed in lieu of the words of the statute'. Unfitness was to be regarded as a 'jury question'.

As mentioned above, the Court of Appeal had a further chance to consider the setting of standards in *Secretary of State for Trade and Industry v. Gray and Another* [1995] 1 BCLC 276 but again failed to determine the relationship between moral culpability and incompetence or to set some measure of competence. In view of the latter failure it is the more surprising that the Court felt able to overturn the lower court's finding that the directors were not unfit and should therefore be disqualified. The Court held that the respondents' conduct fell below the 'standard appropriate' for directors. The three allegations in this case were that the companies involved had (i) been trading while insolvent, (ii) failed to keep proper accounting records and (iii) failed to file accounts on time. This behaviour had also involved the giving of preferences. Other remedies had been pursued in respect of the preferences, so that the judge discounted them. The Court of Appeal held that she was wrong to do so. The language in the case gives support to the argument that this is a penal measure. As described above, the Court held that only the past conduct was relevant. The present state of affairs was irrelevant to the issue of disqualification, as was the future protection of the public. This attitude certainly seems to indicate that the thrust is punishment for past misdeeds. Deterrence is also an aim. Thus Hoffman LJ approved the statement by Sir Donald Nicholls VC in *Secretary of State for Trade and Industry v. Ettinger; Re Swift 736 Ltd* [1993] BCLC 896: 'Those who make use of limited liability must do so with a proper sense of responsibility. The directors' disqualification procedure is an important sanction introduced by Parliament to raise standards in that regard.'

In *Re Barings plc* [1999] 1 BCLC 433, Parker J held that a disqualification would be imposed where there were no allegations relating to honesty and integrity. However the alleged incompetence must be of a 'high degree'. Failure to exercise adequate management control fell into that category.

The length of the disqualification and 'mitigating factors'

In *Re Sevenoaks Stationers* [1991] BCLC 325, the Court of Appeal held that in determining the length of a disqualification under s. 6 Company Directors Disqualification Act 1986, the top bracket of disqualification should be reserved for serious cases. This would involve disqualification of 10 years or more. The Court of Appeal suggested that cases in this bracket might well include cases of imposition of a second disqualification order on a director. Unhelpfully, Dillon LJ suggested that the 'middle bracket of disqualification from 6 to 10 years should apply for serious cases which do not merit the top bracket' [1991] BCLC 325, at p. 328. The minimum bracket of 2 to 5 years of disqualification 'should be applied where, though disqualification is mandatory, the case is, relatively, not very serious'. Unfortunately the Court did not analyse or discuss the matters which were likely to place a case within one of the 'brackets', with the exception of Crown debts. These were said only to be of especial significance where they had caused suffering over and above that caused by other creditors. It is unfortunate that the Court of Appeal did not seize the opportunity to carry out a more comprehensive review of the matters which would cause a case to fall within each bracket. More particularly, the matters which may be viewed as 'mitigating factors' are even more unclear.

There are a number of factors which have caused the court to impose a shorter order than would otherwise be the case. In cases decided under s. 300 Companies Act 1985, the same factors led the court to exercise its discretion not to disqualify. Among those factors are:

Effect on employees

The court may be reluctant to impose a disqualification order where jobs are at stake. In *Re Majestic Recording Studios Ltd* [1989] BCLC 1, the judge made a clear finding that the director was unfit but then went on to permit him to continue to be director of one company under certain conditions, partly because of the hardship that this would otherwise cause to employees. However, this situation is sometimes dealt with by imposing a disqualification and subsequently granting leave to act as a director on certain conditions; see *Secretary of State for Trade and Industry* v. *Rosenfield* [1999] BCC 413. See also the subsection below on 'Leave to act while disqualified'.

Acting on professional advice

This was a significant factor in reducing the period of disqualification in *Re Rolus Properties Ltd & Another*.

The youth of the director

The youth of the director at the time of the failure of the company and evidence that he has learnt from past mistakes may be mitigating factors (see *Re Chartmore*, 12 October 1989 [1990] BCLC 673). However, the status of these cases and factors seems very doubtful in view of the Court of Appeal's clear ruling in *Secretary of State for Trade and Industry v. Gray and Another* that only past behaviour should affect the decision to disqualify. Hoffman LJ, however, recognised that 'whether or not he has shown himself unlikely to offend again' will be relevant to whether or not there will be a grant of leave to act while disqualified. He went on to say: 'it may also be relevant by way of mitigation on the length of disqualification, although I note that the guidelines in *Re Sevenoaks Stationers* [1991] BCLC 325 are solely by reference to the seriousness of the conduct in question.'

Leave to act while disqualified

A curious light is thrown on the mandatory nature of the disqualification under s. 6 by the power of the court to exercise a discretion to permit a director to act as such during the period of disqualification. This could amount to a reversal of the duty to impose a disqualification order, but it seems that the court will often impose quite stringent conditions on the grant of such permission (see *Re Lo-Line Electric Motors Ltd* [1988] BCLC 698). Another example is *Re Chartmore* (see above). In that case a disqualification for two years for 'gross incompetence' was imposed. However, the director was permitted to continue to act for a named company for one year despite these misgivings expressed by Harman J:

> 'The only matter that bothers me is that the failure of the company for which I have disqualified Mr Buckingham, Chartmore Limited, was primarily due to Mr Buckingham having started it with quite inadequate capitalisation and having carried it on unrealising that he was in effect trading on the creditors' backs in such a manner as to show that degree of inadequacy warranting disqualification.
>
> This new company has one hundred pounds paid up share capital and no other equity on its balance sheet at all. There are no other directors' loan accounts which could be subordinated to the trade and other creditors or converted into equity. There is a statement by Mr Buckingham that he and his fellow director have paid fifteen thousand pounds into the company. That worries me because the accounts show no trace of the sum and they therefore cast considerable doubt on Mr Buckingham's sworn statement.'

It is to be hoped that the courts will exercise caution in using this discretion.

Disqualification after investigation

Section 8 Company Directors Disqualification Act 1986 gives power to the court to make a disqualification order, on the application of the Secretary of State, if it appears from a report made to him or from information or documents obtained by him that it is expedient in the public interest that an order should be made against a director or former director of any company. The court must be satisfied that the conduct of the director in relation to the company makes him unfit to be concerned in the management of a company.

It would have been under this section that the Secretary of State could have made an application for disqualification following the House of Fraser enquiry. It is to be noted that not only the unfitness test must be satisfied but that the Secretary of State may only make the application if it appears to be expedient in the public interest that a disqualification order should be made. This gives a very wide discretion to the Secretary of State as to whether he should apply. Presumably he may take into account all such matters as would be considered by the Director of Public Prosecutions when considering whether to exercise his discretion to prosecute. Such matters may well include the wisdom of prolonging an already drawn-out affair as well as the chances of the application being successful. It must be noted that the power of the Secretary of State is limited to application to the court. Contrary to the thrust of some press reports at the time of publication of the House of Fraser report, the power to disqualify lies with the court and not with the Secretary of State. There is a discretion to disqualify under this section. The maximum disqualification period is fifteen years.

Conclusion

The legislation has been widely used and disqualification is made more significant because a register of disqualified directors is kept and can be consulted. Two major difficulties remain in the operation of s. 6: the first is the exact degree to which the penal nature of the provisions should lead to care in protecting the rights of director defendants; the second is the definition of the standard of care to be expected from a reasonable director. The latter needs to be ascertained in order to more clearly identify deviancy. It is to be hoped that care will be taken to define this standard in future cases.

12.2 Insider dealing

The practice of 'insider dealing' or 'insider trading' occurs when a person with information makes use of that information for his own gain or to enable another to gain. Opinions differ as to whether the defendant should have gained the information in some privileged capacity. This aspect makes a fundamental difference to the philosophical basis of the laws forbidding the practice and is discussed below. First the content of the European Community and UK rules will be examined.

In respect of insider dealing or insider trading, UK law applies penal sanctions. There may be other constraints on company directors who contravene insider trading legislation using information gained as a director. They will be in breach of their duties to their company. Company law duties which may be used to control this type of behaviour are also examined below. The UK legislation, as well as much of the legislation in force in other Member States will be driven by the EC Directive on Insider Dealing which was implemented in the UK by the Criminal Justice Act 1993 which came into force on 1 March 1994.

The implementation of the EC Directive on Insider Dealing in the UK

The EC Directive on Insider Dealing was implemented in the United Kingdom by the Criminal Justice Act 1993 of which the relevant provisions came into force on 1 March 1994.

Part V of the Act contains the implementation of the EC Directive on Insider Dealing (89/592/EEC). Section 54 and Schedule 2 define the securities to which the insider trading provisions apply. The implementation of the EC Market Abuse Directive by the UK led to the Financial Services and Markets Act 2000 (FSMA). It had proved extremely difficult to prosecute cases of insider dealing under the criminal law, so the FSMA includes provisions giving the Financial Services Authority (FSA) power to impose civil sanctions, including fines on persons engaging in 'market abuse', which includes insider dealing. The criminal sanctions continue in force.

Securities

There is a double test. The relevant securities must appear in the list in Schedule 2 (which the Treasury may amend by order (s. 54(2)) and must satisfy such other conditions as shall be laid down by Treasury order. Schedule 2 currently lists: stocks and shares, debt securities, warrants, depositary receipts, options, securities futures and contracts for differences.

In the absence of the relevant orders it is difficult to comment on the double test, save to say that it will involve complications. It does not appear from the face of the section that the Treasury approach will be to issue a simple list of securities which are caught, and it would be almost impossible to do so. The introduction of any 'condition' to be satisfied must inevitably cause uncertainty although the approach is perhaps preferable to the approach in the Company Securities (Insider Dealing) Act 1985 which differentiates between deals on a stock exchange and off-market deals. It provides that the prohibitions apply to dealing:

> '(i) through an off-market dealer who is making a market in those securities, in the knowledge that he is an off-market dealer, that he is making a market in those securities and that those securities are advertised securities.'

The burden of proving the three necessary elements of *mens rea* to satisfy this test was clearly considerable. However under the proposed provisions the prosecutor must still show that the defendant knew that the securities fell within the orders to be issued by the Treasury under s. 54, since it is only in that case that information relating to them becomes 'inside information' and so subject to restriction (ss. 56 and 57).

Having established that the securities in question are within the definition and that the defendant knew this, the prosecutor must show that the defendant knew that the information was inside information and that the defendant 'has [the information] and knows that he has it, from an inside source' (s. 57(1)(b)).

'Inside information'

'Inside information' must be information relating to securities as defined for the purposes of this Part (as discussed above). It must also relate to particular securities or a particular issuer of securities and not to securities or issuers in general. It must be specific or precise, must not have been made public and would be likely to have had a significant effect on the price of securities if made public.

Uncertainty must exist over the meaning of 'specific or precise' and 'significant effect' on price. Whether or not the facts of an individual case fit within these definitions will be for the jury to decide. They may well be in considerable difficulties in determining these matters which may involve considerations outside their normal day-to-day experience.

Further difficulties may arise concerning the moment of 'publication' since information may well become available in widening circles rather than to everyone simultaneously. This problem is addressed in s. 58. This provides a non-exhaustive definition of the meaning of 'made public'. Information is made public if it is published in accordance with the rules of a regulated market for the purpose of informing investors and their professional advisers, is in any record open to public inspection, can readily be acquired by those likely to deal in relevant securities or is derived from information which has been made public. The section goes on to permit a wide construction of 'made public' in that information may be treated as made public even though it can only be acquired by persons exercising diligence or expertise, it has only been communicated to a section of the public, it can be acquired only by observation, is communicated on payment of a fee or it is published only outside the UK.

'Insider'

It will be remembered that the prosecutor must prove not only knowledge that the information was inside information but also that the defendant has the information from an inside source and knows that he has it from an inside source (s. 57).

An insider is defined by s. 57 as a person who has the information through:

'(a) being a director, employee or shareholder of an issuer of securities; or
(b) having access to the information by virtue of his employment, profession, office or profession or the direct or indirect source of his information is a person within para. (a).'

This definition replaces the notion of a person 'knowingly connected with a company' under s. 9 Company Securities (Insider Dealing) Act 1985 and those abusing information obtained in an official capacity (s. 2 of that Act). The wording follows Art. 2 of the EC Directive on Insider Dealing which defines the persons prohibited from trading as any person who:

'(i) by virtue of his membership of the administrative, management or supervisory bodies of the issuer,
(ii) by virtue of his holding in the capital of the issuer, or
(iii) because he has access to such information by virtue of the exercise of his employment, profession or duties in the exercise of his employment, profession or duties, possesses inside information.'

This formulation may catch the waiter who gleans the information from overheard conversation as he serves a meal to insiders since he gains the information by virtue of his employment. The loosening of the 'connection' with the company may make the offence too wide. It also puts in doubt the philosophical basis of making this behaviour a criminal offence. If the 'connection' was important, an argument based on breach of trust by individuals was credible. A widening of the offence reduces this credibility. However, it is also arguable that the wording imports a causal link between the employment etc. and the acquisition of the information. (On this point see Takis Tridimas, 'Insider Trading in Europe', 40 ICLQ 919.) By requiring that the 'access' to the information was 'by virtue' of the employment etc., the link required is stronger than in the Commission proposal which defined an insider as any person who 'in the exercise of his employment, profession or duties, acquires inside information'. The wording of the Act follows the wording of the adopted text. However, the wording of both the

Directive and the Act is ambiguous and the necessity for a causal link may well fall to be determined by the European Court of Justice at some future date.

One possible improvement on the present law is the absence of the need to prove an 'obtaining' of the information. The defendant must know that he 'has' the information as insider or that the direct or indirect source of the information was an insider (s. 57). It is clear that unsolicited information is covered. Under the present law it was unclear whether positive action by the defendant was necessary until the decision in *Attorney-General's Reference (No. 1 of 1988)* [1989] BCLC 193 determined that it was not.

Liability of individuals

The offence set out in s. 52 makes it plain that only individuals can be liable.

The exclusion of criminal liability for companies can be explained by reference to the provisions of the Directive which clearly contemplates that companies can be insiders but also expressly provides (Art. 2(2)) that when the status of insider is attributable to a legal person, the prohibition applies to the natural persons who decided to carry out the transaction for the account of the legal person concerned. It was therefore not possible to exclude companies from the definition of insiders but they can and will be excluded from liability as they are not considered to be in a position to commit the offence.

Next the prosecution must show that there was a 'dealing' in the securities, a disclosure of the information or an encouragement of another to deal (s. 52). It should be noted that unlike the other matters we have examined, these are three alternative methods of committing the offence. All other matters pose cumulative hurdles for the prosecution.

(i) Dealing or encouraging dealing

Dealing is further defined by s. 55 and includes acquisition and disposal as principal or agent or the direct or indirect procurement of an acquisition or disposal by any other person. In *Attorney-General's Reference (No. 1 of 1975)* [1975] 2 All ER 684 (at p. 686) 'procure' was held to mean 'produce by endeavour'. The defendant must therefore have caused the prohibited result by his actions. In that case the defendant charged with the procurement had added alcohol to the drink of another without his knowledge. It was held that if the defendant knew that the other man intended to drive and that the ordinary and natural result of the added alcohol was to cause him to have an alcohol concentration above the limit for drivers, the defendant had procured him to commit the drink-driving offence.

The meaning of an 'indirect procurement' must therefore remain rather obscure, particularly so far as the *mens rea* to be proved. Must it be proved that the defendant foresaw or that it was reasonably foreseeable that the defendant's actions would lead to another acquiring or disposing of securities? The relationship between this section and s. 52(2)(a), which prohibits the encouragement of another to deal, is also somewhat obscure. Could there be an indirect procurement which was not an encouragement to deal or vice versa?

Dealing will only amount to an offence if it takes place in the circumstances set out in s. 52(3). They are:

> 'that the acquisition or disposal in question occurs on a regulated market or that he relies on or is himself acting as a professional intermediary.'

This wording follows Art. 2(3) of the EC Directive which permits Member States 'to exempt deals not involving a professional intermediary'.

'Professional intermediary' is defined in s. 59. Essentially it is a person who holds himself out to a section of the public as being someone willing to engage in the acquisition or disposal of securities or act as an intermediary between persons taking part in any dealing in securities.

(ii) Disclosing

Section 52(2)(b) provides that it is an offence to disclose information to another 'otherwise than in the proper performance of the functions of his employment, office or profession'. This section deals with the simple disclosure of information and is perhaps the most likely offence to be limited by the concept of 'taking advantage' discussed below.

(iii) Encouraging others to deal

The third way of committing the offence is by encouraging others to deal. It must be shown that the defendant must know or have reasonable cause to believe that the deal will occur on a regulated market or would be effected through a professional intermediary.

Finally the concept of 'taking advantage' has been used in a limited way in the provision of specific defences.

The defences

If the factors discussed so far can be proved, the defendant is guilty of insider dealing unless he can take advantage of the defences set out in s. 53 or specific defences which appear in Schedule 1. The Act is specific about the burden of proof in that each defence requires that the defendant should 'show' the relevant facts. This will presumably mean that a defendant must establish the defences on a balance of probabilities. The defences available on a dealing charge are that:

(a) he did not at the time expect the dealing to result in a profit attributable to the fact that the information in question was price-sensitive information in relation to the securities; or

(b) that at the time he believed on reasonable grounds that the information had been disclosed widely enough to ensure that none of those taking part in the dealing would be prejudiced by not having the information; or

(c) that he would have done what he did even if he had not had the information.

This exception replaces s. 3 of the 1985 Act and is apt to cover the situation where the profit motive is present but is not a primary purpose. The problem posed by the Directive was to retain this and other exceptions while implementing the Directive which contains no parallels. Use has been made of the 'taking advantage' approach in the Directive to achieve this.

The special trustee exceptions (s. 7 Insider Dealing Act 1986), will also be covered by this exception in the Act.

Section 52(2) provides exactly similar defences for the offence of encouraging another to deal and s. 53(3) provides a defence to the disclosure provision. It is a defence for a defendant accused of insider dealing by disclosure of information to show either that he did not expect anyone to deal as a result of the disclosure or that he did not expect the dealing to result in a profit attributable to the fact that the information was price-sensitive. In all cases the notion of profit includes avoidance of a loss (s. 53(6)).

There are also specific defences for: market makers dealing in good faith in the course of business or employment; dealers whose information is market information concerning acquisition or disposal of certain securities who deal in good faith in circumstances where it was reasonable for them to deal; and price stabilisation operations provided that the individuals carrying them out have acted in conformity with price stabilisation rules made under s. 48 Financial Services Act 1986.

Article 2(4) of the Directive provides an exemption for transactions carried out by Member States or their agents 'in pursuit of monetary, exchange rate or public debt-management policies'. This general exemption is reflected in s. 63 of the Act.

One concern which may be felt is the reversal of the burden of proof in all the above circumstances save for the general exemption in s. 63. The presumption against a defendant and the defence based on motive may be of little comfort where criminal charges are in prospect.

Jurisdiction

By Art. 5 of the Directive, the Member States are to apply the prohibitions 'at least' to actions undertaken within their territory 'to the extent that the transferable securities concerned are admitted to trading on a market of a Member State'. This provision appears to be of impenetrable obscurity but an attempt has been made to reflect the Directive in s. 62 which restricts jurisdiction to acts done within the UK or markets declared by Treasury order to be a market regulated in the UK. It is not necessary that the dealing should have occurred within the UK: 'any act constituting or forming part of the alleged dealing' will be sufficient to found jurisdiction.

Conclusion

Article 13 of the Directive provides that the Member States shall determine the penalties to be applied for infringement of the prohibitions. The only proviso to this discretion is that the 'penalties shall be sufficient to promote compliance'. The maximum penalty provided for in the Act is seven-years' imprisonment and an unlimited fine for a conviction on indictment. The UK would seem to have ignored both the criticism of the use of the criminal law and the possibility of substituting civil remedies. (See Hopt and Wymeersch (eds.), *European Insider Dealing*, Butterworths, 1991 and J. Naylor, 'The Use of Criminal Sanctions by the UK and US Authorities for Insider Trading' (1990) 11 Co. Law 53.) Although the implementation provisions reflect the Directive well, the use of the criminal law probably does not promote compliance with the prohibitions as it is well known to be ineffective.

The sum total of the matters which the prosecution must prove has been set out above and it is plain that the offence is still complex and difficult to prove. It is arguable that putting in place an ineffective convoluted criminal offence is at the same time a misuse of the criminal law and an ineffective implementation of the EC Directive.

Should insider dealing be a crime?

Some argue that this is a 'victimless crime' in that it is not clear if there is actually a loser; others claim that the practice of insider trading increases the volume of sales on a market, so that overall the market gains.

Theories behind control of insider trading

In the USA, regulation of insider dealing dates from the 1930s. A comprehensive ban on dealing passed into UK law in the 1980s. Prior to this, insider dealing by directors might have given rise to an action for breach of fiduciary duties provided that the misfeasance was not ratified by the company's general meeting.

The controversy surrounding the regulation of insider trading starts from a number of theoretical standpoints:

Misappropriation Perhaps the simplest is the misappropriation theory which regards non-public price-sensitive information as a valuable commodity which is the property or akin to the property of a company. The information does not belong to the individuals who make up the company. It is therefore inequitable and akin to theft for those individuals to make use of that information for their own gain. This theory does not require any loss to have been suffered in real terms – the offensive behaviour is seen as the unjustifiable gain or avoidance of loss. This equation of insider trading with misappropriation is perhaps the strongest argument in favour of criminal sanctions. It is to be noted, however, that at this stage practical considerations have not been taken into account. The most compelling practical consideration is that both the offence and the transactions which constitute the *actus reus* are complicated. This makes proof of all of the elements of an offence to the criminal standard extremely difficult. There have been fewer than 20 convictions in the UK since the offence was introduced. Some of these followed pleas of guilty.

Fairness and confidence in the market This argument in favour of the regulation of insider trading rests on the perception that if, of two potential players in a market, one has price-sensitive information available and the other has not, that is unfair.

The argument may be bolstered by, or include reference to, the misappropriation theory and its proponents may or may not assert that the 'victims' suffer loss as opposed to making a profit. The unfairness is said to lead to loss of confidence by investors in the markets and will lead to a diminution in trading.

In fact, there are three closely related approaches which may overlap. The inherent unfairness approach, the misappropriation theory and the idea that insider trading may lead to loss of confidence in the market are all distinct reasons for regulating insider trading. They may be used together as above but the loss of confidence in the market may not necessarily be related to the perception that the market is unfair.

Market efficiency If it could be shown that insider dealing created a more efficient market, then there would be a benefit to all investors at the expense of no one. Manne ('The Economics of Legal Relationships', *Readings in the Theory of Property Rights*, St Paul, 1975) sought to establish that the effect of insider dealing is to produce a gradual change in prices as more and more people receive and rely on the information in question. Only speculative dealers on the market would suffer from insider dealing. The long-term investor will not be interested in the timing of the disclosure but will reap his reward in due course. When such an investor sells, Manne argues that even if he sells in ignorance of information which is causing insiders to trade, the very fact that they are trading increases the price he receives for his shares. Suter (*The Regulation of Insider Dealing in Britain*, Butterworths, 1989, p. 22) has the following to say about that proposition:

> 'Arguments as to the seller's gain will be of little comfort to a seller who argues that had he known what the insider knew, he would not have sold. In deciding to sell, he sells at a lower price than if the information had been disclosed. He is also deprived of information relevant to his investment decision. The fact that the seller's loss is contingent does not mean that the insider's gain is not made at the expense of anyone.'

The gap between the two positions can perhaps be explained by the difference between the economists' approach, which focuses on the efficiency of the market and would regard the improved efficiency of the market and the consequent gain to all investors as outweighing any notions of inequities between individual participants, and the other approaches. This attitude leads to the extreme theory which holds that the ability to use price-sensitive information before it is made public is a legitimate reward for those in a position to be able to do so.

The government's view

However, the view current at present in official circles in the UK is that insider trading undermines confidence in the probity of the market and is unfair. It is a practice also condemned on the ground that it has parallels with those who use information or property belonging to a company to make gains on their own account.

Summary

1. The general fiduciary duties of directors are backed up by specific duties and prohibitions set out in the statutes.

2. These prohibitions include limitations on transactions between the company and directors or their families.

3. There is also a general prohibition on the misuse of price-sensitive information about shares obtained by or from a person in a privileged position. The rule against insider dealing attracts criminal and civil penalties.

Case notes

1. Sections 182, 183, 188, 190, 191, 197, 199 and 215 Companies Act 2006

182 Declaration of interest in existing transaction or arrangement

(1) Where a director of a company is in any way, directly or indirectly, interested in a transaction or arrangement that has been entered into by the company, he must declare the nature and extent of the interest to the other directors in accordance with this section.

This section does not apply if or to the extent that the interest has been declared under section 177 (duty to declare interest in proposed transaction or arrangement).

(2) The declaration must be made –

(a) at a meeting of the directors, or

(b) by notice in writing (see section 184), or

(c) by general notice (see section 185).

(3) If a declaration of interest under this section proves to be, or becomes, inaccurate or incomplete, a further declaration must be made.

(4) Any declaration required by this section must be made as soon as is reasonably practicable.

Failure to comply with this requirement does not affect the underlying duty to make the declaration.

(5) This section does not require a declaration of an interest of which the director is not aware or where the director is not aware of the transaction or arrangement in question.

For this purpose a director is treated as being aware of matters of which he ought reasonably to be aware.

(6) A director need not declare an interest under this section –

(a) if it cannot reasonably be regarded as likely to give rise to a conflict of interest;

(b) if, or to the extent that, the other directors are already aware of it (and for this purpose the other directors are treated as aware of anything of which they ought reasonably to be aware); or

(c) if, or to the extent that, it concerns terms of his service contract that have been or are to be considered –

(i) by a meeting of the directors, or

(ii) by a committee of the directors appointed for the purpose under the company's constitution.

183 Offence of failure to declare interest

(1) A director who fails to comply with the requirements of section 182 (declaration of interest in existing transaction or arrangement) commits an offence.

(2) A person guilty of an offence under this section is liable –

(a) on conviction on indictment, to a fine;

(b) on summary conviction, to a fine not exceeding the statutory maximum.

188 Directors' long-term service contracts: requirement of members' approval

(1) This section applies to provision under which the guaranteed term of a director's employment –

(a) with the company of which he is a director, or

(b) where he is the director of a holding company, within the group consisting of that company and its subsidiaries,

is, or may be, longer than two years.

(2) A company may not agree to such provision unless it has been approved –

(a) by resolution of the members of the company, and

(b) in the case of a director of a holding company, by resolution of the members of that company.

(3) The guaranteed term of a director's employment is –

(a) the period (if any) during which the director's employment –

(i) is to continue, or may be continued otherwise than at the instance of the company (whether under the original agreement or under a new agreement entered into in pursuance of it), and

(ii) cannot be terminated by the company by notice, or can be so terminated only in specified circumstances, or

(b) in the case of employment terminable by the company by notice, the period of notice required to be given,

or, in the case of employment having a period within paragraph (a) and a period within paragraph (b), the aggregate of those periods.

(4) If more than six months before the end of the guaranteed term of a director's employment the company enters into a further service contract (otherwise than in pursuance of a right conferred, by or under the original contract, on the other party to it), this section applies as if there were added to the guaranteed term of the new contract the unexpired period of the guaranteed term of the original contract.

(5) A resolution approving provision to which this section applies must not be passed unless a memorandum setting out the proposed contract incorporating the provision is made available to members –

(a) in the case of a written resolution, by being sent or submitted to every eligible member at or before the time at which the proposed resolution is sent or submitted to him;

(b) in the case of a resolution at a meeting, by being made available for inspection by members of the company both –
   (i) at the company's registered office for not less than 15 days ending with the date of the meeting, and
   (ii) at the meeting itself.

(6) No approval is required under this section on the part of the members of a body corporate that –
   (a) is not a UK-registered company, or
   (b) is a wholly-owned subsidiary of another body corporate.

(7) In this section 'employment' means any employment under a director's service contract.

190 Substantial property transactions: requirement of members' approval

(1) A company may not enter into an arrangement under which –
   (a) a director of the company or of its holding company, or a person connected with such a director, acquires or is to acquire from the company (directly or indirectly) a substantial non-cash asset, or
   (b) the company acquires or is to acquire a substantial non-cash asset (directly or indirectly) from such a director or a person so connected, unless the arrangement has been approved by a resolution of the members of the company or is conditional on such approval being obtained.

For the meaning of 'substantial non-cash asset' see section 191.

(2) If the director or connected person is a director of the company's holding company or a person connected with such a director, the arrangement must also have been approved by a resolution of the members of the holding company or be conditional on such approval being obtained.

(3) A company shall not be subject to any liability by reason of a failure to obtain approval required by this section.

(4) No approval is required under this section on the part of the members of a body corporate that –
   (a) is not a UK-registered company, or
   (b) is a wholly-owned subsidiary of another body corporate.

(5) For the purposes of this section –
   (a) an arrangement involving more than one non-cash asset, or
   (b) an arrangement that is one of a series involving non-cash assets, shall be treated as if they involved a non-cash asset of a value equal to the aggregate value of all the non-cash assets involved in the arrangement or, as the case may be, the series.

(6) This section does not apply to a transaction so far as it relates –

    (a) to anything to which a director of a company is entitled under his service contract, or

    (b) to payment for loss of office as defined in section 215 (payments requiring members' approval).

191 Meaning of 'substantial'

(1) This section explains what is meant in section 190 (requirement of approval for substantial property transactions) by a 'substantial' non-cash asset.

(2) An asset is a substantial asset in relation to a company if its value –

    (a) exceeds 10% of the company's asset value and is more than £5,000, or

    (b) exceeds £100,000.

(3) For this purpose a company's 'asset value' at any time is –

    (a) the value of the company's net assets determined by reference to its most recent statutory accounts, or

    (b) if no statutory accounts have been prepared, the amount of the company's called-up share capital.

(4) A company's 'statutory accounts' means its annual accounts prepared in accordance with Part 15, and its 'most recent' statutory accounts means those in relation to which the time for sending them out to members (see section 424) is most recent.

(5) Whether an asset is a substantial asset shall be determined as at the time the arrangement is entered into.

197 Loans to directors: requirement of members' approval

(1) A company may not –

    (a) make a loan to a director of the company or of its holding company, or

    (b) give a guarantee or provide security in connection with a loan made by any person to such a director,

unless the transaction has been approved by a resolution of the members of the company.

(2) If the director is a director of the company's holding company, the transaction must also have been approved by a resolution of the members of the holding company.

(3) A resolution approving a transaction to which this section applies must not be passed unless a memorandum setting out the matters mentioned in subsection (4) is made available to members –

    (a) in the case of a written resolution, by being sent or submitted to every eligible member at or before the time at which the proposed resolution is sent or submitted to him;

    (b) in the case of a resolution at a meeting, by being made available for inspection by members of the company both –

(i) at the company's registered office for not less than 15 days ending with the date of the meeting, and

(ii) at the meeting itself.

(4) The matters to be disclosed are –

(a) the nature of the transaction,

(b) the amount of the loan and the purpose for which it is required, and

(c) the extent of the company's liability under any transaction connected with the loan.

(5) No approval is required under this section on the part of the members of a body corporate that –

(a) is not a UK-registered company, or

(b) is a wholly-owned subsidiary of another body corporate.

199 Meaning of 'quasi-loan' and related expressions

(1) A 'quasi-loan' is a transaction under which one party ('the creditor') agrees to pay, or pays otherwise than in pursuance of an agreement, a sum for another ('the borrower') or agrees to reimburse, or reimburses otherwise than in pursuance of an agreement, expenditure incurred by another party for another ('the borrower') –

(a) on terms that the borrower (or a person on his behalf) will reimburse the creditor; or

(b) in circumstances giving rise to a liability on the borrower to reimburse the creditor.

(2) Any reference to the person to whom a quasi-loan is made is a reference to the borrower.

(3) The liabilities of the borrower under a quasi-loan include the liabilities of any person who has agreed to reimburse the creditor on behalf of the borrower.

215 Payments for loss of office

(1) In this Chapter a 'payment for loss of office' means a payment made to a director or past director of a company –

(a) by way of compensation for loss of office as director of the company,

(b) by way of compensation for loss, while director of the company or in connection with his ceasing to be a director of it, of –

(i) any other office or employment in connection with the management of the affairs of the company, or

(ii) any office (as director or otherwise) or employment in connection with the management of the affairs of any subsidiary undertaking of the company,

(c) as consideration for or in connection with his retirement from his office as director of the company, or

(d) as consideration for or in connection with his retirement, while director of the company or in connection with his ceasing to be a director of it, from –

(i) any other office or employment in connection with the management of the affairs of the company, or

(ii) any office (as director or otherwise) or employment in connection with the management of the affairs of any subsidiary undertaking of the company.

(2) The references to compensation and consideration include benefits otherwise than in cash and references in this Chapter to payment have a corresponding meaning.

(3) For the purposes of sections 217 to 221 (payments requiring members' approval) –

(a) payment to a person connected with a director, or

(b) payment to any person at the direction of, or for the benefit of, a director or a person connected with him,

is treated as payment to the director.

(4) References in those sections to payment by a person include payment by another person at the direction of, or on behalf of, the person referred to.

2. *Re Dawson Print Group* [1987] BCLC 601

The defendant director was a director of two companies, which were wound up in April and May 1983. The first company (DPG) had assets of approximately £3,850 and debts of approximately £111,000, of which £40,000 was represented by unpaid VAT, PAYE and National Insurance Charges (NIC). The second company (Princo) had assets of approximately £3,450 and debts of approximately £21,000, of which £5,500 was for VAT, PAYE and NIC. A disqualification order was sought under s. 300 Companies Act 1985 which was the predecessor to s. 6 Company Directors Disqualification Act 1986. The Companies Act section differs from its replacement in that disqualification is discretionary. From subsequent cases it appears that this difference has little effect on the courts' view of the behaviour of the directors in question and the courts' judgment of whether they are 'unfit' to be directors.

Hoffman J refused to disqualify the director. He took into account:

(1) the fact of large debts owed to the Crown; he did not consider this of great significance;

(2) the young age of the director (first appointed at twenty);

(3) the fact that there had been no 'breach of commercial morality' or 'really gross negligence';

(4) the fact that this director was now running a successful company; and

(5) some of the losses could be accounted for by unforeseeable bad luck and the behaviour of other people.

3. *Re Stanford Services* [1987] BCLC 607

This was also an application to disqualify a director under s. 300 Companies Act 1985. The two companies in which the director was principally involved were insolvent. The approximate sums involved were as follows. First company: assets £46,200; liabilities £253,880, including £12,400 PAYE, £13,100 NIC and £14,900 VAT. Second company: assets £451,800; liabilities: £779,600, including £29,400 PAYE, £27,700 NIC and £33,800 VAT.

Vinelott J imposed a disqualification order for two years. Important factors were:

(1) the debts to the Crown were large and the companies had only continued to trade by not paying them;

(2) there had been a failure to keep and file proper accounts;

(3) there was evidence of recklessness in acquiring or commencing the companies; and

(4) there was evidence of negligence in carrying on the businesses when a reasonable person would have known them to be insolvent, and in paying himself large sums at such a time.

Exercises

1. Would the transactions prohibited by statute be a breach of directors' duties according to the case law?

2. Should insider dealing be a criminal offence?

Chapter 13

Suing the company, suing for the company, enforcing directors' duties

Key words

▶ **Derivative action** – an action brought by shareholders on behalf of the company (deriving from the company's right to sue).

▶ **Ratification** – voting by the general meeting to forgive directors' breaches of duty.

13.1 Suing the company

One of the reasons for conferring a legal personality on a company was to make it able to sue and be sued in its own name. Consequently a company can be sued for a wrong perpetrated by it, either by a member or by a third party who has been aggrieved by the company's action. Difficulties may sometimes arise when the capacity of the member to sue is in doubt (see the discussion of the articles as a contract in Chapter 5). As a general rule, however, where the wrong has been done to or by a company, the company can sue or be sued. Thus, if a director is in breach of his duties to the company, the company can sue him for redress. However, corporate personality has caused problems as well as solving them. Without controls arrived at by the courts and those now in the 2006 Companies Act, if the majority of the shares in a company were held by those controlling that company (and they often were), those controllers could perpetrate all kinds of wrongdoing to the detriment of the minority and then vote that the company should not take legal action to gain compensation. Suppose, for example, that a director sells to the company land worth £10,000. He and his cronies who together hold a majority of the shares in the company, pay £20,000 for the land. They then pass a resolution to the effect that the company should not take action to get back the money that has been taken unnecessarily from the company. The minority shareholders in the company have had the assets of the company diminished and thus the value of their shareholding in the company goes down. What can they do? In theory it is the company's money to give away and it has done so. This is the type of situation in which the courts made an exception to the corporate personality rule. This exception was known as the exception to the rule in *Foss* v. *Harbottle* (1843) 2 Hare 461.

13.2 Suing for the company (the exceptions to the rule in *Foss* v. *Harbottle* and derivative actions)

The duties which a director owes to the company are only useful if they can be effectively enforced. If a right has been infringed which is in law a right belonging to a company (for example, the misapplication of company property – *Foss* v. *Harbottle*, or indeed any other breach of directors' duties) the only proper plaintiff is the company itself. This rule was known as the rule in *Foss* v. *Harbottle* (see Case note 1, p. 272) because this is the case in which the rule was first clearly established. In *Bamford* v. *Bamford* [1970] Ch 212, Lord Justice Russell said:

> 'it would be for the company to decide whether to institute proceedings to avoid the voidable allotment: and again this decision would be one for the company in general meeting to decide by ordinary resolution. To litigate or not to litigate, apart from very special circumstances, is for decision by such a resolution.'

As a general principle this was admirable because it had the advantage of avoiding the problem of many actions being commenced simultaneously by all members that believed themselves to be aggrieved by a particular action of the management. However, real problems occurred when the alleged perpetrators of the wrong against the company also control the general meeting. In those circumstances, of course, it was most unlikely that the members of the general meeting would resolve to sue themselves. When this happens, if the wrong done was serious enough a shareholder might have been permitted to sue on behalf of the company. However, four major difficulties confronted such a plaintiff:

1. The standing of the plaintiff and his entitlement to sue had to be settled as a preliminary matter before the substantive complaint was heard. This involved the plaintiff in establishing that the alleged wrongdoers are 'in control' of the company. Further, the action had to have been brought *bona fide* for the benefit of the company for wrongs to the company for which no other remedy is available and not for an ulterior purpose. In *Barrett* v. *Duckett and Others* [1995] 1 BCLC 243 the action was brought to harass an ex-son-in-law and thus was not permitted.
2. The plaintiff had to show that the company suffered a wrong of such an order that it would be unfair to permit the general meeting to ratify the wrong. The ambit of this requirement was most uncertain. It seems clear that actions wholly outside the power of the company to perform could not be ratified by ordinary resolution, only by the special procedures under

s. 35 Companies Act 1985 (which provided for ratification of *ultra vires* acts by special resolutions). It is certain that minor wrongs against the company could be ratified. There remained an enormous area of uncertainty providing a potential pitfall to a plaintiff in this sort of action.

3. The plaintiff had to prove the actual commission of the serious wrong against the company by those controlling it. This in itself was a difficult task since the plaintiff is not, by definition, a controller of the company and so he will in all likelihood have limited access to information concerning the internal management of the company.

4. If the plaintiff could surmount these three not inconsiderable hurdles he would succeed in his action. However, during the course of the case he was always at peril as to costs. Even if he succeeded, the principal beneficiary of the action was the company in whose favour judgment was given. The actual gain to the plaintiff might thus be very small. His only gain might be the right to participate in the fortunes of a better-managed company. It is perhaps not surprising that this type of action was infrequently brought, particularly in view of the remedy introduced in 1980 and now to be found at ss. 994–999 of Companies Act 2006. This whole area is now covered by the Companies Act 2006 although it is not wholly clear how much of the case law will remain relevant.

13.3 Ratification

Ratification is now covered by the 2006 Act but that Act has failed to solve some of the more fundamental issues which stem from the whole concept of ratification. The statute covers the issue in a single section. Section 239 states:

Ratification of acts of a director

(1) This section applies to the ratification of a company of conduct by a director amounting to negligence, default, breach of duty or breach of trust in relation to the company.

(2) The decision of the company to ratify such conduct must be made by the resolution of the members of the company.

(3) and (4) prevent the director or a connected person from voting on such a resolution.

(7) This section does not affect any other enactment or rule of law imposing additional requirements for valid ratification or any rule of law as to the acts which are incapable of being ratified by the company.

It is subsection (7) which appears to open the interpretation of the statute to all the uncertainties which existed under the case law as to what actions could or could not be ratified (see below). This used to require a 'fraud on the minority' and whether or not this had occurred was one of the most difficult questions in company law. First, however, the plaintiff must show that he has a right to sue.

The right to sue: who is in control of the company?

Under the case law which preceded Companies Act 2006, in *Birch* v. *Sullivan* [1958] 1 All ER 56 the court said that when an individual plaintiff institutes a derivative action to enforce a right belonging to the company, he must specifically allege in his pleadings, and be prepared to prove, that those in control of the company would prevent the company from suing in its own name. If there is any challenge to that allegation the matter had to be determined as a preliminary issue (*Prudential Assurance Co. Ltd* v. *Newman Industries Ltd (No. 2)* [1982] Ch 204). The great difficulty was in determining an effective test which will embrace all circumstances in which the persons complained about are 'in control' of a company. In *Prudential Assurance Co. Ltd* v. *Newman Industries Ltd (No. 2)* [1982] Ch 204; [1982] 1 All ER 354, the judge who first heard the case believed that the court should examine the realities of the situation. He said:

> 'if the defendants against whom relief is sought on behalf of the company control the majority of votes, the action will be allowed to proceed whether a resolution that no action should be brought by the company has been passed or not; so also, if the persons against whom relief is sought do not control a majority of the votes but it is shown that a resolution has been passed and passed only by the use of their votes ... But there are an infinite variety of possible circumstances ... If shareholders having a majority of votes in general meeting are nominees, the court will look behind the register to the beneficial owners to see whether they are the persons against whom relief is sought: see *Pavlides* v. *Jensen* [1956] Ch 565. There seems no good reason why the court should not have regard to any other circumstances which show that the majority cannot be relied upon to determine in a disinterested way whether it is truly in the interests of the company that proceedings should be brought.'

The judgment of the Court of Appeal in that case left matters most unclear. The suggestion was made that if 'control' was an issue the court should grant an adjournment 'to enable a meeting of shareholders to be convened by the board, so that he can reach a conclusion in the light of the conduct of, and proceedings at, that meeting'. This would seem to imply rejection of the idea that all matters which might in fact affect control of the company should be investigated. The approach suggested by the Court of Appeal would to some extent confine the court to taking into account matters which appeared, so to speak, 'on the face of' the meeting. However, the judgment offers no very clear guidance as to what matters should be taken into account. Even if it did, the Court of Appeal's words would be of doubtful value, since the issue of the *Foss* v. *Harbottle* rule had become irrelevant to the outcome of the case by the time it was heard in that court. The judges had refused to hear counsel's arguments on the proper scope of *Foss* v. *Harbottle* and were careful to point out that they were not expressing a 'concluded' view on the scope of the rule in *Foss* v. *Harbottle*. The extent to which a court can probe the reality of the situation to determine control thus remains uncertain. What is clear from *Smith* v. *Croft (No. 2)* [1988] Ch 114 (see Case note **2**, pp. 272–3) is that a minority shareholder who would otherwise be able to sue on behalf of the company, under an established exception to the rule in *Foss* v. *Harbottle*, may nevertheless be prevented from doing so if a majority of the members, independent of the wrongdoers, is opposed to the litigation. If a majority of the oppressed minority is not prepared to support the action it cannot go ahead.

The Companies Act 2006 retains the need for the plaintiff to apply for permission to bring the action and the scales seem to be quite heavily weighed against him. There are certainly relics of the need to prove that the wrongdoers were in control to be found in s. 263, especially s. 263(4), but it will be a matter for the courts to determine how much of the pre-existing case law will be regarded as relevant.

Section 261 provides:

(1) A member of a company who brings a derivative claim . . . must apply to the court for permission . . . to continue it.
(2) If it appears to the court that the application and the evidence filed by the applicant in support of it do not disclose a *prima facie* case for giving permission, the court –
must dismiss the action.

Section 262 provides:

A member may apply to continue a claim brought by a company if
    (a) the manner in which the company commenced or continued the claim amounts to an abuse of the process of the court;
    . . .
    (c) it is appropriate for the member to continue the claim as a derivative claim.
(3) In considering whether to give permission . . . the court must take into account, in particular
    (a) whether the member is acting in good faith in seeking to continue the claim;
    (b) the importance that a person acting in accordance with s. 172 (duty to promote the success of the company) would attach to continuing it;

(c) whether the company would have been likely to ratify the act or omission;

(d) whether the company had decided not to pursue the claim;

(e) whether the act or omission gives rise to a cause of action that the member could pursue in his own right rather than on behalf of the company.

Section 263 concerns whether permission to be given:

(2) Permission . . . must be refused if the court is satisfied

(a) that a person acting in accordance with s. 172 (duty to promote the success of the company) would not seek to continue the claim;

(b) where the cause of action arises from an act or omission that is yet to occur and the act or omission has been authorised by the company;

(c) where the cause of action arises from an act or omission that has already occurred, that the act or omission –

(i) was authorised by the company before it occurred;

(ii) has been ratified by the company since it occurred.

. . .

(4) In considering whether to give permission . . . the court shall have particular regard to any evidence before it as to the views of members of the company who have no personal interest, direct or indirect, in the matter.

Two other restrictions were that a defendant might raise not only defences which would be valid against an action by the company, but also defences that would only be valid against the plaintiff personally (*Nurcombe* v. *Nurcombe* [1985] 1 All ER 65 (see Case note **3**, p. 273). It has also been held that a minority shareholder may not bring a derivative action when a company has gone into liquidation. Only the liquidator can represent the company after that moment (*Fargo Ltd* v. *Godfroy* [1986] 3 All ER 279).

Serious wrongdoing by those in control

An essential distinction made in the case law was between actions by the controllers of the company which could not be 'ratified' by the majority of the company voting in a general meeting and those that could be ratified. It seems that s. 239(7) retains this case law's relevance. Ratification is a concept borrowed from agency law where it is used to describe the process of retrospective validation of an agent's acts. If an agent acts outside the authority conferred upon him by his principal, the principal can at a later date approve the action of the agent and agree to be legally bound by any transaction entered into by that agent. In company law, if the directors of the company have acted in breach of their duties it is open to the shareholders, on some occasions but not on others, to vote that such directors will not be sued in respect of those breaches of duty. The major difficulty is in identifying what breaches are ratifiable and can be forgiven and which are not ratifiable and will therefore found an action provided the wrongdoers are in control of the company in the sense discussed above. However, there is another curious feature of ratification which must be noted. Under the old law a breach of duty was ratifiable *notwithstanding that the wrongdoers made up part or all of the vote in favour of ratification*. This is no longer the case under ss. 239(3) and 239(4).

What actions make up a wrong which cannot be ratified?

The categories that are identifiable from the cases are:

(1) where the act complained of is *ultra vires* or illegal;
(2) where there is a 'fraud on the minority'.

It is clear in the aftermath of the *Prudential* case that there is to be no exception to the rule in *Foss* v. *Harbottle* simply 'where the interests of justice so require'.

Ultra vires and illegal acts

It was for some time unclear whether an *ultra vires* or illegal act was a wrong done to individual shareholders as well as a wrong done to the company. If it could be regarded as infringing the personal rights of shareholders, each shareholder would have a personal right to sue on his own behalf and would not need to invoke the derivative action. However, it now seems clear, following *Smith* v. *Croft*, that all cases in which compensation is sought on behalf of the company for past *ultra vires* or illegal acts are to be regarded as cases brought on behalf of the company. The court may, however, refuse permission because of s. 262(3) where the action is originally brought by the company. This does not affect the personal right of a shareholder to sue to restrain an action which is about to occur and which will be *ultra vires* or illegal. An example of illegality and *ultra vires* is *Smith* v. *Croft* itself (see Case note 2, pp. 272–3).

Ratification and fraud on the minority

Under case law, ratification was not available if the action amounted to a 'fraud on the minority'. It should be noted that 'fraud' in this context has a special meaning unconnected with any considerations of deceit or of criminal law notions of fraud. Some actions may involve crimes, others may not. Over the years commentators have discerned various categories of fraud on the minority from the cases but all agree that the cases are difficult to reconcile with one another and in some cases behaviour can be found which fits more than one of the categories. Perhaps the proper way to regard the cases is to extract the total wrongdoing of the controllers and ask whether this is behaviour that can be condoned by a majority vote which would now exclude the wrongdoing director and connected persons? Categories which have been identified are:

[handwritten: → derive the owner of its property.]

(1) expropriation of the company's property;
(2) *mala fide* breaches of duty;
(3) negligent acts from which the directors benefit;
(4) use of powers for an improper purpose.

To some extent these categories are merely a way of saying that where there has been a breach of duty by directors the court will examine all the facts to determine whether it is such a serious matter that it cannot be 'forgiven' by ratification. Obviously, taking the company's property is the clearest example of such a situation, so that is an identifiably separate category. With regard to the other instances of breach of duty it is doubtful whether there is value in attempting to do more than look at the sum total of the behaviour of the controllers in order to assess whether a proper case can be made for a derivative action to be permitted to go ahead. For that reason breaches of duty not involving expropriation of company property are divided into non-ratifiable acts which are then distinguished from ratifiable acts. Among the latter are: *bona fide* incidental profit-making; use of powers for an improper purpose; and negligence which does not benefit the directors.

The ambit of s. 262(4) is in some doubt because of case law which preceded the Companies Act 2006. In *Johnson* v. *Gore Wood & Co.* [2000] UKHL 65, Lord Bingham underlined three propositions stemming from previous case law (accessed at:
www.bailii.org/uk/cases/UKHL/2000/65.html

(1) Where a company suffers loss caused by a breach of duty owed to it, only the company may sue in respect of that loss. No action lies at the suit of a shareholder suing in that capacity and no other to make good a diminution in the value of the shareholder's shareholding where that merely reflects the loss suffered by the company. A claim will not lie by a shareholder to make good a loss which would be made good if the company's assets were replenished through action against the party responsible for the loss, even if the company, acting through its constitutional organs, has declined or failed to make good that loss. So

much is clear from *Prudential*, particularly at pp. 222–3; *Heron International* v. *Lord Grade* [1983] BCLC 244, particularly at pp. 261–2; *George Fischer (Great Britain)* v. *Multi Construction Ltd, Dexion Ltd* [1995] 1 BCLC 260, particularly at pp. 266 and 270–1; *Gerber Garment Technology Inc* v. *Lectra Systems Ltd and Another* [1997] RPC 443; and *Stein* v. *Blake* [1998] 1 BCLC 573, particularly at pp. 726–9.

(2) Where a company suffers loss but has no cause of action to sue to recover that loss, the shareholder in the company may sue in respect of it (if the shareholder has a cause of action to do so), even though the loss is a diminution in the value of the shareholding. This is supported by *Lee* v. *Sheard* [1956] 1 QB 192, at pp. 195–6; *George Fischer*; and *Gerber*.

(3) Where a company suffers loss caused by a breach of duty to it, and a shareholder suffers a loss separate and distinct from that suffered by the company caused by breach of a duty independently owed to the shareholder, each may sue to recover the loss caused to it by breach of the duty owed to it but neither may recover loss caused to the other by breach of the duty owed to that other. We take this to be the effect of *Lee* v. *Sheard*, at pp. 195–6; *Heron International*, particularly at p. 262; *R. P. Howard Ltd & Richard Alan Witchell* v. *Woodman Matthews and Co.* [1983] BCLC 117, particularly at p. 123; *Gerber*; and *Stein* v. *Blake*, particularly at p. 726. We do not think the observations of Leggatt LJ in *Barings plc and Another* v. *Coopers and Lybrand and Others* [1997] 1 BCLC 427 at p. 435B and of the Court of Appeal of New Zealand in *Christensen* v. *Scott* [1996] 1 NZLR 273 at p. 280, lines 25–35, can be reconciled with this statement of principle.

In *Walker* v. *Stones* [2001] BCC 757, the court followed the *Johnson* line and stated that when the shareholder in question had suffered a personal loss which is distinct from a loss incurred by the company in which he had a financial stake, he is justified in making a personal claim. Thus, an individual shareholder has a right to bring a personal claim when his loss is separate and distinctive from the losses suffered by the company in cases where a director has breached his fiduciary duty causing damage. On the contrary when his loss is just reflective of the company's general loss, he will not be able to raise a personal claim since these losses would be recoverable only with a derivative action. If on the other hand his losses are just an aspect of the general losses of the company then the former are recoverable only with a derivative action. This appears to be consistent with the line and the argumentation that the court had previously adopted in *Prudential Assurance Co.* v. *Newman Industries* [1982]. In that case it was respectively stated that: 'what a shareholder cannot do . . . is to recover a sum . . . [when] such a loss is merely a reflection of the loss suffered by the company . . . his loss is through the company, in the diminution in the value of the net assets of the company.' This line was also followed in *Day* v. *Cook* [2001] EWCA Civ 592.

In *Giles* v. *Rhind* [2002] EWCA Civ 1428, the principles laid down by Lord Bingham were slightly evolved. In this case the two people involved, *G* and *R*, were former directors of a company which had become insolvent after *R* set up a new business to which he diverted employees and contracts. With these actions he effectively breached a previous shareholder agreement to which himself and *G* were both parties. Since the company was insolvent, its action against *R* was discontinued. In the light of this development *G* decided to pursue personal claims for damages. The question arising was whether *G* was entitled to bring a claim on the loss of value of his shareholding and his future losses of remuneration. At first instance it was held that the aforementioned losses of *G* were reflective of the general losses of the company, thus preventing a personal claim on his part. The company was the legitimate source of action in this case irrespective of the fact that the company had not been able because of insolvency, to pursue the recovery of such losses. Still, the losses in question could be legitimately claimed solely by the company.

The court of appeal had a different opinion. It stated that *G* was indeed entitled to pursue his own personal claim against *R*, since his personal loss was not merely reflective of the company's loss but constituted a separate cause of action. In such a case there will not be a double recovery against *R* since the company itself, because of its state of insolvency, could not recover the losses itself. Therefore, it was justified to let an individual shareholder take action, especially in the light of the recognition that the inability of the company to act was attributed to *R*'s wrongdoing. So, although a company in this case does have a cause of action, an individual shareholder is allowed to pursue a personal action because the company is in no position to exercise its rights and make its own claims for the losses incurred. This seems to depart from the first proposition laid down by Lord Bingham in *Johnson*.

Moreover, the court in *Giles* went a step further by stating that even in respect of those losses of *G* which were reflective of the losses of the company, he could still bring a personal action because the company had been prevented from proceeding with its own action because of *R*'s wrongdoing. Thus, *G*'s claims for loss of future earnings, especially in relation to his remuneration, were not treated as expected, which is losses reflective of the company's losses which prevent any personal action from being raised. The company ceased to exist and, therefore, *G* was left unemployed with no future earnings coming from his remuneration. Even if the company had been able to pursue its claims against *R*, any recovered sums would not have compensated him for the loss of employment. He was allowed, therefore, to raise a personal action, which seems to also depart from the spirit of the three propositions of *Johnson*.

Expropriation of company property

In *Menier* v. *Hooper's Telegraph Works* (1874) LR 9 Ch D 350 a rival company had a controlling interest in the company concerned. It used this controlling interest to settle an impending action between the two companies in its favour. The judge said that the majority had 'put something into their pockets' at the expense of the minority. This fell squarely within the fraud on the minority exception and would not be permitted. Similarly, in *Cook* v. *Deeks* [1916] 1 AC 554, the directors diverted to themselves contracts which they should have taken up on behalf of the company. It was held that directors holding a majority of votes would not be permitted to make a present to themselves. The exact facts of this case could not re-occur as the interested directors would now not be permitted to vote.

A case falling on the other side of the line, where the behaviour was held to be mere incidental profit-making by the directors so that the breach of duty could have been ratified, is *Regal (Hastings) Ltd* v. *Gulliver* [1942] 1 All ER 378. In that case, Regal (Hastings) Ltd owned a cinema. The directors decided to acquire two other cinemas with a view to the sale of the whole concern. They formed a subsidiary company. The owner of the cinemas demanded that the subsidiary should have a paid up capital of £5,000 before he would grant a lease. The directors subscribed for £3,000 of the shares and Regal (Hastings) for £2,000. The concern was then sold and the directors ultimately made a profit on their shares. The court said that the directors were in breach of their duties. As this had involved making a profit out of the fiduciary relationship in which they stood to the company they were bound to repay the profits they had made.

Breaches of duty

Here, as elsewhere, the only clear distinction between breaches of duty which are ratifiable and those which are not lies in the extent to which the behaviour is regarded as villainous. In *Atwool* v. *Merryweather* (1867) 5 Eq 464, a company was formed to acquire a mine from Merryweather. In fact the mine was worthless and the formation of the company and its subsequent flotation were nothing more than a conspiracy to defraud the public. It was held that the company could get back the money it had paid for the worthless mine despite the fact that the majority had voted against this course of action.

Other examples include *Alexander* v. *Automatic Telephone Co.* [1900] 2 Ch 56, where the directors holding the majority of the shares tried to avoid paying the full price for their shares, while requiring all other members to do so; and *Estmanco (Kilner House) Ltd* v. *GLC* [1982] 1 WLR 2. The latter case is interesting, since the judge seemed to take an overall view of the wrongdoing without seeking to put it carefully into categories. The court came to the conclusion that a derivative action would lie where the end result of the breaches of duty was to 'stultify the purpose' for which the company had been formed (see Case note **4**, p. 273).

Negligent acts which benefit a director

In *Daniels* v. *Daniels* [1978] Ch 406 (see Case note **5**, p. 274) the court held that a minority shareholder who has no other remedy may sue where directors use their powers intentionally or unintentionally, fraudulently or negligently in a manner which benefits themselves at the expense of the company.

This last case shows that benefit to themselves provides a dividing line between ratifiable and non-ratifiable actions because it was held in *Pavlides* v. *Jensen* [1956] Ch 565 that an individual plaintiff would not be permitted to sue where the claim was based on negligence alone. No exception to the rule in *Foss* v. *Harbottle* would be made in such a case. Section 260(3) permits a derivative claim where a director is negligent and says nothing about the additional requirement of personal profit. However, it is possible that the court may refuse permission in such a case.

Use of powers for an improper purpose

Clear instances of actions that are ratifiable occur where powers given to the directors for one purpose are misused. An example of this is when shares are issued to fend off a takeover or otherwise to alter the balance of voting power within a company. The courts have held that the power to issue shares must only be used where the primary purpose of the issue is to raise capital (*Bamford* v. *Bamford* [1970] Ch 212). However, where the directors have misused these powers the courts have consistently allowed ratification by a majority vote at a general meeting provided that the holders of the newly-issued shares were not allowed to exercise votes attached to the new shares (*Bamford* v. *Bamford* (as above); and *Hogg* v. *Cramphorn Ltd* [1967] Ch 254).

Further fraud on the minority: alteration of articles

One last category of cases must be mentioned. They are the cases concerned with the alteration of articles (see Chapter 5). It has been held that an individual may prevent the alteration of articles of association where that alteration was not made *bona fide* for the benefit of the company. However, the cases do not make it clear on what basis the action is brought. If it is brought on the basis that a personal right has been infringed, then it could be argued that the preservation of the integrity of the articles is the concern of every shareholder and any breach of those articles could be remedied by a personal action. This would allow the multiplicity of suits which the rule in *Foss* v. *Harbottle* was invented to prevent. However, that rule is rarely mentioned in that series of cases so it may be the case that the upholding of the articles can be achieved by a personal action. However, if that is not the case another category must be added to the 'fraud on the minority' cases. That is where alteration of the articles is attempted by a majority in control of the company but that alteration is not *bona fide* for the benefit of the company (see cases discussed in Chapter 5).

13.4 The statutory remedy in section 994

Sections 994–996 replace ss. 459–461 Companies Act 1985, providing a remedy for a member when 'the company's affairs are being or have been conducted in a manner which is unfairly prejudicial to the interests of its members generally or of some part of its members' (for the full text, see Case note 6, pp. 274–5). The extension may have the effect of including nearly all behaviour which could be litigated under a derivative action although it is as yet not clear that the two are co-extensive. By s. 260 a derivative action for unfair prejudice can only be brought in pursuance of an order of the court made under s. 994. There is little difference between the Companies Act 2006 text and the preceding text of the 1985 text. The case law is therefore assumed to remain relevant.

13.5 Unfair prejudice

Consideration was given to the meaning of unfair prejudice in *Re Bovey Hotel Ventures* (31 July 1981) unreported, quoted in *Re R. A. Noble & Son (Clothing) Ltd* [1983] BCLC 273. Slade J said: 'a member of a company will be able to bring himself within the section if he can show that the value of his shareholding in the company has been seriously diminished or at least seriously jeopardised by reason of a course of conduct on the part of those persons who do have *de facto* control of the company, which was unfair to the member concerned.' He suggested that the test should be an objective one: would the reasonable bystander observing the consequences of their conduct . . . regard it as having unfairly prejudiced the petitioner's interest? This text was adopted by the court in the *R. A. Noble* case. In that case a clear distinction was drawn between the prejudice which was held to have occurred and the unfair element which was not shown. In the case one of the directors had been deliberately and systematically excluded from the running of the affairs of the company. This was conduct which the judge found could have come within the section. However, the circumstances of each particular case had to be examined and in this case the director had brought his exclusion upon himself by disinterest. The conduct was therefore not unfair. This approach was adopted in *Re London School of Electronics Ltd* [1986] Ch 211. In *Re Macro (Ipswich) Ltd* [1994] 2 BCLC 354 the court held that where conduct was unfairly prejudicial to the financial interests of the company then it would also be unfairly prejudicial to the interests of its members. In assessing the fairness of the conduct the court had to perform a balancing act in weighing the various interests of different groups within the company. The court did not interfere in questions of commercial management but where the mismanagement was sufficiently significant and serious to cause loss to the company then it could constitute the basis for finding unfair prejudice. The concept of unfairness is thus capable of being a very broad one indeed. A number of possible limitations have been raised:

(1) What is the 'conduct of the company's affairs'?
(2) Must there be infringement of a legal right in order to show unfair prejudice?
(3) What interest in the company must the petitioner have?
(4) In what capacity must the defendant be complaining?

Conduct of company affairs

In *Re A Company (No. 001761 of 1986)* [1987] BCLC 141 the court held that the acts of a shareholder in a personal capacity outside the conduct of the company's affairs were irrelevant. Thus the court was not interested in 'an attempt to blacken the respondent's name and to make the court look on her with disfavour as an immoral and attractive woman'. See also *Re Leeds United Holdings plc* (discussed below).

In *Re Red Label Fashions Ltd* [1999] BCC 308, the respondent was alleged to be subject to disqualification proceedings as a '*de facto*' director. Although she had been in business with her director husband, the court held that there was no evidence that she had assumed the role of director and exercised management responsibilities. She had acted 'as a dutiful wife' rather than as a director.

The infringement of legal rights

The concept of unfair prejudice is larger than the idea of infringement of legal rights. In *Re A Company* [1986] BCLC 376, Hoffman J said that in a small company 'the member's interests as a member may include a legitimate expectation that he will continue to be employed as a director and his dismissal from that office and exclusion from the management of the company may therefore be unfairly prejudicial to his interests as a member'.

The same view was taken in *Re Sam Weller & Sons Ltd (Re A Company (No. 823 of 1987)* [1990] BCLC 80, where the court refused to strike out a petition alleging unfair prejudice by a failure to declare an adequate dividend. The court emphasised that 'interests' should be considered as wider than 'rights'. It should be noted that this wide view seems to be more easily adhered to in cases where a small company is involved (see *Re Carrington Viyella PLC* (1983) 1 BCC 98) but it has recently been litigated in a number of sporting contexts. In *Re Tottenham Hotspur plc* [1994] 1 BCLC 655 Terry Venables, the chief executive of Tottenham Hotspur, and Alan Sugar, its chairman, originally had a 50/50 interest in the company. Sugar later obtained control and Venables was removed as chief executive. Venables claimed that this removal was contrary to a legitimate expectation that Venables would be involved in managing the company. The court found that there was little if any evidence to support the allegation and did not make any order. In *Re Leeds United Holdings plc* [1996] 2 BCLC 545 the court held that: 'The legitimate expectations which the court has to have regard to under s. 459 must relate to the conduct of the company's affairs, the most obvious and common example being an expectation of being allowed to participate in the affairs of the company.' However, the court went on to dismiss the s. 459 action in that case because it was based on an expectation that a particular shareholder would not sell his shares without the consent of the other shareholders. This was held not to relate to the company's affairs and therefore fell outside s. 459.

The important case of *Re Saul D Harrison & Sons plc* [1995] 1 BCLC 14 contains an extensive analysis of the operation of s. 459 to protect 'legitimate expectations'. Hoffman LJ said:

> 'In deciding what is fair or unfair for the purposes of s. 459, it is important to have in mind that fairness is being used in the context of a commercial relationship. The articles of association are just what their name implies: the contractual terms which govern the relationships of the shareholders with the company and each other ... Since keeping promises and honouring agreements is probably the most important element of commercial fairness, the starting point on any case under s. 459 will be to ask whether the conduct of which the shareholder complains was in accordance with the articles of association ... Although one begins with the articles and the powers of the board, a finding that conduct was not in accordance with the articles does not necessarily mean that it was unfair, still less that the court will exercise its discretion to grant relief. There is often sound sense in the rule in *Foss* v. *Harbottle* (1843) 2 Hare 461. In choosing the term "unfairly prejudicial", the Jenkins Committee (para. 204) equated it with Lord Cooper's understanding of "oppression" in *Elder* v. *Elder and Watson* (1952) SC 49: "A visible departure from the standards of fair dealing and a violation of the conditions of fair play on which every shareholder who entrusts his money to a company is entitled to rely." So trivial or technical infringements of the articles were not intended to give rise to petitions under s. 459.'

Hoffman LJ goes on to point out that technically lawful actions may also be unfair:

'the personal relationship between a shareholder and those who control the company may entitle him to say that it would in certain circumstances be unfair for them to exercise a power conferred by the articles upon the board or the company in general meeting. I have in the past ventured to borrow from public law the term "legitimate expectations" to describe the correlative "right" in the shareholder to which such a relationship may give rise. It often arises out of a fundamental understanding between the shareholders which formed the basis of their association but was not put into contractual form, such as an assumption that each of the parties who has ventured his capital will also participate in the management of the company and receive the return on his investment in the form of salary rather than dividend.'

The judgment emphasised the fact that because the company is small, this is not sufficient to find that there are legitimate expectations above and beyond those in the articles. 'Something more' was needed and was absent in this case. It is clear that some evidence must be brought of an understanding between the parties separate from the articles. In *Re BSB Holdings* [1996] 1 BCLC 155 the Court made it clear that *Re Saul D. Harrison* did not mean that s. 459 was limited to cases of breaches of the articles or other agreements and that the categories of behaviour for which relief could be given were not closed. However, the court followed *Re Saul D. Harrison* in emphasising that 'fairness' meant fairness in a commercial context, which meant that directors had a duty to exercise their powers fairly between different classes of shareholders.

This case was affirmed in *O'Neill and Another* v. *Phillips* [1999] 2 BCLC 1, which was the first case concerning s. 459 to come before the House of Lords. Lord Hoffman held that the existence of a quasi-partnership did not, of itself, give a right to a member to have his shares purchased; 'fairness' usually required some breach of the terms on which the member had agreed that the affairs of the company should be conducted.

O'Neill established the mainstream approach towards the interpretation of s. 459, and its reasoning was found in the basis of other court rulings as well. In *Larvin* v. *Phoenix Office Supplies Ltd* [2002] EWCA Civ 1740, a company appealed against a decision ordering its two remaining directors to purchase at a full price the shares of the third departing director. The latter's decision to leave the company was personal. The remaining directors had refused to buy his shares and did not consent to the provision of any access to him to the accounts of the company. The court of appeal held that a director leaving his place on the board on his own volition was not entitled to demand to have his shares bought at their full undiscounted value. The court underlined that not every quasi-partnership entitled directors to a 'no fault divorce'. Section 459 had a very clear function and that was to protect shareholders against a breach of terms on which they had initially joined the company or from inequity in the sense noted by *O'Neill*. In this case the departing director had assumed the decision to leave the company for his own personal reasons. His departure was not a result of actions performed on the part of the rest of the directors or shareholders of the company. Hence, the remaining directors had not been found to have treated him in an unfairly prejudicial manner just because they excluded him from the company's affairs. The court wanted to prevent the application of s. 459 to all directors who decide on their own will to leave a certain company. If that decision entailed an obligation on behalf of their company to buy their shares, this would mean a severe burden for small companies across the country. The principles applied in *O'Neill* were, therefore, further illuminated.

Another important element in understanding the function of s. 459 was clarified in *Re Legal Costs Negotiators Ltd* [1999] BCC 547. In the case it was revealed that s. 459 remains essentially a minority claim. In this case two partners turned their business into a limited company in which the first possessed 75 per cent of the shares while the other held the remaining 25 per cent of the shareholding. The minority shareholder was accused of inefficiency in carrying out his duties towards the company. The majority shareholder managed to obtain his resignation and removal from the board. In addition to that, the majority shareholder actually managed to dismiss the minority shareholder from the company. The holder of the 75 per cent of the company subsequently wanted to rely on s. 459 in order to force the removed director to sell him the remaining shares. The court did not consent to these demands, and stated that the majority shareholder, by possessing 75 per cent of the shares, was capable of passing any resolution in the company and could terminate any existing prejudicial state of affairs, which he did since he effectively removed the minority shareholder from the board and dismissed him from the company. Because of his initiatives the minority shareholder did not have any say in the company's affairs. Thus, further relying on s. 459 to force the minority shareholder to sell his shares to him would constitute an inappropriate use of the relevant provisions.

What interest in the company must the petitioner have?

In *R & H Electric and Another* v. *Haden Bill Electrical Ltd* [1995] 2 BCLC 280 the court held that a broad view should be taken of the capacity in which a petitioner complained for the purposes of s. 459. In that case a company controlled by P was a major creditor of Haden Bill Electrical (HB). P was a director and chairman of HB until relationships broke down and he was removed at short notice. The court held that P could rely on his interest in having been instrumental in raising the loan through his company and the understandings that flowed from that and was not just confined to his interest as shareholder.

Section 459(2) of the Act allows those to whom shares have been transferred or transmitted by operation of law (for example, by inheritance) to petition. Section 460 gives the same right to the Secretary of State. These powers have not apparently been used. In *Re A Company* (1986) 2 BCC 98 & 952 it was held that those who were not registered as shareholders but who were entitled to the benefit of owning the shares (beneficial owners) could not petition.

In what capacity must the complaint be made?

Under the predecessor section to s. 459 a member had to make his complaint 'in his capacity as member'. This meant that if his real complaint was, for example, that he had been excluded from the office of director, this complaint would not found an action. The same difficulty arose as that discussed in Chapter 5 concerning the enforcement of the articles as a contract. In *Re A Company* [1983] Ch 178 the court seemed at first sight to adopt this line. However, the contrast that was being made in that case was between the interests of a person as a shareholder in a company, and totally incidental interests that the same shareholder might have which could be affected by the company's actions. An example might be if the company gained permission to establish a rubbish tip in close proximity to the private house of someone who happened to own shares in that company. It seems that in the light of the number of cases which have taken into account the 'legitimate expectations' of the members to partake in the management of the company that the courts will be most reluctant to return to the strict division between a member's interest as a member and his interest as an active participant in the management of the company.

Which members?

In a number of cases (*Re Carrington Viyella PLC* (1983) 1 BCC 98; and *Re A Company* (1988) 4 BCC 506) the court ruled that the behaviour would adversely affect all shareholders. There was therefore no 'part' of the shareholders affected so that the petition could not succeed. This curious approach has been reversed by s. 145, Schedule 19, Art. 11 Companies Act 1989, which substituted the words 'unfairly prejudicial to the interests of its members generally or of some part of its members' for the words found in the 1985 Act which referred only to behaviour 'unfairly prejudicial to the interests of some part of the members'.

13.6 The relief that can be granted

Section 996 Companies Act 2006 provides that if a court is satisfied that a petition on the ground of unfairly prejudicial conduct is well founded 'it may make such order as it thinks fit for giving relief in respect of the matters complained of'. Subsections particularise a number of actions which the court might take (see Case note **6**, p. 275). The particularisation of these potential actions is expressly 'without prejudice' to the general discretion contained in subsection 1 and so in no way limits the court's powers. The court has freely used its power to order the sale of shares. This has the virtue of breaking the deadlock in a company where the behaviour complained of is exclusion from management which has caused the shares held by the complainant to lose value. In *Re Brenfield Squash Racquets Club Ltd* [1996] 2 BCLC 184 the court even ordered the majority to sell their shares to the minority shareholders where that (exceptionally) seemed to be the best solution for the company. In such cases the valuation will be backdated to the time before the behaviour complained of commenced.

13.7 Winding-up orders

Section 122(1)(g) of the Insolvency Act 1986 provides that a company may be wound up by the court if the court is of the opinion that it is just and equitable that the company should be wound up. This is qualified by s. 125(2) Insolvency Act 1986, where the company should not be wound up if some other remedy is available to the petitioners, and the court is of the opinion that they are acting unreasonably in seeking to have the company wound up instead of pursuing that other remedy. This proviso is likely to be of much greater importance in the light of the wide jurisdiction exercised by the courts under s. 459 Companies Act 1985. It is a drastic move to destroy the company completely as a remedy for unfairness. Far better to allow an aggrieved party to buy his way out at a fair valuation. The cases prior to 1980 can only therefore afford guidance about the availability of the winding-up remedy now. In the light of s. 459, petitioners might be prevented by s. 125(2) Insolvency Act 1986 from obtaining a winding-up order which they could have obtained before a s. 459 remedy appeared on the statute book. Nor need the 'alternative remedy' necessarily be a s. 459 remedy. In *Re A Company* [1983] 1 WLR 927, the court emphasised that the power to grant a winding-up order on the just and equitable ground was discretionary and should certainly be refused where a reasonable offer to buy the petitioner's shares had been refused.

A petition for s. 994 relief can be combined with a petition to wind up on the just and equitable ground. It should be noted that unfair prejudice or malpractice need not be alleged in order to show that there is a case for winding-up (see, for example, *Re German Date Coffee Co.* (1882) 20 Ch D 169, where the purpose for which the company was formed was no longer attainable). In *Re R. A. Noble & Son (Clothing) Ltd* [1983] BCLC 273, the judge held that malpractice need not be shown provided that the conduct of those in control had been the 'substantial cause' of the lack of mutual confidence between the parties. In that case the judge dismissed the petition for s. 459 relief and made an order for the winding-up of the company on the just and equitable ground.

13.8   When a winding-up order is likely to be made

The leading case on 'just and equitable' winding-up is *Re Ebrahami* v. *Westbourne Galleries Ltd* [1973] AC 360. In that case the petition was brought by Mr Ebrahami, who for many years had been an equal partner with Mr Nazar in a business dealing in Persian carpets. In 1958 it was decided to incorporate the business and Ebrahami (E) and Nazar (N), who were both appointed directors, each held 500 shares. Soon after this N's son was made a director and E and N each transferred 100 shares to the son. After this the Nazars held a majority of the votes. In 1965, the relationship between the Nazars and E began to break down. In 1969, the Nazars used their majority to remove E from his directorship. Thereafter he was unable to take any part in the management of the business and he received no money since all payments were made to the participants in the business by way of directors' salaries rather than dividends. The court held that the removal of E had been lawful. Nevertheless, because the company was in essence an incorporated partnership, the Nazars had abused their power and were in breach of the good faith partners owed to one another. E was therefore entitled to a winding-up order.

This may well now be a situation in which s. 459 relief could be granted and thus a winding-up order would be refused. (For a detailed look at the judgment in this case, see Case note 7, pp. 275–6.)

Other situations in which the remedy has been granted are where deadlock has been reached because shares were equally divided between two factions at odds with each other: *Re Yenidje Tobacco Co. Ltd* [1916] 2 Ch 426 and where the whole purpose or substratum of the company had failed. An instance of the latter is *Re German Date Coffee Co.* (1882) 20 Ch D 169 where the company (mercifully?) failed to obtain the patent to make coffee from dates. That activity had been the major purpose for which the company was formed.

In order for a petition to succeed, a shareholder must show that he has an interest in the winding-up: that is, that there is a probability that the company is solvent and so, after the winding-up, there will be assets to be distributed to the shareholders (*Re Expanded Plugs Ltd* [1960] 1 WLR 514).

13.9   Department of Trade investigations

The Department of Trade and Industry is the government department concerned with the conduct of companies and the law which governs them.

By legislation the department is given various powers to investigate the affairs of companies. One way that this can be done is by the appointment of an inspector to look into the affairs of a company. The appointment can be instigated in a variety of ways:

1. On the order of the court

The Department of Trade must appoint an inspector to investigate the affairs of a company if the court so orders (s. 432(1) Companies Act 1985).

2. On the application of the company

Section 431(2)(c) provides that inspectors may be appointed on the application of the company. The application must be accompanied by evidence showing a good reason why the company's affairs should be investigated and even then the department has a discretion as to whether or not an inspector will be appointed. Few inspectors have been appointed under this power.

3. Fraud, unfair prejudice or withholding of information

The department also has a discretion to appoint inspectors where there is evidence of a company's affairs being conducted in a fraudulent or unfairly prejudicial way, that it proposes to act unlawfully or that 'its members have not been given all the information with respect to its affairs which they might reasonably expect' (s. 432(1)(b)).

Although some inspectors have been appointed under this section, there is grave danger that the mere announcement of the appointment of inspectors will bring lasting damage to the reputation of the company which cannot be reversed even if the allegations prove to be unfounded at the end of the day. Because of this difficulty the Companies Act 1967 introduced a wide range of powers which the Department of Trade and Industry could use more discreetly to determine whether allegations of misconduct were soundly based. Sections 447–452 Companies Act 1985 now enable the department to require the production of books and papers, to ask for a search warrant if there are grounds for suspecting that articles requested have not been forthcoming and to search premises in respect of which a warrant is issued. Criminal penalties are available for providing false statements and for falsifying, mutilating or destroying documents. It is a defence to show that there was no intention to conceal the state of affairs of the company or to defeat the law. The department's officers are acting in a police capacity when they require the production of books and papers. They are not acting in a way similar to judges. The court will therefore not exercise its power to review decisions taken by those who act in a judicial or quasi-judicial capacity. However the notice requiring the production of books and papers must not be unreasonably or excessively wide (*R v. Secretary of State for Trade,* Ex Parte *Perestrello* [1981] QB 19). The Companies Act 2006 does not repeal these sections but ss. 1035–1039 give sweeping powers to the Secretary of State to make regulations concerning the conduct of inspections.

13.10 When inspectors have been appointed

In *Re Pergamon Press* [1970] 3 WLR 792 the Court of Appeal held that inspectors were not acting in a judicial or quasi-judicial way. Nevertheless they have a duty to act fairly. This is important as they have very wide-ranging powers to examine on oath the officers and agents of the company, to require documents and even to require a person who is not connected with the company to attend before them and assist in their inquiry (ss. 433–435 Companies Act 1985). By s. 436, obstruction of officers is treated as contempt of court. Following the investigation the inspectors make a report which will be admissible as evidence in any subsequent legal proceedings (s. 441(1)). The report is only evidence of the opinion of the inspectors with regard to matters investigated by them, not as to the existence of facts.

Human rights and investigations

The whole procedure of investigations may give rise to questions under the Human Rights Act 1998. *Saunders* v. *UK* (Case 43/1994/490/572) [1977] BCC 872 was a judgment by the European Court of Human Rights concerning the use of statements made to DTI inspectors during an investigation. These statements had subsequently been used in a criminal prosecution against Saunders. The ECHR held that Saunders had been deprived of the right to a fair hearing by the use of these statements.

13.11 Following investigations

After an investigation by inspectors or by the department using its powers to require books and documents, the DTI must decide if it is in the public interest to take legal proceedings. If it decides that the public interest will be best served by so doing, it can bring any action the company itself might bring, including petitioning for a winding-up order (ss. 438 and 440).

Summary

1. Directors owe their duties to the company and the company is therefore the proper plaintiff in an action to enforce such duties. This was usually known as the rule in *Foss* v. *Harbottle*. It is now enshrined in the Companies Act 2006.

2. If such a rule was absolute, the majority would have an absolute right to defraud the minority. This is now prevented by the rule that a director (and connected persons) may not vote on a resolution to sue him.

3. Exceptions to majority rule were made first by the courts and subsequently by the Companies Act 2006. Whether the individual shareholder can sue or, on the other hand, whether the majority can prevent the action and forgive the directors (ratification of the directors' actions) depend on the depravity of the wrongdoing in question.

4. An oppressed minority have a wide and flexible action which is procedurally simpler in ss. 994–996 Companies Act 2006.

5. An aggrieved member may also petition the court to wind up a company on the ground that it would be just and equitable to do so.

6. The DTI have wide powers to inspect the books of companies where malpractice is suspected.

Case notes

1. *Foss* v. *Harbottle* (1843) 2 Hare 461

The Vice Chancellor [Sir James Wigram] said:

'It was not, nor could it successfully be, argued that it was a matter of course for any individual members of a corporation thus to assume to themselves the right of suing in the name of the corporation. In law the corporation and the aggregate members of the corporation are not the same thing for purposes like this; and the only question can be whether the facts alleged in this case justify a departure from the rule which, *prima facie*, would require that the corporation should sue in its own name and in its corporate character, or in the name of someone whom the law has appointed to be its representative.'

2. *Smith* v. *Croft* (*No. 2*) [1988] Ch 114

The plaintiff's action claimed that certain payments to directors had been excessive and were therefore *ultra vires*. The court held:

(i) that although excessive remuneration paid to directors might be an abuse of power, where the power to decide remuneration was vested in the board, it could not be *ultra vires* the company;

(ii) that although a minority shareholder had *locus standi* to bring an action on behalf of a company to recover money paid away wrongfully, the right was not indefeasible even if the transaction was *ultra vires*. It was proper to have regard to the views of the independent shareholders, and their votes should be disregarded only if the court was satisfied that they would be cast in favour of the defendant directors in order to support them rather than for the benefit of the company, or if there was a substantial risk of that happening; accordingly since the majority of the independent shareholders' votes would be cast against allowing the action to proceed, the statement of claim should be struck out.

3. *Nurcombe* v. *Nurcombe* [1985] 1 All ER 65

The husband and wife were respectively the majority and minority shareholders in a company. They were divorced in 1974 and in the course of matrimonial proceedings it was disclosed that the husband had breached the fiduciary duty which he owed as a director to the company. The wife continued the matrimonial proceedings after that information came to light and the improper profit made by the husband was taken into account in the matrimonial proceedings. The wife subsequently sought to bring a derivative action. The court would not permit her to do so on the grounds that it would be inequitable to permit the wife to pursue the derivative action when the amount of improper profit had been taken into account in other proceedings.

4. *Estmanco (Kilner House) Ltd* v. *GLC* [1982] 1 WLR 2

A block of flats was in the process of being sold by the Greater London Council (GLC). Once a flat had been sold, the purchasers of the flats became shareholders of the Estmanco company. When all the flats had been sold the company would function to manage the

flats and the shareholders would have voting rights. The policy of selling the flats was discontinued after the political control of the Council changed. Twelve flats had been sold. The new Council resolved upon a new housing policy and decided to break the terms of the agreement and use the unsold flats to accommodate the needy. A shareholder sought to bring a derivative action on the company's behalf against the Council to enforce the covenant. The Council held the only voting shares in the company at that time and had voted that no action should be taken in respect of the breach of the agreement. The action succeeded. Megarry VC said:

'There can be no doubt about the twelve voteless purchasers being a minority; there can be no doubt about the advantage to the Council of having the action discontinued; there can be no doubt about the injury to the applicant and the rest of the minority, both as shareholders and as purchasers, of that discontinuance; and I feel little doubt that the Council has used its voting power not to promote the best interests of the company but in order to bring advantage to itself and disadvantage to the minority. Furthermore, that disadvantage is no trivial matter, but represents a radical alteration in the basis on which the Council sold the flats to the minority. It seems to me that the sum total represents a fraud on the minority in the sense in which "fraud" is used in that phrase, or alternatively represents such an abuse of power as to have the same effect.'

5. *Daniels* v. *Daniels* **[1978] Ch 406**

A husband and wife were the two directors of a company and also the majority shareholders. They caused the company to sell to the wife land owned by the company. Four years later she sold the land for over twenty-eight times what she had paid for it. The judge permitted minority shareholders to claim against the directors. He said:

'a minority shareholder who has no other remedy may sue where directors use their powers, intentionally or unintentionally, fraudulently or negligently, in a manner which benefits themselves at the expense of the company.'

6. Sections 994–996 Companies Act 2006

PART 30

PROTECTION OF MEMBERS AGAINST UNFAIR PREJUDICE

Main provisions

994 Petition by company member

(1) A member of a company may apply to the court by petition for an order under this Part on the ground –

    (a) that the company's affairs are being or have been conducted in a manner that is unfairly prejudicial to the interests of members generally or of some part of its members (including at least himself), or

    (b) that an actual or proposed act or omission of the company (including an act or omission on its behalf) is or would be so prejudicial.

(2) The provisions of this Part apply to a person who is not a member of a company but to whom shares in the company have been transferred or transmitted by operation of law as they apply to a member of a company.

(3) In this section, and so far as applicable for the purposes of this section in the other provisions of this Part, 'company' means –

    (a) a company within the meaning of this Act, or

    (b) a company that is not such a company but is a statutory water company within the meaning of the Statutory Water Companies Act 1991.

995 Petition by Secretary of State

(1) This section applies to a company in respect of which –

    (a) the Secretary of State has received a report under section 437 of the Companies Act 1985 (inspector's report);

    (b) the Secretary of State has exercised his powers under section 447 or 448 of that Act (powers to require documents and information or to enter and search premises);

    (c) the Secretary of State or the Financial Services Authority has exercised his or its powers under Part 11 of the Financial Services and Markets Act 2000 (clause 8) (information gathering and investigations); or

    (d) the Secretary of State has received a report from an investigator appointed by him or the Financial Services Authority under that Part.

(2) If it appears to the Secretary of State that in the case of such a company –

(a) the company's affairs are being or have been conducted in a manner that is unfairly prejudicial to the interests of members generally or of some part of its members, or

(b) an actual or proposed act or omission of the company (including an act or omission on its behalf) is or would be so prejudicial, he may apply to the court by petition for an order under this Part.

(3) The Secretary of State may do this in addition to, or instead of, presenting a petition for the winding up of the company.

(4) In this section, and so far as applicable for the purposes of this section in the other provisions of this Part, 'company' means any body corporate that is liable to be wound up under the Insolvency Act 1986 or the Insolvency (Northern Ireland) Order 1989 (S.I. 1989/2405 (N.I. 19)).

996 Powers of the court under this Part

(1) If the court is satisfied that a petition under this Part is well founded, it may make such order as it thinks fit for giving relief in respect of the matters complained of.

(2) Without prejudice to the generality of subsection (1), the court's order may –

(a) regulate the conduct of the company's affairs in the future;

(b) require the company –

(i) to refrain from doing or continuing an act complained of, or

(ii) to do an act that the petitioner has complained it has omitted to do;

(c) authorise civil proceedings to be brought in the name and on behalf of the company by such person or persons and on such terms as the court may direct;

(d) require the company not to make any, or any specified, alterations in its articles without the leave of the court;

(e) provide for the purchase of the shares of any members of the company by other members or by the company itself and, in the case of a purchase by the company itself, the reduction of the company's capital accordingly.

7. *Re Ebrahami* v. *Westbourne Galleries Ltd* [1973] AC 360

Lord Wilberforce said:

'the foundation of it all lies in the words "just and equitable" and, if there is any respect in which some of the cases may be open to criticism, it is that the courts may sometimes have been too timorous in giving them full force. The words are a recognition of the fact that a limited company is more than a mere legal entity, with a personality in law of its own: that there is room in company law for recognition of the fact that behind it, or among it, there are individuals, with rights, expectations and obligations *inter se* which are not necessarily submerged in the company structure. That structure is defined by the Companies Act and by the articles of association by which shareholders agree to be bound. In most companies and in most contexts, this definition is sufficient and exhaustive, equally so whether the company is large or small. The "just and equitable" provision does not, as the respondents suggest, entitle one party to disregard the obligation he assumes by entering a company, nor the court to dispense him from it. It does, as equity always does, enable the court to subject the exercise of legal rights to equitable considerations, that is, of a personal character arising between one individual and another, which may make it unjust, or inequitable, to insist on legal rights, or to exercise them in a particular way.

It would be impossible, and wholly undesirable, to define the circumstances in which these considerations may arise. Certainly the fact that a company is a small one, or a private company, is not enough. There are very many of these where the association is a purely commercial one, of which it can safely be said that the basis of association is adequately and exhaustively laid down in the articles. The superimposition of equitable considerations requires something more, which typically may include one, or probably more, of the following elements: (i) an association formed or continued on the basis of a personal relationship, involving mutual confidence – this element will often be found where a pre-existing partnership has been converted into a limited company; (ii) an agreement, or understanding, that all, or some (for there may be "sleeping" members), of the shareholders shall participate in the conduct of the business; (iii) restriction upon the transfer of the members' interest in the company – so that if confidence is lost, or one member is removed from management, he cannot take out his stake and go elsewhere.'

Exercises

1. Discuss the advantages and disadvantages of the courses of action open to an aggrieved minority shareholder.

2. What purpose did the rule in *Foss* v. *Harbottle* serve? To what extent has s. 994 replaced derivative actions?

3. Olivia holds 10 per cent of the shares in Unknown Ltd, a private company. Sian, the Chair and Managing Director of Unknown Ltd, owns 60 per cent of the shares and the remaining 30 per cent are held by Lynne and Cynthia, the company's other directors. Olivia is not a Director. Sian's conduct of the company's business over the past two years has caused heavy losses. She has undertaken a number of contracts at a loss, and has bought untested equipment which has proved mechanically unsound. At meetings of the board and at general meetings Sian has attributed this conduct to the need to build up goodwill. Sian is very slow in both paying the company's debt and

presenting its bills. Sian has explained this behaviour as being the result of pressure of work and has given repeated assurances of improvement. Olivia has now had enough. She is not supported by Lynne and Cynthia when she voices her criticisms of Sian at general and board meetings. Olivia seeks your advice on the remedies (if any) which may enable her to:

(i)   compel Sian to compensate Unknown Ltd for the losses she has caused;
(ii) force a change of company policy;
(iii) retrieve her investment in Unknown Ltd.

Advise Olivia.

Chapter 14

Shares

Key words

> ▶ **Variation of share rights** – note that this is a very technical legal term and there can be all sorts of changes to share rights which do not amount to a legal 'variation'.

A share does not confer on its owner a right to the physical possession of anything. Section 541 Companies Act 2006 provides: 'The shares or other interest of a member in a company are personal property ... and are not in the nature of real estate.' A share confers a number of rights against the company (for example, the limited right to enforce the articles – see Chapter 5). The face value of the share is also a measure of the shareholder's interest in the company. In the event of the distribution of the company's assets the amount that will come to any particular shareholder will be proportionate to the face value of the shares owned by him. By s. 542 Companies Act 2006 each share must have a fixed nominal value or the allotment of the share is void.

The interest of the shareowner in the company and his right to uphold the constitution of the company distinguish the shareholder from the owner of a debenture. The holder of a debenture has lent money to the company, so he, as well as a shareholder, has provided money for the company's operations. A debenture-holder's rights are, however, restricted to the remedies given to him by his contract of loan with the company. He has no *interest* in that company.

However, companies have found that to attract different types of investor it is useful to have different types of shares. The various 'classes' of shares all enjoy different rights, which are usually set out in the articles. However, where these rights have not been clearly defined, the law lays down rules which fill in the gaps and determine the rights of the different classes of shareholders. Where the company wishes to alter the rights of any of the classes, strict rules have to be complied with. The alteration of such rights is known as a 'variation' of rights.

14.1 Ordinary shares

Unless the memorandum, articles or the documents describing the shares when they were issued otherwise provide, ordinary shareholders are entitled to receive dividends when they are declared (they cannot force a declaration), and to be paid a proportion of the company's assets after payment of the creditors when the company is wound up. The amount will be proportionate to the size of his shareholding and if the amount to be distributed exceeds the nominal value of the company's shares, each shareholder will participate in this 'surplus' in proportion to the nominal value of his shareholding.

An ordinary shareholder will also normally have the right to exercise one vote for each share he holds at the general meetings of the company.

These rights only subsist if there is nothing to the contrary in the document describing the original issue of the shares, in the articles or memorandum. The rights otherwise given by law to shareholders are often varied by those documents. For example, it is common for a company to have more than one class of ordinary shareholders with different voting rights.

14.2 Preference shares

The holders of preference shares are entitled to have some of a payment out by the company paid to them before the ordinary shareholders are paid. Again, the terms of issue or the memorandum and articles can determine the rights of the holders but the courts have had to provide a network of rules which make up possible gaps in the description of the shareholders' rights which appear in these documents. Rules are usually expressed in terms of 'presumptions', that is, the courts will presume that a particular right does or does not attach to a share unless it can be shown that this cannot be the case because of the way in which the shares are described in one of the documents mentioned. The alternatives are that the preference shares can be preferred over the ordinary shares in respect of:

(i)   dividend; or
(ii) return of capital; or
(iii) both dividend and return of capital.

In all these cases matters are further complicated by the fact that the preferences may be 'cumulative' or 'non-cumulative'. A cumulative right means that if the dividend in one year was less than the shareholder was entitled to expect, the arrears must be made up in a subsequent year before the ordinary shareholders receive anything. Unlike the ordinary shareholders, the preference shareholders do know what sum they should receive because the dividend due to a preference shareholder is generally expressed as a fixed percentage of the par value of the share.

Preference as to dividend

There is a presumption that a fixed preferential dividend is cumulative, that is, arrears from previous years must be made good before any amount is paid to the ordinary shareholders. The presumption may be rebutted by the terms of the documents describing shareholders' rights. The right to have any money paid to them by way of dividend only becomes a right when the directors exercise their discretion to pay a dividend at all. Neither the preference shareholders nor the ordinary shareholders can force the declaration of a dividend, even when the company is doing well.

When the company goes into liquidation a difficult question which sometimes needs to be settled is whether the preference shareholders are entitled to arrears of dividend before anyone else is paid. A number of cases have determined that unless there is an express right to the arrears in the documents, the preference shareholders are not entitled to have these arrears made up (see, for example, *Re Crichton's Oil* [1902] 2 Ch 86; and *Re Wood Skinner & Co.* [1944] Ch 323). The 'express' right need not be very clear, however, as the presumption that they will not be made up is easy to displace.

The other presumption that applies here is that the rights stated in any of the relevant documents are exhaustive. The preference shareholders will have a right to what is expressly stated but no more.

Capital

Just because preference shareholders have a right to be paid dividends before ordinary shareholders does not give them preference when the company is being wound up and the capital of the company is being distributed among the shareholders. A further question that arises is whether the preference shareholders are entitled to participate on an equal footing with the ordinary shareholders if there is a surplus after:

(i) the preference shareholders have had their capital returned (if they have a preference as to return of capital); and
(ii) the ordinary shareholders have had their capital returned.

If after those two operations there is still a surplus for distribution, there is a question as to whether the preference shareholders may participate in the distribution of the surplus.

These two dilemmas are solved by:

(a) the presumption that all shareholders should be treated equally so that unless there is a specific right spelled out in the documents giving the preference shareholders a preference as to the repayment of capital then they have no such preference; and

(b) the rule that where a preference as far as the repayment of capital is expressed, the rights set out in the document describe the totality of the rights as far as capital is concerned. The description of rights is said to be 'exhaustive'. Where a preference as to capital is given to preference shareholders, they will therefore not participate in any surplus remaining after capital has been repaid unless an express right to do so is written into the issue documents, the memorandum or articles.

14.3 Voting rights

The allocation of voting rights is a matter for the constitution of the company and will be found in the company's articles. The articles may provide for one vote per share or may provide for as complicated a structure of voting rights as may be desired. The idea of non-voting shares has been attacked from time to time. An example of the case against non-voting shares is to be found in a Note of Dissent to the 'Jenkins Committee' report. The note of dissent was signed by Mr L. Brown, Sir George Erskine and Professor L. C. B. Gower:

'Feeling as we do, that the development of non-voting equity shares is undesirable both in principle and practice, we find ourselves unable to concur in the failure to make stronger recommendations for their control.

2. In our opinion the growth of non-voting and restricted voting shares (a) strikes at the basic principle on which our Company Law is based (paragraph 3 below), (b) is inconsistent with the principles underlying our Report and the Reports of earlier Company Law Committees (paragraphs 4, 5 and 6) and (c) is undesirable (paragraphs 7 et seq.).

3. The business corporation is a device for enabling an expert body of directors to manage other people's property for them. Since these managers are looking after other people's money it is thought that they should not be totally free from any control or supervision and the obvious persons to exercise some control are the persons whose property is being managed. Hence the basic principle adopted by British Company Law (and, indeed, the laws of most countries) is that ultimate control over the directors should be exercised by the shareholders. This control cannot be exercised in detail and from day to day, but shareholders retain the ultimate sanction in that it is they who 'hire and fire' the directorate.

When the directors own the majority of the equity they are free from outside control, but here they are managing their own money. Hence the interests of the directors and the shareholders are unlikely to conflict, and self-interest should be a sufficient curb and spur (subject to certain legal rules to protect the minority against oppression). When, however, the directors have no financial stake in the prosperity of the company, or only a minority interest, the outside control operates. [Paragraphs 4 and 5 showed that the thrust of most Company Law reports was to increase effective shareholder control.]

6. In recent years, however, control by shareholders has been stultified in two

ways: firstly in a few cases by cross-holdings and circular-holdings within a group of companies [see Chapter 1], and secondly by non-voting equity shares. The first method has already received the attention of the legislature and an attempt has been made to control it by section [23 of the Companies Act 1985]. In our discussion of this section . . . we recognize that it is improper for directors to maintain themselves indefinitely in office, against the wishes of the other shareholders. We also recognize that section [23 Companies Act 1985] does not go far enough in preventing this mischief and we reject an extension of the section with reluctance and only because of the complexity and arbitrary nature of the provisions which would be necessary . . . .The second method of maintaining control by the existing directors, by utilising non-voting shares, is not as yet controlled in any way; it is only of recent years that it has become a major issue. Today non-voting shares are the simplest and most straightforward method whereby directors can render themselves irremovable without their own consent, notwithstanding that they only own or control a fraction of the equity.

7. It is said that shareholder control is ineffective because of the indifference of shareholders. Everyone would probably agree that shareholders are apathetic while all goes well. But, while all goes well, there is no reason why they should not be apathetic; their intervention is only required when things go ill. No doubt it is true that the small individual shareholder has little power even then, but, as we point out . . . the institutional investor has considerable influence; and even non-institutional shareholders are collectively powerful so long as they have votes. It can hardly be doubted that the possibility that a take-over bidder will obtain control by acquiring those votes has caused directors to pay greater heed to the interests of shareholders.

8. It is also said that shareholder control is inefficient, since directors, as a class, know better what is good for business and for the shareholders than the shareholders themselves. In the normal case this is usually true. But if shareholder control is destroyed and nothing put in its place we have to go still further and say that business efficiency is best ensured by allowing the directors to function free from any outside control, except that of the Courts in the event of fraud or misfeasance, and by making themselves irremovable, without their own consent, however inefficient they may prove to be.'

Despite this cogent criticism, nothing has been done to curb the use of non-voting shares. Indeed, the Stock Exchange accepts non-voting shares provided it is made clear at the outset that this is what they are.

Preference shareholders may have restricted voting rights but they often have a right to vote on issues when their dividend is a certain amount in arrears. By statute they have voting rights when the company is trying a 'variation' of their rights. However, we shall see that 'variation' has in this context a special and narrow definition (see p. 284).

14.4   The exercise of voting powers

There are three important restrictions imposed by the courts on the exercise of the right to vote. The vote must be exercised in a way that is *'bona fide* for the benefit of the company as a whole' in situations where the courts permit a challenge to a resolution on that basis (this question principally arises where there is an attempt to alter the articles – see Chapter 5). Secondly, where the member voting belongs to more than one class of shareholder, and he is exercising a vote in the context of a 'class vote', he may not vote with his holdings in another class principally in mind. Both of these principles are aptly illustrated by *Re Holder's Investment Trust Ltd* [1971] 1 WLR 583. In that case, the court was considering an unopposed petition for the confirmation by the court of a reduction of capital. Megarry J said:

> 'The resolution was carried by the requisite majority because nearly 90 per cent of the preference shares are vested in the trustees of three trusts set up by Mr William Hill, and they voted in favour of the resolution. These trustees . . . also hold some 52 per cent of the ordinary stocks and shares . . . [counsel] contends that the extraordinary resolution of the preference shareholders was not valid and effectual because the supporting trustees did not exercise their votes in the way that they ought to have done, namely, in the interests of preference shareholders as a whole. Instead, being owners of much ordinary stock and many shares as well, they voted in such a way as to benefit the totality of the stocks and shares that they held . . . In the *British America* case [*British America Nickel Corporation Ltd* v. *M. J. O'Brien Ltd* [1937] AC 707], Viscount Haldane, in speaking for a strong board of the Judicial Committee, referred to . . . "a general principle, which is applicable to all authorities conferred on majorities of classes enabling them to bind minorities; namely, that the power given must be exercised for the purpose of benefiting the class as a whole, and not merely individual members only" . . . I have to see whether the majority was honestly endeavouring to decide and act for the benefit of the class as a whole, rather than with a view to the interests of some of the class and against that of others . . . [the] exchange of letters seems to me to make it perfectly clear that the advice sought, the advice given, and the advice acted upon, was all on the basis of what was for the benefit of the trusts as a whole, having regard to their large holdings of the equity capital . . . From first to last I can see no evidence that trustees ever applied their minds to what under company law was the right question, or that they ever had the *bona fide* belief that is requisite for an effectual sanction of the reduction. Accordingly, in my judgment there has been no effectual sanction for the modification of class rights.'

The third restriction is in relation to ratification of a breach of duty by directors when the director concerned and any connected person may not vote (s. 239 Companies Act 2006).

14.5 Variation of class rights

If a company wishes to vary the rights attaching to a class of shares or act contrary to the interests of a class of shareholders, special rules must be observed.

Class rights

The protection of the special regime extends to 'rights attached to any class of shares' and it is only when these rights are under threat that it applies. The question as to the meaning of this phrase arose in *Cumbrian Newspapers Group Ltd* v. *Cumberland & Westmorland Herald Newspaper & Printing Co. Ltd* [1987] Ch 1. In that case, a wide definition of the phrase was adopted. Scott J said:

> 'In my judgment, if specific rights are given to certain members in their capacity as members or shareholders, then those members become a class. The shares those members hold for the time being, and without which they would not be members of the class, would represent, in my view, a "class of shares".'

Section 629 Companies Act 2006 broadly follows this definition. It reads:

> '(1) For the purposes of the Companies Acts shares are of one class if the rights attached to them are in all respects uniform.
> (2) For this purpose the rights attached to shares are not regarded as different from those attached to other shares by reason only that they do not carry the same rights to dividends in the twelve months immediately following their allotment.'

In the *Cumbrian Newspapers* case the right in issue was a right given to the plaintiff under the defendant's articles, including a pre-emptive right regarding the transfer of any shares in the defendant and the right to nominate a director to the board of the defendant so long as it held 10 per cent of the issued ordinary shares of the defendant. These rights were held to be class rights, only alterable in accordance with the special procedure set out in s. 125 Companies Act 1985 (now s. 630 Companies Act 2006). This decision means that where particular rights are granted to an individual shareholder they would not be alterable without the consent of that shareholder. In those circumstances the individual concerned would constitute a class of one. It might in some cases be possible to say that the right had not been granted to the individual 'in his capacity as shareholder' but in some other capacity. If that is not so, provisions very common in the articles of private companies will become, for all practicable purposes, unalterable. For the time being it is clear that 'class rights' are to be widely defined.

Variation or abrogation

The special procedures apply where class rights are to be 'varied' or 'abrogated' (s. 630(6)). The courts have, in general, taken a narrow view of what is meant by these words. In general there will be a variation if the alteration directly affects the way the rights are described, but not if the value of the shareholding has been altered in some other way, for example, by varying the rights of another class of shares.

The attitude of the courts can only be understood properly by examining some of the relevant cases.

In *Greenhalgh* v. *Arderne Cinemas Ltd* [1946] 1 All ER 512, the company, by resolution, subdivided some 10s (50p) ordinary shares into five 2s (10p) ordinary shares. The votes created by this were used to pass a resolution for increasing the capital of the company. The effect of this was explained by Greene MR as follows:

> 'As a result of those two resolutions, if they are valid, the voting power of the appellant, which previously gave him a satisfactory measure of voting control, is liable to be completely swamped by the votes of the other ordinary shareholders.'

Despite this, the resolution was held not to have varied the rights of the appellant:

> 'the effect of this resolution is, of course, to alter the position of the ... 2s shareholders. Instead of Greenhalgh finding himself in a position of control, he finds himself in a position where control has gone, and to that extent the rights of the ... 2s shareholders are affected, as a matter of business. As a matter of law, I am quite unable to hold that, as a result of the transaction, the rights are varied; they remain what they always were – a right to have one vote per share *pari passu* with the ordinary shares for the time being issued which include the new 2s ordinary shares resulting from the subdivision.'

In *Re Old Silkstone Collieries* [1954] Ch 169 it was held that a reduction of capital by repaying preference shareholders, so that they would lose their right to any compensation due to them under the government's compensation scheme, did constitute a variation of their rights. However, by no means will any elimination of a class of shares constitute a variation. Where capital is repaid in accordance with the par value of the shares, and no well-defined right is taken away, the special procedure need not be invoked. The most usual of these will be a clearly defined right to participate in surplus assets on a winding-up.

The protection intended by the statute has not been forthcoming in the following cases:

1. In *Re Mackenzie & Co. Ltd* [1916] 2 Ch 450, where a reduction of capital was carried out by the cancellation of paid-up capital in two cases to an equal extent. The practical result was to reduce the amount payable under the fixed preferential dividend to the preference shareholders, while the ordinary shareholders could share the larger remainder of any declared dividend. Because the percentage of the dividend was not affected, that is, the actual description of the rights, on the face of it, were not altered, there was held to be no variation.

2. In *Re Schweppes Ltd* [1914] 1 Ch 322, an issue of shares ranking equally with existing shares was held not to be a variation.
3. In the *Greenhalgh* case (see p. 285) subdivision of shares and consequent dilution of voting rights was held not to be a variation.
4. In *White v. Bristol Aeroplane Company* [1953] Ch 65, an issue of bonus shares to one class which greatly increased its voting power as opposed to another class was held not to be a variation.
5. In *Dimbula Valley (Ceylon) Tea Co.* v. *Laurie* [1961] Ch 353, an issue of bonus shares to one class which would substantially reduce the amount which it would receive when participating in surplus assets on a winding-up was held not to be a variation.

Thus, it is only in the most obvious cases, usually when the rights attaching to shares have been altered by alteration of the actual wording describing those rights, where the special protection afforded by s. 630 will come into play. This seems to be an unnecessarily technical and legalistic approach to interpretation of legislation. It seems particularly strange when deciding what is meant by a law operating in the business sphere that a hard distinction should be drawn between 'affecting rights as a matter of business' and 'varying rights as a matter of law'. One reason for this cautious approach which can be discerned from the cases is the fear that by using a wide definition of 'variation' the courts would be allowing one class a veto over a scheme which might benefit the company as a whole. It would seem, however, that in this instance the courts have been rather overcautious.

Where there is a true 'variation'

Once it has been determined that a class right will be varied by a scheme put forward by a company, the correct procedure depends on the procedure set out in ss. 630–634 which represents a very welcome simplification of the complex regime under the 1985 Companies Act. Where the company has a share capital rights may be varied either:

'(a) in accordance with provision in the company's articles for the variation of those rights, or
(b) where the company's articles contain no such provision, if the holders of shares of that class consent to the variation in accordance with this section.
(4) The consent required for the purposes of this section on the part of the holders of a class of a company's shares is –
(a) consent in writing from the holders of at least three-quarters in nominal value of the issued shares of that class . . .
(b) a special resolution passed at a separate general meeting of the holders of that class sanctioning the resolution.'

Similar provisions apply to a company without a share capital and in both cases there is a right to object to the variation (ss. 633 and 634). If holders of more than 15 per cent of the shares object to the variation then, provided they did not vote for it, they may apply to the court to cancel the variation.

14.6 Alteration of articles to insert a variation clause

Section 125(7) Companies Act 1985 provides:

> 'Any alteration of a provision contained in a company's articles for the variation of rights attached to a class of shares, or the insertion of any such provision into the articles, is itself to be treated as a variation of those rights.'

14.7 Statutory right to object

Section 630(5) Companies Act 2006 gives a right to apply to the court to have a variation cancelled. The right to apply is surprisingly limited. One inbuilt limitation is the very narrow definition of 'variation' which was discussed above (see p. 284). As well as that, the statute requires that the application must be made by the holders of not less than 15 per cent of the issued shares of the class of shares whose rights are being varied, provided that they did not consent to or vote for the alteration. An application must be made to the court within 21 days after the variation was apparently made and may be made by one of the shareholders who must be appointed in writing (s. 633(4) Companies Act 2006). If such an application is made the variation has no effect until it is confirmed by the court. On hearing the application the court has a discretion to disallow the variation if it is satisfied, having regard to all the circumstances of the case, that the variation would unfairly prejudice the shareholders of the class represented by the applicant.

The narrow ambit of this minority right may account for the fact that the courts have indicated that a minority shareholder affected by a variation would have a common law right to challenge a variation on the grounds that the resolution to achieve the variation was not passed in good faith (see *Carruth* v. *Imperial Chemical Industries Ltd* [1937] AC 707 at 756, 765). There would be no necessity for the holders of 15 per cent of the shares of the class to agree on such an action. The matter could also come before the court in an action under ss. 994 *et seq*. for unfairly prejudiced shareholders (see Chapter 13).

Summary

1. Shares confer on a shareowner a number of rights in a company. Shares are often divided into different classes, ordinary and preference shares being commonplace.

2. The rights attaching to shares are usually to be found in the articles of association. Any lacunae in the description of share rights are made good by various presumptions of law.

3. Shares may or may not have voting rights.

4. Changing class rights will be considered a 'variation' only if the description of the rights is changed.

5. Where there is a true variation the correct procedure must be followed or the variation will be open to challenge. The procedure is largely set out in s. 630 Companies Act 2006.

Exercises

1. What are the arguments for and against non-voting shares?

2. Are the courts too restrictive in their definition of variations?

3. What are the usual differences between ordinary and preference shares?

Chapter 15

Lending money and securing loans

Key words

- **Crystallisation** – the moment at which a floating charge becomes fixed, that is, attaches to specific items owned by the company.
- **Debenture** – the document which sets out the terms of a loan to the company.
- **Floating charge** – when a loan is secured by a floating charge it is possible to deal with the property over which the charge 'floats' without the consent of the lender until the charge 'crystallises'.

A company can finance its activities by selling shares or by raising money from banks or other money-lending institutions. If the company is granted a loan, the lender may become a debenture-holder. A debenture has never been satisfactorily defined. The Companies Act 2006 provides (s. 738):

'In the Companies Acts "debenture" includes debenture stock, bonds and any other securities of a company, whether or not constituting a charge on the assets of the company.'

In *Levy* v. *Abercorris Slate and Slab Co.* (1883) 37 Ch D 260, Chitty J said:

'In my opinion a debenture means a document which either creates a debt or acknowledges it, and any document which fulfils either of these conditions is a "debenture".'

Shareholders are members of the company and their rights have been described elsewhere in this book. Debenture-holders are creditors of the company and their rights are normally defined in the contract made between them and the company. It is interesting to note that, unlike shares, debentures can be issued at a discount unless they are convertible into shares, when such an issue at a discount would be an invitation to evade the rule that shares may not be issued at a discount (*Mosly* v. *Koffyfontein* [1904] 2 Ch 108). The lender may wish to secure his position by taking a charge over the property of the company, that is, creating a legal relationship between himself and the company which will ensure he is paid in priority at least to some of the other claimants against the company.

15.1 Debenture-holder's receiver

The power of a debenture-holder to appoint a receiver will be determined by the terms of the debenture itself. In the circumstances in which a receiver may be appointed, he will be appointed to collect the assets of the company with a view to the repayment of the debt due to the debenture-holder. He must, however, pay creditors whose claim should be paid before the debenture-holder, for example a preferential creditor as set out in Schedule 6 of the Insolvency Act 1986 (see s. 754 Companies Act 2006 and Chapter 17).

15.2 Fixed and floating charges

It may be important for the purposes of determining the priority of charges to decide whether a particular charge is a 'fixed' or a 'floating' charge. Essentially a fixed charge gives the holder the right to have a particular asset sold in order to repay the loan that he has given the company. This means that the company may not deal with the property subject to the fixed charge without the consent of the holder of the charge. A floating charge gives the holder the right to be paid in priority to others after the sale of the assets subject to the charge, but in this case the assets over which the charge floats are not specified. The company may continue to deal with them without the permission of the holder of the charge and it is only on the happening of certain events (such as non-payment of an instalment of interest or repayment of capital) that the charge will become fixed. On the happening of the event in question (which will be specified in the contract for the loan) the charge is said to 'crystallise' and will become fixed on the particular assets that the company holds at that moment which answer to the general description of the property over which the charge originally 'floated'. It then becomes indistinguishable in form from a fixed charge. Thus, if the original charge 'floated' over all stock-in-trade and a crystallising event occurred, the goods subject to the crystallised charge would be the stock the company owned on that particular day. After the crystallisation, the company would not be able to sell these assets without the permission of the debenture-holder.

The court in *Re Yorkshire Woolcombers Association Ltd* [1903] 2 Ch 284 (see Case note, p. 301) grappled with the definition of floating charges. In the Court of Appeal, Romer J said:

> 'I certainly do not intend to attempt to give an exact definition of the term "floating charge" nor am I prepared to say that there will not be a floating charge within the meaning of the Act, which does not contain all the three characteristics that I am about to mention, but I certainly think that if the charge has the three characteristics that I am about to mention it is a floating charge: (1) if it is a charge on a class of assets of a company present and future; (2) if that class is one which,

in the ordinary course of the business of the company, would be changing from time to time; and (3) if you find that by the charge it is contemplated that, until some future step is taken by or on behalf of those interested in the charge, the company may carry on its business in the ordinary way as far as concerns the particular class of assets I am dealing with.'

Thus, the idea of a 'floating' charge is that the company is unhindered from dealing with its assets despite the fact that an outsider has a legal interest in those assets.

When the charge is created, the nature of the charge as a fixed or floating charge depends on its characteristics and not on whether the parties have described it as a fixed or floating charge. Thus in *Re Armagh Shoes Ltd* [1982] NI 59, the charge being considered by the court was described in the document that created it as a 'fixed' charge but was held by the court to have been a floating charge. The document included the following:

'the mortgagor pursuant to every power and by force of every estate enabling it in this behalf and as beneficial owner hereby charges in the favour of the bank by way of fixed charge all receivables debtors plant machinery fixtures fittings and ancillary equipment now or at any time hereafter belonging to the mortgagor.'

Hutton J said:

'the authorities establish that the description of a charge as a fixed or specific charge does not, in itself, operate to prevent the charge from being a floating charge; and the deed in this case contains no express provision restricting the company from dealing with the assets charged. In my judgment in the present case it is a necessary implication from the deed that the company was to have the right or licence to deal with the assets, comprised within the ambit of the charge, in the ordinary course of its business until the bank decided to enforce the charge. I can see no basis for the implication that it was the intention of the company and the bank that the company would deal with the charged assets in breach of its contract with the bank, to which breaches the bank would turn a blind eye, and that if a third party asked the company if it was entitled to transfer some of the charged assets to him the company would have to tell him to obtain the bank's consent to the transfer.'

In *Re Keenan Brothers Ltd* [1986] BCLC 242 the parties tried to create a fixed charge on money that was due to be paid to the company in the future, that is, 'book debts'. Two questions arose: (i) whether it was possible in law to create a fixed charge on future book debts – the court answered in the affirmative; and (ii) whether the charge that had in fact been created in this case was a fixed charge or a floating charge. On this point, McCarthy J, giving judgment in the Irish Supreme Court, emphasised the term in the agreement that read:

'The company shall pay into an account with the Bank designated for that purpose all moneys which it may receive in respect of the book debts and other debts hereby charged and shall not without the prior consent of the Bank in writing make any withdrawals or direct any payment from the said account.'

He said:

'In my view, it is because it was described as a specific or fixed charge and was intended to be such, that the requirement of a special bank account was necessary; if it were a floating charge payment into such an account would be entirely inappropriate and, indeed, would conflict with the ambulatory nature of the floating charge . . . In *Re Yorkshire Woolcombers Association Ltd* Romer LJ postulated three characteristics of a floating charge, the third being that, if you find that by the charge it is contemplated that, until some future step is taken by or on behalf of those interested in the charge, the company may carry on its business in the ordinary way as far as concerns the particular class of assets I am dealing with. Counsel for the banks has argued that this latter characteristic is essential to a floating charge and that the banking provision in the instruments here negatives such a characteristic; I would uphold this view.'

This case can be contrasted with *Re Brightlife Ltd* [1987] Ch 200, where Hoffman J held that the charge in question was a floating charge. It was a charge over (among other things) future book debts. Hoffman J held that the existence of a floating charge is not dependent on the company over whose property it floats having complete freedom of action. He said:

'It is true that clause 5(ii) does not allow Brightlife to sell, factor or discount debts without the written consent of Norandex [who had the benefit of the charge]. But a floating charge is consistent with some restriction on the company's freedom to deal with its assets. For example, floating charges commonly contain a prohibition on the creation of other charges ranking prior to or *pari passu* with the floating charge. Such dealings would otherwise be open to a company in the ordinary course of its business. In this debenture, the significant feature is that Brightlife was free to collect its debts and pay the proceeds into its bank account. Once in the account, they would be outside the charge over debts and at the free disposal of the company. In my judgment a right to deal in this way with the charged assets for its own account is a badge of a floating charge and is inconsistent with a fixed charge.'

See also *New Bullas Trading Ltd* [1993] BCC 251, in which the Court of Appeal found that the debenture in question in that case had created a fixed charge over book debts which would become a floating charge over the proceeds once they had been collected and paid into a specified account. The debenture-holder had power to give directions as to the application of the money once it had been received but had not exclusive control over that money unless a direction had actually been given. There were thus circumstances in which the company could dispose of the money and the charge was a floating charge. Before the money was collected the company had an absolute obligation to pay any proceeds of book debts into a particular account. At this stage there was therefore a fixed charge over the book debts. In *William Gaskell Group* v. *Highley* [1994] 1 BCLC 197 the issue of whether the charge was fixed or floating turned on whether a clause requiring payment of the proceeds of debts into an account which could not be drawn on without the consent of the Midland Bank remained valid after the Midland assigned the debenture. The court held that it was still commercially viable to require the Midland's consent, the clause remained valid and the restriction meant that the charge was a fixed charge.

The court will look carefully at the substance of the charge and will not be bound by the wording adopted by the parties. In *Re G. E. Tunbridge Ltd* [1995] 1 BCLC 409 a charge described as a fixed charge which purported to be over all the assets of the company except those covered by a floating charge was held not to create a fixed charge over intangible assets such as book debts or tangible assets which were likely to be changed or sold over time. This was despite the fact that the company was not permitted to dispose of the assets subject to the fixed charge without the consent of the chargee. However, in *Re Climex Tissues* [1995] 1 BCLC 409 a charge was held to be properly described as a fixed charge despite the fact that the company was apparently permitted to deal with the property subject to the charge 'in the ordinary course of business'. The court held that this wording must be taken to refer to the stock (toilet rolls) and not the capital machinery but also held that the existence of a limited power to deal with property was not necessarily inconsistent with a fixed charge. Each case therefore turns on its precise facts and the degree of liberty with which the company is able to deal with the property which is subject to the charge. See also *Re Cosslett (Contractors) Ltd* [1998] 2 WLR 131 (CA); *Clark* v. *Mid Glamorgan County Council* [1996] 1 BCLC 407; and *Royal Trust Bank* v. *National Westminster Bank plc and Another* [1996] 2 BCLC 682.

15.3   The characteristics of fixed and floating charges

The cases examined above show that the greater the interference with the freedom to use and dispose of the assets affected by the charge the more likely it is the courts will hold the charge to be a fixed charge, however the parties have described it. Because of the huge variety of clauses to be found in documents creating charges, it is impossible to arrive at an exhaustive definition of the difference between the two types of charges; the whole of the nature of the restrictions must be examined. The difference is important when the priority of various claimants has to be decided.

15.4   Crystallisation of the floating charge

A charge will certainly crystallise on the happening of the following:

(i)   the appointment of an administrative receiver by the chargeholder;
(ii) the appointment of an administrator;

(iii) the commencement of liquidation;
(iv) the cessation of business.

The document which creates the floating charge will provide for certain events which will cause the floating charge to become a fixed charge. Prior to the Companies Act 1989 there was much discussion as to whether this 'crystallisation' could be 'automatic', that is, could occur without any action on behalf of the debenture-holders or their agents, merely because an event specified in the debenture had occurred. There was some authority to the effect that this could occur (*obiter* in *Re Brightlife*, see above). In *Re Woodroffes (Musical Instruments) Ltd* [1986] Ch 366, it was held that the crystallisation of a first floating charge did not occur automatically when a subsequent charge was crystallised. However, it was also held that a floating charge did automatically crystallise on the cessation of a company's business. Whether the cessation of business and the moment at which a business ceases to be a going concern are different was unclear to Nouse J. He said: 'My own impression is that these phrases are used interchangeably in the authorities . . . but whether that be right or wrong, I think it clear that the material event is a cessation of business and not, if that is something different, ceasing to be a going concern.' The moment of crystallisation in that case was important, because if the floating charge had crystallised before the appointment of a receiver, the preferential creditors would have lost the priority that they enjoy under s. 175 Companies Act 1985 over the holders of a 'floating charge' created by the company. The charge would be a fixed charge at the relevant date. This effect was confirmed in *Re ELS Ltd; Ramsbottom v. Luton Borough Council* [1994] BCC 449. The court held that on crystallisation the goods subject to the charge ceased to be goods of the company and became the goods of the chargee. Consequently it was not possible for bailiffs acting for the local authority to seize the goods because of rates owed by the company to the local council.

Section 410 Companies Act 1985 gives power to the Secretary of State to make regulations concerning the automatic crystallisation of floating charges. This appears to be statutory recognition of automatic crystallisation. However, until regulations are made there remains a degree of uncertainty in the law.

15.5 Legal and equitable charges

The order in which competing claims against company property will be paid will depend on whether the creditor holds a legal or equitable charge. A legal charge will commonly only occur:

(i) when there is a charge by way of legal mortgage of land under s. 85(1) or s. 86(1) Law of Property Act 1925, or

(ii) where the legal interest in the charged property is transferred to the chargee by way of security for an obligation, on condition that the interest will be transferred back to the surety if and when the secured obligation is met.

All other charges are equitable charges. In the absence of registration, equitable charges take priority in order of creation. However, a legal charge created after an equitable charge will take priority over it unless the chargee had notice of the prior charge. For the effect of registration, see p. 299.

15.6 Floating charges and other claims against the company

Subsequent fixed charges

For a comprehensive survey of these provisions see *AIB Finance Ltd* v. *Bank of Scotland* [1995] 1 BCLC 185. The same result is achieved in England by the case law (see *Wheatley* v. *Silkstone and Haigh Moor Coal Company* (1885) 29 Ch D 715). In the absence of actual notice of a restriction on the creation of later charges (sometimes called a 'negative pledge clause') the fixed charge will take priority over a previous floating charge. This, of course, is subject to the effects of non-registration of registrable charges. The legislation appears to produce an odd result in that the registration rules affect priority as against those subsequently acquiring an interest in the same property. It would seem that a subsequent fixed charge will rank in priority over a registered floating charge, even if the fixed charge is not registered.

Subsequent floating charges

A company will not be able to create a second floating charge ranking equally or having priority over an existing floating charge, in the absence of words permitting this in the instrument creating the first floating charge (*Re Benjamin Cope & Sons* [1914] 1 Ch 800). However, permission to create a subsequent charge ranking equally or in priority to an earlier one may be construed out of a clause reserving power to create charges over specific property. The theory seems to be that reserving a general power to charge property when a first charge is created will not permit the erosion of the value of the first charge by creation of a second charge. However, such erosion is permitted where the reservation of the right to charge is confined to specific property. In *Re Automatic Bottle Makers Ltd* [1926] Ch 412, Sargant LJ said:

'Great stress has, however, been laid for the respondents on a decision of my own as a judge of first instance in *Re Benjamin Cope & Sons* [1914] 1 Ch 800, and it has been argued that that case decides that a general floating charge is necessarily incompatible with the subsequent creation under a special charging power of a floating charge to rank in priority or *pari passu* with the earlier floating charge. I have examined that decision with great care, and have no reason to think that it was wrong, particularly in view of the fact that it appears to be in accord with an earlier decision of Vaughan-Williams J in *Smith* v. *England and Scottish Mercantile Investment Trust* [1896] WN 86 and not to have been questioned since. But the facts in that case were very different. There the original charge was on the whole undertaking and property for the time being of the company, and the reservation of a power to mortgage was in quite general terms; and it was held that such a power could not have been intended to authorise a competing charge on the entirety of the property comprised in the earlier charge. Here the reservation of the power to mortgage is precise and specific in its terms, and extends only to certain particular classes of the property of the company.'

In certain circumstances charges can be overturned when a company is liquidated. For a discussion of this see Chapter 17.

Set-offs

If an outsider has a right which is enforceable against the company at the time when a floating charge crystallises, he can resist any claim which the receiver has against him to the extent of his right against the company, that is, he can set off his right against the amount being claimed by the receiver (*Robbie* v. *Whitney Warehouses* [1963] 3 All ER 613).

Judgment creditors

Once a receiver has been appointed by debenture-holders, the claim of the debenture-holders will take priority to the claim of the creditor despite the fact that he has obtained judgment in his favour (*Re Cairney* v. *Black* [1906] 2 KB 746).

15.7 Retention of title clauses

These clauses are sometimes known as Romalpa clauses after the case of *Aluminium Industrie Vaassen BV* v. *Romalpa Aluminium Ltd* [1976] 1 WLR 676, which established their validity. A clause is inserted in a sale of goods contract which provides that the goods purchased shall remain the property of the seller until the purchase price is paid. If a receiver is appointed under the terms of a floating charge before the purchase price is paid, an unpaid purchaser would be able to recover 'his' goods from the company; the receiver may not treat them as the property of the company. The unpaid seller's rights continue only until the goods are identifiable and in the possession of the buyer. Thus in the case of *Borden (UK) Ltd* v. *Scottish Timber Products* [1979] 3 WLR 672, the material sold under the contract was resin. This was processed with other materials into chipboard. The unpaid seller had no rights over the chipboard. A simple retention of title clause does not at present require registration (see also *Clough Mill Ltd* v. *Geoffrey Martin* [1985] 1 WLR 111; and *Specialist Plant Services Ltd* v. *Braithwaite Ltd* [1987] BCLC 1).

However where more complicated clauses have been used a registerable charge may be created. See *Re Bond Worth* [1980] Ch 228 and *Re Curtain Dream plc* [1990] BCLC 925.

15.8 Registration of company charges

The law in this area seems to be permanently in a state of flux. The 1989 Companies Act contained new rules but they were never brought into force. The DTI Company Law Review Committee issued a consultation document concerning registration of charges (*Modern Company Law for a Competitive Economy: Registration of Charges*, October 2000), and the Companies Act 2006 contains a new set of rules on the issue (ss. 860–877 for England and Wales; there is a separate regime for Scotland). However, these relate principally to the keeping of the register and are not yet in force so, in view of the consistent failure to implement legislation in this field, the regime under the 1985 Act is described. Much of the difficulty in this area is that it is problematic to radically change the system of registration of company charges without a complete overhaul of other areas. Many hope that the Diamond Report's recommendations (Professor Diamond, *A Review of Security Interests in Property* (HMSO, 1989)) will be implemented. The Diamond Report's radical proposals for a review of the whole of the law relating to security over property other than land are still under consideration. If implemented there would be a single register of security interests created by companies, partnerships and sole traders in the course of business. Determination of priority would be by date of filing. The register would cover retention of title clauses, hire purchase and chattel leases for more than three years. It would replace the present scheme and create a single register for these charges.

15.9 Which charges are registrable?

By ss. 395(1) and 396(1) Companies Act 1985 the following charges must be registered with the Registrar of Companies within 21 days of being created by a company registered in England and Wales. If the Companies Act 2006 is implemented, s. 860 repeats this list:

- a charge securing an issue of debentures;
- a charge on uncalled share capital of the company;
- a charge created or evidenced by an instrument which, if executed by an individual, would require registration as a bill of sale;
- a charge on land or any interest in land, other than a rent charge;
- a charge on book debts of the company;
- a floating charge on the undertaking or property of the company;
- a charge on calls made but not paid;
- a charge on a ship or aircraft, or any share in a ship;
- a charge on goodwill, or on any intellectual property.

15.10 Salient points

Of these complicated provisions the most notable factors are:

(i) Book debts are registrable although, as we have seen, the designation of book debts as fixed or floating charges is highly controversial.

(ii) In *Re Brightlife* [1987] Ch 200, Hoffman J decided that a bank account fell outside the definition of book debts so that a charge over a bank account did not require registration. The Registrar has, however, accepted such charges for registration. Because of the changed role of the Registrar it will still be possible in the future to register such charges. However, whether the registration of them should become obligatory will depend on a clearer definition of book debts. The Diamond report contains the view that it is unnecessary to include such charges, at least until the implementation of Part II of its recommendations. Because bank accounts are usually secret, other creditors will not be misled by the existence of an undisclosed charge over one. This controversy does not affect the situation where the charge over the bank account is registrable in its own right, for example as a floating charge.

(iii) *Paul & Frank Ltd* v. *Discount Bank (Overseas) Ltd* [1967] Ch 348, in which it was held that a charge on an insurance policy before a claim arose was not a book debt, remains good law. The Diamond report recommended registration of such charges (paragraph 23.5) but this might be done when book debts are more clearly defined.

(iv) Charges over shares are not registrable *per se*.

15.11 Delivery of particulars and priorities

Prescribed particulars must be delivered to the Registrar within 21 days of the creation of the charge (s. 395(1)).

The date of creation of a charge is the date of execution of the instrument creating the charge or of fulfilment of conditions if executed conditionally, or the date of an enforceable agreement conferring a security interest forthwith or on the acquisition by the company of property subject to the charge.

15.12 Priorities under the registration system

The fundamental rule regarding priority, gives priority in accordance with the date of creation of a charge. This is despite the inadequate protection which is given by a system which bases priority on the date of creation of a charge and then permits registration within 21 days. The Diamond report recommendations for a system of registration based on date of registration, coupled with a provisional registration system or for a certificate of guarantee from the Registrar, have never been implemented.

15.13 Effect of registration

Registration of a charge in the register is notice to everyone that a charge of a particular type exists but it does not constitute notice of the terms and conditions of the charge (*Wilson* v. *Kelland* [1910] 2 Ch 306). Section 398(4) provides that the Registrar will merely file the statement of particulars delivered by the parties. The charge will not be produced so there is no question of checking the particulars. Registration of a charge will continue to be sufficient to give notice of the charge to anyone subsequently taking a charge over the company. Although the doctrine of constructive (deemed) notice has been generally abolished by s. 711A(1), s. 711A(4) provides that it is subject to s. 416. Section 416(1) provides:

'A person taking a charge over a company's property shall be taken to have notice of any matter requiring registration and disclosed on the register at the time the charge is created.'

Section 416(2) provides thus:

'Otherwise, a person shall not be taken to have notice of any other matter by reason of its being disclosed on the register or by reason of his having failed to search the register in the course of making such inquiries as ought reasonably to have been made. This is clear so far as additional information which is not discovered by the person taking the charge. It is also clear that where such a person has in fact discovered the additional information he is not deemed to know it merely because it is on the register. The section does not seem to preclude proof of actual knowledge of such information.'

15.14 Duty to register and effect of non-registration

Section 398 provides that it is the duty of a company which creates a charge, or acquires property subject to a charge, to deliver particulars of the charge to the Registrar within 21 days of the creation of the charge. Anyone interested in the charge may deliver the particulars but if no one does so the company and any officer of the company in default commit an offence and will be liable to a fine.

The most important consequence of failure to deliver, however, is that by s. 395(1) it becomes void against the liquidator or administrator and any creditor of the company. This means that a subsequent chargee can ignore an unregistered charge even if he has actual notice of it, unless such subsequent chargee has expressly agreed to be subject to the unregistered charge. These provisions change the situation of a purchaser from the company of the property subject to the charge. Such a purchaser will now take the property free of the charge even if he knew of the charge provided he has not agreed to take the property subject to the charge.

15.15 Payment of money secured by unregistered charge

Section 395(2) provides that money secured by an unregistered demand becomes repayable on demand when the charge becomes void to any extent. Such money is automatically repayable at the end of the 21-day period.

Summary

1. Money lent to a company will normally be secured by a fixed charge over definite property or by a floating charge which will enable the company to deal with the assets involved until crystallisation of the floating charge turns it into a fixed charge.

2. Crystallisation of a floating charge will normally occur when the lender (debenture-holder) intervenes to assert his rights, often at the appointment of a receiver.

3. It is still unclear whether a floating charge can 'automatically' crystallise on the happening of an event specified in the debenture or whether intervention by the debenture-holder is required.

4. Charges must be registered if they are to be valid against others taking security from a company. They must be registered within 21 days of creation but priority is in order of creation rather than order of registration.

5. The registration provisions cover the situations where there is late delivery of particulars of a charge or errors or omissions in particulars.

Case note

Re Yorkshire Woolcombers Association Ltd [1903] 2 Ch 284

By a trust deed of 23 April 1890, the Yorkshire Woolcombers Association Ltd specifically mortgaged all its freehold and leasehold properties to trustees to secure its debenture stock, and, as beneficial owner, charged in favour of the trustees 'by way of floating security all its other property and assets both present and future, and its undertaking, but not including capital for the time being uncalled'. The deed contained a power enabling the association to deal with the property and assets which were subject to the charge. The question before the court was whether the charge was a fixed or floating charge, since it had not been registered; if it was a floating charge, it would be void as against the receiver. Farwell J said at first instance:

> 'The very essence of a specific charge is that the assignee takes possession, and is the person entitled to receive the book debts at once. So long as he licenses the mortgagor to go on receiving the book debts and carry on the business, it is within the exact definition of a floating security.'

The Court of Appeal upheld this judgment: part of the speech of Romer J is reproduced in the text.

Exercises

1. Would a system of priority of charges depending on order of registration be better than the present system (which depends on order of creation)?

2. If a floating charge is created does (i) a subsequent fixed charge and (ii) a subsequent floating charge expressed to rank equally, have priority over it?

Chapter 16

Takeovers, reconstructions and amalgamations

Key word

▶ **Takeover** – this happens when the shares of one company are bought by another company. The two companies continue to exist; what has changed is control in the company whose shares have been bought; the buyer company can use its shares to control the bought company by voting.

A great number of company reconstructions occur as a result of the takeover of one company by another. This will often be achieved by the company which is effecting the takeover offering to buy the shares held by the shareholders in the target company. Such reconstructions are governed by a mixture of rules, some found in the statutes and others to be found in the City Code on Takeovers and Mergers. The rules of the Financial Services Authority and the London Stock Exchange also require disclosure of a number of matters when a takeover is attempted and a company listed on the Exchange is involved. Such a company must disclose detailed information concerning the company making the offer and the precise terms of the offer in the document which sets out the takeover proposal. This document is known as the 'offer document'.

16.1 Public offers

If the offeror company proposes an exchange of its shares for the target company's shares, that is, the price for the shares of the target company is shares in the offeror company, this will be a public issue of shares and will be governed by the rules explained in Chapter 7.

16.2 Monopolies

Some takeover bids may be regarded as bad for the general public because the end result would be a company which had such a large share of the market as to be able to dominate that market and set the terms on which the items it dealt with changed hands. If a company was alone in a particular market it would have a monopoly of that market. In fact, the authorities normally intervene some time before a monopoly situation is reached. A number of the rules in this area have been made under the Enterprise Act 2002 and Article 82 of the EEC Treaty. The competition authorities of the UK and EU will consider the possible effect of the takeovers on the relevant market. If a takeover has implications for the EC market, the EC Commission will assess its probable effect.

16.3 The Takeover Panel

The Panel supervises takeover of public and other large companies. For the first time the Takeover Panel is given powers by statute under the Companies Act 2006. Sections 942–946 give the Panel very wide powers and responsibilities. These will be subject to judicial review by the courts. In the past the Panel was not a body established by statute and the argument has always been that turning it into a statutory body would hinder its flexibility and the speed with which it could take decisions. The width of the powers given by the Companies Act 2006 means that this is not a likely outcome although it will be necessary to wait and see exactly what happens in the future. In *R* v. *Panel on Takeovers* Ex Parte *Datafin* [1987] 2 WLR 699, the Court of Appeal held that the decisions of the Panel should be reviewable by the court, although a review was refused in that particular case. The court was reluctant to hinder the work of the Panel and so held that resort to the court should not be made during the course of the events on which the Panel was ruling. The court should allow the Panel to make decisions and allow events to take their course, intervening, if at all, later, in retrospect, by declaratory orders. In *R* v. *Panel on Takeovers and Mergers* Ex Parte *Guinness PLC* [1989] BCLC 255 the Court of Appeal confirmed that the Panel's decisions would only be subject to judicial review where something had gone wrong with its procedure so as to cause real injustice and require the intervention of the court.

16.4 General principles and rules

The Companies Act 2006 requires the Panel to make rules to implement the EU Directive on Takeovers (ss. 943(1) and 943(2)). Rules made by the Panel may also make provision:

(a) for, or in connection with, the regulation of –
   (i)   takeover bids
   (ii) merger transactions, and
   (iii) transactions (not falling within sub-paragraph (i) or (ii) that have or may have, directly or indirectly, an effect on the ownership or control of companies.

By subsection (3) of s. 943, the provision that may be made under subsection (2) includes, in particular, provision for a matter that is, or is similar to, a matter provided for by the Panel in the City Code on Takeovers and Mergers as it had effect immediately before the passing of this Act.

It seems, therefore, that the Act does not envisage a significant change in the responsibilities or mode of operation of the Panel, which has operated by issuing the Code mentioned in s. 943(3).

The Code sets out general principles 'of conduct to be observed in takeover and merger transactions'. There are also more detailed rules and notes which provide guidance as to the way in which the rules should operate. The Code requires that the spirit of the general principles and rules as well as the precise wording should be observed. The Code seeks to ensure fair treatment of all shareholders, including equal treatment of different classes of shares, as well as equal treatment of members of each class. To this end there is: a requirement of disclosure of the financial soundness of the offeror company; a duty on directors of both companies to consider their shareholders' interests and not to have regard to their personal interests; a requirement that information given to shareholders is sufficient to enable a properly informed decision to be made; and a requirement that any information supplied must be available to all shareholders. There are also rules preventing the use of tactics by an offeree board which would tend to frustrate a takeover bid. Section 952 Companies Act 2006 provides that the Panel rules may contain provisions imposing sanctions on any person who has:

(a) acted in breach of the rules, or
(b) failed to comply with a direction [of the Panel].
(c) The Panel also has power to apply to the court for an order to secure compliance with its rules (s. 955).

16.5 Partial offers

One of the key rules of the Code requires that where 30 per cent or more of the shares in a company have been acquired by some one concern or by a number of concerns or persons 'acting in concert', then, except in exceptional circumstances and with the permission of the Panel, an equivalent offer must be made for the remainder of the shares. This seeks to prevent the situation where there is acquisition of sufficient shares to ensure control of the company, followed by a much lower offer to remaining shareholders. This rule is backed up by s. 793 Companies Act 2006 which permits a company to require the disclosure of interests in shares in certain circumstances.

16.6 Compulsory purchase provisions

If the takeover bid has as its object the acquisition of all the shares in a company, a small dissentient minority could prevent this by refusing to sell their shares. Section 979 Companies Act 2006 therefore provides that if the offeror has acquired or contracted to acquire not less than 90 per cent of the shares to which the takeover offer relates, he may give notice to the holder of any other such shares that he desires to acquire those. The notice can only be given within three months of the day after the last day on which the offer can be accepted unless the time limit for acceptance is not governed by the EU Directive on Takeovers, in which case the period is six months. If a notice is served under these provisions the offeror can and must purchase the shares (s. 981) unless an application is made to the court by a shareholder under s. 986 for an order that the offeror may not exercise his power of compulsory acquisition. In fact, the court is unlikely to look upon such an application with favour. In *Re Grierson, Oldham and Adams Ltd* [1968] Ch 17, Plowman J said:

> 'The first, general observation is that the onus of proof here is fairly and squarely on the applicants, and indeed they accept that is so. The onus of proof is on them to establish, if they can, that the offer was unfair . . . I notice . . . that at first instance in *Re Bugle Press Ltd* [1961] Ch 270, Buckley J, whose decision was upheld by the Court of Appeal, said:
>
> > "In the ordinary case of an offer under this section, where the 90 per cent majority who accept the offer are unconnected with the persons who are concerned with making the offer, the court pays the greatest attention to the views of that majority. In all commercial matters, where commercial people are much better able to judge of their own affairs than the court is able to do, the court is accustomed to pay the greatest attention to what commercial people who are concerned with the transaction in fact decide."'

This view was confirmed in *Re Lifecare International PLC* [1990] BCLC 222. This scheme for compulsory purchase may not be used in a situation which is not a true takeover situation and which therefore ought to proceed under one of the other schemes discussed below (*Re Bugle Press*, see Case note, p. 311).

16.7 Sell-out right

Section 983 Companies Act 2006 provides for the right of a minority shareholder to require an offeror to acquire his shares. This arises where the offeror has already acquired shares amounting to 90 per cent in value and carrying 90 per cent of the voting rights in the company.

16.8 Reconstructions

Sections 902–941 Companies Act 2006 set out a procedure which envisages major reconstruction of a company. One of the situations in which these sections may be used is where a merger of two companies is proposed. Such a reconstruction will affect the rights of members and creditors. Care must be taken to ensure that all interests are taken into account. The schemes of compromise or arrangement, for merger and division set out in these sections provide a more streamlined version of previous requirements, permitting the court to dispense with some of the formalities in certain cases and providing exceptions to the requirement to hold meetings of members in some limited circumstances (ss. 934, 931 and 932 (division) and 917 (merger)).

A scheme of arrangement, a merger or division require the consent of 75 per cent 'in value of the members of each class of shareholders in the affected companies'. If there are conflicting interests within a class, meetings of 'sub-classes' must be held. In *Re Hellenic and General Trust Ltd* [1976] 1 WLR 123 the shares which belonged to the wholly-owned subsidiary of the offeror company were held to belong to a different class from those which belonged to independent shareholders. It was held that where different shareholders have different interests they must be regarded as belonging to a separate class.

16.9 Meetings

Notices summoning the meetings will be sent out to shareholders and (if relevant) to creditors. The notices must explain the scheme and the material interests of the directors of the company. The meeting must have draft terms of the scheme, a report by the directors explaining the scheme and an independent expert's report on the financial consequences of the scheme. At the meeting of each class a majority in number representing 75 per cent in value of those present and voting in person or by proxy must approve the scheme if it is to go further. If the necessary approval is achieved, the approval of the court may be sought under s. 939.

16.10 Approval of the court

The court will normally accept the verdict of the substantial majority required at the meetings and approve the scheme. However, the principle that at the meetings the votes must be cast 'with a view to the class as a whole' has evolved to prevent the scheme being approved because of the vote of someone who had a special interest to protect or further. If such a person is not neutralised by the requirement that persons with different interests should have different class meetings, the scheme may fail at the approval stage because the vote was carried by a voter seeking to further his own interests at the expense of the class as a whole. Thus in *Re English, Scottish and Australian Chartered Bank* [1893] 3 Ch 385, Lindley LJ said:

> 'If the creditors are acting on sufficient information and with time to consider what they are about and are acting honestly, they are, I apprehend, much better judges of what is to their commercial advantage than the Court can be. I do not say it is conclusive because there might be some blot on a scheme which had passed that had been unobserved and which was pointed out later. If, however, there should be no such blot, then the court ought to be slow to differ from [the creditors].'

However, in *Carruth* v. *Imperial Chemical Industries Ltd* [1937] AC 707, Lord Maugham said:

> 'The Court will, in considering whether a scheme ought to be approved, disregard a majority vote in favour of it if it appears that the majority did not consider the matter with a view to the interests of the class to which they belong only.'

The situation appears to be that the court has an unfettered discretion to upset a vote if it is unhappy about whether the outcome is fair to the minority.

16.11 Reconstruction in a liquidation

Under ss. 110–111 Insolvency Act 1986 a company which is in a member's voluntary liquidation (see Chapter 17) may empower its liquidator by special resolution to transfer a whole or part of its business or property to another company in return for shares in that company. The shares must be distributed among the shareholders of the original company in strict accordance with their rights to share in the assets in a winding-up. Such a scheme does not require the approval of the court. However, if shareholders with one-quarter of the voting power do not agree with the scheme, they may express their dissent to the liquidator and require him either to abstain from carrying out the scheme or to purchase their shares at a price agreed or fixed by arbitration. This right cannot be excluded by the memorandum of association (see *Bisgood* v. *Henderson's Transvaal Estates* [1908] 1 Ch 743). The relationship between the s. 425 Companies Act 1985 procedure and the Insolvency Act procedure was explained in *Re Anglo Continental Supply Co.* [1922] 2 Ch 723, where Astbury J said [current section numbers inserted]:

> '(1) When a so-called scheme is really and truly a sale etc. under s. 110 *simpliciter* that section must be complied with and cannot be evaded by calling it a scheme of arrangement under s. 425.
>
> (2) Where a scheme cannot be carried through under s. 110 though it involves (*inter alia*) a sale to a company under that section ... the Court can sanction it under s. 425 if it is fair and reasonable ... and it may, but only if it thinks fit,

insist as a term of its sanction, on the dissentient shareholders being protected in a manner similar to that provided for in s. 110.

(3) Where a scheme of arrangement is one outside s. 110 entirely the Court can also and *a fortiori* act as in proposition 2, subject to the conditions therein mentioned.'

Hot Topic . . .

INTERNATIONAL TAKEOVERS

The story of the Vodafone–Mannesman takeover is remarkable in many respects. Most importantly it was the first successful unsolicited takeover bid made against a German company. Because of this it raised the question of whether barriers to takeover bids, which are inherent in the structure of large German firms, were about to be overcome. This is of significant importance as it would alter the fundamental attitudes towards companies and their regulation, bringing German law more into the Anglo/American mould. The Anglo/American model of company law is a 'contractual' model which gives primacy to the 'contract' made by shareholders to invest their money in the company. The prime agent for controlling managers is therefore the shareholders who elect directors and may remove them by a simple majority vote. This shareholder control is (at least in theory) backed by the takeover mechanism (see pp. 303–4). German law, however, has a more inclusive model of company structure. The shareholders may elect as few as one-third of the supervisory board and it is the supervisory board which appoints and dismisses the members of the management board and thus has a considerable

share in its control. Other members of the supervisory board are elected by employees and sometimes by 'a party named in the constitution' which is often a bank. A simple sale of shares does not therefore mean an automatic change of control. That this model is important to German society in general is clear from the protests which the Vodafone takeover produced. The dislike of the German system in the USA has been equally clear for many years. It is said to be a creaking, stultified system which prevents market flexibility and provides unfair barriers to foreign takeovers. The voices praising the primacy of the US way of doing business have, however, become more muted in the aftermath of various scandals, including ENRON.

The contractual theories: market for corporate control

Contractual and in particular free market economic theories are underpinned by a theoretical control mechanism known as the market for corporate control (Easterbrook and Fischel, 1991). 'The contractarian model sees the hostile takeover as a particularly important device for reducing monitoring costs' (Deakin and Slinger, 1997). If a wealthy

company's assets are not being fully utilised by lazy or inefficient managers, then the company presents a tempting target for a predator company who may make an offer for the shares (which will be undervalued because of the poor performance of management), acquire control of the company, put in an efficient management and restore the efficiency and profitability of company. 'Executives fear takeover bids since they usually lose their jobs after a successful offer. This anxiety has, however, a beneficial by-product: managers, with their jobs potentially on the line, have an incentive to run their companies in a manner which maximises shareholder wealth' (Cheffins, 1996). Further benefits are said to be given by providing an efficient reallocation of productive assets away from declining industries (Jensen, 1988). This theory shows the free market creating its own efficiency police but unfortunately it works in a far from systematic way (Cheffins, 1996): 'the selection of takeover targets is not well correlated with levels of managerial performance' (Deakin and Slinger, 1997), and

'Evidence concerning post-bid performance also casts doubt on the disciplinary hypothesis. Several studies have identified long-term share-price declines following mergers, whether resulting from a hostile or an agreed bid and the most comprehensive study has found that this negative effect intensifies over time . . . earlier research which, rather than taking share price movement as the benchmark of company performance, was based on accounting data concerning companies' sales, assets and profits . . . found that companies which were acquired by tender offers had slightly below industry-average cash flow and sales performance both before and after takeover, so that "the hypothesis that takeovers improve performance is not supported".' (Deakin and Slinger, 1997)3

Further, its claim to reallocate production may cause the sudden decline of a geographically disadvantaged region. The Law Society of Scotland challenged the assumption that takeovers were beneficial in a DTI consultation document:

'The view that the shareholders are invariably in the best position to determine what is in the best interests of the company, and that therefore the market in companies' capital should be allowed to operate with the least hindrance possible, is not universally adhered to among Scottish commentators. The consequences of a free market in takeovers are seen to be potentially serious not only for the workforce directly involved but also for the wider community, and this may justify a more cumbersome regulatory structure if that is what is required to enable these

competing interests to be taken into account.' (Law Society of Scotland, 'Memorandum on the Thirteenth Directive on Takeovers', 1989)

Again, much vaunted efficiency considerations may siphon wealth away from poorer areas into wealthier ones.

History of the bid

11 November 1999
The original offer of €102.3 billion was rejected by Mannesman. The shareholders decide to defend the unprecedented hostile takeover.

19 November 1999
Vodafone launched a €124 billion bid for Mannesman which openly opposed the bid. It was rejected unanimously by Mannesman's supervisory board. It was reported that Mannesman might look to Vivendi as a 'white knight' to fend off the Vodafone bid. Chancellor Schroeder declared that 'hostile takeovers destroy a company's culture'. The German press actively campaigns against the bid. *Das Bild* newspaper 'was squealing in apprehension at the prospect of a "pearl of German industry" falling "prey to greed".' Gerhard Schroeder 'made it quite clear that he was opposed to the bid. Attempted hostile takeovers, he said, should be viewed with "the utmost possible caution". They destroyed corporate culture. They harmed not only the target firm, but also the predator company.' The bid opened up 'a fundamental clash of corporate cultures . . . it pits, in the struggle to come to terms with globalisation, the Anglo-Saxon model of relatively unfettered capitalism in which the shareholder is king against the

Rhineland model of "a social market economy", based on a consensus among stakeholders: workers, unions and politicians as well as shareholders' (*Guardian*, 23 November 1999).

An attempt to hold up the bid by allegations that American bank Goldman Sachs, which was acting as Vodafone's adviser, was subject to conflicts of interest failed in the UK High Court. Goldman Sachs had advised Mannesman on a new equity issue in 1998 and had been involved in the acquisition of Orange. Mannesman alleged that it was therefore privy to confidential information about Mannesman. Despite this the action was unequivocally dismissed.

23 November 1999
Mannesman, via Chief Executive Klaus Esse, 'is expected to declare its £19 billion acquisition of rival mobile phone operator Orange unconditional in terms of shareholder votes and to set out plans to spin off the group's automotive and engineering businesses' (Chris Barrie and David Gow, *Guardian*, 23 November 1999). This move was a poison pill attempt to ditch the businesses where most savings could be made and involve the EU's competition authorities in scrutinising the takeover. Mario Monti, Competition Commissioner, made it clear that the deal required close scrutiny. (See analysis of competition aspects, below.)

December 1999
The Vodafone bid is formally submitted. Klaus Essler, Mannesman's Chairman, declares that the offer is less than the value of Mannesman. The European Commission confirms that it has

no objection to Mannesman's purchase of Orange.

January 2000
Resistance to the offer continues.

February 2000
The bid succeeds. Last minute changes of mind by the supervisory board of Mannesman permitted the bid to go through. Total value of Vodafone estimated to be $365 billion, making it the first company in value on the London Stock Exchange and the fourth internationally. Orange had to be sold. (For other competition consequences see below.)

27 March 2000
Formal offer accepted by 98.62 per cent of Mannesman's shareholders.

17 February 2003
Six people charged in connection with receiving allegedly illegal payments during the takeover. All six were members of Mannesman's supervisory board. The charges are denied. Since this case is *sub judice*, comments on its possible ramifications regarding corporate governance and executive pay must await a final outcome.

Thirteenth Directive on takeovers

The Vodafone–Mannesman takeover was one of the main reasons for the failure of a previous draft of the Thirteenth Directive on takeovers. This was rejected in the European Parliament on 4 July 2001, after the German Government withdrew its support following pressure from German industry worried that the proposed directive banned defensive measures without the consent of

shareholders. The High Level Group of Company Law experts suggested a so-called 'breakthrough' rule which would have significantly diluted the blocking power of the supervisory board. However, the draft under discussion at present has omitted this rule. Although the Commission has declared the Directive to be a priority, difficult negotiations lie ahead, not least because the draft still contains Article 9(2) which provides that during the currency of the bid: 'the board of the offeree company must obtain the prior authorisation of the general meeting of shareholders given for this purpose before taking any action other than seeking alternative bids which may result in the frustration of the bid and in particular before issuing any shares which may result in a lasting impediment to the offeror in obtaining control over the offeree company.'

Adoption of a German Takeover Act

A direct consequence of the Vodafone takeover was the adoption of a German Act of Takeovers (Gesetz zur Regelung von Offenlichen Angeboten zum Erwerb von Wertpapieren und von Unternehmensubernahmen) which came into force on 1 January 2002. Defensive measures may be taken after the publication of the offer in four cases:

(1) on the basis of a prior (general) authorising resolution of the shareholder's meeting;
(2) on a specific resolution of the shareholder's meeting;
(3) with the approval of the supervisory board;
(4) to look for a white knight.

Without the relevant approvals the management board may only take 'such measures as would be carried out by a diligent and conscientious manager of a company not subject to a takeover bid'.

The Act clearly allows more defensive measures than the proposed Directive; note in particular no. 3. It is also unclear how far a diligent etc manager would also seek to adopt defensive measures even if there is no bid actually looming.

And finally

A number of the directors of the supervisory board of Mannesman were prosecuted after the takeover as it was suspected that they had accepted bribes to agree to the takeover. However, they were all acquitted.

Notes

1. See also J. Macey and G. Miller, 'Corporate Governance and Commercial Banking: A Comparative Examination of Germany, Japan and the United States' (1995) 48 *Stanford Law Review* 73.

2. See also A. Cosh, A. Hughes, K. Lee and A. Singh, 'Institutional Investment, Mergers and the Market for Corporate Control' (1989) 7 *International Journal of Industrial Organisation* 73.

3. See T. Langeteig, 'An Application of a Three-factor Performance Index to Measure Stockholder Gains from Merger' (1978) 6 *Journal of Financial Economics* 365; E. Magenheim and D. Mueller, 'Are Acquiring Firm Shareholders Better off After an Acquisition?', in J. Coffee, L. Lowenstein and S. Rose-Ackerman (eds.), *Knights, Raiders and Targets: The Impact*

of the Hostile Takeover, Oxford University Press, New York, 1988; A. Agrwal, J. Jaffe and G. Mandelker, 'The Post Performance of Acquiring Firms: A Re-examination of an Anomaly' (1992) 47 *Journal of Finance* 1605; D. Ravenscraft and F. Scherer, 'Life After Takeover' (1987) 36 *Journal of Industrial Economics* 147; F.

Scherer, 'Corporate Takeovers: the Efficiency Arguments' (1988) 2 *Journal of Economic Perspectives* 69.

References

Cheffins, *Company Law*, Oxford University Press, 1996, 119.
Deakin, S. and Slinger, G., 'Hostile Takeovers, Corporate Law, and the Theory of the Firm' (1997)

24 *Journal of Law and Society* 124 and 126.
Easterbrook, F. and Fischel, D., *The Economic Structure of Corporate Law*, Harvard University Press, Cambridge, Mass., 1991.
Jensen, M., 'Takeovers: their causes and consequences' (1988) 2 *Journal of Economic Perspectives* 21.

Summary

1. Takeovers by the purchase of shares are regulated by a code which has a new statutory basis under the Companies Act 2006: the City Code on Takeovers and Mergers, administered by the Panel on Takeovers and Mergers.

2. Submission to the rulings of the Panel is now backed by sanctions which the Panel has authority to impose under the Companies Act 2006.

3. The Panel seeks to protect shareholders, in particular by requiring equal treatment of the shareholders in a target company.

4. If 90 per cent of the shares in a company have been acquired, the remainder of the shares may be purchased compulsorily (s. 459 Companies Act 1985).

5. A minority shareholder may require the offeror to purchase his shares.

6. The minority whose shares may be purchased in this way may object to the scheme but will generally receive an unsympathetic hearing.

7. Sections 110–111 Insolvency Act 1986 provide a method of reconstruction of a company through liquidation.

Case note

Re Bugle Press Ltd **[1961] Ch 270**

Two majority shareholders in a company formed a new company and put forward an arrangement simply for the purpose of obtaining a 90 per cent majority and getting rid of a dissentient minority by way of compulsory purchase under what is now s. 459 Companies Act 1985. The court would not permit this.

Exercises

1. Whose interests are likely to be damaged by reconstructions of companies? Are they all adequately protected?

2. What are the advantages and disadvantages of the methods of reconstructing a company?

3. Do shareholders have a duty to others when exercising a vote in a shareholders' meeting?

Chapter 17

Insolvency

Key words

▶ **Dissolution** – the 'death' of a company, the moment at which it ceases to exist.
▶ **Liquidation** – the process of collecting in the assets of a company and paying all the debts.

The Insolvency Act 1986 revised and updated the law in this area, introducing two new procedures with a view to encouraging corporate rescues. Amendments to these procedures are likely following the publication of a new Insolvency Bill whose clauses are at present under discussion.

17.1 Voluntary arrangements

This is a scheme for making arrangements with creditors which will be legally binding on all creditors, even if not all of them agree. This has the advantage that where a company has sensible plans which are likely to avoid a liquidation, those plans cannot be upset by a single creditor insisting on a liquidation of the company. The disadvantage of the scheme under the Insolvency Act 1986 is that the scheme may not be approved for some weeks and there is nothing, until creditor approval is gained, to prevent such a liquidation from occurring. For this reason s. 1A and Schedule 1A Insolvency Act 1986 which came into force on 1 January 2003, enable an 'eligible company' (basically, a small company) to obtain a moratorium on creditor action while a proposal for a voluntary arrangement is considered.

17.2 Proposal

The first step towards approval of an arrangement is a proposal to the company and the creditors. The proposal is made by the directors unless the company is in administration or liquidation, when it is made by the administrator or liquidator (s. 1 Insolvency Act 1986). A receiver or administrative receiver is not empowered to propose a voluntary arrangement. The arrangement must be supervised by a qualified insolvency practitioner. The most likely proposals will be the acceptance by each creditor of a percentage of their claim, or a moratorium on enforcement of claims for a certain period.

17.3 The involvement of the court

If the supervisor of the scheme is someone other than the liquidator or administrator, he must report to the court within 28 days as to whether the proposal should be considered and, if so, the dates and times when he would call the relevant meetings (s. 2(2) Insolvency Act 1986). He is then obliged to summon those meetings.

17.4 Contents of the proposal

The rules lay down the matters which must be set out in the proposal. As might be expected, the company's assets and liabilities must be set out in detail, as must the proposed arrangement itself.

17.5 Meetings

Meetings of the company members and the creditors must be summoned. For the members' meeting the requisite majority for any resolution is more than one-half of the members present in person or by proxy and voting (Insolvency Rules, r.1.20(1)).

As far as the creditors' meeting is concerned, there are two requisite majorities – more than 75 per cent for the resolution to pass any proposal or any modification of the proposal, and more than 50 per cent for other resolutions. The percentages are of votes of creditors present in person or by proxy and voting. There are detailed rules by which certain votes must be ignored in order to prevent the majorities being made up of persons connected with the company. If the arrangement is approved it binds everyone who was entitled to have notice of and vote at the meeting.

17.6 Challenges

An arrangement can be challenged on the grounds of unfair prejudice or material irregularity at either of the meetings (s. 6(1) Insolvency Act 1986).

17.7 Administrative receivership

An administrative receiver is appointed by a secured creditor. The court does not normally need to be involved in the procedure. An administrative receiver will take control of the whole of the company's property in order to realise it so that the creditor who was responsible for his appointment will be paid. Theoretically this procedure does not involve the liquidation of the company, but in practice the receiver will not be appointed unless there are serious concerns as to the solvency of the company and the appointment of the receiver will often be the last straw for the company.

From the time of his appointment the receiver has authority to deal with the property which is the subject matter of the charge. The authority of the directors to deal with that property disappears. However, the directors remain in office for other purposes, for example to fulfil the company's duty to provide the Registrar with information. The directors also retain their power to bring legal proceedings in the company's name. *Newhart Developments Ltd* v. *Co-operative Commercial Bank Ltd* [1978] QB 814 provided that their exercise of that power does not interfere with the receiver in realising the charged assets.

The powers of the receiver will be found in the contract which creates the charge. However, all receivers will also have the powers conferred by s. 42(1) and Schedule 1 Insolvency Act 1986 (see Case notes, pp. 325–6).

17.8 Liquidations

A company will cease to exist by being liquidated and struck off the register of companies. A company may be wound up by the court or voluntarily by the members.

A company may be wound up by the court if:

(i) the company has by special resolution resolved that the company be wound up by the court;

(ii) the company was originally registered as a public company but has not been issued with a certificate that it satisfies the minimum capital requirement, and more than a year has passed since its registration;

(iii) it is an old public company within the meaning of the Consequential Provisions Act 1985;

(iv) the company does not commence its business within a year from its incorporation, or suspends its business for a whole year;

(v) the number of members is reduced below two (unless the company converts itself into a single member company in accordance with the Companies (Single Member Private Limited Companies) Regulations 1992;

(vi) the company is unable to pay its debts;

(vii) the court is of opinion that it is just and equitable to wind up the company (see Chapter 13).

The court will wind up a company after the successful presentation of a winding-up petition which may be presented by the company, the directors, any creditor or any person liable to contribute to the assets of the company in the event of a winding-up (contributory), the supervisor of a voluntary arrangement, or in some circumstances by a receiver. All shareholders are contributories even if they have no further money to pay on their shares and are not actually liable to contribute to the assets of the company.

A member's petition will only succeed if he can show that he has a tangible interest in the winding-up. He must show that he would gain an advantage or avoid or minimise a disadvantage.

A creditor, contributory, the Official Receiver or the Department of Trade and Industry may seek a compulsory winding-up order even if the company is in voluntary liquidation.

17.9 Voluntary winding-up

A company may be wound up voluntarily when the members resolve by special resolution to wind it up or if it resolves by extraordinary resolution that it cannot, by reason of its liabilities, continue its business and that it is advisable to wind it up (s. 84 Insolvency Act 1986). If the directors, after a full investigation, believe that the company will be able to pay its debts in full (with interest) within twelve months from the commencement of the winding-up, the liquidation is a 'members' voluntary winding-up' (s. 89 Insolvency Act 1986). If no declaration of solvency is made the liquidation becomes a creditors' voluntary winding-up. In this case a creditors' meeting must be summoned and the liquidator must attend the creditors' meeting and give a report on any exercise of his powers. Section 107 provides that in a voluntary winding-up, the property of the company is to be applied first in paying the preferential debts, then in satisfaction of its liabilities, and lastly it is to be distributed among the members according to their rights and interests as determined by the articles.

The directors of the company can petition for its winding-up as can a receiver. The Secretary of State may also petition for a winding-up if it appears that it may be in the public interest to do so (s. 124A Insolvency Act 1986).

17.10 The liquidator

With the commencement of the winding-up of the company, the directors cease to control its affairs and the liquidator manages the company with a view to collecting all the assets of the company. The winding-up will normally commence at the time of the presentation of the petition for winding-up. However where a resolution for voluntary winding-up has been passed, the date of the resolution will (in the absence of fraud or mistake) be the relevant date (s. 129 Insolvency Act 1986). The liquidator must be an insolvency practitioner (s. 390(1) Insolvency Act 1986). His eventual aim will be to pay the costs of the winding-up, pay the debts of the company and distribute any surplus among the members (ss. 107 and 143

Insolvency Act 1986). He has a considerable array of powers conferred for this purpose (see Rajak, *Company Liquidations*, para. 903 *et seq.*).

In a winding-up by the court, the liquidator is subject to the control of the court. All liquidators are subject to substantial duties both equitable and statutory (see Rajak, *Company Liquidations*, para. 922 *et seq.*).

If, during a members' voluntary winding-up the liquidator forms the opinion that the company will be unable to pay its debts within the period specified in the directors' declaration of solvency, he is obliged to summon a creditors' meeting and from the date of that meeting the liquidation becomes a creditors' voluntary winding-up (ss. 95 and 96 Insolvency Act 1986).

17.11 Order of payment of debts

The assets (which will be diminished by the enforcement of any fixed charge) are applied in the following order:

(1) The proper expenses of the winding-up.
(2) The preferential debts. These appear in s. 386 and Schedule 6 Insolvency Act 1986 (see Case notes, pp. 326–9). If the company has not enough money to meet these debts in full, preferential creditors take priority over the holders of floating charges (s. 175 Insolvency Act 1986).
(3) Floating charge holders.
(4) Ordinary creditors.
(5) Members.

17.12 Avoiding antecedent transactions

The liquidator may be able to avoid certain transactions entered into by a company in order to increase the fund available to the general body of creditors.

Transactions at an undervalue

An administrator or liquidator may apply to the court where the company has entered into a transaction at an undervalue (s. 238 Insolvency Act 1986). The court has an unfettered discretion to make such order as it thinks fit. The Act lays down the time limits within which the transaction must have occurred for it to be vulnerable to this application. So far as a company going directly into liquidation is concerned these periods are: the period counted back from the date of the resolution to wind up or the date of the presentation of the winding-up petition. The liquidator must establish that at the time of the transaction the company was unable to pay its debts.

Under s. 241 the court has a wide discretion to make orders to transfer property in order to correct the situation but may not affect the rights of a *bona fide* purchaser of property (s. 241 Insolvency Act 1986). This latter restriction has been clarified and extended by the Insolvency (No. 2) Act 1994 which came into force on 26 July 1994 in relation to interests acquired and benefits received by third party purchasers after that date. It applies both to transactions at an undervalue and to preferences and protects a subsequent purchaser if he has acted in good faith for value. This extends protection to those who knew that there has been a transaction at an undervalue or a preference at some time but nevertheless acted in good faith at the time of the transaction. However, where the purchaser has knowledge both of the preference or undervalue transaction and 'relevant proceedings' there is a rebuttable presumption that the purchaser is not in good faith. Lack of good faith is also presumed where the subsequent purchaser is connected with or is an associate of the company. 'Relevant proceedings' mean administration or liquidation within certain time-scales set out in the Act.

person who takes
responsibility for the fulfilment
of anothers obligation

Preferences

There are similar provisions for the upsetting of a preference, which is the doing of anything by the company which has the effect of putting either one of its creditors, or someone who is a surety or guarantor of one of its debts, in a position which, in the event of the company going into insolvent liquidation, will be better than the position he would have been in if that thing had not been done (s. 239(4)(b) Insolvency Act 1986). The relevant periods during which preferences can be upset are: (i) two years if the other party to the transaction was connected with the company; or (ii) six months if the other party was not connected.

The court has the same discretions here as it has with regard to transactions at an undervalue. In *Re M. C. Bacon Ltd* [1990] BCLC 324 the court (Chancery Division) gave some guidance on the interpretation of the Insolvency Act sections concerning transactions at an undervalue and preferences. In that case a company had carried on business as a bacon importer and wholesaler. It had been profitable until it had lost its principal customer. The company continued trading on a smaller scale for some time but eventually had to go into liquidation. During the time when it was trading on a small scale a debenture was granted to the bank. At this time the company was either insolvent or nearly so. The validity of the debenture was challenged. Miller J held that the debenture was not invalid as a preference under s. 239 Insolvency Act 1986 because the directors in granting it had not been motivated by a desire to prefer the bank but only by a desire to avoid the calling in of the overdraft and their wish to continue trading. Nor was the debenture invalid as a transaction at an undervalue under s. 238 because the giving of the security had neither depleted the company's assets nor diminished their value.

In coming to the conclusion about the preference under s. 239, Miller J drew a clear distinction between the 'desire' of the directors and their 'intention'. The section requires desire and this was interpreted as synonomous with motive. If intention had been the test the debenture would surely have been invalid as the court would have needed only to be satisfied that the directors knew that the bank would be put in a better position than before by the debenture. In view of the introduction of objective tests elsewhere (for example, s. 214 Insolvency Act 1986, see below), this extremely subjective approach is perhaps surprising.

Transactions defrauding creditors

A transaction at an undervalue may also be challenged under s. 423 Insolvency Act 1986. Under this provision there are no time limits and the company need not be in liquidation or even insolvent. It is necessary to show that the transaction was entered into for the purpose of putting assets beyond the reach of a creditor or potential creditor or of prejudicing the interests of such a person. In *Arbuthnot Leasing International Ltd* v. *Havelet Leasing Ltd (No. 2)* [1990] BCC 636 a company's business and assets had been transferred on legal advice to an off-the-shelf company shortly before it went into receivership. The court ordered the reversal of the transaction. In *Chohan* v. *Saggar and Another* [1994] 1 BCLC 706 the court held that the proper purpose of an order under s. 423 was both to restore the position to what it would have been if the transaction had not been entered into and to protect the interests of the victims of the transaction.

Extortionate credit transactions

Section 244 Insolvency Act 1986 permits companies to set aside credit transactions which are deemed to be extortionate. This can only occur when the company is in liquidation or administration. The transaction must have been entered into at any time during the three-year period ending with the day on which an administrator was appointed or the day on which the company goes into liquidation (either the date on which the winding-up resolution is passed or the date on which a winding-up order is granted).

A credit transaction is extortionate if it either:

(1) requires grossly exorbitant payments to be made whether unconditionally or only in certain events in exchange for credit; or
(2) it grossly contravenes ordinary principles of fair dealing.

The court must, however, take account of the risk that was taken by the creditor in providing credit. This may be important as companies in this situation may have been bad risks even some considerable time previously.

The court may set such an agreement aside in whole or in part, or vary the terms.

Avoidance of floating charges

A floating charge can be successfully challenged by a liquidator or administrator under s. 245 Insolvency Act 1986 if:

(1) It was a floating charge within s. 251 Insolvency Act 1986. This defines a floating charge as 'a charge which, as created, was a floating charge'. (This definition prevents crystallisation by notice converting the charge into a fixed charge and giving debenture-holders priority over preferential creditors.)
(2) It was created within two years of the commencement of the winding-up or administration where it was created in favour of a connected person; one year where it was in favour of a person unconnected with the company and if it was created in favour of an unconnected person only if it was created when the company was unable to pay its debts.
(3) To the extent that the company has received nothing in exchange. This means that a charge which would otherwise be invalid under s. 245 Insolvency Act 1986 will be valid to the extent of any value in money paid, or goods and services supplied to the company or in discharge or reduction of the company's debts provided this was done by the chargee at the time of or after the creation of the charge. Thus a new loan to pay off and replace an old loan will not be exempt under this section unless made in good faith to enable the company to carry on business (see *Re Destone Fabrics* [1941] Ch 319; and *Re Matthew Ellis* [1933] Ch 458).

Connected persons

For the purposes of the provisions which may result in the avoidance of prior transactions, s. 249 Insolvency Act 1986 provides a definition of persons 'connected with' a company. It reads:

'a person is connected with a company if –
(a) he is a director or shadow director of the company or an associate of such a director or shadow director, or
(b) he is an associate of the company.'

'Associate' has the meaning given by s. 435 Insolvency Act 1986. This is reproduced in the Case notes to this chapter (pp. 329–30) and it can clearly be seen that the net is spread very widely indeed.

17.13   Fraudulent trading

Fraudulent trading is actionable both as a civil offence (s. 213 Insolvency Act 1986) and as a criminal offence (s. 993 Companies Act 2006). In both cases it is necessary to establish trading with 'intent to defraud'. This requires the court to find that the directors were acting dishonestly, not just that they were acting unreasonably (*Re L. Todd (Swanscombe) Ltd* [1990] BCC 125). The difficulty of establishing this has made this remedy little used. It is wider than wrongful trading, however, in that it is available against 'any persons who were knowingly parties to the carrying on of the business' of the company. For a comprehensive discussion of the law concerning fraudulent trading see *R* v. *Smith* [1996] 2 BCLC 109.

Only a liquidator may apply under the civil remedy, but criminal proceedings can be instituted for fraudulent trading outside the insolvency context, regardless of whether a company is wound up or not. The court has power under the civil remedy to make an order that the respondent 'make such contribution (if any) to the company's assets as the court thinks proper'.

17.14   Summary remedy against delinquent directors – Section 212 Insolvency Act 1986

Section 212 Insolvency Act 1986 provides a means by which any person concerned in the management of a company may be made liable if it can be shown that he has:

> 'misapplied or retained, or become accountable for, any money or other property of the company, or been guilty of any misfeasance or breach of any fiduciary or other duty in relation to the company.'

This section was given a wide interpretation by Hoffman LJ in *Re D'Jan of London Ltd* [1993] BCC 646 where he held a director liable for a breach of the duty of skill and care, using as a standard that imposed in respect of wrongful trading. For the possible effect of this judgment on directors' duties see Chapter 11.

17.15   Wrongful trading

This is only a civil remedy. In essence it consists of continuing to trade when the company is known to be insolvent. It may, if successful, lead to the same order for a contribution as an order under the fraudulent trading provisions (see 17.13). As with fraudulent trading, an application may only be made by the liquidator.

In the case of wrongful trading, an application can only be made when the company has gone into an insolvent liquidation (s. 214(2) Insolvency Act

1986), that is, going into liquidation at a time when its assets are insufficient for the payment of its debts, other liabilities and the expenses of its winding-up. An application can only be made against a director or shadow director. In *R v. Farmizer (Products) Ltd* [1995] 2 BCLC 462 it was held that an action under s. 214 was subject to s. 991 Limitation Act 1980 which imposes a six-year limitation period for bringing a claim. Time runs from the time when the company goes into insolvent liquidation.

Standard

The contrast with fraudulent trading is clear when it is realised that the director is judged by what he ought to have known as well as by what he did know and there is no question of having to establish dishonesty. Thus, wrongful trading applies at a time when a director at some time prior to the commencement of the winding-up, knew or ought to have concluded that there was no reasonable prospect that the company would avoid going into insolvent liquidation. There is a defence: the relevant person escapes where by the standard of the 'reasonably diligent person' he satisfies a court that he took every step with a view to minimising the potential loss to the company's creditors after he had the first knowledge of the insolvent state of the company.

The standard of knowledge and skill required is a cumulative blend of the subjective and objective, and includes:

(a) the general knowledge, skill and experience that may reasonably be expected of a person carrying out the same functions as are carried out by that director in relation to the company; and

(b) the general knowledge, skill and experience that director has (s. 214(5) Insolvency Act 1986).

The thinking of the courts was well explained by Knox J in *Produce Marketing Consortium Ltd* [1989] 1 WLR 745. He said:

'It is evident that Parliament intended to widen the scope of legislation under which directors who trade on when the company is insolvent may in appropriate circumstances be required to make a contribution to [a company's creditors] . . . the test to be applied by the Court has become one under which the director in question is to be judged by the standards of what can reasonably be expected of a person fulfilling his functions and showing reasonable diligence in doing so . . . The general knowledge, skill and experience postulated will be much less extensive in a small company in a modest way of business with simple accounting procedures and equipment than it will be in a large company with sophisticated procedures. Nevertheless certain minimum standards are assumed to be attained . . . [Wrongful trading is] an enhanced version of the right which any company would have to sue its directors for breach of duty – enhanced in the sense that the standard of knowledge, skill and experience required is made objective.'

Although much academic discussion has focused on wrongful trading, it is not used frequently by practitioners who usually consider that the money which will be clawed back will not be worth the time and effort involved in proceedings.

17.16 The destination of the money

Assets recovered by the liquidator in connection with transactions at an undervalue, voidable preferences, extortionate credit transactions, wrongful and fraudulent trading and misfeasance proceedings under s. 212 Insolvency Act 1986 are paid into the general pool of the company's assets. They are not available for the payment of particular creditors. However, where a floating charge is invalidated the effect will often be to give priority to another charge which has been validly created over the same assets (*Capital Finance Co. Ltd v. Stokes* [1968] 1 All ER 573).

17.17 Dissolution

A company ceases to exist when it is dissolved. This can only happen when its affairs are completely wound up.

In a winding-up by the court, the liquidator sends notice of the final meeting of creditors and vacation of office by him to the Registrar of Companies, the notice is registered and the company is normally dissolved at the end of the period of three months from the date of registration.

On completion of a voluntary winding-up the liquidator presents his final accounts to meetings of the company's creditors and/or members. Within a week after that has been done, the liquidator must send copies of the accounts and a return of the holdings of the meetings to the Registrar of Companies. The Registrar registers them and the company is normally deemed to be dissolved three months later (ss. 94 and 205 Insolvency Act).

Sections 201 and 205 contain provisions which permit delaying dissolution on the application of an interested party. By s. 651 the court has a discretion to declare a dissolution void at any time within twelve years. Section 652 provides that dissolution does not affect the liability of officers and members of the company to be sued.

Summary

1. Voluntary arrangements are schemes for coming to an arrangement with creditors. By a majority agreeing to the scheme, it becomes binding on all the creditors. The purpose is to prevent a minority of creditors from precipitating a liquidation where there is a hope that the company can be saved.

2. A company may be wound up by a court or by a voluntary creditors' or members' winding-up. The last course is only available where the company is solvent.

3. So far as the distribution of property is concerned, holders of fixed charges have a right to enforce their security. After that, other property is distributed as follows:

    (i) for the proper expenses of the winding-up;
    (ii) to preferential creditors, who take priority over floating chargeholders where there is not enough money to satisfy them in full;
    (iii) to creditors with floating charges by way of security;
    (iv) to ordinary creditors; and
    (v) to members.

4. There are a number of provisions for avoiding transactions which took place before the liquidation. In certain circumstances the following can be avoided:

    (a) transactions at an undervalue;
    (b) preferences;
    (c) extortionate credit transactions; and
    (d) floating charges;

5. Anyone may be liable to criminal or civil penalties if they have been involved in fraudulent trading. Directors or shadow directors may be liable for wrongful trading if they continued to trade when they knew or ought to have concluded that the company was insolvent.

Case notes

Insolvency Act 1986

14. General powers

(1) The administrator of a company –

    (a) may do all such things as may be necessary for the management of the affairs, business and property of the company, and

    (b) without prejudice to the generality of paragraph (a), has the powers specified in Schedule 1 to this Act;

and in the application of that Schedule to the administrator of a company the words 'he' and 'him' refer to the administrator.

(2) The administrator also has the power –

    (a) to remove any director of the company and to appoint any person to be a director of it, whether to fill a vacancy or otherwise, and

(b) to call any meeting of the members or creditors of the company.

(3) The administrator may apply to the court for directions in relation to any particular matter arising in connection with the carrying out of his functions.

(4) Any power conferred on the company or its officers, whether by this Act or the Companies Act or by the memorandum or articles of association, which could be exercised in such a way as to interfere with the exercise by the administrator of his powers is not exercisable except with the consent of the administrator, which may be given either generally or in relation to particular cases.

(5) In exercising his powers the administrator is deemed to act as the company's agent.

(6) A person dealing with the administrator in good faith and for value is not concerned to inquire whether the administrator is acting within his powers.

SCHEDULES

SCHEDULE 1

Section 14.42

POWERS OF ADMINISTRATOR OR ADMINISTRATIVE RECEIVER

1. Power to take possession of, collect and get in the property of the company and, for that purpose, to take such proceedings as may seem to him expedient.

2. Power to sell or otherwise dispose of the property of the company by public auction or private contract or, in Scotland, to sell, feu, hire out or otherwise dispose of the property of the company by public roup or private bargain.

3. Power to raise or borrow money and grant security therefor over the property of the company.

4. Power to appoint a solicitor or accountant or other professionally qualified person to assist him in the performance of his functions.

5. Power to bring or defend any action or other legal proceedings in the name and on behalf of the company.

6. Power to refer to arbitration any question affecting the company.

7. Power to effect and maintain insurances in respect of the business and property of the company.

8. Power to use the company's seal.

9. Power to do all acts and to execute in the name and on behalf of the company any deed, receipt or other document.

10. Power to draw, accept, make and endorse any bill of exchange or promissory note in the name and on behalf of the company.

11. Power to appoint any agent to do any business which he is unable to do himself or which can more conveniently be done by an agent and power to employ and dismiss employees.

12. Power to do all such things (including the carrying out of works) as may be necessary for the realisation of the property of the company.

13. Power to make any payment which is necessary or incidental to the performance of his functions.

14. Power to carry on the business of the company.

15. Power to establish subsidiaries of the company.
16. Power to transfer to subsidiaries of the company the whole or any part of the business and property of the company.
17. Power to grant or accept a surrender of a lease or tenancy of any of the property of the company, and to take a lease or tenancy of any property required or convenient for the business of the company.
18. Power to make any arrangement or compromise on behalf of the company.
19. Power to call up any uncalled capital of the company.
20. Power to rank and claim in the bankruptcy, insolvency, sequestration or liquidation of any person indebted to the company and to receive dividends, and to accede to trust deeds for the creditors of any such person.
21. Power to present or defend a petition for the winding-up of the company.
22. Power to change the situation of the company's registered office.
23. Power to do all other things incidental to the exercise of the foregoing powers.

SCHEDULE 6

THE CATEGORIES OF PREFERENTIAL DEBTS

Category 1: Debts due to Inland Revenue

1. Sums due at the relevant date from the debtor on account of deductions of income tax from emoluments paid during the period of 12 months next before that date.

   The deductions here referred to are those which the debtor was liable to make under section [203 of the Income and Corporation Taxes Act 1988] (pay as you earn), less the amount of the repayments of income tax which the debtor was liable to make during that period.

2. Sums due at the relevant date from the debtor in respect of such deductions as are required to be made by the debtor for that period under section [559 of the Income and Corporation Taxes Act 1988] (sub-contractors in the construction industry).

Category 2: Debts due to Customs and Excise

3. Any value added tax which is referable to the period of 6 months next before the relevant date (which period is referred to below as 'the 6-month period').

   For the purposes of this paragraph –
   (a) where the whole of the prescribed accounting period to which any value added tax is attributable falls within the 6-month period, the whole amount of that tax is referable to that period; and
   (b) in any other case the amount of any value added tax which is referable to the 6-month period is the proportion of the tax which is equal to such proportion (if any) of the accounting reference period in question as falls within the 6-month period;

   and in sub-paragraph (a) 'prescribed' means prescribed by regulations under the Value Added Tax Act 1983.

4. The amount of any car tax which is due at the relevant date from the debtor and which became due within a period of 12 months next before that date.

5. Any amount which is due –

(a) by way of general betting duty or bingo duty, or

(b) under s. 12(1) of the Betting and Gaming Duties Act 1981 (general betting duty and pool betting duty recoverable from agent collecting stakes), or

(c) under s. 14 of, or Schedule 2 to, that Act (gaming licence duty),

from the debtor at the relevant date and which became due within the period of 12 months next before that date.

Category 3: Social security contributions

6. All sums which on the relevant date are due from the debtor on account of Class 1 or Class 2 contributions under the Social Security Act 1975 or the Social Security (Northern Ireland) Act 1975 and which became due from the debtor in the 12 months next before that date.

7. All sums which on the relevant date have been assessed on and are due from the debtor on account of Class 4 contributions under either of those Acts of 1975, being sums which –

(a) are due to the Commissioners of Inland Revenue (rather than to the Secretary of State or a Northern Ireland department), and

(b) are assessed on the debtor up to the 5th April next before the relevant date,

but not exceeding, in the whole, any one year's assessment.

Category 4: Contributions to occupational pension schemes, etc.

8. Any sum which is owed by the debtor and is a sum to which Schedule 3 to the Social Security Pensions Act 1975 applies (contributions to occupational pension schemes and state pension scheme premiums).

Category 5: Remuneration, etc. of employees

9. So much of any amount which –

(a) is owed by the debtor to a person who is or has been an employee of the debtor, and

(b) is payable by way of remuneration in respect of the whole or any part of the period of 4 months next before the relevant date,

as does not exceed so much as may be prescribed by order made by the Secretary of State.

10. Any amount owed by the way of accrued holiday remuneration, in respect of any period of employment before the relevant date, to a person whose employment by the debtor has been terminated, whether before, on or after that date.

11. So much of any sum owed in respect of money advanced for the purposes as has been applied for the payment of a debt which, if it had not been paid, would have been a debt falling within paragraph 9 or 10.

12. So much of any amount which –

(a) is ordered (whether before or after the relevant date) to be paid by the debtor under the Reserve Forces (Safeguard of Employment) Act 1985, and

(b) is so ordered in respect of a default made by the debtor before that date in the discharge of his obligations under that Act,

as does not exceed such amount as may be prescribed by order made by the Secretary of State.

Interpretation for Category 5

13. – (1) For the purposes of paragraphs 9 to 12, a sum is payable by the debtor to a person by way of remuneration in respect of any period if –

    (a) it is paid as wages or salary (whether payable for time or for piece work or earned wholly or partly by way of commission) in respect of services rendered to the debtor in that period, or

    (b) it is an amount falling within the following sub-paragraph and is payable by the debtor in respect of that period.

(2) An amount falls within this sub-paragraph if it is –

    (a) a guarantee payment under s. 12(1) of the Employment Protection (Consolidation) Act 1978 (employee without work to do for a day or part of a day);

    (b) remuneration on suspension on medical grounds under s. 19 of that Act;

    (c) any payment for time off under s. 27(3) (trade union duties), 31(3) (looking for work, etc.) or 31A(4) (ante-natal care) of that Act; or

    (d) remuneration under a protective award made by an industrial tribunal under s. 101 of the Employment Protection Act 1975 (redundancy dismissal with compensation).

14. – (1) This paragraph relates to a case in which a person's employment has been terminated by or in consequence of his employer going into liquidation or being adjudged bankrupt or (his employer being a company not in liquidation) by or in consequence of –

    (a) a receiver being appointed as mentioned in s. 40 of this Act (debenture-holders secured by floating charge), or

    (b) the appointment of a receiver under s. 53(6) or 54(5) of this Act (Scottish company with property subject to floating charge), or

    (c) the taking of possession by debenture-holders (so secured), as mentioned in s. 196 of the Companies Act.

(2) For the purposes of paragraphs 9 to 12, holiday remuneration is deemed to have accrued to that person in respect of any period of employment if, by virtue of his contract of employment or of any enactment that remuneration would have accrued in respect of that period if his employment had continued until he became entitled to be allowed the holiday.

(3) The reference in sub-paragraph (2) to any enactment includes an order or direction made under an enactment.

15. Without prejudice to paragraphs 13 and 14 –

    (a) any remuneration payable by the debtor to a person in respect of a period of holiday or of absence from work through sickness or other good cause is deemed to be wages or (as the case may be) salary in respect of services rendered to the debtor in that period, and

    (b) references here and in those paragraphs to remuneration

in respect of a period of holiday include any sums which, if they had been paid, would have been treated for the purposes of the enactments relating to social security as earnings in respect of that period.

[*Category 6: Levies on coal and steel production*

15A. Any sums due at the relevant date from the debtor in respect of:

(a) the levies on the production of coal and steel referred to in Articles 49 and 50 of the ECSC Treaty, or

(b) any surcharge for delay provided for in Article 50(3) of that Treaty and Article 6 of Decision 3/52 of the High Authority of the Coal and Steel Community.]

Orders

16. An order under paragraph 9 or 12 –

(a) may contain such transitional provisions as may appear to the Secretary of State necessary or expedient;

(b) shall be made by statutory instrument subject to annulment in pursuance of a resolution of either House of Parliament.

Part XVIII

INTERPRETATION

435. Meaning of 'associate'

(1) For the purposes of this Act any question whether a person is an associate of another person is to be determined in accordance with the following provisions of this section (any provision that a person is an associate of another person being taken to mean that they are associates of each other).

(2) A person is an associate of an individual if that person is the individual's husband or wife, or is a relative, or the husband or wife of a relative, of the individual or of the individual's husband or wife.

(3) A person is an associate of any person with whom he is in partnership, and of the husband or wife or a relative of any individual with whom he is in partnership; and a Scottish firm is an associate of any person who is a member of the firm.

(4) A person is an associate of any person whom he employs or by whom he is employed.

(5) A person in his capacity as trustee of a trust other than –

(a) a trust arising under any of the second Group of Parts or the Bankruptcy (Scotland) Act 1985, or

(b) a pension scheme or an employees' share scheme (within the meaning of the Companies Act),

is an associate of another person if the beneficiaries of the trust include, or the terms of the trust confer a power that may be exercised for the benefit of, that other person or an associate of that other person.

(6) A company is an associate of another company –

(a) if the same person has control of both, or a person has control of one and persons who are his associates, or he and persons who are his associates, have control of the other, or

(b) if a group of two or more persons has control of each

company, and the groups either consist of the same persons or could be regarded as consisting of the same persons by treating (in one or more cases) a member of either group as replaced by a person of whom he is an associate.

(7) A company is an associate of another person if that person has control of it or if that person and persons who are his associates together have control of it.

(8) For the purposes of this section a person is a relative of an individual if he is that individual's brother, sister, uncle, aunt, nephew, niece, lineal ancestor or lineal descendant, treating –

(a) any relationship of the half blood as a relationship of the whole blood and the stepchild or adopted child of any person as his child, and

(b) an illegitimate child as the legitimate child of his mother and reputed father;

and references in this section to a husband or wife include a former husband or wife and a reputed husband or wife.

(9) For the purposes of this section any director or other officer of a company is to be treated as employed by that company.

(10) For the purposes of this section a person is to be taken as having control of a company if –

(a) the directors of the company or of another company which has control of it (or any of them) are accustomed to act in accordance with his directions or instruction, or

(b) he is entitled to exercise, or control the exercise of, one third or more of the voting power at any general meeting of the company or of another company which has control of it;

and where two or more persons together satisfy either of the above conditions, they are to be taken as having control of the company.

(11) In this section 'company' includes any body corporate (whether incorporated in Great Britain or elsewhere); and references to directors and other officers of a company and to voting power at any general meeting of a company have effect with any necessary modifications.

Exercises

1. Describe the roles of liquidators and receivers.

2. Consider the possible liabilities of directors on a winding-up of a company (see Chapters 11, 12 and 13 as well as this chapter).

3. In what circumstances and on what time-scale can transactions prior to a liquidation be avoided?

Chapter 18

The effect of the EU on English company law

Key words

> **Direct effect** – the legal position when a European Directive is effective in the law of Member States without implementation.
>
> **European Company Statute** – a new form of cross-border company which will be available in all 25 Member States of the European Union.
>
> **Implementation** – the translation of European Directives into the domestic law of Member States.

The Member States of the European Community (EU) (now numbering 25) have agreed to move towards a 'single European Market'. This means that as many as possible of the barriers to trading freely across national frontiers will be removed. One difficulty of trading internationally occurs when companies involved in trading are themselves subject to different rules. They are more likely to be suspicious of each other and require complicated legal safeguards in their contracts. These will have to be drawn up with reference to several systems of law. Because of this the EU has tried to harmonise a number of rules relating to companies. This has generally been done by 'Directives'. These are laws which have been adopted by the Council of the European Community. After this adoption they become part of UK law by *implementation*. This is achieved by the relevant government department (in this case almost always the Department of Trade and Industry) drafting a statute which translates the provisions of the Directives into terms which will be understood in the UK. The statute is then dealt with by the UK Parliament in the ordinary way except that, because there is an obligation to implement the Directive, the scope for making amendments to the legislation is necessarily limited.

18.1 The making of a Directive

The procedure followed for making a Directive is as follows. The Commission (the EU's civil servants) discuss the proposal with officials from Member States and other interested parties (such as, in the UK, the Confederation of British Industry, the Institute of Directors, the Chartered Accountants' professional bodies, the Stock Exchange and the Law Society). During this period the Commission will issue a number of drafts and receive comments on those drafts from the interested parties. The Commission will then adopt the final draft as a formal proposal.

The formal proposal is then submitted to the Council, the European Parliament and the Economic and Social Committee (ECOSOC). A Council working group, made up of officials from Member States, then discusses the proposal in detail before referring it to the Committee of Permanent Representatives (COREPER) which in turn refers it to the Council. Depending on the Article of the original Treaty on which the proposal is based, different procedures may apply. Usually the legislation is adopted via a complex co-decision procedure which involves the Parliament to a much greater extent than was the case in previous years.

Eventually the proposal returns to the Council for final adoption. It is after the final adoption of the measure that the Member States must go through the implementation process described above. The Maastricht Treaty resulted in increased powers for the Parliament which has resulted in active co-operation between it and the other institutions rather than Parliament merely giving reports on proposed legislation.

Company law may be also affected by an EU Regulation. This is a method of making law which is different from passing Directives, because a Regulation will apply directly throughout the Community. It will not require a statute to implement it but may need legislation to translate its effect into ideas which are familiar in the UK, and to fill in gaps.

18.2 The extent of the influence of EU rules

The changes brought about by the EU mostly become law in the UK by passing a statute in the usual way. Many people do not realise that a large number of the recent changes to our law are in fact 'Directive-driven', that is, they were only included in company law reform measures because of an obligation to implement a Directive. The extent of the EU's influence has therefore been partially hidden. Because these measures are now part of general company law, it is not necessary to deal with them in detail here. More discussion of them will be found in the chapters dealing with the particular topics involved. However, the importance of EU measures can be seen from the summary of those Directive-driven measures already introduced. The continuing and increasing influence of the EU is shown by the number of measures which are progressing through the steps towards becoming Community law. The time taken to complete the procedure depends on many things: the more complex and controversial the measure the longer it will take. The progress of some measures may also depend on whether an influential figure, such as the President of the Commission, is particularly keen to see the measure adopted during his term of office.

It is also important to note that many Directives have been held by the European Court of Justice to be of 'direct effect' and where this has happened the Directive is similar to a Regulation in having immediate binding effect as law in the Member States, without needing implementing legislation.

Note: Because this is an area where law is changing, this text will quickly become out of date. The Department of Trade is usually able to help enquirers with information about the latest position in respect of any particular Directive, or consult the EU website http: //**europa.eu.int/** and look for internal market.

18.3 Sources of EU law

Primary sources

The primary source of EU law is the Treaty of Rome, signed by the original six Member States in 1957 and to which the UK became a party in 1972 by signing one of the Acts of Accession. The Treaty contains a large number of Articles, some of which have in themselves the content of the relevant law, for example, Arts. 85 and 86 concerning competition law, and others which lay down the framework of laws, the detail of which is made by secondary community legislation.

The scope of the Treaty of Rome was enlarged by the Single European Act (SEA) signed in 1986. In line with the desire to speed up European integration and achieve a common internal market, the SEA also introduced a number of important procedural changes, in particular allowing for more measures to be passed by the Council of Ministers (see p. 335) by majority vote. The Treaty of Maastricht, which came into force from 1 November 1993, also makes significant amendments from the original Treaty as already amended by the SEA. One of the more obvious changes is that the community is now generally known as the European Union. It is important to note, however, that the European Union does not replace the European Community. The European Union is the collective name for the governments of the Member States, whereas the power to initiate and enforce community-wide legislation remains with the institutions of the European Community.

The Amsterdam Treaty which came into force on 1 May 1999 further amends the founding Treaties, in particular extending the scope of majority voting. It also renumbers all the Treaty Articles which are now referred to in this chapter by their post-Amsterdam numbering, although in pre-1999 cases they will, of course, be referred to by their old numbers. There will be significant changes if the EU is able to agree on a constitution.

Secondary EU legislation

Article 249 of the EU Treaty specifies a number of ways in which the council and the Commission can legislate. These are collectively referred to as 'Acts'. They are:

(1) Regulations

These are binding from the time of agreement and are 'directly applicable' in a Member State; in other words they have the force of law in all Member States from the time of making.

(2) Directives

These are addressed to the Member States, which are bound by them as to the results to be achieved, but have a discretion as to how they achieve the results. In other words, they have to be implemented by domestic legislation. A period of time is usually specified within which the Member States are obliged, so far as is necessary, to change their domestic laws. The UK has implemented Directives by means of both Acts of Parliament and secondary legislation (a general power to implement by statutory instrument is given under s. 2 European Communities Act 1972).

Sometimes Directives have been regarded as directly effective or directly applicable in the law of a Member State. For example, in Joined Cases C19 and C20/90, *Karella v. Minister of Industry, Energy and Technology* (1991) ECR I-02691 (judgment of 30 May 1991), OJ C166/12; [1994] 1 BCLC 774, it was held that certain provisions of the Second Company Law Directive were of direct effect. It is also possible that failure to implement a Directive may give rise to an action by an individual, resulting in the award of damages against the Member State in default. This was the situation in Joined Cases C6 and C9/96, *Francovich and Boniface v. Italian Republic* ([1992] ECR 133, discussed on pp. 346–7). Where there is a relevant EU Directive which has not been correctly implemented, specialist legal advice needs to be sought as to whether it is effective to override the UK law on the particular point or might give rise to a remedy in damages.

(3) Decisions

These may be addressed to a Member State or to an individual, and are directly binding on the addressee.

(4) Recommendations and opinions

These are not binding, but of persuasive authority.

Regulations, Directives and some decisions are published in the *Official Journal*.

18.4   The institutions of the EU

The principal institutions provided for in the Treaty of Rome, as amended, are the Parliament, the Council, the Commission, the Court of Justice and the Economic and Social Committee.

The European Parliament

The Parliament is not a true legislative body, although in recent years it has played a more important role because of the introduction of the co-decision procedure.

It must be consulted by the Council of Ministers over proposed legislation, including the legislation relating to the internal market, and, since the SEA, it has had the chance, having once disagreed with proposed legislation, to have a second look at the draft. If it maintains its objection, the Council can still proceed but must do so unanimously. Following the Maastricht Treaty, there is a provision for acts to be jointly adopted by the European Parliament and the Council and provision for the intervention of a Conciliation Committee where Parliament and Council differ. The Commission also reports regularly to the Parliament. The Treaty of Maastricht increased the powers of the Parliament, but it will not become a legislative body with powers equivalent to that of the UK legislature.

The Council of Ministers

The Council is the primary law-making body of the EU, although it can act only on the basis of a recommendation from the Commission and must consult the Parliament and the Economic and Social Committee. It consists of representatives from the governments of each Member State, with different representatives for different sorts of business. Thus the UK government may for different purposes be represented by, for example, the Prime Minister, the Foreign Secretary or the Secretary of State for Trade and Industry.

Originally, and for many years, the Council could proceed only by unanimous agreement. However, the SEA and the Maastricht and Amsterdam Treaties now allow the Council to act by what is called a 'qualified majority' in respect of many items of legislation relating to the completion of the internal market. For this purpose, Member States have 'weighted' voting rights according to their size, and legislation can be passed by a majority which works out at just over two-thirds. By itself, the UK cannot veto legislation requiring only a qualified majority.

In practice, much of the work of the Council is delegated to the Committee of Permanent Representatives or to Management Committees.

The European Commission

There are 30 Commissioners chosen from the Member States to act essentially as the guardians of the Community interest. The Commission has three primary functions. First, it brings forward proposals for legislation in the form of draft regulations, Directives etc. Secondly, it is charged with enforcing community law against Member States, if necessary by bringing proceedings before the Court of Justice. It is also the sole policeman of EU competition law. Thirdly, the Commission acts as the EU executive or civil service, implementing decisions of the Council.

The European Court of Justice and the Court of First Instance

The European Court of Justice (ECJ) is the ultimate arbiter of European Law. Over many years of interpreting the Treaty of Rome and other EU legislation, it has revealed itself to be almost as much of a law-making body as the other institutions. It is clear that it works in a radically different way from the courts in the UK, in particular in its willingness to make law and in not regarding itself bound by its previous decisions.

Litigation can reach the Court in a number of ways. The most relevant for the purposes of this work are: (1) actions taken against other Member States by the Commission or by a fellow Member State, for example alleging a failure to implement or an outright breach of EU legislation, and (2) issues of Community law referred to the Court by a national court under Art. 177 of the Treaty. The latter is particularly important because individuals (and companies) have very limited rights to bring direct actions in the Court of Justice against Member States or the EU institutions, and no right to bring actions alleging breach of EU law against other individuals. Their best remedy is to try to raise EU law indirectly in proceedings in the national court. Any national court has the power to refer the point to the Court of Justice for a preliminary ruling. Courts of last resort have a *duty* to refer.

The Court of First Instance is part of the European Court of Justice. It has 12 judges and deals with cases other than those where the constitution of the Community or the Union is an issue. It is therefore mostly concerned with cases involving the staff of the European Community institutions but its jurisdiction has recently been extended to cover all cases except those of constitutional significance and anti-dumping cases.

The Economic and Social Committee

This body consists of persons appointed by the Council to represent a variety of sectional interests throughout the community. Essentially it plays a consultative role.

Community jurisprudence and community law

Recent cases show that it is not possible to ignore any area of EC law. The Treaty articles dealing with such diverse matters as competition law and free movement may be relevant in a company law context. Three cases make the point. In *Alpine Investments BV* v. *Minister van Financien* [1995] 2 BCLC 214 the issue was whether rules in the Netherlands preventing cold-calling of clients in another Member State were contrary to Art. 59 of the EC Treaty, which prohibits restrictions on the free movement of services between Member States. *Oakdale (Richmond) Ltd* v. *National Westminister Bank plc* [1997] 1 BCLC 63 concerned the compatibility of loan arrangements with Arts. 85 and 86 of the EC Treaty (prohibition of anti-competitive measures). *Chequepoint SARL* v. *McClelland and Another* [1997] 1 BCLC 117 concerned the compatibility of orders for security for costs made against companies in another Member State of the Community with Community prohibitions preventing discrimination against nationals of another Member State.

Of particular interest for companies is *Centros Ltd* v. *Erhuerus- og Selskabsstyrelsen* (Case C212/97) [2000] 2 BCLC 68 which concerned the freedom of establishment of companies, where the ECJ held that natural law could not prevent the establishment of a branch in a Member State even when the foreign parent was not carrying on business in the state of registration.

18.5 The EU Company Law Harmonisation Programme

The following is a summary of legislation which has been passed, and the most important of the proposals currently being considered by the EU legislators. The programme is considered in sections according to their format or subject matter. The sections are:

(1) Regulations;
(2) Company Law Directives;
(3) Securities regulation; and
(4) Insolvency.

Regulations

European Economic Interest Grouping (EEIG) Regulation (OJ 28 L199/1)

This creates a new instrument for business which may be formed by persons from at least two Member States. It must not have as its primary purpose the making of profits, and it may only employ 500 employees. When it was a proposal it was envisaged that one of the purposes for which it would be most used was joint research and development, but it is being utilised for a wide variety of purposes (see Anderson, *European Economic Interest Groupings* (Butterworths, 1990), p. 9). There are over 800 EEIGs in existence.

Hot Topic . . .

THE EUROPEAN COMPANY (SE)

On 8 October 2001 the EU Council of Ministers formally adopted the Regulations and Directive which create the European Company Statute (Regulation (EC) 2157/2001, OJ 2001 L294/1; Directive 2001/86/EC, OJ 2001 L294/22).

This legislation creates a new business organisation governed partly by the European law contained in the Statute and partly by the law of the Member State in which it registers. It creates a new option for businesses – no company need convert into a European company, and no amendment of company law is required, save to add a European company as an extra choice for businesses.

This type of company can only be formed by a group of persons from more than one Member State, but there is no restriction on its profit-making capacity, nor on the number of employees it may have. The earlier proposals required all European companies to have a system of worker involvement in the important decisions made by the company. This requirement was contained in a draft Directive linked to the regulation which contains the company's structural provisions.

The requirement for worker participation caused the Statute to be blocked as it was unpopular, not least in the UK. The worker participation proposals were considered by the Davignon working group which published its report in May 1997. This report emphasised the importance of fixing only the framework for negotiation and permitting the employees and the company to arrive at the type of worker participation best suited to the individual company.

The current Directive follows a diluted version of the recommendations of the Davignon group. It establishes machinery for negotiation of worker participation in an SE with the primary purpose of avoiding the dilution of rights which are already enjoyed by employees of participating companies. However, the Directive does require the establishment of rules for participation by Member States and provides a minimum content for those rules.

A 'special negotiating body' must be established with 'the task of determining by written agreement, arrangements for the involvement of employees within the SE'. Article 7 provides that Member States must lay down standard rules on employee involvement. In the absence of agreement to the contrary, the rules established by the Member State of registration will apply. The Member State rules must satisfy criteria set out in the Annex to the Directive. These require the establishment of a representative body composed of employees of the SE, members to be elected in proportion to the number of employees in relevant companies in each Member State. The representative body has the right to be informed and consulted by the relevant decision-making organ of the company on the basis of regular reports drawn up by that organ. The reports must detail the company's current and future business plans, production and sales levels, implications of these for the workforce, management changes, mergers, divestments, potential closures and layoffs. Meetings between the employees' body and the decision-making body of the company must concern 'the structure, economic and financial situation, the probable development of the business and of production and sales, the situation and probable trend of employment, investments and substantial changes concerning organisation, introduction of new working methods or production processes, transfers of production, mergers, cut-backs or closures of undertakings, establishments or important parts thereof and collective redundancies'.

The representative body also has a right to be informed and to require a meeting where exceptional circumstances are likely to affect the employees' interests 'to a considerable extent' particularly in the event of 'relocations, transfers, the closure of establishments or undertakings or collective redundancies'. An SE will be able to transfer its registered office from one Member State to another without having to be wound up.

18.6 Company Law Directives

It should be noted that the European Court of Justice appears to be increasingly vigilant in detecting poor implementation of Directives and will not hesitate to substitute its interpretation of the Directive for a Member State provision which it regards as a defective interpretation of EU law.

The First Directive (68/151/EEC). This provides a system of publicity for all companies. Member countries must ensure disclosure of the following:

(1) the memorandum and articles;
(2) officers of the company;
(3) paid-up capital;
(4) balance sheet and profit and loss account;
(5) winding-up; and
(6) appointment of liquidators.

The Directive also provides that a third party who enters into a contract with the company may presume that the Act is within the objects of the company. This latter provision was badly implemented by s. 9 European Communities Act 1972, and re-enacted as s. 35 Companies Act 1985. A further measure in this field was introduced by s. 108 Companies Act 1989, which inserted a new s. 35 into the Companies Act 1985. Many of the other provisions were implemented by the Companies Act 1980, a statute which was almost entirely Directive-driven, and both the 1980 and 1989 amendments are now consolidated in the 1985 Act. All Member States have implemented this Directive. Its major achievement is the introduction of a uniform disclosure system of company information in all Member States. Article 11 was the subject of an important ECJ decision in Case 16/89, *Marleasing SA* v. *La Comercial International de Alimentation SA* (1990) ECR I-4135).

The Second Directive (OJ 1977 L26/1). This applies to public companies and lays down minimum requirements for the formation of the company and the maintenance, increase and reduction of capital. Companies must disclose their corporate form, name, objects, registered office, share capital, classes of shares and the composition and powers of the various organs of the company. The minimum subscribed capital of a public limited company must exceed 25,000 ecu. Capital subscribed in kind must be valued by an independent expert. There are other maintenance of capital provisions, and the Directive provides for pre-emptive rights for shareholders. Like the First Directive, the Second Directive was part of the driving force behind the Companies Acts of 1980 and 1981, now consolidated. All Member States have implemented this Directive.

The interpretation of the Second Directive was the subject of examination by the European Court of Justice. Two cases came before the court: Joined Cases C19 and C20/90, *Karella* v. *Minister of Industry, Energy and Technology* (1991) ECR I-02691 (judgment of 30 May 1991), OJ C166/12; [1994] 1 BCLC 774 and Case 381/89, *Syndesmos EEC, Vasco et al.* v. *Greece et al.* (1992) ECR I-2111 (judgment of 24 March 1992). In these cases the Court held that Arts. 25 and 29 of the Second Directive which relate to the increase of capital had direct effect in the laws of the Member States and applied not only when a company was functioning normally, but also when the company was the subject of a rescue operation. The effect of the decisions was to prevent the allocation of new shares without taking into account the rights of existing shareholders and to prevent an increase in share capital before consideration of the scheme to do so by the general meeting. The Greek government could not override the interests of shareholders by pleading reasons of social policy.

This case is of dubious value to company law, since it relies heavily on the idea of shareholder democracy which seems to be bolstered at the expense of the 'revitalisation of companies of particular social and economic importance'. Further, in Case C441/93, *Panagis Pafitis and Others* v. *Bank of Central Greece and Others* (12 March 1996), Lexis 6244, an increase in the capital of a bank which was made by the Greek government without the approval of the general meeting was held to be contrary to Arts. 25–29 of the Second Directive. The Court rejected the argument that banks were not subject to the Directive.

The Third Directive (OJ 1978 L295/36). This regulates mergers between public companies where the assets and liabilities of the acquired company are transferred to the acquiring company. The shareholders of the acquiring and acquired companies receive an equivalent stake in the merged company. The necessary valuations are carried out by an independent expert. The rights of employees are covered by Directive 77/197, part of EEC Social Affairs and Employment Law. This has been implemented in the UK by the Companies (Mergers and Divisions)

Regulations 1987 (SI 1987 No. 1991). A study carried out at the behest of the Commission shows that merger and division activity is not very common, particularly in the UK.

The Fourth Directive (OJ 1978 L222/11). This contains detailed rules regarding the drawing up of the accounts of individual companies, and was implemented by statutes which are now to be found in Part VII of the Companies Act 1985, but which were mostly introduced into UK law by the Companies Acts of 1980 and 1981. There are amendments to this Directive and the Seventh Directive, which go some way to lift the burden from small companies, but also include partnerships within the ambit of these Directives (Directive 90/605/EEC, OJ 1990 L317/60 and Directive 90/604/EEC, OJ 1990 L317/57, for which see below). The Directive has been implemented in all Member States, although there is increasing doubt as to whether the 'true and fair' provisions in particular bear the same meaning in different Member States; however, the ECJ has had an opportunity to set out some general principles in *Tomberger v. Gebruder von der Wettern GmbH* (Case C234/94) [1996] 2 BCLC 457.

The Sixth Directive (OJ 1982 L378/47). This covers the division of an existing public company into entities. Member countries are not obliged to introduce this form of reconstruction but, if it is used, the process must be in conformity with the Directive. The allocation of assets and liabilities among the various beneficiary companies requires specific provisions to protect creditors. On any increase in capital, the existing shareholders must be given pre-emptive rights. This Directive has also been implemented by the Companies (Mergers and Divisions) Regulations 1987 (SI 1987 No. 1991). This Directive has also been implemented in all Member States.

The Seventh Directive (OJ 1983 L193/1). The Seventh Directive specifies how and in what circumstances consolidated accounts are to be prepared and published by companies with subsidiaries. In the UK, the Companies Act 1989 has implemented this Directive. The provisions of the Directive were considered in *Tomberger v. Gebruder von der Wettern GmbH* (Case C234/94) [1996] 2 BCLC 457 (see above).

Amendments to the Fourth and Seventh Directives. There are amendments to the Fourth and Seventh Directives. The first (Directive 90/605/EEC, OJ 1990 L317/60) seeks to prevent avoidance of the provisions of those Directives by the use of partnerships. The preamble makes clear the aims. Noting that the Fourth and Seventh Directives apply only to companies, it continues:

'Whereas, within the Community there is a substantial and constantly growing number of partnerships and limited partnerships all of the fully liable members of which are constituted either as public or as private limited companies; Whereas these fully liable members may also be companies which do not fall within the law of a Member State but which have a legal status comparable to that referred to in Directive 68/151/EEC [First Directive];

Whereas it would run counter to the spirit and aims of those Directives to allow such partnerships and partnerships with limited liability not to be subject to Community rules . . .'

To this end, the amending Directive requires a name, head office and legal status of any undertaking of which a limited liability company is a fully liable member to be indicated in the accounts of such member, and imposes the obligation to draw up accounts on the members of partnerships, and to have them audited and published. The Directive also attempts to fit such partnerships into the consolidated account framework and provides jurisdictional rules for this purpose.

The second amendment is to the rules for small and medium enterprises with the aim of lessening the burdens placed on small enterprises by burdensome accounting requirements. The amending Directive (SI 1992/2452) changes the definition of enterprises which may qualify for exemption from the full requirements of the Directive. It does this by amending Art. 11 of the Fourth Directive, which was further amended in 1994 when the European Council adopted Directive 94/8 on 21st March 1994. This revision constitutes the third five-yearly revision provided for under Art. 53(2) of the Fourth Directive. After amendment that Article will read:

'The Member States may permit companies which on their balance sheets dates do not exceed the limits of two of the three following criteria:
– balance sheet total: 250,000 ecu (replacing 200,000 ecu)
– net turnover: 5,000,000 ecu (replacing 4,000,000 ecu)
– average number of employees during the financial year: 50
  to draw up abbreviated balance sheets . . .'

The Article also permits Member States to waive the application of Arts. 15(3)(a) and 15(4) to the abridged accounts. These paragraphs require that movements in the various fixed asset items be shown in the balance sheet or in the notes on the accounts.

This Directive has been implemented in the UK by the EC Companies (Accounts of Small and Medium-Sized Enterprises and Publication of Accounts in ecu) Regulations 1992 (90/604 EEC, OJ 1990 L317/57).

The Eighth Directive (OJ 1984 L126/30). The Eighth Directive places an obligation on Member States to ensure that auditors are independent and properly carry out their task of vetting company accounts. It lays down minimum requirements for the education and training of auditors. This has also been implemented by the Companies Act 1989.

The Eleventh Directive on the disclosure requirements of branches of certain types of company (OJ 1989 L395/36). This Directive deals with disclosures to be made in one Member State by branches of companies registered in another Member State or in non-EEC countries (that is, in UK terms – an 'oversea company'). The Directive recognises that a branch does not have a legal personality of its own, and it would therefore require disclosure of information concerning the company of which the branch is part, including its accounts, drawn up in accordance with the Fourth and Seventh Directives, that is, in a manner consonant with ss. 228–230 Companies Act 1985, that company accounts must give a true and fair view of the state of affairs within that company or group of companies. This Directive has been implemented in the UK by the Oversea Companies and Credit Financial Institutions (Branch Disclosure) Regulations 1992.

The Twelfth Directive (OJ 1989 L395/40). The Twelfth Company Law Directive embodies a proposal adopted by the European Council in December 1989 (OJ 1989 L395/40). The idea was to introduce legislation in Member States to permit single member companies with limited liability. This Directive has now been implemented in the UK by the Companies (Single Member Private Limited Companies) Regulations 1992 (SI 1992/1699).

The idea is simple in essence. The single shareholder company will be introduced throughout the Community. The Commission believes that the availability of company status without the need to find another shareholder will encourage individuals to set up businesses. There is also the advantage that such businesses will have a separate legal personality, thus allowing continuity of the business even if the owners change.

The effect of the Directive is to require Member States to allow private limited companies to have a single member who could be either a natural person or a legal person, that is, a company. All the shares will have to show the name of the person owning them and be held by a single shareholder.

The sole member will have to: exercise personally the powers of the general meeting; record in minutes the decisions taken under those powers; and draw up in writing any agreement between the sole member and the company. Otherwise, the company will be subject to the restraints of company law in the usual way.

An alternative scheme is provided for in Art. 7 of the Directive. Member States are given the option of introducing legislation which would enable an individual businessman to set up an undertaking whose liability was limited to 'a sum devoted to a stated activity'. This appears to be similar to a company limited by guarantee. The detailed rules will be found in the Companies (Single Member Private Limited Companies) Regulations 1992.

Directive on the information to be published when a major holding in a listed company is acquired or disposed of. The effect of this Directive on UK law will be minimal as the current UK disclosure requirements are more stringent than those contained in the Directive. This Directive has been welcomed by interested UK parties as a harmonisation measure which will 'pull up' other systems towards the UK standard. This Directive has been implemented by the Disclosure of Interests in Shares (Amendment) Regulations 1993, which came into force on 18 September 1993 (SI 1993/1819), and the Disclosure of Interests in Shares (Amendment) (No. 2) Regulations 1993, which came into force on 29 October 1993.

The Tenth Directive (OJ 1985 C23 28/11). This Directive concerns cross-border mergers and is progressing no further because fears have been expressed that a cross-border merger could be a way of escaping from worker participation provisions. Thus it awaits agreement on that issue. However, the Commission sees cross-border mergers as very important in achieving harmonisation and is considering further initiatives in this field.

Draft Proposal for a Ninth Directive (not formally adopted by the Commission). In 1984 a draft of a proposal which would be concerned with the conduct of groups of companies was circulated. There is no immediate prospect of work on this project resuming.

18.7 Securities regulation

Prospectus Directive (2003/71/EC; OJ L345, 31 December 2003)

On 15 July 2003 the Council adopted a new Prospectus Directive. This lays down detailed requirements as to the information that must be published before a company's securities may be admitted to trading on a stock exchange. The Directive also requires the listing particulars to be approved before publication by a competent authority. Once the listing particulars have been approved by the competent authorities in one Member State, the Directive requires other Member States to recognise the listing particulars as sufficient. In a change from the previous regime, Member States may not require additional information specific to the market within its jurisdiction. Approval may only be granted if prospectuses meet common EU standards for what information must be disclosed and how. This Directive deals with initial trading. Directive 2001/34/EC deals with obligations for continuing disclosure.

Market Abuse Directive (2003/6/EC)

This Directive supersedes the Insider Dealing Directive and creates a single set of rules for all types of market manipulation, including insider dealing. It includes a detailed set of rules which will impose liability on legal or natural persons if they misuse information about companies where that information is price-sensitive.

18.8 Insolvency

The Council of Europe Bankruptcy Convention

This is not an EU initiative but emanated from the Council of Europe. The intention of the Convention is to provide a framework for insolvencies where assets are situated within the territory of more than one signatory. The idea is to establish a primary liquidation or bankruptcy conducted by a 'liquidator' with powers to act in other States where assets are situated. If the need arises for a 'secondary' bankruptcy proceeding in another State, this could be established but would normally be subordinate to the main procedure.

The EC Regulation on Insolvency Proceedings (1346/2000 OJ L160/1)

Based on Arts. 61 and 67 of the Treaty, this Regulation applies to insolvency proceedings involving the disinvestment of the debtor. This will exclude rescue procedures such as Administration in the UK. Both this Regulation and the Council of Europe Convention deal with company insolvency as well as the insolvency of individuals.

Jurisdiction

Jurisdiction to open insolvency proceedings is given to the Member State in whose territory the centre of the debtor's main interests is situated. There is a presumption that the centre of main interests of a company or other legal person is at the place of registered or statutory office.

Applicable law

The law applicable is to be the law governing insolvency in the State where the proceedings are opened. There is a reference to national law as opposed to internal law in the relevant Article, so it is presumed that conflict of laws rules will apply. Nevertheless, the Convention permits the opening of secondary bankruptcies in certain situations and thus opens the possibility of proceedings being started in two or more jurisdictions with differing laws applying to the whole bankruptcy. This means that the principle of universality (that is, a single law applying to the whole proceeding) has been abandoned and conflicts between different priority rules will inevitably arise.

Recognition of insolvency proceedings

The Regulation provides that an insolvency proceeding, once validly commenced, shall be recognised in all other contracting States. The insolvency proceeding is to have the effect which it has in the State where the proceeding was commenced. If this had been unqualified it would have imported true universality. However, as already mentioned, it is subject to the right to open secondary insolvency proceedings.

Liquidator's powers

The liquidator is to have in all Member States the powers which are conferred on him by the State where the proceedings are opened. Further, the liquidator will have the power to remove assets from any Member State.

Relationship between main and secondary jurisdictions

Having strayed from the principle of universality, the Regulation has the difficult task of determining the relationship between the two sets of proceedings. There is a duty laid on the primary and secondary liquidators to communicate promptly with one another. Further, a secondary liquidation can be stayed for up to three months at the request of the liquidator in the main proceedings provided that interest is paid to preferential or secured creditors. A composition in the secondary proceedings may not become final without the consent of the liquidator in the main proceedings. Such consent cannot be withheld if the financial interests of the creditors in the main proceedings are not affected by the composition. Any surplus remaining in a secondary bankruptcy after payment of all claims must be passed to the main liquidator.

The Francovich Directive (Directive 80/987/EEC)

This Directive concerns the protection of employees in the event of the insolvency of their employer (OJ 1980 L283/23). It was the non-implementation of this Directive that led to the European Court of Justice's decision in Joined Cases C6 and C9/90 (*Francovich and Boniface* v. *Italian Republic* [1992] ECR 133). An Italian company went into insolvent liquidation leaving the plaintiff and others with unpaid arrears of salary. Italy had not set up a compensation scheme to cover this situation. It was required to do so by the terms of Council Directive 80/987/EEC of 20 October 1980 on the approximation of the laws of the Member States relating to the protection of employees in the event of the insolvency of their employer (OJ 1980 L283/23).

According to Art. 11 of the Directive, Member States were bound to bring into force the laws, regulations and administrative provisions necessary to comply with the Directive by 23 October 1983. The Commission, in its role as Community policeman, brought an enforcement action against Italy under Art. 169 of the EEC Treaty. In its judgment in that case (Joined Cases C140/91, C141/91, C278/91 and C279/91 *Commission* v. *Italy* (1992) ECR I-06337), the ECJ found that the Italian Republic had failed to comply with its obligations under the Directive.

From the plaintiff's point of view the situation remained unsatisfactory. He had still received no money. He brought proceedings in Italy claiming compensation from the Italian State for failure to implement properly Directive 80/987/EEC. The Italian courts submitted the question of Mr Francovich's entitlement to damages to the ECJ by way of a preliminary reference under Art. 177 of the EEC Treaty. The ECJ held that in these circumstances the plaintiff was entitled to compensation.

The Money Laundering Directive (Directive 91/308 EEC, OJ 1991 L166/77)

This is a Council Directive on the prevention of the use of the financial system for the purpose of money laundering.

Money laundering is the intentional:

(a) conversion or transfer of property, in the knowledge that such property is derived from criminal activity, for the purpose of concealing or disguising the illicit origin of the property, or of assisting any person who is involved in such activity to evade the legal consequences of his action;

(b) concealment or disguise of the nature, source, location, disposition, movement, rights with respect to, or ownership of, property, in the knowledge that such property is derived from criminal activity, or from an act of participation in such activity;

(c) acquisition, possession or use of property in the knowledge, at the time of receipt, that such property was derived from criminal activity, or from an act of participation in such activity; and

(d) participation in, association or conspiracy to commit, attempts to commit and aiding, abetting, facilitating and counselling the commission of any of the actions established in the previous paragraphs.

Implementation in the UK is by the Criminal Justice Act 1993 and regulations made in accordance with the Act (Money Laundering Regulations 1993 SI 1993 No. 1933).

The Directive for informing and consulting employees of groups (Directive 94/95)

This Directive has been adopted by the Council (OJ 1994 L254/64). Based on Art. 100 of the EEC Treaty, the proposal has its roots in the Social Charter. Indent 5 of the preamble provides:

> 'Whereas point 17 of the Community Charter of Fundamental Social Rights of Workers provides, *inter alia*, that information and consultation for workers must be developed along appropriate lines, taking account of the practices in force in the various Member States; whereas the Charter states that "this shall apply especially in companies having establishments in two or more Member States . . .".'

The preamble also stresses the likelihood of increased merger and cross-border activity and continues:

> 'if economic activities are to develop in a harmonious fashion, this situation requires that undertakings and groups of undertakings operating in more than one Member State must inform and consult the representatives of their employees affected by their decisions.'

The Directive is historically linked to the 'Vredling' Directive, which laid down procedures for informing and consulting employees of undertakings with 'complex structures' (OJ Vol 26C 217/3). The Directive lays down requirements for informing and consulting employees in all undertakings, or groups of undertakings, which operate in more than one Member State and employ more than 1,000 employees within the Community, including at least 100 employees at two different establishments in different Member States.

Such undertakings must set up a European works council which will be the channel for informing and consulting employees. The Directive does not now apply to UK companies .

18.9 Conclusion

It is clear from the above summary that a great deal has been done. Company law harmonisation is aimed at the realisation of a complete freedom of establishment. It is said to be necessary in order to avoid distortions in the market, which may result from the use of freedom of establishment in such a way that Member States which have a well-developed company law are put into a disadvantageous position. Unless a minimum degree of harmonisation has taken place, a 'Delaware effect' is feared, that is, companies will prefer to incorporate in a Member State because of the liberal company law in that State, in the same way that a majority of public companies incorporate in the State of Delaware in the USA. However, it is by no means clear that freedom of establishment can be achieved by harmonisation of the sort described above. A significant difficulty is the failure to harmonise tax regimes. There has been some progress in this field recently (Council Directive of 23 July 1990 on the Common System of Taxation Guidelines in the Case of a Parent Company and Subsidiaries of Different Member States and Council Directive 91/308 EEC, OJ 1991 L166/77). Even leaving that problem aside, the mode of harmonisation by Directive will not create a completely uniform set of laws and a completely 'level playing field'. The importance of companies, and the importance of increasing their freedom of establishment, are undeniable. Two problems have arisen from the Directives which have sought to achieve harmonisation. First, in order to make sure that implementing legislation has a harmonising effect, the Directive must itself be detailed and inflexible. It has been argued that the Directives are too detailed, and that they risk petrifying company law. Even so, it is likely that there will be minor differences in Member States after implementation. The detailed provisions may lead to a 'blocking effect'. The procedure for modifying an adopted Directive is burdensome. The danger that the law will not accord with business practice is therefore very real. Despite the detail in the Directives, there remain significant differences between company regimes in Member States. The burden of regulations on companies has also increased.

Secondly, the harmonisation programme has been unable so far to create a 'European outlook' for companies. Harmonisation by Directive is unlikely to do so, as implementation is by incorporation into national laws. An alternative approach has, as a herald, the introduction of the EEIG. This cross between a small company and a partnership with non-profit motives is remarkable as it is a supra-national 'European' institution. It may be that the new European Company Statute will achieve more effective harmonisation, in the sense that all countries would have available the same basic structure for a company. The current proposal for a European company is unlikely to achieve this aim, however, as the laws of the Member States are relied on heavily to fill in gaps left by the Statute. There is a grave danger of creating 25 different 'European companies'.

Hot Topic . . .
TAKEOVER DIRECTIVE

European Parliament and Council Directive 2004/25/EC of 21 April 2004 on takeover bids

The Directive sets out to establish minimum guidelines for the conduct of takeover bids involving the securities of companies governed by the laws of Member States, where all or some of those securities are admitted to trading on a regulated market. It also seeks to provide an adequate level of protection for holders of securities throughout the Community, by establishing a framework of common principles and general requirements which Member States are to implement through more detailed rules in accordance with their national systems and their cultural contexts. Member States are required to transpose the Directive no later than two years after its entry into force.

Scope

The Directive lays down measures co-ordinating the laws, regulations, administrative provisions, codes of practice and other arrangements of the Member States, including arrangements established by organisations officially authorised to regulate the markets relating to takeover bids for the securities of companies governed by the laws of Member States (hereinafter referred to as 'rules'), where all or some of those securities are admitted to trading on a regulated market

General principles

The Member States must ensure that the following principles are complied with:

- All holders of securities of the offeree company must be given equal treatment; if a person acquires control of a company, the other holders of securities must be protected; the addressees of the bid must have sufficient time and information to be able to reach a properly informed decision on the bid; where it advises the holders of securities, the board of the offeree company must give its views on the effects of implementation of the bid on employment, the conditions of employment and the locations of the company's places of business.

- The board of the offeree company must act in the interests of the company as a whole and must not deny the holders of securities the opportunity to decide on the merits of the bid.

- False markets must not be created in the securities of the offeree company, of the offeror company or of any other company concerned by the bid in such a way that the rise or fall in the prices of the securities becomes artificial and the normal functioning of the market is distorted.

- An offeror must announce a bid only after ensuring that he can fulfil in full any cash consideration, if such is offered, and after taking all reasonable measures to secure the implementation of any other type of consideration.

- An offeree company must not be hindered in the conduct of its affairs for longer than is reasonable by a bid for its securities.

For the regulation of bids, Member States may lay down additional conditions and provisions more stringent than those of the Directive.

Supervisory authority and applicable law

Member States are to designate the authority or authorities competent to supervise bids. The authorities thus designated must be either public authorities, associations or private bodies recognised by national law or by public authorities expressly empowered for that purpose by national law. Member States must inform the Commission of those designations. They must ensure that those authorities exercise their functions impartially and independently of all parties to a bid.

The authority competent to supervise a bid is that of the Member State in which the offeree company has its registered office if that company's securities are admitted to trading on a regulated market in that Member State. In all other cases (for example, where securities are not admitted or are admitted to trading on more than one regulated market), the Directive lays down rules for deciding the competent supervisory authority.

Member States must ensure that all persons employed or formerly employed by their supervisory authorities are bound by professional secrecy. The supervisory authorities and the authorities responsible for supervising capital markets must co-operate and supply each other with information. Information thus exchanged will be covered by the rules of professional secrecy.

Protection of minority shareholders, mandatory bid and equitable price

Where a natural or legal person, as a result of his own acquisition or the acquisition by persons acting in concert with him, holds securities of a company which give him a specified percentage of voting rights in that company, giving him control of that company, Member States must ensure that such a person is required to make a bid as a means of protecting the minority shareholders of that company. Such a bid must be addressed at the earliest opportunity to all the holders of those securities for all their holdings at the equitable price.

Where control has been acquired following a voluntary bid to all the holders of securities for all their holdings, the obligation to launch a bid no longer applies.

The percentage of voting rights which confers control and the method of its calculation must be determined by the rules of the Member State in which the company has its registered office.

Information concerning bids

Member States must ensure that a decision to make a bid is made public without delay and that the supervisory authority is informed of the bid. They must also ensure that an offeror is required to draw up and make public in good time an offer document containing the information necessary to enable the holders of the offeree company's securities to reach a properly informed decision on the bid.

The Directive lays down the minimum information that the offer document must contain. It must, for example, state the terms of the bid, the identity of the offeror, the consideration offered and the maximum and minimum percentages or quantities of securities which the offeror undertakes to acquire; it must also state the conditions to which the bid is subject, the offeror's intentions with regard to the future business of the offeree company, the time allowed for acceptance of the bid and the national law which will govern the contract.

Summary

1. The EU harmonisation programme is composed of a number of measures designed to create a uniform company law throughout Europe.

2. Although a number of measures have become law, the harmonisation that has been achieved is not considerable because a number of obstacles have become apparent.

3. The most significant of these has been the inability of the Member States to agree on taxation of companies, the treatment of groups of companies and worker participation provisions.

4. Other problems have appeared because the programme has consisted mostly of Directives which need implementation in each of the Member States. Some of them contain options which means that even after implementation of the Directives there is no consistency in company law throughout the Member States.

5. In other cases there have been differences in implementation measures with the same result. Much still needs to be done to remove the obstacles to companies operating easily throughout the Member States.

Exercises

1. Describe the process by which a Directive becomes law in the UK.

2. Identify three major changes which have been or will be brought about by the harmonisation programme.

3. What is the value of the new European company?

Chapter 19

Transglobal corporations and world development

Key words

> ▶ **Transnational companies (TNCs) or multinational companies (MNEs)** – these terms are often used to refer to companies which operate in more than one jurisdiction; in fact, there is no such thing; companies must be formed individually in each separate country; they may be linked by shareholding or by agreements but they are many separate entities, not one single body.

Many studies have highlighted a growing polarisation of world resources. More than 1.3 billion people live in absolute poverty (see United Nations Development Programme, *Human Development Report 1996*; and Third World Network, 'A World in Social Crisis: Basic Facts on Poverty, Unemployment and Social Disintegration', *Third World Resurgence*, No. 52, 1994).

Wealth is increasingly being concentrated in the hands of the few, both in terms of disparities among nations and within nations. The United Nations *Human Development Report 1992* found that the 20 per cent of people who live in the world's wealthiest countries receive 82.7 per cent of the world's income; only 1.4 per cent of the world's income goes to the 20 per cent who live in the world's poorest countries. There is a simultaneous and linked environmental crisis. Few studies doubt that the giant transnational corporate enterprises have played their part in creating both strands of this 'globalisation of poverty'. In 1990 there were at least 212 million people without income or assets to guarantee the necessities for a basic existence (see United Nations Development Programme, *Human Development Report 1992*; and United Population Fund, *The State of World Population 1992*). This is caused particularly by companies' adherence to free-market classical economic theories and the economic contractual model of companies. The immense power of corporations is indicated by a comparison between the economic wealth generated by corporations, measured by sales, compared with a country's gross domestic product (GDP). On this basis, 51 of the largest 100 economies are corporations (S. Anderson and J. Cavanaugh, *The Rise of Global Corporate Power*). Further, the number of transnational corporations (TNCs) jumped from 7,000 in 1970 to 40,000 in 1995, and these account for most of the world's trade.

However the phenomenon of globalisation of the world economy is a complex one, and this chapter looks briefly at some of the themes which have been the subject of recent studies. Within this part, some attention will be paid to the role of institutions which have a regulatory capacity, such as the World Trade Organisation (WTO) and the International Monetary Fund (IMF). In order to cover the multitude of issues with some coherence, they are considered under the following headings:

(1) the effect of TNCs on development;
(2) the displacement of domestic production;
(3) the effects of the banking and international money systems;
(4) the undermining of political systems and the absence of control of transnationals;
(5) environmental issues;
(6) labour issues.

Each of these issues has given rise to individual lengthy, scholarly and lively disputes. It will be appreciated that, because of the length of the list, they can only be dealt with here in outline.

19.1 Development issues

Production of goods and provision of services are inherently valuable and beneficial processes, since such goods and services are distributed widely throughout society, and it has been shown that the benefits outweigh any detrimental effects.

David Korten points out, in *When Corporations Rule the World*, that measurements of GNP ignore calculations that would indicate the true benefits of transnationals to the population of societies, and 'the results are sometimes ludicrous'. For example, the costs of cleaning up the *Exxon Valdez* oil spill on the Alaska coast and the costs of repairing the damage from the terrorist bombing of the World Trade Center in New York both counted as net contributions to economic output. The transnationals have been successful in diverting attention from their production of environmentally damaging wastes to 'end of pipeline' clean-up solutions, as a result of which a study prepared for the Organisation for Economic Development and Co-operation (OECD) forecast an 'environmental industry' of $300 billion by the year 2000.

However, it is clear that for developing countries the arrival of a powerful international company 'offers considerable attractions ... The prime advantage is that they help the balance of payments with an immediate inflow of capital' (P. Harrison, *Inside the Third World*, p. 356). But the disadvantage of welcoming TNCs is the fact that 'their purpose is to maximise profits for Western owners, not to promote the welfare of their host nations' (p. 358). Thus TNCs 'make money and send it back home, for that, after all, is their *raison d'être*' (p. 358).

The movement of corporations into a global situation means that national interests, whether of home or host state, are irrelevant to their operations:

> 'Because they span national borders, many MNEs are less concerned with advancing national goals than with pursuing objectives internal to the firm – principally growth, profits, proprietary technology, strategic alliances, return on investment, and market power.' (Office of Technology Assessment, US Congress, *Multinationals and the National Interest: Playing by Different Rules*, pp. 1–4, 10)

Further, 'despite numerous attempts by local and national governments, spurred by citizens' movements, to limit corporations' power and increase their accountability to the public, today these economic powerhouses maintain a firm grip on many key aspects of political life in their home countries, corrupting the democratic process' (J. Karliner, *The Corporate Planet*), and 'they [TNCs] are also using the accelerating process of globalisation to gain an increasing degree of independence from governments' (Karliner). Indeed, it is their duty to be focused on these concerns and not national or local interests if their foundations are in free-market economist theory.

The assessment of TNCs' contribution to development therefore depends on a more fundamental debate about whether growth of wealth is equivalent to development and can be measured in simple terms such as an increase in GNP. In order to take this assessment further, it is necessary to examine the impact of TNCs on other areas of concern to host countries.

19.2   The displacement of domestic production

Harrison (*Inside the Third World*) observes that: 'Multinationals . . . can come to dominate the commanding heights of local industry, as their immense advantages of resources and knowhow give them a massive start on local firms.' There are countless stories of the displacement of indigenous peoples resulting from the exploitation of natural resources by large corporations. This is perhaps the simplest mechanism by which local industries are displaced. However, the drive for ever increased profitability (here again, the echo of our free-market economists) creates other mechanisms which displace local industries and create unemployment.

The arrival of a powerful corporation with modern technology displaces traditional manufacturing and agriculture, driving those ousted from the land into cities:

'Most [governments] have worked on the theory that the traditional sector will wither away naturally and its workers get absorbed into the modern sector. They are certainly right on the first count, but dangerously wrong on the second.' (Harrison, *Inside the Third World*)

An example of the mechanisms involved is given by Karliner in *The Corporate Planet*:

'In the 1980s, US free-market farm policies lowered price supports for the small farmer. As a result, a large number of family farms went into bankruptcy, while major food corporations enjoyed record profits. At the same time, Mexico, in preparation for NAFTA [the North American Free Trade Agreement], wiped out important protections for its small, food producing farmers. Consequently US agribusiness transnationals moved into the lucrative Mexican market. They effectively took over land dedicated to subsistence agriculture there, converting it to pesticide-intensive crops such as strawberries, broccoli, cauliflower and cantaloupes for export to the world market. They then turned round and began selling Mexican farmers corn and beans grown in the Midwest. In theory this is a more "efficient" system, with large corporations growing the most productive crops on both sides of the border and distributing them in a businesslike way. However, such efficiency not only undermines Mexico's food security, increases the use of pesticides and threatens the viability of organic agriculture, but it has also caused thousands of farm families in both the United States and Mexico to lose their land.'

19.3 The effects of the international money and banking systems

According to M. Chossudovsky in *The Globalisation of Poverty*, pp. 68–9:

'The IMF–World Bank reforms brutally dismantle the social sectors of developing countries, undoing the efforts and struggles of the post-colonial period and reversing "with the stroke of the pen" the fulfilment of past progress. Throughout the world, there is a consistent and coherent pattern: the IMF–World Bank reform package constitutes a coherent programme of economic and social collapse.'

It is not possible here to analyse in depth the complex interlocking factors which have led to these claims of serious failure but a pattern can be discerned. The fundamental starting point is the adherence of the most powerful institutions (including transnationals) to the creed of growth.

The second step is the consequent call for global free markets in which the huge transnationals are able to dominate small producers. The establishment of the World Trade Organisation in 1995, with a mandate to regulate freedom of trade, marked a turning point in this process. Thus, even without the assistance of the IMF–World Bank packages, transnationals were on a winning ticket as their vertical integration and relatively small overhead costs, as well as global mobility and huge reserves, enable them to cushion any sudden market movement. However the IMF–World Bank packages for developing nations assist transnationals in a number of ways. The sequence works as follows.

Large amounts of corporate debt in developed countries have been transferred to the state because countries were lent money to reimburse the private-sector banks (M. Chossudovsky, *The Globalisation of Poverty*). In more than 100 debtor nations, the IMF and World Bank work together to impose 'structural adjustment programmes' which appear to directly benefit transnationals. Korten quotes a Philippine Government advertisement:

> 'To attract companies like yours . . . we have felled mountains, razed jungles, filled swamps, moved rivers, relocated towns . . . all to make it easier for you and your business here.'

How does it work? Following the oil price rises imposed by the OPEC countries in the mid-1970s, the foreign debts of developing countries increased enormously. From 1970 to 1980 the long-term external debt of low-income countries increased from $21 billion to $110 billion and that of middle-income countries rose from $40 billion to $317 billion (World Debt Tables 1992–93: External Finance for Developing Countries (World Bank, Washington DC, 1992), p. 212). With default on these loans, inevitably the IMF and World Bank were put into a position to impose structural adjustment packages to ensure that payments were made: 'Each structural adjustment package called for sweeping economic policy reforms intended to channel more of the adjusted country's resources and productive activity toward debt repayment and to further open national economies to the global economy. Restrictions and tariffs on both imports and exports were reduced, and incentives were provided to attract foreign investors' (Korten).

J. Cahn argues that the World Bank is a governance institution, and it is exercising its power:

> 'through its financial leverage to legislate entire legal regimes and even . . . [altering] the constitutional structure of borrowing nations. Bank-approved consultants often rewrite a country's trade policy, fiscal policies, civil service requirements, labor laws, health care arrangements, environmental regulations, energy policy, resettlement requirements, procurement rules, and budgetary policy.'

It is well documented that the consequent 'austerities' cause cuts in all social and in particular health programmes, a move of the population away from rural areas into cities, the vicious-circle effects of poor health and lack of proper food and education, and a consequent willingness of a population to work at any task however ill-paid and poorly regulated (see Bibliography at end of book). This is a situation tailor-made for a transnational corporation seeking to locate its plant at the least expensive site globally. Negative externalities in the form of health, safety and environmental regulations will either be minimal or can be negotiated in that direction with a government which needs the transnational investment in order to be able to repay its debts. At the end of the day, however, the result is a huge disparity in income within the developing countries between those who were 'in on the act' of development and associated with the incoming transnationals, and the majority whose conditions worsen. Further, the export of profits to the developed world and the repayment of debt amount to a huge subsidy by the poor nations of the rich ones, and lead to the growing disparity of incomes and living conditions between nations. While transnationals base their *raison d'être* on profit maximisation they will remain an integral part of this process unless it can in some way be regulated.

19.4 The undermining of political systems and the absence of control of transnationals

A starting point for this section is to remember how tenuous are the controls over companies operating in a single country. Shareholders and governments are unable or unwilling to exert much control. Even internal company controls are difficult to maintain over speedy operations involving large sums of money. Add to this the emphasis in managerial training on global rather than national or regional issues and we begin to get a picture of absence of control. If we then add in the temptation to export dirty or labour-intensive work to avoid stringent environmental controls or labour standards, and remember that 51 of the largest economic units are corporate groups rather than nation states and that the exporting will be done to the poorest of the nation states, the power picture is almost complete – save for the intervention of the international money system which obligingly pressurises countries into playing host to the global corporations in order to attempt to pay off debts owed to the rich nations of the world.

The imposition of conditions attached to loans which require 'good governance' and the holding of multi-party elections are seen by many as a sham (see Bibliography at end of book). The very nature of the economic reforms imposed causes such poverty, illness and despair that the mass of the people are likely to cause unrest so that a 'civilian government takes more and more powers to cope with civil strife' (Harrison). Thus 'the poorer a nation is the more likely it is to suffer from deprivation of political and civil rights'.

Further, the poorest are likely to be under-educated and more concerned with finding the next meal than with a discussion of politics and exercising an informed right to vote. The path to democracy is undermined by global economics, ably assisted by the global groups. Even the recent adoption of so-called 'sustainable development' models by corporations creating 'stakeholder' constituencies may be seen as anti-democratic, since 'it redefines citizens and their communities as constituencies of transnational corporations in the world economy' (Karliner), rather than encouraging pursuit of democracy through the ballot box. Further, the 'needs' of transnationals for stable political conditions in host countries may well persuade governments to repress protest at the behest of corporations, whether the protest has legitimate roots or not. Karliner quotes the general manager of Shell Nigeria as saying in 1995: 'for a commercial company trying to make investments, you need a stable environment ... Dictatorships can give you that.'

If we turn, then, to the other side of the coin, which is to see whether controls can be placed on global corporate operations, we can see immediately how poor a position nation states are in. Even the wealthy nations have considerable difficulty in collecting taxes from global companies. Poor host countries are in a very difficult position indeed.

19.5 Environmental issues

Here we can start with an insight of Kenneth Boulding. In 'The Economics of the Coming Spaceship Earth' (in Henry Jarrett (ed.), *Environmental Quality in a Growing Economy*) he suggests that many problems are rooted in acting like 'cowboys' on an open frontier when in fact we are inhabiting a living spaceship with a finely balanced life support system:

> 'Astronauts live on spaceships hurtling through space with a human crew and a precious and limited supply of resources. Everything must be maintained in balance, recycled; nothing can be wasted. The measure of well-being is not how fast the crew is able to consume its limited stores but rather how effective the crew members are in maintaining their physical and mental health, their shared resource stocks and the life support system on which they all depend. What is thrown away is forever inaccessible. What is accumulated without recycling fouls the living space. Crew members function as a team in the interests of the whole. No-one would think of engaging in non-essential consumption unless the basic needs of all were met and there was ample provision for the future.'

Korten explains how this translates into the concept of a 'full world'. In the past, 'cowboy' behaviour has permitted countries which exceeded their national resource limits to obtain what was necessary for expansion by 'reaching out to obtain what was needed from beyond their own borders, generally by colonising the resources of non-industrial people. Although the consequences were sometimes devastating for the colonised people, the added impact on the planetary ecosystem was scarcely noticed by the colonisers.'

Korten believes that the world is now full, so that continuing such behaviour will impoverish everyone. 'Cowboy' behaviour has two basic effects. It acts as colonialism did to 'transfer income from the middle to the upper classes', increasing the disparity of income within and between nations, and it means that absolute environmental limits have been reached as the world has become full.

On the latter front, acid rain and global warming present two examples and, of course, transglobal companies play their part in exacerbating these problems:

> 'Economic globalisation has greatly expanded opportunities for the rich to pass their environmental burdens to the poor by exporting both wastes and polluting factories.' (Korten)

It is the failure to regulate companies which continue to operate on a 'cowboy' basis, exporting their environmental degradation to countries which have no power to regulate them, since they fear losing inward investment or are unable to pay back debts due to the world financial system, which has exacerbated the disparity between rich and poor nations. The exact extent of this effect is a matter of debate but a few instances can be given:

> 'One of the keys to understanding the global problem of waste and pollution, however, is that much of its incidence in the developing world is due to developed nations' illegal shipment of their own waste to these regions ... trucks entering Eastern Europe [from Germany] export hundreds of thousands of tons of waste that Westerners find too expensive or too inconvenient to dispose of themselves. The pressure is mostly financial. Under US and European environmental laws today, the cost of disposing of hazardous industrial and mining waste can be as high as several thousand dollars per ton ... Shipping such materials abroad is often much cheaper.' (Czinkota, Ronksinen and Moffett)

The exporting nations can pose as environmentally aware:

> 'Japan has reduced its aluminium smelting capacity from 1.2 million tons to 149,000 tons and now imports 90 per cent of its aluminium. What this involves in human terms is suggested by a case study of the Philippine Associated Smelting and Refining Corporation (PASAR). PASAR operates a Japanese-financed and constructed copper smelting plant in the Philippine province of Leyte to produce high grade copper cathodes for shipment to Japan. The plant occupies 400 acres of land expropriated by the Philippine Government from local residents at give-away prices. Gas and waste water emissions from the plant contain high concentrations of boron, arsenic, heavy metals, and sulfur compounds that have contaminated local water supplies, reduced fishing and rice yields, damaged the forests, and increased the occurrence of upper respiratory diseases among local residents. Local people whose homes, livelihoods and health have been sacrificed to PASAR are now largely dependent on the occasional part-time or contractual employment they are offered to do the plant's most dangerous and dirtiest jobs.' (Korten)

Karliner chronicles the migration of the chlorine industry from developed nations to Brazil, Mexico, Saudi Arabia, Egypt, Thailand, India, Taiwan and China, and similar strategies being followed by the nuclear power industry, the automobile industry and tobacco marketing.

Mark Hertsgaard, in *Earth Odyssey*, gives graphic accounts of industrial conditions in developing nations which would not be tolerated in developed nations, including the chlorine discharged from the Chongqing Paper factory:

> 'a vast roaring torrent of white, easily thirty yards wide, splashing down the hillside from the rear of the factory like a waterfall of boiling milk . . . Decades of unhindered discharge had left the rocks coated with a creamlike residue, creating a perversely beautiful white-on-white effect. Above us, the waterfall had bent trees sideways; below, it split into five channels before pouring into the unfortunate Jialing.'

These are just a few instances of the many horrific accounts to be found in environmental studies.

There is no doubt that increased awareness of environmental issues, international conferences, international accords and codes of conduct, the rise of corporate environmentalism (if it is not all 'greenwash') and the concept of sustainable development have created a debate that will not go away. However, there is no legal mechanism affecting the governance of groups likely to be effective in lessening the frightening ability of transnationals to act without constraint.

19.6 Labour law issues

The impact on employees of the push for ever greater efficiency is a repetition of the effects on the environment and is part of the picture creating ever increasing globalisation of poverty.

Hot Topic . . .

SARO-WIWA FAMILY v. ROYAL DUTCH/SHELL

A. Parties to the case

Plaintiffs are three former citizens and residents of Nigeria, as well as a Nigerian citizen identified only as Jane Doe. Plaintiff Ken Wiwa, who brings this action individually and as executor of the estate of his father, Ken Saro-Wiwa, is a citizen and resident of Great Britain (Amended Complaint Against Royal Dutch/Shell, dated April 29, 1997 ['Am. Compl.'] p. 7). Plaintiff Owens Wiwa, the brother of Ken Saro-Wiwa, remains a Nigerian citizen but resides in Canada (Am. Compl., p. 8). Plaintiff Blessing Kpuinen, who brings this action individually and as administrator of her husband John Kpuinen's estate, remains a Nigerian citizen but resides in the United States (Am. Compl., p. 9).

Defendants Royal Dutch Petroleum Company and Shell

Transport and Trading Company [collectively, 'Royal Dutch/Shell'] are incorporated and headquartered in the Netherlands and the United Kingdom respectively (Am. Compl., pp. 11–12). Royal Dutch/Shell wholly owns The Shell Petroleum Company, Ltd, which in turn wholly owns Shell Petroleum Development Company of Nigeria, Ltd ['Shell Nigeria'] (Am. Compl., p. 19).

Defendant Brian Anderson was the country chairman of Nigeria for Royal Dutch / Shell and managing Director of Shell Nigeria. (Complaint Against Brian Anderson, dated April 4, 2001 ['Anderson Compl.'], p. 9). According to plaintiffs, Anderson resides in China. According to Anderson, however, he is a citizen of the United Kingdom and Northern Ireland who maintains residences in Hong Kong and France (Declaration of Brian Anderson, dated March 26, 2001 ['Anderson Decl.'], pp. 2, 4).

B. Plaintiffs' factual allegations

Plaintiff's factual allegations are as follows. Ken Saro-Wiwa was the leader of the Movement for the Survival of the Ogoni People ['MOSOP']; John Kpuinen was the deputy president of MOSOP's youth wing. MOSOP formed in opposition to the coercive appropriation of Ogoni land without adequate compensation, and the severe damage to the local environment and economy, that resulted from Royal Dutch/Shell's operations in the Ogoni region.

Defendants, operating directly and through Shell Nigeria, recruited the Nigerian police and

military to suppress MOSOP and to ensure that defendants' and Shell Nigeria's development activities could proceed 'as usual'. The corporate defendants, through Anderson, provided logistical support, transportation, and weapons to Nigerian authorities to attack Ogoni villages and stifle opposition to Shell's oil-excavation activities. Ogoni residents, including plaintiffs, were beaten, raped, shot, and/or killed during these raids. Jane Doe was beaten and shot during one raid in 1993, and Owens Wiwa was illegally detained.

In 1995, Ken Saro-Wiwa and John Kpuinen were hanged after being convicted of murder by a special tribunal. Defendants bribed witnesses to testify falsely at the trial, conspired with Nigerian authorities in meetings in Nigeria and the Netherlands to orchestrate the trial, and offered to free Ken Saro-Wiwa in return for an end to MOSOP's international protests against defendants. During the trial, members of Ken Saro-Wiwa's family, including his elderly mother, were beaten.

C. Plaintiffs' claims

1. Claims against Royal Dutch/Shell

Plaintiffs allege that corporate defendants' conduct violated international and common law, and is actionable under the Alien Tort Claims Act ['ACTA'], 28 U.S.C. § 1350 (1993). Specifically, plaintiffs assert claims for the following tortious acts: (1) summary execution with respect to the hangings of Ken Saro-Wiwa and John Kpuinen; (2) crimes against humanity, in that

general acts perpetrated against plaintiffs were 'inhumane ... [and] of a very serious nature ... committed as part of a ... systematic attack against [a] civilian population or persecutions on political, racial or religious grounds' (Am. Compl., p. 105); (3) torture with respect to Ken Saro-Wiwa, John Kpuinen, and Jane Doe; (4) cruel, inhuman, or degrading treatment in that the acts allegedly perpetrated against plaintiffs 'had the intent and effect grossly humiliating and debasing the plaintiffs, forcing them to act against their will and conscience [sic], inciting fear and anguish, breaking physical or moral resistance, and forcing them to leave their home and country and flee into exile' (Am. Compl., p. 113); (5) arbitrary arrest and detention with respect to Ken Saro-Wiwa, John Kpuinen, and Owens Wiwa; and (6) violation of the rights to life, liberty and security of person and peaceful assembly and association with respect to Ken Saro-Wiwa, John Kpuinen, Owens Wiwa, and Jane Doe. Plaintiffs also assert the following common law claims under New York, Nigerian, and United States law: (7) wrongful death with respect to Ken Saro-Wiwa and John Kpuinen; (8) assault and battery with respect to all plaintiffs; (9) intentional infliction of emotional distress with respect to all plaintiffs; (10) negligent infliction of emotional distress with respect to all plaintiffs; and (11) negligence with respect to all plaintiffs. Plaintiffs Owens Wiwa and Jane Doe also assert (12) a RICO (Racketeer Influenced and Corrupt Organizations Act) claim.

2. Claims against Anderson

Plaintiffs' claims against Anderson differ in three respects from their claims against the corporate defendants. First, plaintiffs allege that some of Anderson's conduct violates, not just the ACTA but also the Torture Victim Protection Act of 1991 ['TVPA'], 28 U.S.C. §1350, note (1993). Second, Jane Doe is not a plaintiff in the action against Anderson. Third, plaintiffs do not assert a RICO claim against Anderson.

Bibliography and further reading

General
Cheffins, *Company Law*, Oxford University Press, 1996.
Dine, *Criminal Law in the Company Context*, Dartmouth, 1995.
DTI Publications, *Modern Company Law for a Competitive Economy*, DTI, 2000.
Farrar, *Company Law*, 4th edn, Butterworths, 1998.
Gore-Brown on Companies, Jordans (looseleaf), 1986.
Gower, *Principles of Modern Company Law*, 6th edn, Sweet & Maxwell, 1996.
Mayson, French and Ryan, *Company Law*, 15th edn, Blackstone Press, 1999.
Rajak, *A Sourcebook of Company Law*, 2nd edn, Jordans, 1996.
Rider (ed.), *The Corporate Dimensions*, Jordans, 1998.
Rider (ed.), *The Realm of Company Law*, Kluwer, 1998.
Sealy, *Cases and Materials in Company Law*, 6th edn, Butterworths, 1996.

Chapter 1   The reasons for forming companies
Fraser, 'The Corporate as a Body Politic' (1983) *Telos*, no. 57, 5.
Rajak, *A Sourcebook of Company Law*, 2nd edn, Jordans, 1996.
Wedderburn, 'The Social Responsibility of Companies' (1985) 15, *Melbourne U L Rev*, 4.
Wolff, 'On the Nature of Legal Persons' (1983), 54 *LQR* 494.

Chapter 2   Starting a company
Sealy, *Cases and Materials in Company Law*, 6th edn, Butterworths, pp. 1–10.
Secretarial Administration, Jordans (looseleaf).

Chapter 3   Corporate personality
Dine, *The Governance of Corporate Groups*, Cambridge University Press, 2000.
Fraser, 'The Corporation as a Body Politic' (1983) *Telos*, no. 57, 5.
Hart, 'Definition and Theory in Jurisprudence' (1954) 70 *LQR* 37.
Kahn-Freud, 'Some Reflections on Company Law Reform' (1944) 7 *MLR* 54.
Pickering, 'The Company as a Separate Legal Entity' (1968) 31 *MLR*.
Smith and Hogan, *Criminal Law*, 8th edn, Butterworths, 1996.
Twining (ed.), *Legal Theory and Common Law*, Oxford, 1996.
Wedderburn, 'The Social Responsibility of Companies' (1985) 15, *Melbourne U L Rev*, 4.
Wolff, 'On the Nature of Legal Persons' (1983) 54 *LQR* 494.

Chapters 4 and 5   The memorandum and articles of association
Drury, 'The Relative Nature of the Shareholders' Rights to Enforce the Company Contract' (1986) *CLJ* 219.
Gregory, 'The Section 20 Contract' (1981) 44 *MLR* 526.

Leader and Dine, in Patfield (ed.), *Perspectives on Company Law, I*, Kluwer, 1995.
Wedderburn, 'Shareholders' Rights and the Rule in *Foss* v. *Harbottle*' (1958) *CLJ* 193.

Chapter 6   Power to represent the company
T. Reith, 'The Effect of Pre-incorporation Contracts in German and English Company Laws' (1987) 37 *ICLQ* 109.

Chapters 7 and 8   Public issue of securities and regulation of investment business
Alcock, *The Financial Services and Market Act 2000*, Jordans, 2000.
Andenas and Kenyon-Slade (eds.), *Financial Market Regulation*, Sweet & Maxwell, 1993.
Gore-Brown on Companies, Jordans (looseleaf), 1986, ch. 12.
Page and Ferguson, *Investor Protection*, Butterworths, 1992.
Pennington, 'The Stock Exchange (Listing) Regulations 1984' (1984) 5 *Co Law* 2003.
Plender and Wallace, *The Square Mile: A Guide to the New City of London*, Century Publishing, 1985.
Review of Investor Protection, Part I, Cmnd 9125, 1984.
Rider, Chaikin and Abrams, *Guide to the Financial Services Act 1986*, CCH editions, 1987.
Streight, *Futures Markets*, Blackwell, 1983.
Welch, 'The King is Dead: Long Live the King' (1985) 6 *Co Law* 246.

Chapter 9   Maintenance of capital
Green Paper, *The Purchase by a Company of its Own Shares*, Cmnd 7944, 1980.
Milman (ed.), *Regulating Enterprise*, Hart, 1999.
Sealy, *Cases and Materials in Company Law*, 6th edn, Butterworths, ch. 7.

Chapter 10   The balance of power inside the company: corporate governance
Anderman, *Labour Law*, 4th edn, Butterworths, 2000.
Berle and Means, *The Modern Corporation and Private Property*, American Institute for Public Policy Research, New York, 1932.
Boyle, 'The Minority Shareholder in the Nineteenth Century' (1965) 28 *MLR* 317.
Wedderburn, 'Shareholders' Rights and the Rule in *Foss* v. *Harbottle*' (1958) *CLJ* 193.

Chapters 11 and 12   Directors' duties
Dine, 'Disqualification of Directors' (1991) 12 *Co Law* 6.
Dine, *Criminal Law in the Company Context*, Dartmouth, 1995.
Gore-Brown on Companies, Jordans (looseleaf) ch. 27.
Griffin, *Personal Liability and Disqualification of Company Directors*, Hart, 1999.
Guidelines for Directors, Institute of Directors, 1990.
Hopt and Wymeersch (eds.), *European Insider Dealing*, Butterworths, 1991.
Law Commission Report No. 261, *Company Directors: Regulating Conflicts of Interest and Formulating a Statement of Duties*, DTI.
Sealy, *Company Law and Commercial Reality*, Sweet & Maxwell, 1984.
Sealy, *Disqualification and the Personal Liability of Directors*, 4th edn, CCH editions, 1992.
Suter, *Insider Dealing in Britain*, Butterworths, 1989.

Chapter 13   Suing the company

Boyle, 'The Minority Shareholder in the Nineteenth Century: A Study in Anglo-American Legal History' (1965) 28 *MLR* 317.

Boyle, 'Minority Shareholders' Suits for Breach of Directors' Duties' (1980) 1 *Co Law* 3.

Law Commission Report No. 246, *Shareholder Remedies*, 1997.

Prentice, (1973) 89 *LQR* 107.

Rider, 'Amiable Lunatics and the Rule in *Foss* v. *Harbottle*' (1978) *CLJ* 270.

Wedderburn, (1957) *CLJ* 194 and (1958) *CLJ* 93.

Chapter 14   Shares

Gore-Brown on Companies, Jordans (looseleaf), ch. 14.

Gower, *Modern Company Law*, 4th edn, Stevens, 1979, pp. 562–3.

Chapter 15   Lending money and securing loans

Boyle, 'The Validity of Automatic Crystallisation Clauses' (1979) *JBL* 231.

Farrar, 'The Crystallisation of a Floating Charge' (1976) 40 *Conveyancer* 397.

Robbie and Gill, 'Fixed and Floating Charges: A New Look at the Banks' Position' (1981) *JBL* 95.

Chapter 16   Takeovers, reconstructions and amalgamation

Deakin and Hughes (eds.), *Corporate Governance*, Blackwell, 1997.

Gore-Brown on Companies, Jordans (looseleaf), ch. 29.

Patfield and Snaith, 'Regulating the City', ch. 5 of *The Changing Law*, Leicester University, 1990.

Weinburg and Blank, *Takeovers and Mergers*, 4th edn, Sweet & Maxwell, 1979.

Chapter 17   Insolvency

Gore-Brown on Companies, Jordens (looseleaf), part VII.

McCormack, *Proprietary Claims and Insolvency*, Sweet & Maxwell, 1996.

Rajak, *Company Liquidations*, CCH editions, 1988.

Rajak (ed.), *Insolvency Law*, Sweet & Maxwell, 1993.

Chapter 18   The effect of the EU on English company law

Anderson, *European Economic Interest Groupings*, Butterworths, 1990.

Buxbaum and Hopt, *Legal Harmonisation and the Business Enterprise*, Walter de Gruyter, 1988.

Dine and Hughes, *European Community Law*, Jordans (looseleaf).

House of Lords Select Committee on the European Communities, *19th Report on the European Company Statute* (HL Paper 71), 1989–90.

Van Gervan and Aalders, *European Economic Interest Groupings*, Kluwer, 1990.

Wachter, van Hulle, Lanau, Schaafsma and Raaijmakers, *Harmonisation of Company and Securities Law*, Tilbury University Press, 1989.

Wooldridge, *EC Company Law*, Athlone, 1991.

Chapter 19   Transglobal corporations and world development

Anderson and Cavanaugh, *The Rise of Global Corporate Power*, Institute for Policy Studies, Washington DC, 1996.

Bornschier and Stam, 'Transnational Corporations', in Wheeler (ed.), *The Law of the Business Enterprise*, Oxford University Press, 1994, p. 333.

Cahn, 'Challenging the New Imperial Authority: The World Bank and the Democratization of Development' (1993) 6 *Harvard Human Rights Journal* 160.

Chambers, *Whose Reality Counts?*, Intermediate Technology, 1997.

Chossudovsky, *The Globalisation of Poverty*, Zed Books, 1997.

Czinkota, Ronksinen and Moffett, *International Business*, 4th edn, Dryden, 1996.

Harrison, *Inside the Third World*, 3rd edn, Penguin, 1993.

Heerings and Zeldenrust, *Elusive Saviours*, International Books, Utrecht, The Netherlands, 1995.

Hertsgaard, *Earth Odyssey*, Abacus, London, 1999.

Jarrett (ed.), *Environmental Quality in a Growing Economy*, Johns Hopkins University Press, Baltimore, 1968.

Karliner, *The Corporate Planet*, The Sierra Club, San Francisco, 1997.

Korten, *When Corporations Rule the World*, Kumarian Press, 1995.

Office of Technology Assessment, US Congress, *Multinationals and the National Interest: Playing by Different Rules*, US Government Printing Office, Washington DC, 1993.

Third World Network, 'A World in Social Crisis: Basic Facts on Poverty, Unemployment and Social Disintegration', *Third World Resurgence*, No. 52, 1994.

United Nations, *Human Development Report 1992*, New York, 1992.

United Nations, *Human Development Report 1996*, New York.

United Nations, *Human Development Report 1997*, New York, 1999.

United Population Fund, *The State of World Population 1992*, New York, 1992.

Index

Accounts   134–9, 182
  annual   135
  directors' report   138–9
  duty to prepare   136–7
  FREDs   135
  FRSs   135
  group   137–8
  keeping records   136
  medium-sized companies   137
  obligation to prepare   136
  small companies   136–7
  small groups   136–7
  'true and fair view'   136–7
Administrative receivership   314–15
Agency
  corporate personality, and   37–9
  ultra vires rule, and   51
Agent
  power to represent company   80–2
Annual general meeting   144–5
Articles of association   59–74
  alteration   60, 67–72
    adjustment of conflicting interests   70
    benefit of company as a whole   68
    bona fide for benefit of company   68–71
    breach of contract, and   67–8
    cautious view of courts   70-1
    compulsory purchase of shares   68
    damages   72
    discrimination, and 71
    injunction   71–2
    intervention by court   70
    non-variation   67
    rectification   72
    remedies   71–2
    special resolution   67
    subjective belief of shareholders   69–70
  contents   59–60
  contracts, as   60–1
  enforceable, whether   60
  entrenched provisions   65
  evidence of contract, as   65–7
    contradictory clauses in contract and articles   66

  key document, as   59
  rights governed by   61–2
    Law Commission proposals   64
    line between shareholders' and outsiders' rights   64
    outsiders, and   62–4
    shareholders   61–2
    third persons   62–4

Bonus shares   127
Borrowing powers
  object, whether   54–5

Canada
  company law reform   2–3
Charges, *see also* Equitable charge;
    Fixed charge; Floating charge;
    Legal charge
  registration, *see* Registration of charges
Charities
  memorandum of association   46
City Code on Takeovers and Mergers   304
  partial offers   304
Class rights
  meaning   284
Community interest companies   19
Companies
  importance of   1
Company secretary   162, 181
Constructive notice
  ultra vires, and   47
Corporate governance   7–9, 141–84
  alteration of share capital   170–1
  balance of power   141
  calls on shares   168–9
  capitalisation of profits   182–3
  DTI consultation process   141–2
  forfeiture   168–9
  general meetings   171
  'inclusive approach'   142
  indemnity   184
  international debate on corporate social responsibility   164–5
  lien   167–8
  minutes   181

notice of general meetings   171–2
notices   183
proceedings at general meetings
    172–3
purchase of own shares   171
Regulations   166–84
seal   181
transfer of shares   169–70
transmission of shares   170
votes of members   173–5
winding-up   184
Corporate personality   21–45
    advantages   2, 4
    civil liability, and   39
        alter ego doctrine   42
        vicarious liability   42
    constituency model   25
    contractual theory   23–4
    criminal liability, and   39–41
        alter ego doctrine   39
        justifications for   40–1
        limitations   39–40
        scope   39–40
        vicarious liability   39
    effects   27–8
    enterprise model   26
    essence of   21
    exceptions   26–7
        interests of justice   26–7
    fundamental importance of   23
    groups of companies   31–7
        agency   37–9
        Community law   32–3
        EC proposed Ninth Directive
            33–4
        'enterprise', concept of   32–3
        fairness   34–5
        German law   33–4
        guidelines   36–7
        'letters of comfort'   32
        procedural requirements   34–5
        trust   37–9
        'undertaking', concept of   32–3
        United Kingdom   36–7
        United States of America   34–5
    identification of company's *alter ego*
        41
    interests of shareholders, and   24
    interests of the company   24
    legal basis   22–3
    lifting the veil   27–30
        fraud   30–1
        justice, and   28–9
        personal liability, and   30
    limitations of liability   21
    problems caused by doctrine   26–7
    problems created by   21–2
    separation of ownership and control
        24–5

stakeholder model   25
statutory intervention   27

Damages
    alteration of articles, and   72
    fraudulent misrepresentation, for   87
    promoters, and   87
Debenture
    meaning   289
Debenture-holder's receiver   290
    judgment creditors   296
Department of Trade investigations
    269–71
    action following   271
    application of company   270
    fraud   270–1
    human rights, and   271
    inspectors appointed, when   271
    order of court   270
    unfair prejudice   270–1
    withholding of information   270–1
Development issues   354–5
Directives   331–2, *see also* European
        Union
    procedure for making   331–2
Directors   149–50, 151–62
    age   153
    alternate   175–6
    appointment   151, 176–7
    board ceasing to function   161–2
    'connected persons'   153
    definition   152–3
    disqualification   157, 177–8, *see also*
        Disqualification of directors
    expenses   178
    gratuities   179
    interests   178–9
    meetings   157–8
    number of   151–2, 175
    pensions   179
    power to bind company   75–80, *see*
        also Power of directors to bind
        company
    powers   176
    proceedings   179–81
    public issue of securities, and   94
    relationship with general meeting
        159–61
    removal   155–7, 177–8
    remuneration   153–5, 178
        quantum meruit   154–5
        resolution   155–6
    retirement   176–7
    shareholders, and   4
    ultra vires, and   49
    validity of acts   157
Directors' duties   185–218
    act within powers   200–2
    avoid conflicts of interest   203

Directors' duties (*cont.*)
  breach, consequences of   211
  Cadbury Committee   187–8
  categories of duties   200–11
  Combined Code   188–9
  company, meaning   190–2
    creditors   190–2
    employers   190
    members   190
  company, owed to   189
  declare interest in proposed
      transactions or arrangements
      203–10
    case law   203–10
    competing company   209–10
    employment contract   206–7
    personal profit   205–6
    resignation, after   208
  duties of care and skill   192–7
    Delaware Corporation Law   195
    objective standard   194–5
    reasonable man   193–4
  executive directors   185
  exercise independent judgment   202
  fiduciary   197–9
    duty to act *bona fide*   197–8
    duty to promote success of
      company   198–9
    prohibitions absolute, whether
      199–200
  Hampel Committee   188
  nature of decisions   186
  non-executive directors   185
  specific   219–49
  standard of conduct   185
  types of company   186
Directors' report   138–9
Displacement of domestic production
  355–6
Disqualification of directors   220–33
  acting on professional advice   232
  conviction of indictable offence
    220–1
  duty to disqualify   222–3
  employees, effect on   231
  fraud discovered in winding-up
    221–2
  incompetence   230
  insolvency   223
  investigation, after   233
  leave to act while disqualified
    232
  length   231
  mitigating factors   231
  moral culpability   230
  persistent default   221
  probable effect on directors' duty of
    care   223–4
  unfitness   224–5
    factors in determining   226–8

    objective   228
    standard of care   225–6
    subjective   228–31
    youth of director   232
Distributions   121
  members' liability   123
  permitted payments to members
    123–4
  public companies   123–4
  rules governing   121
Dividends   122–3, 185–6
  profits available for purpose   122
  realised profits   122, 123
  unrealised profits   122, 123

Elements of a company   3–5
Employees   5–6, 162–3
  EC, and   163
Environmental issues   359–61
  corporations operating on 'cowboy'
    basis   359–60
Equitable charge   294–5
European Company   338
European Union   331–52
  Community jurisprudence   337
  Community law   337
  company law Directives   339–44
    amendments to Fourth and
      Seventh Directives   341–2
    Directive on information to be
      published when major
      holding in listed company
      acquired or disposed of   344
    draft proposal for Ninth Directive
      344
    Eighth Directive   342–3
    Eleventh Directive   343
    First Directive   339
    Fourth Directive   341
    Second Directive   339–40
    Seventh Directive   341
    Sixth Directive   341
    Tenth Directive   344
    Third Directive   340–1
    Twelfth Directive   343–4
  Company Law Harmonisation
      Programme   337–9
    Regulations   337–8
  Council of Europe Bankruptcy
      Convention   345
  Council of Ministers   335
  Court of First Instance   336
  Decisions   334
  Directive for informing and
      consulting employees of
      groups   348
  Directives   334, *see also* Directives
  EC Regulations on Insolvency
      Proceedings   345
    applicable law   345–6

jurisdiction   345
liquidator's powers   346
recognition of insolvency
        proceedings   346
relationship between main and
        secondary jurisdictions
        346
Economic and Social Committee
        336
effect on English company law
        331–52
European Commission   336
European Court of Justice   336
European Parliament   335
extent of influence of rules   332–3
Francovich Directive   346–7
harmonisation   348–9
insolvency   345–8
institutions   335–7
Market Abuse Directive   345
Money Laundering Directive   347–8
Opinions   334
primary sources of law   333
Prospectus Directive   344–5
Recommendations   334
Regulations   334
securities regulation   344–5
sources of law   333–4
Takeover Directive   350–1

Financial assistance for purchase of
        shares   130–4
complexity of arrangements   131–2
exceptions   133–4
involvement of company   130–1
meaning   130
'principal purpose' exception   132–3
Financial Services Authority, see
        Regulation of investment business
Fixed charge   290–3
characteristics   291–3
meaning   290
subsequent   295
Floating charge   290–3
characteristics   291–3
crystallisation   293–4
meaning   290
set-offs   296
subsequent   295–6
Fraud
corporate personality, and   30–1
promoters, by   84–5
Fraud on minority
ratification, and   256–60
Fraudulent misrepresentation
damages for   87

Globalisation of world economy
        353–4
Groups of companies   15–16

corporate personality, and   31–7

Incorporation   18
Injunction
alteration of articles, and   71–2
Insider dealing   233–42
confidence in market   241
crime, whether   240–2
dealing or encouraging dealing
        237–8
defences   238–9
disclosing   238
encouraging others to deal   238
fairness   241
government's view   242
implementation of EC Directive   234
inside information   235–6
insider   236–7
jurisdiction   240
liability of individuals   237
market efficiency   241–2
meaning   233–4
misappropriation   241
securities   234–5
theories behind control   240–2
Insolvency   313–30
International Monetary Fund   356–7
International money and banking
        systems
effects   356–8
Investment business
meaning   106

Judgment creditors
debenture holders, and   296
labour law issues   361–3

Legal charge   294–5
Lending money   289–301
Limited companies   11–12
advantages   11
company limited by shares   12
registration   12
Limited liability
meaning   2
Liquidations   315–23
avoidance of floating charges   320
avoiding antecedent transactions
        317–21
connected persons   320
dissolution   323
extortionate credit transactions
        319–20
fraudulent trading   321
liquidator   316–17
order of payment of debts   317
preferences   318–19
reconstruction in   307
summary remedy against delinquent
        directors   321

Liquidations (*cont.*)
  transactions at undervalue   317–18
  transactions defrauding creditors
      319
  wrongful trading   321–3
Listing particulars   95–9
  compensation exemptions   103–4
  contents   95–6
  continuing obligations   96
  defective, remedies for   96–9
  disclosure, duty of   96–7
  exemptions from liability   98
  misstatements in, liabilities for
      99–100
    damages   100
    deceit   100
    negligence   100

Maintenance of capital   119–40
  accounts   134–9, *see also* Accounts
  acquisition by company of own
      shares   119–20
  bonus shares   127
  distributions   121
    members' liability   123
    permitted payments to members
        123–4
    public companies   123–4
  dividends   122–3
  financial assistance for purchase of
      shares   130–4, *see also*
      Financial assistance for
      purchase of shares
  fundamental rule   119–20
  illegal transactions   130–4
  payment of money to members
      120–1
  purchase of own shares   129
  redeemable shares   127–9
  serious loss of capital by public
      company   134
Management of the company   149–51
  Combined Code   150
  directors   149–50, *see also* Directors
Manager
  meaning   222
Managing director   158–9
Meetings   143–9
  adjournments   148
  application of court to order   144
  class meetings   145
  formality of procedure   143
  notice of   145
  quorum   145–6
  resolutions   146
  voting   146–8
    minimum standard   147
    shareholder agreements   148–9
Memorandum of association   16,
      46–58

charities   46
objects   52–5
  borrowing powers   54–5
  giving away money   53–4
  knowledge by outsider that
      transaction is outside   54
  'long list' approach   52–3
objects of association   46
powers   52–3
ultra vires   47–52, *see also* Ultra vires

Name of company   16–17
  passing off   17

Off-the-shelf companies   19
Offer to the public
  meaning   101–2
Outsiders   5–6

Parent companies   6, 15–16
Passing off
  name of company   17
Political systems
  undermining of   358–9
Power of directors to bind company
      75–80
  common law   75–6
  section 40, Companies Act 2006
      76–7
    dealing   78
    'decided on by directors'   78
    good faith   78–80
    protection   78
    'third parties'   79
    transaction   78
  section 41, Companies Act 2006   77
  section 161, Companies Act 2006   77
  Turquand's case   75, 76
Power to represent company   75–90
  pre-incorporation contracts, *see* Pre-
      incorporation contracts
  promoters   83–7, *see also* Promoters
  unauthorised agents   80–2
    actual authority   81–2
    apparent authority   81–2
    ostensible authority   81–2
    relevant questions   82
    usual authority   83
Pre-emption rights   93
Pre-incorporation contracts   87–9
  common law   88
  enforceability   88–9
  liability of company   89
  ratification   89
  section 51, Companies Act 2006   88
Preference shares   279–81
  capital   280–1
  preference as to dividend   280
Private companies   12–14
  change of status to public   14–15

public companies distinguished
12–14
Promoters 83–7
actions for damages 87
disclosure 85–6
duties 83, 84–5
fraud by 84–5
meaning 83–4
property acquired after promotion
commences 85
property acquired before promotion
commences 85
remuneration 87
rescission, and 86–7
secret profit 85–6
who are 83–4
Prospectus 99–102
defective, remedies for 99
EC Directive 101–2
fraudulent 30–1
misstatements in, liabilities for
99–100
damages 100
deceit 100
negligence 100
Proxy voting 142–3
solicitation of proxies 142–3
Public companies 12–14
change of status to private 14–15
minimum capital requirements 14
private companies distinguished
13–14
Public issue of securities 91–105
admission to Stock Exchange listing
95
authority to issue shares 94
direct offers 92
directors' duties 94
issuing houses 92
listing particulars 95–9, see also
Listing particulars
offer to the public 91
offers for sale 92
placing 93
pre-emption rights 93
restricted rights offer 92–3
rights offer 92–3
shares 92
structure of rules 94
two regimes 92
Purchase of own shares 129

Ratification 252–62
actions which cannot be ratified
256–62
acts of director 252–3
breaches of duty 260–1
expropriation of company property
260
fraud on minority, and 256–60

alteration of articles 261
categories 257
negligent acts which benefit director
261
pre-incorporation contracts 89
right to sue: who is in control of
company? 253–5
serious wrongdoing by those in
control 255–6
ultra vires acts 50, 256
use of powers for improper purpose
261
Reasons for forming companies 1–10
Reconstructions 306–7
approval of court 306–7
liquidation, in 307
meetings 306
Rectification
alterations of articles, and 72
Redeemable shares 127–9
directors' declarations 128–9
implications for capital 128–9
Reductions of capital 124–7
confirmation by court 124, 125–6
creditors, interests of 126
procedure 126–7
special resolution 124
Registrar, duty of 18
Registration of charges 297–300
charges registrable 297–8
delivery of particulars 298–9
Diamond Report 297
duty to register 299–300
effect 299
non-registration effect 299–300
payment of money secured by
unregistered charge 300
priorities 298–9
salient points 298
Regulation of investment business
106–18
complaints 114–16
Financial Ombudsman 114–15
Financial Services Authority 106–7
authorisation provisions 113–14
counterparties 110
operating framework 110
protection of consumers 109–10
regulatory toolkit 111–12
risk assessment process 110–11
strategies 109
threshold conditions 113–14
use of range of regulatory tools in
practice 112–13
Financial Services and Markets Act
2000 106
exemptions 108
regulated business 108–12
Financial Services and Markets
Tribunal 114

Regulation of investment business
        (cont.)
    Human Rights Act 1998   115–16
    Investment Services Directive   116
    Market Code   115
    regulated activity   107
    risk assessment
        impact factors   117
        probability factors   117
Rescission
    promoters, and   86–7
Resolutions   146
    special   146
    unanimous consent   146
Retention of title clauses   296–7

Saro-Wiwa family v. Royal
        Dutch/Shell   361–3
Securing loans   289–301
Shadow director   152–3
Share capital   167
Share certificates   167
Shareholders
    creditors, and   4–5
    directors, and   4
    rights and liabilities   3–4
Shares   278–88
    exercise of voting powers   282–3
    nature of   278
    ordinary   278–9
    preference   279–81, see also
        Preference shares
    variation of class rights   283–7
        alteration of articles to insert
                variation clause   287
        class rights, meaning   284
        statutory right to object   287
        true 'variation'   286–7
        variation or abrogation   284–6
    voting rights   281–2
Single European market   331
Single member companies   6–7
Starting a company   11–20
Stock Exchange listing
    admission to   95
Subsidiary companies   6, 15–16
Suing company   250–1
Suing for the company   251–2
    derivative actions   251–2
    Foss v. Harbottle, exceptions to rule
        251–2

Takeover Panel   303
    general principles   303–4
    rules   303–4
Takeovers   302–12
    compulsory purchase provisions
        305
    international   308–11
    meaning   302

monopolies   302–3
public offers   302
sell-out right   305
Transglobal corporations   353–63
    absence of control of   358–9
Trust
    corporate personality, and   37–9

Ultra vires   47–52
    agency, and   51
    basic rule   56
    cases decided in 1980s   55–7
    constructive notice   47
    determination of   48–9
    'elevation' clause   55–6
    justification of act   57
    justification of doctrine   48
    'main objects' rule   48–9, 51–2
    new law   49
    old case law   50–2
    old law   47–9
    powers of directors   49
    ratification   50, 256
    'regulated sector'   57
    subjective element   52
    true construction of memorandum,
        and   56
Unfair prejudice   262–7
    capacity in which complaint made
        267
    conduct of company affairs   263
    infringement of legal rights
        263–6
    legitimate expectations   263–6
    members affected   267
    petitioner's interest in company
        266–7
    relief that can be granted   267–8
    test for   262–3
Unlimited companies   11–12

Voluntary arrangements   313–14
    challenges   314
    contents of proposal   314
    involvement of court   314
    meetings   314
    proposal   313
Voluntary winding-up   316

Wealth
    concentration of   353
Winding-up by court   315–16
Winding-up orders   268–9
    petition for   268–9
    when likely to be made   269
World Bank   356–7
World development   353–63
Wrongful trading   321–3
    destination of money   323
    standard   322–3